Creative State

Creative State

Forty Years of Migration and Development
Policy in Morocco and Mexico

Natasha Iskander

ILR Press
an imprint of
Cornell University Press
Ithaca and London

First published 2010 by Cornell University Press
First printing, Cornell Paperbacks, 2010

Printed in the United States of America

Library of Congress Cataloging-in-Publication Data

Iskander, Natasha N. (Natasha Nefertiti), 1972-
   Creative state : forty years of migration and development policy
in Morocco and Mexico / Natasha Iskander.
      p. cm.
   Includes bibliographical references and index.
   ISBN 978-0-8014-4872-0 (cloth : alk. paper)—ISBN
978-0-8014-7599-3 (pbk. : alk. paper)
   1. Morocco—Emigration and immigration—Economic aspects.
2. Mexico—Emigration and immigration—Economic aspects.
3. Morocco—Emigration and immigration—Government policy.
4. Mexico—Emigration and immigration—Government policy.
5. Emigrant remittances—Morocco. 6. Emigrant remittances—
Mexico. 7. Morocco—Economic policy. 8. Mexico—Economic
policy. I. Title.

   JV8978.I84 2010
   325'.264—dc22

                                                      2010010708
Cornell University Press strives to use environmentally responsible
suppliers and materials to the fullest extent possible in the
publishing of its books. Such materials include vegetable-based,
low-VOC inks and acid-free papers that are recycled, totally
chlorine-free, or partly composed of nonwood fibers. For further
information, visit our website at www.cornellpress.cornell.edu.

Cloth printing   10 9 8 7 6 5 4 3 2 1
Paperback printing   10 9 8 7 6 5 4 3 2 1

For Maria

Contents

Acknowledgments

This book is about how we collaborate to create realities we have as yet to imagine, and as I wrote it, it began to embody its central tenet in ways that I had not expected. It became something very different from what I had initially envisioned, in terms of both its form and significance in my life. It grew into an expression of the relationships, personal and intellectual, that supported this book's development, and into an articulation of the quality of attention those relationships challenged me to cultivate.

Among the most significant of these was my relationship with Michael Piore. I thank him for being a teacher in the broadest sense of the term. From the beginning, he encouraged me to trust my instincts and explore ideas that were still only nebulous hunches, and showed by example that insight depends on compassion and patience. I also thank Richard Locke for his penetrating critique and his constructive advice; Paul Osterman for his fairness, his support, and his intellectual guidance; and Alice Amsden for her discerning comments and criticism, and for demonstrating that creativity often demands irreverence. I also extend my gratitude to Judith Tendler, Wanda Orlikowski, Pablo Boczkowski, Susan Slyomovics, and Richard Lester for challenging me with a few difficult and well-timed questions that caused me to reexamine assumptions of mine so deeply held that they had become invisible to me. Timothy Mitchell exhorted me to be ambitious and to walk boldly into whatever controversy the book might spark. Rogan Kersh generously shared his careful reflection on the book's argument and structure, and provided advice that was keen but gentle on how to bring this book to completion. I am grateful to Ellen Schall for her steadfast support of this project.

I thank Janice Goldman, Sumila Gulyani, Monica Pinhanez, Sean Safford, Nichola Lowe, Janice Fine, Vicky Hattam, Ruth Milkman, Zeynep Gursel, Jennifer Brinkerhoff, and Jonathan Murdoch for reading sections of this book at various stages in my writing. Their perceptive comments improved the book immeasurably.

Two anonymous reviewers read the manuscript in its entirety. I thank them both for the care they took in evaluating the book, and for thoughtful and meticulous comments they provided me. The book is much stronger for their attention, and I very much appreciate their investment in this project.

I also thank many colleagues who generously shared their thoughtful comments and criticisms with me, especially Liesl Riddle, Kathleen Newland, Yevgeny Kutznetsov, Michael Clemens, Carlos Martinez, Sarah Kaplan, Karim Lakhani, Andrew Schrank, Roger Waldinger, and Devesh Kapur. I owe them all an intellectual debt.

The fieldwork on which this book rests was as collaborative as the process of reflection that spun its narrative thread. I am extremely grateful to the many people who took the time to speak with me, who went out of their way to help me understand local political and economic realities, and who guided me as I tried to reconstruct local and transnational histories. In Mexico, government officials in numerous municipal, state, and federal agencies generously took the time to talk with me and graciously opened their archives to me. I am grateful to them all, but I extend special thanks to Carlos Gonzalez Gutierrez, Elizabeth Chavolla, Pedro Barrios, Diana Alvarez, Dante Gomez, Samuel Delgado, and Placido Morales. I also express my warm gratitude to the migration studies group at the University of Zacatecas, especially to Rodolfo García Zamora, Raul Delgado Wise, and Miguel Moctezuma Longoría; their reception and support of me during my stay in Zacatecas, and even after I left, stand out as a standard of academic and personal generosity. I also thank the many migrants and migrant activists who shared their experiences with me, *y gracias a David para las buenas comidas*. Brandie Maxwell collaborated with me on interviews in Guanajuato, and her cheerfulness made dusty trips to remote villages enjoyable. I also owe a special debt to Manuel Orozco, who invited me to participate in an early project on migration and development policy and allowed me to join him on a whirlwind trip through more than half a dozen Mexican states, enabling me to complete my initial case selection.

In Morocco, I received a gracious welcome from the vibrant community of scholars who study migration, including the Moroccan Association for the Study and Research of Migration (AMERM) and the National Institute for Applied Economics and Statistics (INSEA). I am also deeply indebted to several migrant organizations and activists in Morocco and in Europe for the openness and detail with which they shared their experiences and for the hospitality with which they received me. In particular, I thank Hassan Boussetta, Nouria Ouali, Youssef Haji, Jamal Lahoussain, Zakya Daoud, and especially Nadia Bentaleb and Jacques OuldAoudia (*merci pour les conversations auprès du feu*). I also thank members of the Moroccan government who generously provided me with their frank reflections about policy changes, especially Nouzha Chekrouni, Mohammed Sajid, and the staff at the Hassan II Foundation (who also patiently helped me navigate the foundation's archives). Special thanks also go to Jean-Pierre Garson of the Organization for Economic Cooperation and Development, who provided me with invaluable assistance in Paris and lifted my spirits with his unfailing sense of humor.

The research for this book was generously supported by grants from the Institute of Work and Employment Research at the Sloan School of Management at MIT, the Social Science Research Council, the Institute for International Education, and the Industrial Performance Center at MIT. I extend special thanks to Tom Kochan at MIT for authorizing a seed grant for exploratory research even before the direction of this project became clear. I express my gratitude to the Industrial Performance Center for providing me with a supportive space for writing. Anita Kafka and Richard Lester nurtured a culture of friendly intellectual exchange that transformed the Industrial Performance Center's office suite into a center for constructive personal and academic collaboration. New York University's International Center for Advanced Studies hosted workshops in which portions of this work were considered. I thank the participants for their intelligence, their perceptiveness, and their enthusiasm. I am grateful to the Social Science Research Council Book Fellowship, offered in partnership with Columbia University Press, for editorial support (many thanks to Adi Hovav) and for the window it provided onto the world of academic publishing. Peter Dimmock at Columbia University Press was especially encouraging.

Portions of chapter 5 were previously published in N. Iskander, "Diaspora Networks for National Infrastructure: Rural Morocco, 1985–2005," in *Diasporas and Development: Exploring the Potential*, edited by J. M. Brinkerhoff (Washington, DC: Lynne Rienner Publishers, 2008); and in N. Iskander and N. Bentaleb, "Assets, Agency, and Engagement in Community Driven Development," in *From Clients to Citizens: Communities Changing the Course of Their Own Development*, edited by A. Mathie and G. Cunningham (Rugby, UK: Practical Action Publishing, 2008); used with kind permission of both publishers.

At Cornell University Press, I thank Fran Benson, who believed in this book from the beginning and skillfully shepherded it through to publication. Throughout, she evinced grace, tenacity, and generosity. Thanks also to Emily Zoss and Susan Specter, who provided guidance and meticulous attention to production details. Kathryn Gohl helped with careful and insightful copyediting and Nairn Chadwick with indexing.

Katherine Scheuer tightened my prose with efficient dexterity. I am indebted to her for her editorial help. Thanks also to Bill Nelson for drawing the maps of Morocco and Mexico included in this book. Martha Bowen not only painstakingly verified and organized my sources, but also read the manuscript in its entirety and made many helpful improvements. Vivian Yela provided indispensable formatting and proofreading assistance. Jayati Vora got me out of a pickle by helping with some last-minute details.

Although this book was in many ways a collaborative exercise, those who participated in its creation, wittingly or not, are only responsible for improving the book and not for any errors or oversights that may remain, or for the views the book expresses.

Researching and writing this book was a process that spanned several years, and along the way, I experienced an illness that required me to live the claim I make in the book: it compelled me to hold the ambiguity of the present moment while trusting that a useful answer would eventually emerge. Thanks to Elaine Stern, Susannah Carleton, Lori Dechar, Anthony Weiss, Sylvia Perrera, and Alba Cabral for helping me cultivate that ability and the strength on which it depends.

This book is, in an important if implicit sense, an homage to my family, Egyptian, Czech, and Mexican, and to the ways they have been able to sustain ties of love and nourish currents of understanding across many places and historical times. My father, Magdi Rashed Iskander; my mother, Marta Czernin von Chudenitz née Ruzova; my aunts, Hoda, Mona, Samia, and Laila (who reminded me that home is not a place—it is the people who love you); Uncle Nasser; my sisters, Mai and Yasmine; and my adopted family, Robin Chaflin (and now Ella and Aria), Nils Fonstad, Alejandro Neut, and Silvia Sagari, and others not named here have all taught me more than I can say about interpretation, forgiveness, and care. Finally, I offer my most heartfelt thanks to Maria Elosua. She has accompanied me on every step of this journey, embracing adventures, discoveries, and occasional misfortunes with her indulgent laughter, her patience, and her engagement.

Acronyms

ADEME	Agence de l'Environment et de la Maîtrise d'Énergie
ADS	Agence de Développement Sociale (Agency for Social Development)
AFME	Agence Française pour la Maîtrise de l'Énergie
AMF	Association des Marocains en France (Association of Moroccans in France)
ATMF	Association des Travailleurs Marocains en France (Association of Moroccan Workers in France)
BCP	Banque Centrale Populaire
CFDT	Confédération Française Démocratique du Travail (French Democratic Confederation of Workers)
CTM	Confederación de Trabajadores Mexicanos (Confederation of Mexican Workers)
DACGE	Dirección General de Atención a Comunidades Guanajuatenses en el Extranjero
DGCME	Dirección General para las Comunidades Mexicanas en el Extranjero
EDF	Électricité de France
FCZSC	Federación de Clubes Zacatecas del Sur de California (Federation of Zacatecan Clubs from Southern California)
FND	Frente Nacional Democrático (National Democratic Front)

IME	Instituto de los Mexicanos en el Extranjero (Institute for Mexicans Abroad)
IRCA	Immigration Reform and Control Act
MALDEF	Mexican American Legal Defense Fund
M/D	Migrations et Développement (Migration and Development)
MECHA	Movimiento Estudiantil Chicano de Aztlán
MRE	Marocains Résident à l'Étranger (Moroccans Living Abroad)
MTA	Mouvement des Travailleurs Arabes (Movement of Arab Workers)
OFAM	Oficina de Atención a Migrantes y Sus Familias (Agency for the Support of Migrants and Their Families)
ONE	Office Nationale de l'Électricité (National Office of Electricity)
PAGER	Programme d'Approvisionnement Groupé en Eau Rurale (Program for the Collective Provision of Water in Rural Areas)
PAN	Partido Acción Nacional (National Action Party)
PCME	Programa para Comunidades Mexicanas en el Extranjero (Program for Mexican Communities Abroad)
PERG	Programme d'Électrification Rurale Globale (Total Program for Rural Electrification)
PNCRR	Programme Nationale de Construction de Routes Rurales (National Rural Roads Program)
PNER	Programme Nationale pour l'Électrification Rurale (National Program for Rural Electricity)
PPER	Programme pour la Pre-Électrification Rurale (Program for Rural Pre-Electrification)
PRD	Partido Revolucionario Democrático (Democratic Revolutionary Party)
PRI	Partido Revolucionario Institucional (Institutional Revolutionary Party)
SEDESOL	Secretaría de Desarrollo Social (Secretariat for Social Development)
SRE	Secretaría de Relaciones Exteriores (Secretariat of Foreign Relations)
UMT	Union des Travailleurs Marocains (Moroccan Workers' Union)
UNAM	Universidad Nacional Autónoma de Mexico (National Autonomous University of Mexico)

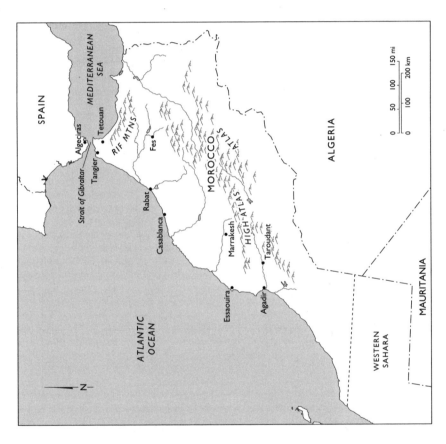

Map of Morocco

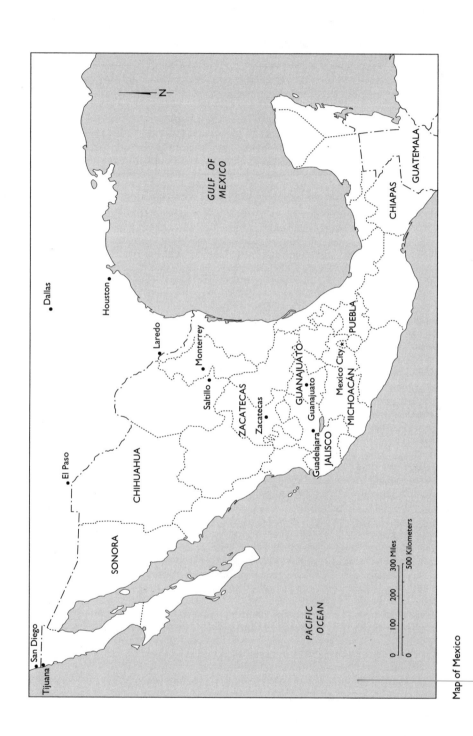

Map of Mexico

Morocco   # Mexico

Morocco	Year	Mexico
Hassan II becomes king	1961	
Labor export agreements signed with European countries	**1963**	Bracero program renewed for last time by U.S. government
	1964	Bracero program ends
	1968	Government fires on student protestors
Banque Centrale Populaire offers bank accounts to emigrants	1969	MECHA sends its first delegation to Mexico City
Unsuccessful coup attempts against Hassan II	1971	
	1972	
European countries adopt restrictive policies for labor immigration	1974	
Green March into Western Sahara	1975	
	1982	President de la Madrid declares moratorium on debt payments
Emigrants instated as parliamentary representatives for Moroccan migrants	1985	

1986	◆	Immigration Reform and Control Act passed in U.S. Congress; informal matching-funds program for migrants launched in Zacatecas (One-for-One)
1990	◆	Government establishes Hassan II Foundation, Ministry for the Moroccan Community Abroad, and Bank el-Amal for migrant investors — Program for Mexican Communities Abroad (PCME) established
1992	◆	One-for-One formalized as Two-for-One program in Zacatecas
1993	◆	Casas Guanajuato program begins
1994	◆	Ministry for the Moroccan Community Abroad downgraded to subministry — NAFTA goes into effect; Zapatista rebellion begins; Proposition 187 passed in California
1997	◆	Ministry for the Moroccan Community Abroad abolished — Two-for-One program augmented to Three-for-One in Zacatecas
1998	◆	
1999	◆	Mohammed VI becomes king
2000	◆	Fox elected president of Mexico; Three-for-One program applied nationwide
2002	◆	Subministry for the Moroccan Community Abroad created — Institute for Mexicans Abroad (IME) established
2005	◆	Mexican emigrants acquired right to vote in Mexican elections via absentee ballots
2006	◆	
2007	◆	Council for the Moroccan Community Abroad established — Four-for-One program begins in Zacatecas in partnership with Western Union

Creative State

1

Introduction

Interpretive Engagement in Morocco and Mexico

In late August of 1989, a Spanish immigration officer observed the crush of Moroccans returning to Europe by ferry from Tangier at the end of their summer vacations. "Morocco is becoming to Spain what Mexico is to the United States," he complained (as quoted in Riding 1989). For decades, Moroccan migrants had pushed on through to Europe's wealthier countries, but as Spain's economy started to expand, Moroccans began to stay and fill the growing demand for cheap labor. They took the same kinds of menial jobs in Spain's fields, factories, restaurants, and homes that they had worked in for more than a generation in France, Belgium, Germany, and the Netherlands. These jobs were strikingly similar to the low-wage jobs, an ocean away, that Mexicans crossed into the United States to fill. Morocco added Spain to the list of countries to which it could export its unemployed youth and also, when possible, the men who made up the political opposition that mounted occasional but serious threats to Morocco's fragile monarchy. Mexico, meanwhile, continued to let millions of its unemployed and underemployed seep north past its border, just as it had for over twenty years, with its autocratic one-party government quietly grateful for the economic relief as the country lurched from crisis to crisis.

"We're separated by water, but people still keep coming," remarked the same Spanish immigration officer as he surveyed the narrow Strait of Gibraltar. In response to increased immigration, Spain had built higher walls around its outposts in Morocco, Melilla, and Ceuta, and it had begun to draw on the arsenal of restrictive immigration policies its European counterparts had been honing for years. Likewise, the United States steadily tightened its own immigration policy, launched increasingly virulent raids, and began erecting a fortress wall in San Diego that would, for the next two decades, advance doggedly east, progressively girdling the belly of the continent.

People kept coming, however. As they came, they began to transform the places that they had left as well as those to which they traveled. The same longing that had propelled them across increasingly dangerous borders provided them with the motivation, political power, and resources to change the places they left behind. "Each year, I traveled back with a van filled with things for the poor," remembered a Moroccan migrant I spoke with over a decade later, in 2000. "It never erased my memory of need, of not having shoes, of going to bed hungry. But I built my house and my parents' house, and this year, I am bringing back supplies for the clinic we opened in my village three years ago" (interview, Tangier, July 2000). His sentiments were echoed in the reflections a Mexican migrant shared with me at a border crossing halfway across the globe, in San Diego. "I went for three years without seeing my children; I was gone when my eldest sister died in childbirth. That absence still sits heavy in my heart," he said, "but now, there is a sign with my name on it at the entrance to the road that I helped pave. It connects my town to the hospital an hour away" (interview, San Diego, August 1999).

This book tells the political story of how migrants from Morocco and Mexico changed the communities they left, and how their initiatives, small and bold, would ultimately transform the nations from which they had emigrated. Accounts of the ways migrants have changed their communities of origin for the better have become widespread; in their most celebratory versions, migrants' philanthropic efforts at community development offer reassuring confirmation that small is indeed beautiful and that economic change can occur far outside the reach of the state. These laudatory portrayals omit a central protagonist. They minimize, when not completely obscuring, the role of governments in shaping the impact that migrants' efforts to improve the lives of their families have on their communities and, more broadly, on their nation. However, the clinic in the mountain village in Morocco was not built nor was the road between the isolated Mexican town and the modern hospital paved without government support. In both cases, government policies mediated migrant investment in their communities of origin. In Morocco, government guidelines for medical equipment and the nursing staff the government provided turned the small concrete room into a working health center. In Mexico, municipal officials with maps of the potential roads in hand sought out migrants and asked them to raise funds for the project, with the promise that any road paved with migrant dollars would serve as a permanent symbol of their strong commitment to their communities, despite the border that kept them far from home.

This book rehabilitates the place of the state in the narrative about the relationship between migration and development. It argues that the impact that migrants had on the welfare of their communities and countries of origin grew directly out of their involvement with the very governments that had—discreetly in the case of Mexico, enthusiastically in that of Morocco—encouraged their departure while actively neglecting the development of the areas they came from.

Whether the migrants of Morocco and Mexico elbowed their way into everyday practices of governing or whether the governments of those countries sought out their counsel, their exchanges would rework the patterns of state interaction with migrants and their communities of origin. As migrants and state bureaucrats worked together, they came up with new ways for migrants to contribute to development and new ways for the state to support their initiatives. Over time, the engagement between migrants and government bureaucrats became so dense that it began to blur the line between state and society. But it also grew so vital that it transformed the state in this context from a solid structure into a verb. From being a set of agencies and fixed policies, the state dissolved into fluid practices that both migrants and state actors renegotiated and reinterpreted as they went along. Out of the engagement between migrants and their states emerged policies, striking in their creativity, that tied emigration to development. Over time, these policies revolutionized the way the governments of Morocco and Mexico perceived migration, crafted their national economic development plans, and reacted to migrant petitions for a greater political voice.

The Paradox of Success

At the turn of the twenty-first century, the impact of emigration on the places migrants left behind had begun to catch the attention of policymakers around the world, and the experiences of Morocco and Mexico in this domain acquired salience overnight. Conversations about globalization and development that had formerly focused on trade, foreign direct investment, and multinational production began to appraise international migration—the movement of people across borders—as a key determinant of local and national development. After the terrorist attacks of September 11, 2001, the increased vigilance of governments that strove to track formal and, especially, informal flows of money made remittances newly visible. It became clear that migrant remittances worldwide had risen to stratospheric levels, mushrooming from an estimated $11 billion in 1975 to over $150 billion in 2004—a sum already almost triple the amount of international development aid and one that would, in a couple of years, surpass even foreign direct investment (Chami et al. 2005; International Monetary Fund 2005). For many developing countries, migrant remittances emerged as an indispensable source of capital, a flow of cash that could literally make or break their economic fortunes.

Over and above these infusions of hard currency, international migration had provided sending countries with other critical factors for economic development. Migration had sparked knowledge and learning transfer across national boundaries; it had woven social networks that served as infrastructure for international production and exchange, and laid the foundation for powerful political lobbies that influenced the policies of both the countries migrants had left and those they adopted as their new home. Through countless small transfers of savings and innumerable social exchanges, migrants were transforming the places they had left in fundamental and irrevocable ways. Community by community, they were changing their countries, redefining nationhood itself, and opening new avenues for economic development.

The sheer magnitude of migration's effect on economic development made it impossible to ignore, and governments of migrant-sending countries around the world began searching for ways to capitalize on it for economic growth. As they cast about for policy solutions, many looked to the experience of a handful of nations with long-standing policies that tied migration to development. Morocco and Mexico featured prominently as sources of "best practice" in this area. In 2001, they ranked as two of the top recipients of remittances in the world, with Mexico placing second behind India and Morocco ranking a decent fourth behind the Philippines. But the impact of emigration on the national development of both countries had less to do with the volume of those financial flows, or the flows of ideas and networks that accompanied them, than with the way both governments engaged with those resources and with the migrants that produced them. The governments of both countries had policies to forge a relationship between the emigration of low-skilled workers and economic development that were effective and well established; some had been functioning successfully for decades.

Morocco pioneered financial institutions and services that met the needs of large numbers of emigrants with no previous exposure to banking and formal money transfer services. The financial tools it created, administered through a state-controlled bank, the Banque Centrale Populaire, allowed migrants to send money home, to save and invest, while at the same time making remittances available to the government for monumental national development projects, ranging from dams to industrial parks. The Moroccan government also collaborated with migrants and their communities of origin to design better and cheaper systems to deliver basic infrastructure, such as roads and electricity, to rural areas; once supplied with services that linked them to the rest of Morocco, formerly isolated villages were brought into the national economy. The Moroccan government complemented these economic and structural interventions with initiatives to support emigrants' participation in the cultural and political life of their country of origin: it established several agencies, including a royal foundation and a ministerial office for emigrants, which nurtured emigrants' sense of belonging to their homeland.

In Mexico, after a couple of false starts, the government launched a major national program to encourage emigrant investment in communities of origin. The program matched migrant contributions to the provision of basic services, ranging from sewage to drug rehabilitation clinics to the beautification of village squares, with government monies; the program not only led to the development of migrants' communities of origin but it also supported organizing efforts by migrants on both sides of the U.S.-Mexico border. The Mexican government expanded and refined its consular services to make them among the most attentive in the world: their offerings spanned everything from health counseling to legal advocacy to cultural and language programs for children. It opened new channels for migrants to exercise political influence in Mexico and in the United States: it afforded Mexicans abroad the ability to vote in Mexican elections and created a representative body for migrants so that they could help to shape the policies on both sides of the border that affected their lives and the development of their communities.

Despite their different emphases, the policies of Morocco and Mexico shared two important characteristics that made them remarkable among attempts worldwide to link emigration and development. First, they were innovative in their design. They embodied groundbreaking ways of drawing the resources generated by emigrants into national economic development. In particular, both governments' policies involved migrants, either directly or indirectly, in economic development planning, especially in the envisioning of new possibilities for—and even new definitions of—economic transformation. Second, the policies were dynamic. Less like tools, they were more like expressions of changing patterns of interaction. They improved over time as the engagement between migrants and government deepened; they manifested the new ways of relating that migrants and government bureaucrats discovered. As a result, the policies became more responsive to the specific and emerging needs that migrants felt as their experience of migration changed, and more attuned to the possibilities for development that migration represented.

Even as they evolved—or rather, because they did—Moroccan and Mexican policies remained consistently innovative, sometimes exceptionally so, propelling government into new functions, extending it into unfamiliar geographic territory, and enlisting aspects of migration as slippery as cultural identity for political and economic ends. They also proved impossible to replicate. When governments new to policy making in the field of migration and development mimicked Moroccan and Mexican policies, the results they saw were decidedly mixed. In the best cases, the imitations were not as effective as they had been in their original settings, and on numerous occasions they turned out to be counterproductive, alienating emigrants and stunting economic growth, and had to be abandoned. Rarely tailored to the specific needs of these other economies and their emigrants, the borrowed templates often constrained the possibilities for positive transformation that migration could hold.

My project was to move beyond this problematic "best practice" approach to policy making that migrant-sending countries seemed to be adopting as they eyed Moroccan and Mexican migration and development policy. Whereas a "best practice" approach congealed a broad, evolving, contextualized set of practices into a policy instrument, identified it as better than all the rest, and then applied that instrument indiscriminately in contexts that were very different from the place where it had emerged, I wanted to understand the processes by which governments made sense of migration and then designed policies to seize on the opportunities that it offered for economic transformation. More pointedly, I wanted to get to the bottom of how those processes had emerged in Morocco and Mexico decades before the potential of migration as a catalyst for economic development caught the attention of other governments, scholars, and development institutions. Why—and more importantly, how—were their governments able to perceive the changes caused by out-migration, some of them very subtle and diffuse, and how were they able to translate those perceptions into innovative policies, often reframing their own role and mission in the process?

What I found was that, paradoxically, the Moroccan and Mexican policies emulated as models of excellence were never designed with a view to using migration for economic development, or at least not a version of economic development that included migrants and their communities in any meaningful way. Instead, they were initially devised to respond to domestic political crises. Both the Moroccan and Mexican governments dealt with migrants when doing so seemed likely to shore up their own often shaky political legitimacy. They engaged with migrants on an international level in order to strengthen their domestic hold on power. Furthermore, even though Morocco's and Mexico's policies fundamentally—even radically—redefined nationhood, development, and citizenship for both countries, the process of policy development was so iterative and improvisational that neither the governments nor their migrant constituencies ever predicted, much less intended, their outcomes.

This book chronicles how these policies, used as blueprints for building bridges between migration and economic development in the early years of the twenty-first century, came to be, and argues that it was precisely the indeterminacy surrounding their emergence that was the source of their originality. For the governments of Morocco and Mexico, the conceptual connection between migration and development became clear only when the policies to link them were already well established and being copied by other sending states. The question—how to link migration and development—and the answer—the policies that did so—arose in tandem. The welter of contradictory ideas and nascent understandings that permeated the process of policy development may have made it impossible for government planners, and the migrants they engaged with, to see where they were going, but it was also what allowed them to get there.

The Politics of Ambiguity

Rarely are the terms "creative" and "state" used in the same phrase. The state has generally been portrayed as a creaking behemoth badly in need of overhaul. The prescriptions for reform have focused on making sure the state fulfills its tasks with as little wastage as possible. Transparency, accountability, and efficiency have dominated as catchphrases of the day, and efforts to refurbish dreary state bureaucracies have combined a free market–inspired drive to reduce the size of government with a bureaucrat's obsession for standardizing the procedures that remain. Cultivating the ability of government to come up with new ways of doing things—to innovate—has almost never made it onto the reformers' agenda. Instead, the handful of policies tapped as successes have been carefully scrutinized in order to identify why exactly they worked. An analytic scalpel has been taken to them, and they have been meticulously dissected to pinpoint exactly which elements can be replicated in other settings. *How* the new policy instruments are invented, however, has received far less analysis, if any.

This tendency to overlook the process behind government innovations stems from an assumption that the political process by which novel ideas are embraced and fashioned into policy is too unpredictable to chart. Analyses of policy innovations characterize them as the product of random events or political maneuvers, with causal antecedents that are impossible to model: a bureaucrat serendipitously stumbles onto a new solution for an old problem (Tendler 1997); under political pressure from their constituents, legislators institute a policy that turns out, fortuitously, to be successful, although not at addressing the problem it was designed to target (March 1994); a political crisis on the scale of a war or national fiscal default unexpectedly comes to a head and forces a reluctant government to consider policy suggestions that it previously had disregarded or actively suppressed, and even then, the approaches adopted are likely to have only a loose correspondence with the crisis that compelled their consideration (Schon 1971).

Ever since policy analysts began debunking the notion in the 1970s that the state followed any sort of linear or rational model in designing policy (Schon 1971; Cohen et al. 1972; Nakamura 1987), uncertainty and ambiguity have figured prominently in theories about policy development (Kingdon 1995; Feldman 1989). The cause of the ambiguity is the fact that there are as many takes on any given social problem as there are different actors, institutions, and political camps involved in policy making (Feldman 1989; Zahariadis 2007). The ensuing confusion can rarely be remedied with additional data, especially if those data reflect only one particular worldview. The issue is not a lack of information but an abundance of viewpoints.

According to policy analysts, this ambiguity provides a platform, a wide-open stage, on which policymakers or social movements can push their agendas, and it is their political skill and the power that they accrue, rather than rational choice or impartial analysis, which sways the outcome. How this political pressure manifests itself depends on who you ask: institutional analysts tend to focus on bureaucracies and social rules, such as laws and norms (Ostrom 2000; Powell and DiMaggio 1991); observers of coalitions and social movements stress the contingent relationships and identities that political actors form to advance their agendas (Jansen 1991; Marsh and Smith 2000; Skocpol 1992; Fantasia and Voss 2004); proponents of punctuated-equilibrium theories of policy making, who argue that policy change occurs in brief heady bursts that interrupt long stretches of stasis, attend to the political factors that make government susceptible to lurching policy shifts (True et al. 2007). There is, however, broad consensus that shaping meaning in this ambiguous political field is the most potent means of applying pressure. "Decision making," concludes March, "may in many ways be better conceived as a meaning factory than as an action factory" (1997: 23).

Yet despite the careful stratagems or social momentum behind meaning-making tactics, the policy outcome still remains uncertain. Policies are the product of competing efforts at political persuasion, to be sure, but they are also the product of a haphazard, even chaotic, collision of events and actors. Who will win the struggle to author policy is always far from clear. Cohen, March, and Olsen (1972) go so far as to call the decisions that go into policy making an expression of "organized anarchy" in which different ideas, problems, and solutions are dumped into a proverbial "garbage can." With those different elements jostling around in the can, policies are the product of solutions that actors opportunistically attach to problems, of viewpoints that interest groups muscle onto platforms where they can be aired, and, more prosaically, of policymakers finding work to justify their presence on the payroll.

Confronted with so many confounding variables, policy observers of all stripes tend to derive the meanings used to push a given policy agenda retrospectively. Meanings are "read off" policies once they have already been instated. But policy innovations, because they—by definition—represent a break from past practice, often cannot be traced backed to a well-worn set of meanings in this way. Consequently, they are represented as the product of a process that is especially opaque and random—one that is hopelessly indecipherable. Narratives about policy innovation reach back only to the point in the policy development process where the conceptual building blocks for the new policies have already been clearly articulated and adopted by the relevant bureaucracies, and the practices they embody have already been well rehearsed, if not already formalized into a policy intervention. These accounts start after the action is already over.

The experiences of Morocco and Mexico suggest that we need to pay attention to the murky, unruly ambiguity that is the prologue to policy innovation. Both countries demonstrate that far from being an institution resistant to change, the state can be a remarkable site of creativity. They also show that to understand the state's potential for creativity and to nurture it, we need to delve into the messy and disorienting confusion that characterizes policy making and explore the processes through which state and nonstate actors make sense of the conflicting, hazy, incomplete meanings that are found there. In Morocco and Mexico, ambiguity did not just provide the stage on which political power struggles were played out, where competing constituencies jockeyed to advance well-defined agendas or pushed to get their policies adopted. Instead, ambiguity was the stuff of which policy innovations were made. The dislocation, the complexity, and the contradictions caused by large-scale migration swept away the meanings that the Moroccan and Mexican states had used to understand both migration and development. Out of the morass of incomplete and conflicting understandings that resulted, policymakers, migrants, and their communities drew out the nascent concepts and practices they needed to create new ways of engaging in the living present. The new ways of interacting that grew into policy were more than mere accidents of chance. Based on only hunches and wary exchanges, they were leaps of imagination, completely unforeseeable, and indeed, inconceivable until they came to be.

Emigration and Interpretation

It can take time for flickering insights and hesitant exchanges to grow into policies we recognize. Indeed, it took forty years for the migration and development practices explored in Morocco and Mexico to gel into the policy forms that other countries tried to copy. Their stories began in 1963. That year the governments of Morocco and Mexico radically changed the policies that governed the emigration of their citizens. Morocco launched an ambitious program to export workers to European nations that were still rebuilding after World War II. Mexico, meanwhile, swallowed the United States' formal termination of a two-decades-long guest worker arrangement through which hundreds of thousands of Mexicans had been hired to work in U.S. agriculture. Mexican officials made the strategic decision to ignore the movement of people northward across the border, and emigration, no longer hemmed by formal regulation, increased substantially. Moroccan and Mexican policymakers soon found themselves acting in changing social and economic contexts molded by migration patterns that were new, constantly evolving, and massive. Migrant by migrant, community by community, both nations were being stretched across international borders. The four decades of heavy emigration that began in 1963 changed local and national economic activities and redefined prospects for economic growth: rural areas in both countries hemorrhaged residents and became increasingly desolate. Meanwhile, the fortunes of industries in Moroccan and Mexican urban centers became linked to the labor of migrants who toiled in the factories and fields to the north, as those industries began to depend, albeit indirectly, on the capital migrants sent home.

The number of Moroccans who crossed into Europe and Mexicans who went north to the United States in search of work or to join their families grew steadily during the second half of the twentieth century, and by 2000 at least 10 percent of both nations' populations lived beyond their borders. For Morocco and Mexico, the economic impact of labor migration was substantial: while it undeniably created rude dislocation in many sending areas, it also infused local and national economies with cash, skill, and social capital. In 2002, the 2.6 million Moroccans living outside the kingdom's borders—20 percent of the active workforce—sent home US$3.6 billion, gifting their country with a sum equivalent to a little under 10 percent of GDP (Morocco, Office des Changes 2002). It was the largest single source of Moroccan national income. A similar proportion of Mexicans living abroad, an estimated 8–12 million of the country's 100 million citizens, sent home almost US$9 billion in 2001 (Central Bank of Mexico 2002; World Bank 2002). Although that amount represented a smaller slice of Mexico's GDP, at only 1.5 percent, the flow of money across the border was highly concentrated, disproportionately benefiting 9 out of 32 sending states (Woodruff and Zenteño 2001). For those 9 states, remittances represented close to 10 percent of their income, almost as large as the proportion in Morocco (Woodruff and Zenteño 2001).

While the financial benefits of migration buoyed the economies of Morocco and Mexico—at the very least dampening the painful spikes in poverty caused by periodic economic crises—emigration steadily eroded the foundations on which the political legitimacy of both governments rested. From almost the first day that Morocco began to send workers to Europe in 1963, emigrants circumvented the Moroccan government's repressive strategies, which were designed to confine their existence in Europe to that of docile laborers, and resisted its efforts to control the communities they left behind. From the time Morocco secured its independence from France in 1957 until the late 1990s, its government functioned as a constitutional monarchy in theory and as an authoritarian sultanate in practice. The king, Hassan II, claimed to be the temporal and spiritual leader of the Moroccan people: the monarch appropriated broad legislative and executive powers, including the right to dissolve parliament at will and to issue binding royal decrees, and he invoked his lineage, traced back, according to Moroccan tradition, to the Prophet Mohammed, to assert his role as "commander of the faithful" (*amir al-mu'mininnin*), a religious leader whose person is considered sacred and who is above the secular norms of the constitution. Hassan II, whose reign from 1961 to 1999 covered most of the period considered in this study, ruled through a mix of concentration of powers, repression of the opposition, and manipulation of the parliament (Layachi 1998: 28). Nevertheless, so insecure was his hold on power that in 1974, the *New York Times* gave the sultan the tagline of "Never sure he'll be king by nightfall." Moroccan emigrants were cognizant of how shallow the roots of his legitimacy ran, especially in the rural regions they were from, and they called into question the political rhetoric of his unending and divine supremacy. They challenged, vociferously at times, the allegiance required of the king's subjects and the obedience the king demanded of them, regardless of where they resided (Layachi 1999; Tozy 1999).

The Mexican government's system of patronage, its decades-long tradition of doling out social benefits in exchange for political support, also suffered as migration, with the economic alternatives it offered, sapped both its appeal

and its constituency. Until 2000, Mexico was governed through the compara-
tively benign dictatorship of a single political party, the Institutional Revolutionary Party (PRI). In a profoundly corporatist system, the PRI had maintained
dominance since its founding in 1929 through the cultivation of strategic alliances with key sectors of society, most critically organized labor, and the performance of regular, but largely symbolic, elections. The PRI functioned as a
mammoth, hegemonic political machine. The voluble revolutionary rhetoric
the party churned out to mask what were essentially clientelistic relationships
rang increasingly false to emigrants, who found that their labor grievances,
their families, and their communities of origin were consistently neglected by
their government (Middlebrook 1995; Roett 1993).

More threatening to both governments than the newly transgressive political identities among migrant workers and their communities were the new strategies of political resistance that migration supported. Migrants backed their
critiques of their governments with political organizing, adapted in many cases
from labor mobilization on assembly lines in Europe and from civil rights struggles in the United States. Moroccan workers staged rallies and street marches in
the 1970s and 1980s in France and Belgium to protest their government's harassment and brutalization of emigrant labor leaders and used the language of human rights to press their cause. Mexican migrants demanded that their government pay them the same attention it extended to the Mexican Americans it
was courting as a potential lobby in the United States and, in the late 1980s,
forged alliances with Mexico's fledgling opposition parties to drive home the
message that they would chip away at the PRI's political dominance unless the
party addressed their concerns about subpar working conditions and the increasing hardships they faced in the United States.

In addition to shaking up the political landscape, long-standing emigration
also challenged social norms in Morocco and Mexico. The new prospects for
economic advancement that migrants enjoyed abroad upended class hierarchies and gender relations in contexts as intimate as the family and as broad as
the nation. Emigration reconfigured individual and community aspirations in
small towns where the only work to be had was across a national border, but
it did so just as radically in large cities, where emigration not only emerged as
an escape from chronically high unemployment but as a living critique of government economic policy. In Morocco and Mexico, emigration meant different
things to different people at different times, but it always meant something,
something powerful, to everyone—and more often than not, something alarm-
ing to the state.

Confronted with emerging political and economic realities that were confus-
ing and always shifting, policymakers at various levels of government in both
countries found themselves compelled to engage with migrants and their communities to try and make sense of the social and economic changes that migration had set in motion, if only to contain them. Migrants and their communities, striving to take advantage of the new possibilities that migration offered

but also to cope with the new constraints it also produced, engaged with the state in an attempt to compel it to address their changing needs. Sometimes migrants were reluctant participants in a conversation too important to ignore, but just as often they were the initiators of the exchange, determined to get their governments to pay attention to the way migration was impacting their lives.

Initially, state and nonstate actors brought perspectives to the conversations that were mutually incomprehensible. The wide variety of meanings produced misunderstandings so acute that they strained already tense exchanges to the breaking point. This ambiguity, however, was precisely the attribute that enabled the conversations to yield new insights: as participants struggled to understand what their interlocutors were saying, as they probed the slippages between the different understandings brought to the exchanges, as they reflected on why they saw things the way they did, they brought buried meanings to the surface. They made them explicit enough so that they could be spliced together in new ways, recombining them in unexpected hybrids that recycled old beliefs into concepts that were entirely novel. The conversations that policymakers and migrants used to interpret their shifting contexts were at times collaborative, at times combative, and most often colored by mutual suspicion, but they also generated new meanings, gave rise to new identities, and forged new relationships.

To tolerate the intense but generative ambiguity that characterized their exchanges, policymakers and migrants depended on a certain quality of engagement characterized by dense interactions and a deliberate attentiveness to the nascent meanings that participants attempted to articulate. This interaction, which I call *interpretative engagement*, produced the insights that served as the basis for new patterns of state-society relations that would come to be regarded as major policy innovations because of the way they linked migration to development. Less celebrated but more important is the fact that these policies also opened institutional spaces in which the state, migrants, and their communities could reenvision local and national development in an ongoing manner and could produce generation after generation of conceptual and institutional breakthroughs. The policies made room for the state, migrants, and their communities to continue reinventing themselves and to continue imagining previously unthinkable possibilities for local development and state support. Stated differently, Moroccan and Mexican policies provided shelter for ongoing state creativity.

In this sense, the Moroccan and Mexican experiences with migration and development policy illustrate that policy innovations and the processes that generate them must be considered together. They show that when we sever policy from process, we obscure the extent to which the effectiveness of a given policy flows from the way it supports the continuing creative process that gave rise to it. So critical was the practice of interpretation to the effectiveness of both countries' migration and development policies that any time the spaces for it were closed, the policies atrophied to brittle structures, drying from the inside out until they were little more than empty husks. At that point, the policies invariably began to fail. Without a careful consideration of the relationship between both countries' migration and development policies and the creative practices they supported, the policies' success, as well as their occasional failure, remains incomprehensible and appears as random and as unpredictable as processes of policy innovation are widely deemed to be.

Interpreting Innovation

Interpretation can be thought of as the process of establishing functional communication between two or more interlocutors who do not share the same language, the same practices, or the same experiences. It is the act of revealing and explaining meanings that are familiar, and of developing new relationships to concepts that are foreign by conceiving them in light of an existing set of beliefs, judgments, or circumstances (Lakoff 1987). In this sense, it is the process of creating new meanings by exploring the distance between understandings, by mining the gaps between concepts expressed as misinterpretation, ambiguity, or even conflict, and discovering the possibilities for new understanding and imagination held in those spaces.

Increasingly, studies on creativity and on organizational innovation identify interpretation as central to the process through which new ideas are conceived and new products are imagined (Cook and Brown 1999; Orlikowski 2002; Nootebloom 2000; Lester and Piore 2004; Fonseca 2002; Amabile 1996). These studies use the analogy of interpretation as a "conversational process" to describe how it supports creativity (Fonseca 2002); although they refer to both actual speech and enacted practices, they characterize interpretation as a exchange among people and organizations with different backgrounds, areas of expertise, and cognitive frameworks who are trying to reach a common understanding about the possibilities and constraints for the development of a given product or practice (Cornelissen 2006; Katloft et al. 2006; Sawyer 2007; Ganz 2009). These conversations are unpredictable, sometimes even unwieldy, in their form and in their duration, and in retrospect, participants may find themselves unable to explain why the conversations evolved as they did (Lester and Piore 2004). But it is precisely the ambiguity that characterizes them, the blurriness of meaning and direction, that makes the interpretive conversations generative. As participants engage with others who perceive opportunities where they see obstacles, and who ascribe different implications to both, they borrow their interlocutors' perspective and view the problem they understand themselves to be faced with from a different angle. In this sense, interpretation can be thought of as a process of *problem finding*, as opposed to a process of *problem solving* (Weisberg 2006).

Morocco and Mexico produced generation after generation of policy innovation by engaging in just such a process of interpretation and problem finding.

In much the same way as innovators studied by organizational scholars, migrants, and policymakers found themselves compelled to engage with one another about the significance of migration, the role of the state in development, and the boundaries of citizenship and sovereignty. The meanings that surfaced through interpretation allowed them to consider the dynamic phenomenon of migration from multiple angles, and to redefine the economic and political potential it represented.

Thus, interpretive engagement, as defined here, is not negotiation. At its base, negotiation begins with the premise that the parties know what their position is, or can figure it out, and will then enter into rounds of bargaining in order to secure an outcome that is as close to their objectives as possible. In Morocco and Mexico, however, neither the state nor the migrants could articulate what they were seeking. It was only through their conversations that they were able to begin to define their needs and comprehend how migration was changing the political and economic spaces woven together by the movement of people. In negotiation, the goal is to reach an agreement between the parties involved; in interpretive engagement, the aim, if it can be articulated at all, changes along the way and is often radically different toward the end of an engagement than at its beginning. Instead of reaching an agreement, interpretive engagement is driven by a pressing policy need to make sense of social changes and to discover what possibilities for action they offer. In Morocco and Mexico, the impetus was different for the governments that sought to control migrants than it was for the emigrants who sought to improve their lives, but the quest for understanding brought them together to interpret what migration meant and how to build on it for change, regardless of whether the change envisioned was national political consolidation or community development.

Interpretive engagement is also not the same as deliberative democracy. Broadly defined, deliberative democracy refers to the process of citizens engaging in reasoned debate over a public issue through clearly established procedures (Cohen 1997; Elster 1998; Gutmann and Thompson 2004). Those deliberations often shift public preferences, causing participants to reevaluate their stance in favor of one outcome or another (Gutmann and Thompson 2004; Fung and Wright 2003). Sometimes, note observers of the process, deliberative democracy can also produce new insights and spin off original solutions for addressing social problems (Heller 2001). The scope of public discussion in deliberative democracy, however, and the range of new ideas it can produce are well demarcated. Its boundaries are established by the requirements that arguments be reasonable and that deliberation follow a set process that is agreed upon, explicit, and often formalized. This is different from interpretive engagement, in which what constitutes a reasonable approach remains as ambiguous as the social dynamic that participants are trying to understand. Moreover, the practices that shape how people engage are as emergent and mercurial as the meanings the process yields; they are constantly evolving, changing in response to new understandings that arise. In Morocco and Mexico, being reasonable was secondary to the urgent task of trying to sort through the implications that migration patterns would have for personal livelihoods and national economic growth. The ways that migrants from both countries and their governments engaged varied dramatically as interpretation yielded new understandings, new opportunities, and most importantly, new sources of power.

The Politics of Engagement

The ambiguity, the search for meaning, and the embryonic and fluid nature of the processes through which people engage make interpretive conversations extremely generative. These qualities also make them very fragile. With no straightforward mandate, with no question to answer or problem to solve that is clear to all participants, no agreed-upon conflict to negotiate, interpretive conversations are extremely vulnerable to being shut down (Lester and Piore 2004). Often it is not the process of interpretation itself that is difficult; rather it is tolerating the confusion and indeterminacy involved that represents the greatest challenge for people and organizations. Indeed, as organizational scholars have noted, the ambiguity that results when parties armed with different sets of understanding come together often incites anxiety and paralysis so intense that it provokes people into searching for new ways of interacting in the present moment, and new meanings that allow them to move forward (Fonseca 2002).

The fragility of interpretive conversations also makes them highly political. Precisely because interpretive engagement allows participants to reconsider meanings that are taken for granted and to imagine new concepts and new ways of doings things, the conversations that make it up become moments in which different, and often transgressive, political possibilities can be envisioned and the practices to make them into realities can be explored. Consequently, opening up spaces to hold those conversations—to say nothing of nurturing, renewing, and enriching them (Lester and Piore 2004)—becomes a matter of fierce political contest.

In Morocco and Mexico, the state entered into interpretive conversations with migrants in an effort to capture the resources that they had acquired because they had crossed into Europe or the United States. Migrants' newfound or newly created wealth and political clout were what drew the state into conversations with persons whom it had been only too happy to ignore or actively oppress before they emigrated. How state actors perceived migrant resources informed whether they initiated conversations with migrants. Governments of both countries approached migrants when policymakers were able to see their assets and viewed them as means to further state priorities. Governments of both countries initiated conversations with migrants when they could see the resources that migrants held and viewed those assets as important for state priorities. The central government of Morocco and local governments in Mexico began conversations with migrants when they sought to capture remittances for economic development initiatives, projects that often bypassed the communities that migrants were from.

Likewise, migrants were able to draw government into interpretive exchanges only when they succeeded in making the resources they held visible to the state. Sometimes those resources were monetary remittances, but just as often, they were the political power that migrants had cultivated and the new knowledge they had created. In both countries, migrants pulled government actors into an interpretive engagement by organizing themselves into a movement so politically powerful that it threatened to derail state development plans, or by generating practices through their own interpretive processes that became irresistibly attractive to the state as solutions to long-standing development challenges.

Once the interpretive exchanges began, the relative power of state and migrant participants shaped the twists and turns their engagement would take; it determined when the conversations would be sustained, when they would be abandoned, and when they would be revived. Those power dynamics were specific and situated: they grew out of the particular historical moments in which the interpretive conversations occurred, and they reflected the specific places in which the conversations unfolded, as well as the places to which these conversations referred.

During moments of political vulnerability, the governments of both Morocco and Mexico focused on shoring up their political legitimacy and stamped out sources of political challenge, including their engagement with migrants. The coup attempts and the popular rebellions that threatened to unseat Hassan II from his throne during the 1970s made the Moroccan government strident in its response to any emerging ideas it viewed as disloyal. Similarly, when the PRI's margin of victory in national elections grew so slim in the late 1980s and early 1990s that it had to rely on increasingly blatant fraud to stay in power, its patience with migrant petitions evaporated. Migrants were shut out, and the extent to which their engagement with the state was contingent on the government's goodwill was made searingly clear.

In contrast, the economic crises that periodically convulsed both countries made their governments more attentive to the ideas that migrants were articulating: in times of economic freefall, Morocco's need for remittances grew more acute, and its willingness to engage with migrants to find ways to capture those funds more pronounced. Mexico's need for harmonious relations with its northern neighbor, perennially ambivalent about Mexican migrants, grew more desperate, and its receptiveness to ideas about how to create a political lobby that could shape policy in Washington grew more explicit.

The optimism surrounding the postwar economic boom in the United States and Europe and the robust need for migrant workers to fill new jobs made the conversations expansive and hopeful. Later the decay of the industries that had been the economic backbone of western Europe and the United States, and the layoffs, immigration restrictions, and xenophobic outbursts that accompanied it, strained interpretive exchanges. Migrants and their governments had more at stake, and their positions, the meanings to which they held fast, grew more entrenched.

In addition to the political and economic turbulence that shaped them, the conversations were saturated in the more prosaic everyday experiences of their participants. They invoked migrants' communities of origin and were spoken in the intimate argot of identity and responsibility that kept migrants bound to their families, but they sometimes took on a weariness that reflected the relentless pace of the assembly lines that migrants manned and the harsh conditions in the fields where they worked. They were laden with the bureaucratic jargon of government offices and with the political platitudes that became more formulaic during periods of political insecurity.

The power dynamics that moved through interpretive conversations in Morocco and Mexico were also situated within the interactions that made them up. Over time, repeated exchanges wove their own patterns of power, ones that were specific to the conversations themselves, and interpretations took on significance not only from their place in the flow of meanings but from their place in the flow of power. In Morocco, for example, conversations that the state had opened with migrants about their financial needs allowed it to create banking services that met those needs but also to channel remittances into state coffers. As the state came to rely on direct access to migrant wages, the leverage that migrants could exercise over the direction of the conversation grew: they were able to insist that the state address not just how they remitted their wages but the working conditions under which they earned them. In Mexico, migrants' engagement with local government produced matching funds agreements for community development. Those arrangements, embryonic and informal as they were at the beginning, provided a structure around which migrants could organize into clubs and then federations of clubs. Soon, migrants who had mobilized into a movement grew too powerful for the federal government to rebuff.

These interpretive conversations, and the power relations they embodied, could allow for the imagining of possibilities regarding the link between migration and development that were not just technically innovative but politically radical precisely because they were situated in specific contexts and in specific exchanges. The meanings that the conversations produced in these two countries became intrinsic sources of power, but it was their "situatedness" that made them useful to migrants and their communities. Migrants were able to use them to challenge the particular brands of state rhetoric used to marginalize them, and to assert the particular rights that they needed in order to be able to author their own futures. The meanings became crowbars that allowed them to pry open the space to act as agents of development and political transformation. Had they not emerged from these defined contexts, they would not have been specific enough to resist those particular practices of state control that migrants and their communities confronted.

In Morocco and Mexico, the interpretive engagement between migrants and policymakers, and the intensive interactions it comprised, would ultimately redefine the state, blurring the boundary between state and society and revealing the state as a set of practices that permeated society rather than a freestanding (and impervious) institution. Over time, the repeated exchanges began to scuff out the political line that kept the state separate from the society it governed. Soon, it was no longer a case of the state *acting on* society but rather a matter of *relationships* between state and society that were producing new institutions, new policies, and new visions for economic development. Identifying who was "acting on" whom became impossible, and attributing authorship to actions, and to meanings behind those actions, became a futile exercise. Not only did these circumstances transform policy formulation from the act of designing policy to the art of forging relationships, but they opened up new avenues for political change. Once the thick wall between state and society was eroded through the repeated back-and-forth of interpretive exchange, the decision to open up the practices of governing to nonstate actors no longer remained the prerogative of the state. Furthermore, when state practices were reinterpreted and enacted in new ways, ascertaining precisely who had reinvented them was often simply not possible, and thus exacting political retribution became a hopelessly inexact and pointless endeavor. Political resistance shifted from a strategy of opposition to one of engaging with the state in order to change its practices, and the meanings on which they were based, from within.

The interpretive engagement between migrants and the state in Morocco and Mexico would eventually become so durable that it would survive the political transitions that occurred in both countries at the turn of the century. It also helped to ensure that those shifts would represent a move toward political openness that was unprecedented in the modern histories of both countries. As of 1999, Morocco had a new king, the young Mohammed VI; hailed as a political modernizer, he presided over the most open and competitive parliamentary elections since Moroccan independence. In the Mexican presidential elections of 2000, an opposition party, the National Action Party (PAN), was elected to power, unseating the PRI and ending its seventy-one-year monopoly of formal political control. In both countries, emigration continued apace, even under new political stewardship, but, thanks to their intensive engagement with the state, emigrants were afforded a larger role in determining how their governments would manage emigration itself. This book follows Moroccan and Mexican migration and development policies through this period of political transition at the turn of the twenty-first century and documents their consolidation, as well as the deepening of the interpretive engagement that gave rise to them, over the five years that followed. By the end of 2005, both countries' policies would begin to reflect the inclusion of new interlocutors in interpretive conversations. At that point, new actors, such as multilateral donor organizations, private companies, and other governments took those conversations global, and past the analytic scope of this book.

Processing Impact

Any consideration of migration and development policy risks getting caught up in an overly categorical debate about whether migration can actually foster positive economic transformation. For the most part, international labor migration, and low-skilled labor migration in particular, has been celebrated as globalization from below, benefiting those whom the bonanza of international trade has bypassed. The millions who cross national borders each year, legally and illegally, in search of work or opportunity, to join family, or to escape political or social oppression have been portrayed as a popular force that countervails the rapid and rapacious movement of capital around the globe. In a characterization that has increasingly garnered political and academic appeal, migrants are described as having set in motion flows that rival those of investment capital in scale and in impact, through their own movement across borders but also through the money that they remit (M. Orozco 2001; Garza and Lowell 2002), the knowledge that they transfer (Saxenian 2007; Guarnizo 2003), and the social values and cultural norms that they transmit (Levitt 2001; Brinkerhoff 2009). Moreover, migrants have been characterized as resisting a global order that enables maximum mobility of capital while confining labor to national territories and enclosing workers behind the high (and increasingly material) walls of national borders. A growing body of literature on transnational communities fills in the details of this general picture by documenting "the initiatives of common people to establish durable economic and other ties" that stretch across national boundaries (Portes 2003: 875).

Even as this view has taken hold, a more sober evaluation counters that migration reproduces and reinforces global inequalities and stalls economic development. Studies of this ilk caution that remittances, for all their volume, have an unclear impact on poverty and may actually stunt long-term economic growth in migrant-sending communities (Glytsos 2002; Ouaked 2002). Similarly, skepticism has emerged about whether migrants bring back knowledge that actually fosters development, or whether instead they merely join, and even slow, processes of political and economic transformation already under way (Obukhova 2009). Accounts of the social disruption caused by migration have challenged that portrayals of transnational communities as cogent and integrated are hopelessly quixotic and have pointed to the painful breaches that have opened in communities, with migration privileging one group of residents to the exclusion of another (Suárez-Orozco et al. 2005; Haour-Knipe and Rector 1996).

Despite their divergent views, the two sides of this debate share two pivotal traits. The first is that they attribute the effects of migration on development to some intrinsic quality of migrants themselves, and implicitly base their conclusion on an analysis of migrant behaviors and motivations. In their baser versions, these representations homogenize migrants, portraying them as all cut from one cloth, but most accounts acknowledge that while migrants are often altruistic, productive, and invested in the political futures of their countries of origin, they can also be venal, self-interested, and economically manipulative. Similarly, these analyses recognize that the resources that migrants remit— be they monies, knowledge, political influence, or social networks—can have complex effects, but they attribute the impacts of those flows to migrant choices. In other words, the positions staked out in this debate focus on who migrates and what they contribute—or don't—to development, and recommendations concentrate on how to change migrant priorities. What they overlook is how migrants affect development and how they infuse the resource they remit with value.

Second, the scholarship that buttresses these different stands has tended to overlook the state, implicitly suggesting that migrants have been able to "rise above" state constraints and pressures for assimilation to create vital and coherent communities that exist in "transnational social fields" (Levitt 2001), seamless and seemingly suspended above borders (Basch et al. 1994; Kearney 1991; Portes et al. 1999; M. Smith and Guarnizo 1998). When scholars have turned their attention to the state, they have theorized about how migrant social practices, along with the identities and relationships they embody, traverse a terrain made challenging, even treacherous, by the institutions and policies that not just one but several states erect to establish control and legitimacy (Goldring 2002; R. Smith 2003; Levitt 2001; Guarnizo 1998). Their accounts have shown either how state structures have directed migrants' political activities and social identities (Kastoryano 2002; Brand 2002; Taylor 2002), or how migrants have challenged and even torn down state obstacles—set up in both sending and receiving countries—that have prevented them from accessing political rights and achieving economic security (R. Smith 2003; Goldring 2002; Moctezuma Longoría 2003; Argun 2003). For all of their richness and subtlety, these accounts firmly maintain state structures as analytically and actually separate from migrant community practices.

This book steps outside the debate about whether migration in fact produces development. Instead of taking sides, it concentrates on the processes by which migration sometimes does. It shows how certain kinds of interaction and certain qualities of engagement support creativity in policy making, and it considers how those processes emerge, intensify, and condense into durable institutional structures that foster a synergy between migration and development. Consequently, the primary analytic attention in the study is trained on practices of interpretive engagement rather than on which particular actors participated in the processes of creative policy making and what their motives were.

This focus on process allows the narrative presented here to eschew the two assumptions that confine the current debate on the relationship between migration and development. First, while this account acknowledges that the specific actors who author interpretive processes have multiple and complex motivations, the concern is not with defining or judging the intentions of migrants, or of state bureaucrats for that matter, but rather with the ways those actors engage with one another to generate new ideas and insights for policy. This account shows how the resources migrants remit become useful for economic development because of the ways they and their state partners draw them into their interpretive exchanges. Second, the attention paid in this book to the specifics of the processes though which Morocco's and Mexico's migration and development policies were fashioned necessarily entails a recognition of the extent to which the policies were woven out of interactions between the migrants and the state. By showing how intense and prolonged were the exchanges that produced the policies that mediated emigrants' relationships to their countries of origin, it reveals the extent to which the distinction between migrant practices and state structures is more often a matter of semantics than lived experience.

The processes I examine are those that produced policy innovations. Many exchanges between migrants and the states that governed their countries of origin did not. The argument made here is that the state can be a site of creativity—not that it always or even generally is. This study dissects only those processes that produced policy innovations, even if those processes faltered at times; it should not be read as a comprehensive account of all interactions between migrants and their state. It should, however, be taken as evidence of the potential for radical policy transformation that those interactions often hold.

Institutional Archeology

To study the processes that produced policies linking migration and development in Morocco and Mexico, I used an approach best described as institutional archeology—a case-study method applied through time and across space. Most definitions of this method view it as an exploration of a specific policy or phenomenon in a given place at a given moment in time (Van Maanan 1988; Vaughan 1992). My method differs in that I extended the case-study approach retrospectively through time and across multiple geographic and political spaces. My study was defined by the scope of the processes that I was trying to understand. In order to identify the processes that had created migration and development policy and to trace their evolution, I followed them backward, exploring them through the various iterations of the policies they produced. I pursued them across national borders to sites in the United States and Europe, just as I followed them back to hamlets in isolated areas of Mexico and Morocco. Through this perspective, policies that today appear coherent and well developed unraveled into multiple and disparate threads that reached back into numerous physical places and political events, and policies that had seemed to be breakthrough innovations were revealed as merely the last in a long series of iterations of a given approach. As I followed the process of innovation, I uncovered layer upon layer of institutional structure, some well documented and some partially in ruins and almost forgotten. I also encountered various generations of meaning that emerged through interpretive engagement between migrants and the state in Mexico and Morocco. Finally, I came to know of policies that had once existed but had been abandoned along the way, and I tried to discern why fully formed policies and institutions had been discarded. (For a more detailed discussion of the methods I used, please refer to the appendix at the end of this book.)

As I continued this research, the political nature of the data became increasingly clear to me. States construct social and political categories through the ways they tabulate and classify people and actions. Similarly, political discourses shape the way states conduct their counts and devise their taxonomies (Nobles 2000). In Morocco and Mexico, the political and economic significance with which migration was infused determined the kind of data both states collected, and those data in turn bolstered certain views of migration, both figuratively and literally. The data both governments produced made certain aspects of migration visible, whereas data they did not generate left other aspects out. In Morocco, because the government promoted large-scale labor emigration as an important economic strategy for the kingdom, the state kept meticulous records of worker emigration. It periodically conducted extensive surveys of Moroccans living abroad, tracking everything from demographic information to plans for investment. In its most recent survey, the government specified that its study included not only Moroccans *living* abroad but also Moroccans *from* abroad in order to capture trends among second- and third-generation Moroccans who may have never set foot in the kingdom. In Mexico, by contrast, the government's political decision to ignore emigrants for much of the four decades since 1963 has led to a dearth of data. What is available is produced through comprehensive household surveys conducted as a precursor to poverty reduction interventions. Although Mexico is short on demographic data, its government archives are both more complete and more accessible than those of Morocco, where documentation and public access to records of government practices tends to be markedly more restricted.

In my own data production practices, I have endeavored to be as cognizant as possible of the political context in which I worked. In this book, this effort may be most palpable in what is not said and, more specifically, in who is not named. The character of interpretive engagements documented here has vacillated between collaborative and adversarial. Many of those who participated did so at some political and personal peril. As a result, the confidentiality of the persons I interviewed is maintained throughout. Where appropriate, the organization, place, and month in which the interviews were conducted are noted. There are a few notable exceptions, however, to this general rule. In some cases, the participation of certain persons in interpretive conversations determined whether the relationships and insights they generated would in fact become policy; governors, for example, fall into this category. All of my interviews with high-ranking government officials were "on the record," and they agreed to be referred to by name. I identify those officials where appropriate in the text. Persons cited in newspaper, magazine, or journal articles appear as they do in the printed media, and speeches by public officials at public events, designed for public consumption and quotation, are attributed to the person who delivered them.

Last, I use the terms "emigrant" and "migrant" almost interchangeably. "Emigrant" defines migrants in relationship to the country or to the communities they have left. The practices of interpretation this book documents took place in numerous locations, on both sides of national borders, and sometimes the interpretation focused on migrants' relationship to the places to which they had migrated and on the ways that they were "immigrants." As a reflection of the multiplicity of political spaces that that interpretation touched on, literally and figuratively, I use the term "migrant" purposefully and often.

Mirrors and Windows: Overview of Chapters

The central claim of this book is that the policy innovations linking migration to development in Morocco and Mexico were produced through *interpretive engagement* between state and nonstate actors. The purpose of the book is to reclaim the messy ambiguity that supports interpretation as a resource worthy of analysis and, even more, worthy of cultivation and protection, especially early on, when its policy value is still far from clear.

How interpretative conversations began depended on whether or not the state perceived emigrants as valuable interlocutors. Whether the state had deployed administrative measures to make migrants visible or whether, instead, emigrants had to organize to make themselves visible to the state determined the genesis and the progression of the interpretive conversations that then took place. This book, therefore, begins with an exploration of how and why the states of Morocco and Mexico perceived migrants as they did, and outlines the consequences these perceptions had for the ways that both governments chose to engage with their nationals abroad. Chapter 2 describes the shift in emigration policy both countries experienced in 1963 and provides a historical overview of the political and economic events that led up to that change.

Because Morocco and Mexico applied contrasting policy regimes to emigration, their investment in interpretive engagement with their migrants evolved along divergent paths. Comparing them side by side brings into relief various aspects of the strategies that each government used to try to exert control over migrants and dominate any interpretive engagement with them. The Moroccan government was keen to engage with emigrants in order to capture their wages and eagerly deployed institutions to initiate conversations. When the exchanges began to produce criticisms of government policy and of the king's autocratic rule, however, the state attempted to curb the emerging meanings by controlling the process of interpretive engagement, steering it with a heavy hand toward topics it viewed as safe. Mexico, by contrast, was skittish about engaging with emigrants that it had been loath to acknowledge in the first place, and the federal government tried to limit engagement to short periods of time when it viewed enrolling the support of its emigrants as politically expedient. Migrants tried to maintain their conversations with the government, and to thwart their efforts, federal bureaucrats stubbornly refused to create the structures necessary to shelter the fragile process of collective interpretation.

In both countries, migrants wrested the process of interpretation from government control by initiating conversations that were more local, situated in the rural areas where they were from, and that they knew so well. As their interpretive engagement with local government began to thrive, spinning off innovation after innovation, they brought their conversations and their politics to the capital. In Morocco, migrants initiated a process of interpretive engagement around infrastructure that was so generative of new ideas that the central government was forced not just to recognize its value but to respect the unnerving directions it took. Meanwhile, in Mexico, migrants developed policy structures to hold interpretive conversations with municipal and state governments, which proved so useful and robust that the federal government found itself compelled not only to adopt them but to extend them to the nation as a whole.

In Morocco and Mexico, the conditions that the central government imposed on interpretive conversations with migrants were contested and discredited by meaning produced through local, and primarily rural, processes of interpretation between local bureaucrats and migrants, and in both countries, the fusion of those two streams of conversation ultimately led to the redefinition of economic development at the local and national levels. The organization of this book captures this mirroring effect and dedicates the first half to the Moroccan experience, the second half to the Mexican. Chapters in both halves offer a window onto a slightly different aspect of interpretive engagement and reflect on the lessons it offers for how we think about policy making and innovation.

The section on Morocco details the assertive steps needed to initiate and sustain an interpretive engagement with Moroccan nationals abroad. Chapters 3 and 4 depict the evolution of that engagement from the mid-1960s through the end of the 1980s. These chapters show how that engagement led to the creation of a series of highly sophisticated financial services tailored to a population of emigrants traditionally considered unbankable, as well as to new understandings of the political influence that emigrants, when they organized, could wield both in Morocco and in Europe.

In response to the chronic state neglect of their communities of origin, emigrants initiated interpretive conversations in their villages to generate new solutions for the provision of infrastructure but also, more broadly, to elaborate new visions of development that included their isolated villages. Chapter 5 describes the emergence and evolution of those local interpretive processes and shows how emigrants deliberately drew the state into those conversations in a bid to pressure the government to provide services as basic as electricity, water, roads, and education. Moreover, emigrants were able to call into question the national development model that classified rural areas as useless and had prevailed in the kingdom for over three decades. Their success in demonstrating that areas represented as economic wastelands could be centers of economic transformation speaks to the relationship between interpretive practices and power, and chapter 5 elucidates that connection.

Chapter 6 chronicles how the Moroccan state, in the mid-1990s, began to view the interpretive processes that emigrants had set in motion as resources in and of themselves, and, as a result, established new institutions in an effort to capture those processes. The chapter describes these institutions and their implications for theories about how firms and governments can draw on "user-driven innovations"; it also describes the interpretive processes emigrants have launched more recently in an attempt to discover new ways to resist state cooptation of their creative processes.

Chapters 7–9 cover the evolution of interpretive engagement in Mexico. In the late 1960s, Mexican Americans approached the Mexican government with a desire to engage with it politically, as an extension of political mobilization in the U.S. civil rights movement. Chapter 7 depicts how the Mexican state, for the next three decades, joined in interpretive conversations with Mexican Americans on a sporadic basis, whenever it appeared that doing so would provide it with resources to resolve its latest political or economic crisis. Its engagement with Mexican Americans stood in sharp contrast with the treatment it reserved for Mexican migrants. As part of its policy of pretending that Mexican emigration did not exist, the Mexican federal government rebuffed all overtures from the migrants. Chapter 7 shows the vast difference in policy results that the two approaches yielded.

At the state level, however, a distinct pattern of engagement between migrants and government began to emerge. From the mid-1970s and throughout the 1980s, municipal and state authorities began to seek out migrants and engage them in interpretive conversations. This trend was most pronounced in Zacatecas, and chapter 8 describes how an arrangement between migrants and the government of that agricultural state to provide basic infrastructure in migrants' communities of origin became an institutional container for ongoing engagement. It explains how that engagement provided emigrants with new sources of political power and how they drew on that power to redefine economic development in Zacatecas and ultimately in the whole country.

Finally, chapter 9 depicts how migrants brought interpretive exchanges that had flourished at the state level to the Mexican federal government. Migrant activists used the political opening offered by Vicente Fox's presidential campaign in 2000 to demand that the Mexican government engage with them in ways more meaningful than the arms-length approach it had used up until that point. Migrants marshalled their political power to sweep away stock definitions of who they were and what role they could play in Mexico's political and economic development, and to make themselves indispensable participants in interpretive discussions about their nation's future, a claim that was underscored when they won the right to vote in the Mexican presidential election of 2005.

Drawing on the multiple perspectives that the case material provides on interpretive processes, the conclusion lays out the implications that interpretation, as the source of state creativity, has for the way we think of accountability, how we evaluate policies, and whether we can view imagination as a source of political power.

2

Discretionary State Seeing

Emigration Policy in Morocco and Mexico until 1963

The year 1963 marked a turning point in the emigration policies of both Morocco and Mexico. That year, Morocco began concluding a battery of guest worker agreements with European nations. With the ratification of the labor export conventions, the Moroccan state departed from the haphazard approach that had characterized its administration of worker emigration since independence in 1956 and embarked on an ambitious program of state-managed labor export. Mexico, by contrast, saw its participation in the largest guest worker program in history end in 1963. When the United States discontinued its massive recruitment of Mexican workers for agribusiness after twenty years, the Mexican state withdrew from the direct management of worker emigration and, through its disengagement, quietly enabled the continued large-scale movement of workers across its northern border.

This cardinal shift in the emigration policies of both nations would cause an equally radical change in the way the two states perceived emigration and emigrants. The policy changes would determine the visibility—or invisibility—of emigrants to the state for decades to follow. This (in)visibility would be crucial to the elaboration of Morocco's and Mexico's policies to link migration and development. The way the state discerned migration—the specific ways in which state administrations chose to see migrants—informed how the state engaged with them. It defined the tenor and the boundaries of the conversations between migrants and the state—conversations that would ultimately generate the policy innovations that tethered migration to economic development. In sum, state policies to send migrants out would shape state policies to bring migrants back in.

Increasingly, analysts of the state have focused on the practices of state "seeing" and the relationship of those practices to policy design and political control

(Foucault 1994; Dean 1999; Scott 1998; Hansen and Stepputat 2001). They have demonstrated how the state intervenes in local contexts to make realities and social processes that were opaque and unintelligible to it visible and legible to the state apparatus. They have shown how bureaucratic practices, such as standardization and legal codification, are deployed to simplify complex local realities and to slot their infinite details into a set of reductive categories on which the summary descriptions, comparisons, and aggregations of social diagnostics are based (Scott 1998: 77; Gupta 1998). Multifaceted and often contradictory social phenomena are reduced to data points that the state can "see" and act upon.

As these theorists note, the state *does* act on what it "sees." State practices make social phenomena visible to the state so that those social processes can then be subject to state intervention. The knowledge collected and produced in this fashion is critical to the state's ability to impose its jurisdiction and maintain control. The control is often direct, through the immediate state manipulation of social processes (Scott 1998). Control, however, is even more potent in its more subtle, implicit, and indirect forms, in the production of knowledge through state practices and state "seeing" that invests only certain ways of thinking with rationality, makes specific forms of political discourse reasonable and intelligible, and concludes that only a limited subset of policies are plausible (Hansen and Stepputat 2001: 4; Foucault 1994; Dean 1999).

So critical is state "seeing" to governance that most of its observers share a bias about this form of statecraft that smacks of historical determinism. Their nuanced observations of the historically specific practices through which the state makes social processes visible notwithstanding, many analyses of the production of state knowledge associate the bureaucratic practices that enable the state to see with the modern state and make an implicit assumption that the range of state "sight" in a given bureaucratic administration will remain. What the state sees now, it will continue to see. Moreover, there is an implicit characterization of the state as having an inexorable drive to increase what it can measure, categorize, and control. Because its legitimacy is based on the ability to govern, and because the ability to govern is delimited by what it can "see," the push to render society, in all its local detail, legible to the state is viewed as rooted in the state's institutional need for self-replication and self-preservation. The state, or more precisely the state practices that constitute the institutions that make up the state, will make more and more social phenomena visible, expanding the universe that the state can manage, manipulate, and govern in the process.

The history of Moroccan and Mexican emigration policies calls into question these assumptions about state "seeing." The practices that Morocco and Mexico used to govern the emigration of citizens did not uniformly or consistently make emigration and emigrants visible to state bureaucracies. Nor did their state practices push to amplify what the state could see. At various moments in time, the state practices of both nations were designed to detect, measure, direct, and control the movement of migrants. At others, they reflected reluctance on the part of the state to make emigration visible and thus subject to state management. Through their emigration policies, both states expanded and contracted their field of vision as it pertained to migrants. In a sense, both exercised a kind of discretionary seeing.

Whether Moroccan and Mexican emigration policy made emigrants visible depended very much on the political and economic significance of migration at any given historical moment. State seeing was contingent and strategic. It depended on the political usefulness and ramifications of emigration for the state's ability to maintain its hold on power and protect its legitimacy; it depended on the economic consequences of emigration for the nation as a whole, and sometimes for sending areas in particular; and it depended on the fit between emigration and the nation's economic growth policy. Furthermore, it was informed by both countries' historical experience with migration policy and the bureaucratic tools, already honed through previous engagement with emigration, at their disposal.

The political and economic conditions that affected whether state practices made migration visible were not exclusively those of the migrant-sending state. Mexican and Moroccan experiences with emigration policy suggest that state "seeing" is not exclusively a national affair. Both Morocco's and Mexico's rapport with the countries that received their migrants was as pivotal in determining the extent to which their state practices would make migration visible as domestic concerns. When and how their state practices made migration apparent reflected an understanding that the mechanisms that make social dynamics visible to one state are likely to make them visible to another—and thus subject to its control.

This chapter provides a historical overview of Moroccan and Mexican emigration policies. The narrative for both begins in 1963 with the implications their shift in policy had for the way that both states saw their emigrants and then traces the historical events that led both to change the way they managed migration. I focus on the relationship between both countries' emigration policies and their national economic growth strategies; I pay particular attention to how the changing role of agriculture for national development informed their administrative approach to emigration. Both nations' economic priorities and the ways they translated into emigration policy were deeply influenced by politics, and this chapter looks at how economic growth and emigration policies were shaped by domestic political crises as well as by the relationships between the migrant-sending countries and the countries that received their emigrants. In both cases, political interactions were structured by power imbalances and infused with historical experiences of both concord and conflict.

The account of the historical events covered in this chapter draws mostly, but not exclusively, on secondary materials. The historical record for many of the events is incomplete, so what I offer here is reconstruction. Some information is unavailable, in part because it relates to social phenomena that the states in this story were not interested in "seeing" and therefore did not monitor, measure, and translate into data that were recorded and preserved. Some information has been suppressed or deliberately made invisible because of its political sensitivity at various historical moments. This chapter shows how government practices to manage emigration made different aspects of migration visible at different times, and why.

Morocco: Managing Emigration

The year 1963 marked the beginning of political crisis for Morocco. Long-simmering tensions between the urban political parties that had won independence in 1956 and the monarchy that they had adopted as their nationalist symbol of resistance to French rule finally erupted into a full-blown struggle. Urban nationalists' vision for Morocco as an industrialized country headed by an elected government, perhaps, but not necessarily, in the form of a constitutional monarchy, came head to head with the crown's determination that the kingdom should be stewarded by a strong sultan, a Prince of the Faithful, to whom Morocco's people would owe their political allegiance and religious devotion. The public fight between the two factions would determine Morocco's future into the next century.

The political storm of 1963 started gathering after Mohammed V's untimely death two years before. When his son, the young King Hassan II, ascended the throne in 1961, he began quietly but systematically consolidating power into his own hands. By late 1962, he had authored a new constitution that gave new unchecked powers to the king. In campaigning for its ratification, he addressed the nation and proclaimed that this new regal authority was vital "for the good of the people and glory of the motherland" and represented "a renewal of the sacred pact that has always united the people and their King" (radio address, November 18, 1962, as quoted in Palazzoli 1974: 76).

Urban-based political parties and affiliated labor unions that held fast to plans for a democratically elected government bristled at declarations such as these and, once the constitution was passed in December 1962, spent the next several months publicly rebelling against the concentration of executive authority in the king's hands. The left-leaning Union des Forces Nationales Populaires derided the king's call for national unity, declaring that "no national unity is possible around a feudal power, of a spirit that is fundamentally reactionary, and . . . has given proof of its contempt for principled action" (as quoted in Palazzoli 1974: 263). The right-leaning Istiqlal Party, while slightly more measured in its criticism, nevertheless went so far as to publish a tract titled "White Book on Repression in Morocco" (Palazzoli 1974: 161). Newspapers shot back at the legislative changes with headlines that read "No to the Return to Despotism and Feudalism" and a steady stream of critical articles (*AlDoustour*, as quoted in Bennani 2004: 72). Editorial pages lambasted the "personification of the monarchy" and explicitly opposed the move from constitutional monarchy to increasingly autocratic rule, holding it directly "responsible for the inequalities that exist in [Moroccan] society" (Bennani 2004: 78). The year 1963 would be the last for many decades that such direct critiques of the king could appear in print (Entelis 1980; Zerrouky 2004; Dalle 2001; Clement and Paul 1984).

Within a few short months, Hassan II had the midyear parliamentary elections rigged in his favor, stacking the legislative body with yes-men. To cement his electoral coup, the sultan, claiming to have discovered a plot to overthrow the monarchy, had over a hundred opposition leaders arrested, including twenty-one parliamentary representatives. Dozens of them were tortured, thrown into solitary confinement, and condemned to death. For good measure, the king also purged the armed forces of opposition sympathizers and brought the military to heel as the enforcer of his regime (Entelis 1980; Zerrouky 2004; Dalle 2001; Clement and Paul 1984).

Despite these authoritarian moves, Morocco's burgeoning cities continued to simmer with unrest. More ominously, the countryside saw several instances of peasant revolt. In a trend profoundly disquieting to large landowners, dispossessed peasants occupied tracts of land and had to be removed by force (Farsoun and Paul 1976).

Popular discontent at the kingdom's lurch toward authoritarianism and its economic direction would come to a head two years later, in March 1965, when student and worker riots rocked Casablanca, Fez, and Rabat, Morocco's major urban centers. After putting down the protests in a bloody wave of repression that left four hundred dead and thousands more wounded, the king proclaimed a "state of exception": he recessed the parliament indefinitely, suspended the constitution, and assumed full legislative and executive powers. The aspirations of those who had expelled the French to replace the colonial power with a deliberative constitutional monarchy were definitively crushed (Entelis 1980; Zerrouky 2004; Dalle 2001; Clement and Paul 1984).

In the midst of the political turbulence of 1963, the Moroccan government, under the king's increasingly authoritarian direction, began signing formal agreements for the export of its workers. In May, Morocco and West Germany ratified a convention allowing for the recruitment of Moroccans to work in German heavy industry. In full postwar expansion, Germany faced labor shortages so severe that they threatened to slow down industrial production. A similar agreement with France followed only a month later, and Moroccan workers were exported in large numbers to man the republic's assembly lines and to cultivate its fields. Suffering a serious labor shortfall in its mining industry, Belgium would also turn to the kingdom, finalizing a labor convention in February 1964. In May 1969, the Netherlands, finding the supply of Moroccan labor that it siphoned off from France and Belgium insufficient, would sign its own labor agreement (Khachani 2004; Frennet–De Keyser 2004; Morocco, Ministry of Labor 1963a, 1963b, 1964, and 1969).

The timing was not coincidental. A number of European nations, with France taking the lead, had approached Morocco repeatedly since its independence to negotiate possible guest worker programs, but the reaction of the Moroccan government had been noncommittal at best. Moreover, Morocco's attitude toward the emigration of its nationals since independence had been lackadaisical and indifferent; the state granted emigration permits in a haphazard fashion, processing applications as they were submitted and using no specific criteria to approve or deny requests. Yet in 1963, in what appeared to be an abrupt reversal of policy, the government became suddenly amenable to European overtures (Belguendouz 1987).

In fact, the labor accords were a key component of Hassan II's response to the political crisis. Faced with an increasingly discontented urban opposition, which was backed by mobilized, committed, and sometimes violent public support, Hassan II turned to rural elites as a countervailing source of political legitimacy (Leveau 1976). He sought to cultivate a base of rural support loyal enough and weighty enough to counteract urban middle-class demands for political representation and direct access to legislative and executive power. In adopting this strategy, the king fell back on the same political structures and networks the French colonials had used to maintain power in Morocco. The French, in a classic divide-and-rule tactic, had delegated the task of exerting control over a restive rural population to rural elites and used the mercenary allegiance of its new agents to build a countervailing political force against urban demands that they quit the territory. Hassan II tore a page from France's book and, to gain the support of rural elites that the French had propped up, abandoned plans for industrial modernization that would have benefited the urban middle class, shifting instead to a model of economic growth based on commercial agriculture, which heavily favored large landowners. In doing so, he resuscitated the colonial dream, still largely unrealized, of turning Morocco into the California of Africa, where large farms would grow grain and produce for export. More important, he delayed indefinitely the project of land redistribution, which had been one of the central political promises of the independence movement (Leveau 1976; Daoud 1981).

The Achilles' heel of this solution was that the California model of agricultural development would only deepen the rural poverty already fueling popular unrest—in the countryside as well as in cities. In the rural areas, the poor who had been dispossessed and pauperized under fifty years of colonial rule and who had fought starvation after a series of bad harvests in the 1960s were mobilizing to demand access to land, resorting to armed revolt to underscore their claims (American University 1965; Farsoun and Paul 1976). Legions of rural poor also migrated to cities, where, faced with stagnating urban economies and high unemployment, they joined the ranks of urban protestors (Clement and Paul 1986).

At its core, the problem was that the California model of agricultural production was structurally organized around the existence—and, if necessary, the creation—of rural indigence and displacement. In this latifundiary approach to commercial agriculture, growers tended to eschew important technological advances in agricultural production, depending instead almost exclusively on the availability of abundant low-wage labor for the profitability of their enterprise. Moreover, they required a labor force that could be recruited on very short notice and in great numbers to harvest crops that often ripened all at once on vast estates that specialized in a narrow range of products for export. But the interdependence between the profitability of this low-wage mode of agricultural production and rural poverty rendered the California model fundamentally unstable. Rural poverty had to be pervasive enough to keep wages depressed, but not so acute as to drive people to leave the countryside in search of work, or to rise up in protest against the system—and the rural elites—that exploited them. After independence, the severity of rural poverty, aggravated by a series of political and economic shocks, upset the colonial style of agricultural production. Rural peasants rebelled, and rural elites pressed the king for relief.

The guest worker accords were the crown's response to the rural poverty that, in its intensity, had destabilized the regime and disrupted large-scale commercial agriculture. They paved the way for the kingdom's return to the colonial California model of agricultural development and to the alliance with rural elites that it promised. Over their duration, Morocco would ship hundreds of thousands of rural poor to labor markets in Europe. The crown would effectively reduce rural poverty by exporting some of it, while at the same time generating a source of income for the remaining rural poor, through migrant remittances, that would allow them to stay in the countryside where they would be available to labor periodically on large agricultural estates. Moreover, rural residents receiving steady income from abroad would be less likely to migrate to cities, where they might have otherwise swelled the ranks of urban agitators. The crown also used the guest worker accords to sap burgeoning rebellions of their momentum: the government directed labor recruiters to areas where popular resistance to the monarchy's policies was strong and exported workers from areas that it considered restive in significantly larger numbers than from areas it viewed as subjugated (Atouf 2004). The guest worker accords became the lynchpin that made Hassan II's designs to solidify his position as authoritarian monarch politically and economically feasible.

The central role that guest worker accords played in Hassan II's new political strategy catapulted the bureaucratic management of labor emigration high up the list of state priorities and kept the state's attention trained on emigrant workers abroad. The Moroccan state exercised careful control over the movement of rural labor, meticulously planning, targeting, and supervising the disbursal of guest worker contracts. Because the state managed emigration so deliberately, Moroccan emigrant workers would remain clearly visible to it. The way they would be visible, however, as well as the bureaucratic techniques used to sustain this visibility stemmed directly from the colonial model of commercial agriculture to which Morocco reverted. The government simply retooled the optics the French colonial administration had used before it. The techniques the state used to track workers and control their movements would determine how the government engaged with them in the decades following the signing of the guest worker accords. A look at how the colonial administration deployed earlier iterations of these policies to exercise political control over Moroccans not only elucidates the tenor of the engagement between the government and migrants but also reveals how ready Hassan II's desperate regime was to revive colonial tactics to maintain its rule.

Building California in Africa: Land, Labor, and Rural Elites

Soon after being appointed resident general of France's protectorate in Morocco in 1929, Maréchal Lucien Saint sent a delegation to California on a fact-finding mission. Its task was to discover the methods of arboriculture and irrigation that made Californian commercial agriculture both bountiful and profitable, so that the French protectorate could copy them. To the cultivation of wheat, already well established in Morocco thanks to two decades of colonial subsidies and bonuses, the colonial administration wanted to add the production of fruits and early vegetables for export to Europe (Swearingen 1985). The vision of vast fruit and nut orchards stretching across the valleys of southern Morocco and across its northern plains, and of large farms striated with rows of early vegetables, took firm root in the colonial imagination. French publicity materials on the Souss valley in the south of Morocco promoted agricultural investment in the area to potential colonists with romantic descriptions that reported "veritable natural parks" of fruit trees, including almond, apricot, cherry, pomegranate, quince, and fig, and waxed lyrical about the foothills of the High Atlas, lined with "magnificent orchard forests of olive and argan trees" (Hoisington 1985: 317). Renowned French geographers appraised Morocco as having "fat" soils, which, they predicted, would make it "one of the most fertile grain producing regions in the world" (Swearingen 1985: 248). (In an ironic testament to the power of the colonial imagination, it was later discovered that these dark, so-called fat soils owed their rich color not to organic content but to iron salts that made them barely cultivable [Swearingen 1985: 248]). Merchants of this colonial idyll also affirmed that Morocco, caressed by temperate ocean breezes, would support the cultivation of spring vegetables and the expansion of existing citrus groves (Hoisington 1985: 317).

While this representation of Morocco as the agricultural El Dorado of the French empire may have inspired the French political class, its administrators' efforts to make this quixotic vision a reality had permanent consequences for the rural areas. The model of agricultural production that underpinned the romantic ideal was organized around vast estates that employed cheap labor for the large-scale production of goods for export. Protectorate policies to foster it profoundly reshaped the distribution of land, restructured the configuration of local power relations, and transformed the rural peasantry from one made up of communities engaged in subsistence agriculture to landless laborers exploited by large agriculturalists (Hoisington 1985; Swearingen 1985). The three pillars on which the California model of production rested—the concentration of land, the allegiance of powerful rural elites, and the availability of cheap labor—would later prop up Hassan II's regime and keep it from crumbling under the weight of political opposition (Daoud 1981; Leveau 1976).

The French government began by promoting the consolidation of large tracts of land. The colonial administration specifically recommended that farms in the new protectorate be no less than 400 hectares in size. The land grant policy that France applied to its protectorate was designed to foster large-scale farming:[1] in contrast to its policy in neighboring Algeria, where it had summarily expelled peasants from their land in order to redistribute it in modest parcels to small colonial farmers—the infamous *petits colons*—the colonial administration in Morocco gave preference in land allocation to French elites and large companies that had the means and the desire to purchase vast tracts. The administration encouraged long-term investments using the latest agricultural technologies, and production for export to supply the metropole, as well as other European markets, if France's needs were satisfied (Swearingen 1985).[2]

During the forty-four years of French rule over Morocco, between 1912 and 1956, 1.2 million hectares of Morocco's richest agricultural areas—approximately one-fourth of all cultivable land—were transferred into French hands. Colonial land grants between 1917 and 1931 were large, averaging 250 hectares, somewhat shy of the 400-hectare ideal due to a shortage of available land. Private holdings, purchased from Moroccans under extremely advantageous terms enforced by the colonial administration, also between 1917 and 1931, were concentrated in farms that averaged 370 hectares (Swearingen 1985: 350; Daoud 1981; Safi 1990).

To make land available for these vast estates, the French colonial administration dispossessed hundreds of thousands of small farmers, using both military and administrative means. On numerous occasions, particularly in areas where peasants rebelled, residents were summarily and violently expelled from their lands. More frequently, however, the administration simply refused to recognize traditional property rights, many of which were communal and held by Berber tribes, almost none of which had legal written documentation. The land thus became ownerless under the terms of the colonial legal system, available for colonists to appropriate or purchase at prices far below the market value.[3] In addition, the colonial administration expropriated large tracts belonging to the crown. Before the protectorate, all land in Morocco that was not privately or tribally owned was considered royal property by default. The French administration thus regarded it as state property that could be confiscated for the repayment of national debt. Although no accurate data are available on the total amount of land transferred from royal to French ownership under the protectorate, historical records suggest that it was not insignificant. By 1924, the administration had surveyed much of the land considered royal property and had already placed a lien on at least 50,000 hectares of it (Bidwell 1973: 200–205; Safi 1990; Daoud 1981).

The colonial administration was able to carry out this massive transfer by "sharing the spoils" with Moroccan rural elites. In what it would call its *politique indigène*—policy toward the natives—intended to subjugate rural Morocco, France forged alliances with tribal governors, called *caïds*, and endowed them with the administrative power and material resources to participate—through purchase and confiscation—in large-scale land acquisition. The French resident general retained the caïds as "collectors of taxes, supervisors of public order, and judges in civil and criminal cases" in rural areas (American University 1965: 32), governing through them in a system Leveau has called "a bureaucracy of tentacles" (1976: 14). In the process, the French administration created a class of firmly entrenched rural notables who became avid supporters of the system of agricultural exploitation on which France's imperial project was built and staunch defenders of the protectorate that served their political and economic interests so well.

In exchange for their allegiance and submission, the French invested the caïds with "quasi discretionary powers over the persons and goods" in the jurisdictions allocated to them (Leveau 1976: 11). Under the cover of French rule, these rural elites swallowed up the communal lands belonging to their own tribes as well as to their rivals, confiscated private farms, and multiplied their wealth through independent and arbitrary taxation. A number of them accumulated properties as vast as those of the largest colonial landowners in Morocco.[4] The protectorate would "transform [the rural notables] from armed resistance leaders and tribal chiefs into latifundiary landowners" (Leveau 1976: 11; American University 1965).

The rural elites coalesced into a base of support that the French could use as a political counterweight to the king's resistance to the protectorate and to the independence movement that had begun to rally behind the sultan. Under the protectorate, the king's powers had been significantly diminished, but the French were never able to solidify their control sufficiently to supplant him completely. Moreover, France's continued presence and increasingly invasive penetration of the kingdom's social and economic structures strengthened the movement against foreign rule. The nationalist movement was primarily made up of the educated middle classes in Morocco's cities, who, as one historian dryly stated, "had shown a marked reluctance to collaborate with the French" (Hoisington 1985: 321). Over time, the urban nationalists became more organized, confronting the French with increasingly open defiance, in expressions that ranged from written tracts to violent rioting in the streets. The colonial administration responded to the nationalist challenge by cementing their allegiance with rural elites and implementing a series of policies to make sure the California model of agricultural development took firm hold in the countryside. The French viewed a well-entrenched system of commercial agriculture—controlled by

French landowners but aided and abetted by Moroccan rural elites—as the most effective guarantee that France would maintain its long-term presence in a country that it had come to view as an inalienable part of *une France prolongée*—"an extended France" (Leveau 1976; Hoisington 1985).

Colonial land policy, with its wholesale dispossession of small landholders and tribesmen, transformed rural farmers into a ready workforce, landless and available to work for commercial agriculturalists at low wages. What the colonists left unfinished, the caïds completed with their ruthless taxation and land enclosure. "This oppression, particularly in the areas of the Great Caids, was an important factor in causing the tribesmen to forsake their homes," concludes Robin Bidwell (1973: 301) in his account of French rule in rural Morocco. By 1935, close to 100,000 displaced peasants, a full 2 percent of the rural population at the time, worked as full-time and seasonal laborers on the large colonial farms (Daoud 1981).

In the 1930s, French publicity material for colonial investment in Morocco boasted the success of colonial policies, noting that labor was abundant and cheap (Hoisington 1985). To calibrate the supply of agricultural labor to the requirements of the California model and to make the movement of workers visible and thus subject to state control, the colonial administration crafted a series of measures to check the free travel of rural laborers. It also methodically regulated the supply of labor to ensure that the availability of workers was sufficient to meet the needs of agricultural production but not so overwhelming as to destabilize areas where the French authorities governed by proxy, through the caïds they retained. As Bidwell summarizes, "tribesmen could not get permission to leave areas where the colons were short of labour, while in others, having lost their land, they were forced to join the proletariat in the great cities" (1973: 214).

Colonial Emigration Policy

During the Great War, from 1914 to 1918, France recruited 35,000 Moroccans as soldiers and an additional 30,000 as laborers to dig trenches and work in the munitions industry. At the war's end, many were repatriated or returned on their own, but at least an equivalent number remained in France to work in industries in full postwar expansion. After 1920, when land enclosures in Morocco began in earnest and displaced many tens of thousands, emigration from the protectorate rose dramatically, largely of its own accord, using the infrastructure of transnational social networks fostered by French labor recruitment of Moroccans during the war. Commercial agriculturalists in Morocco, aggressively ramping up their production on newly acquired land, complained of labor shortages. In concert with industrialists setting up factories in coastal cities, they pressed the colonial administration to restrict emigration. In response, the colonial authorities instituted a set of regulations in 1923 designed to make emigration visible to the state, so that it could be limited to areas with a demonstrated labor surplus: candidates had to fulfill a series of bureaucratic requirements that were not only daunting but that made their point of origin and their destination conspicuous to the state.[5] Additionally, candidates needed to obtain approval of their emigration petition from regional colonial authorities, who had to certify that the worker's departure would have no injurious effect on local agriculture or industry.

With commercial agriculture experiencing rapid growth, particularly in wheat production, French agriculturalists complained that these controls were insufficient. They continued to report serious labor shortages, and many took matters into their own hands by forcibly conscripting labor.[6] In response, the colonial administration in 1925 added another set of conditions to restrict emigration, extending many of them to cover migration within Moroccan territory. The most draconian of these were penalties, including a sizable fine and six months' imprisonment, levied against any worker who left employment in Morocco, and a requirement that his village provide a worker to replace the deserter. In 1928 the colonial administration, having discovered that many Moroccans were circumventing restriction on emigration by first crossing over the porous border into Algeria, considered a French territory at the time, in order to then continue on to France, issued a blanket prohibition against any emigration whatsoever, regardless of the destination. Registered emigration dropped to only 71 Moroccans in 1929 (Belguendouz 1987; Atouf 2004).

By 1929, however, commercial agricultural production in Morocco, particularly in wheat cultivation, was entering a phase of overexpansion. With the exception of 1930, when an invasion of locusts devoured much of the yield, Morocco harvested bumper wheat crops from 1929 through 1934. The colonial harvest flooded an already depressed French wheat market. France, suffering from the effects of the Great Depression, reacted by erecting highly restrictive quotas for Moroccan wheat. Moroccan agriculturalists were devastated economically—almost one-fourth of all colonial growers in Morocco went bankrupt during this period (Swearingen 1985: 355). In response to this agricultural crisis and to the destabilizing labor surpluses it created in rural Morocco, the colonial administration rescinded all controls on emigration in 1931. In a short time, however, Moroccan agriculture bounced back: agriculturalists diversified their crops, growing more fruits and vegetables, and French demand increased as its national economic health improved. By 1938, agriculturalists were again reporting that labor shortages were affecting their profitability, and the colonial administration quickly reinstated a complete ban on labor emigration. Within the year, the colonial administration reversed its policy dramatically. France was at war and needed men. Emigration controls were suspended, and France began to recruit workers and soldiers aggressively, contracting with 100,000 workers and drafting an additional 200,000 men for combat. When Moroccans could not be persuaded to "complete their social duty and defend the nation" (Belguendouz 1987), the French conscripted workers and soldiers by force. At the end of the war, France showed equal resolve in repatriating

Moroccans; by 1947, their number in France had dropped to 10,000. Emigration restrictions were reapplied and would remain in force until Morocco's independence (Belguendouz 1987; Atouf 2004; American University 1965).

In addition to restricting the movement of rural Moroccans to meet growers' labor needs, the colonial administration used its emigration policy to mollify resistance to its rule. It systematically directed military drafters and recruiters from French industry to areas that were classified as "not pacified," while at the same time forbidding emigration from any region considered "pacified." In issuing emigration guidelines in 1918, Resident General Lyautey (1912–26) specified that "workers must only be recruited from the regions of Marrakesh and Mogador, zones of dissidence" (as quoted in Belguendouz 1987: 38), thus directing recruiters to the Souss region of the Moroccan south. The Soussis persevered in their armed rebellion against the French occupiers until 1936. Not coincidentally, over 80 percent of Moroccan workers recruited for work or combat were from the Souss, with that proportion approaching 100 percent at various times (Atouf 2004). Lyautey congratulated himself on his policy, saying, "every departure of a Moroccan immigrant removed one rifle [from battle] and every return was propaganda that increased France's tranquility [in Moroccan territory]" (as quoted in Belguendouz 1987: 38). The French viewed the remittances that migrants sent or brought home as an equally beneficial means to foster the acquiescence of rural populations to colonial land and agricultural policies. "The Moroccan South received from France a large proportion of the resources that allowed it to live, and its pacification occurred almost as much in our factories as in its mountains," concluded J. Ray, interwar analyst of Moroccan emigration and considered the foremost expert on the matter during that period (as quoted in Belguendouz 1987: 73; Atouf 2004).

Independence, the Rise of the Urban Middle Class, and the California Model

The excesses of the colonial model of agricultural exploitation began, over time, to corrode its political foundation. Opposition to the displacement and impoverishment of rural laborers, as well as to the immoderation of the rural caïds, emerged with the rise of nationalist resistance against French rule. As early as 1934, Moroccan nationalists included in a list of petitions for reform a demand that the judicial and administrative functions of caïds be eliminated (American University 1965: 37). Dispossessed peasants who were forced to migrate to coastal cities in search of work were "a ready audience" for the nationalist rejection of latifundiary exploitation, and many of them joined the anti-occupation riots that rocked Morocco's cities in the 1930s and 1940s (Joffe 1985: 294). After a series of failed harvests in the mid-1940s compounded the effects of wartime rationing, which, predictably, heavily favored French settlers, armed rebellion against the French erupted in the countryside, coalescing by the 1950s into the Armed Liberation Movement operating out of the Rif Mountains (Waterbury 1970: 33–57).

Ultimately, however, the downfall of the California model of agricultural production was caused by the dissonance between the latifundiary political structure on which it depended and a post–World War II shift in France's economic agenda for its protectorate. The colonial administration began to view investment in industry as key to the economic growth of its Moroccan territories. But as France would discover in a gamble that cost it a fair piece of its *France prolongée,* caïds, through their brutality, had weakened France's political hold over Morocco, and the system that enabled the dramatic expansion of large-scale agriculture had become too enfeebled to enforce the political stability demanded by foreign investors.

For most of the protectorate's existence, foreign investment in industry was far outstripped by agricultural investment, but in the early 1950s it soared: in 1952, an estimated US$570 million (at 1952 values) entered Morocco, with the lion's share going to industry in urban areas. By 1953, foreign investment represented 18 percent of Morocco's GDP (World Bank 1966: 13–14). To create a system of governance that would allow colonial investors greater say over policy in the protectorate, the colonial administration proposed local and regional councils in which half the members would represent 300,000 settlers and the other half 12 million Moroccans. King Mohammed V flatly refused to sign the law. In response, the French summoned their loyal caïds, who surrounded the royal palace with their militias on horseback and in borrowed tanks, and deposed the king on August 20, 1953. The French exiled the king to Madagascar in his nightshirt and replaced him with a puppet caïd from central Morocco. This move generated a political crisis and popular upheaval so great that France was never able to reassert its suzerainty. Peasants and small farmers, exhausted by decades of exploitation by rural elites and French colons, joined urban nationalist parties in a nationwide revolt against the caïd usurpers. Unable to withstand the momentum of the independence movement any longer, France flew Mohammed V back from exile in 1955 and recognized Morocco's independence in 1956 (Lugan 1992; Joffe 1985; Waterbury 1970; American University 1965).

The denouement of France's rule over Morocco precipitated the kingdom's political and economic shift from the predominance of commercial agriculture to an emphasis on modern industrial production. Newly reinstated, Mohammed V sidelined the caïds, summarily divesting them of any formal administrative or judicial power. Cognizant, however, of their immense informal political power and vast resources, and perhaps hoping to co-opt them in due course as the French had before him (Leveau 1976), he did not move to destroy them, provided they did not challenge his authority, but neither did he defend their economic interests.

The urban nationalist parties that had spearheaded the independence movement dominated parliament in the newly established system of constitutional monarchy, where the king found himself increasingly sidelined into a symbolic role. At the top of their agenda was a new direction for Morocco's economic policy, with the goal of promoting heavy industry and infrastructure in littoral cities. Moreover, most of the parties favored land redistribution and the promotion of new models of agricultural production that privileged small farmers. In a rejection of vast estates, the powerful—and right-leaning—Istiqlal (Independence) Party adopted the slogan "Land to the tiller!" and its manifesto on economic policy called for "the transformation of the economic and social structures" that affected "the rural masses" (as quoted in Palazzoli 1974: 144). Independent Morocco's first five-year National Development Plan for 1960–64 codified this new direction. It outlined an ambitious state investment program for heavy industry and in primary resource transformation, and forecast "an agrarian reform in order to promote the rationalization of [agricultural] exploitation" (*Plan Quinquennal, 1960–64*, as quoted in Leveau 1976: 61).

The 1960–64 National Development Plan was never implemented. Hassan II, in the throes of the political crisis precipitated by his power grab after his father's death, annulled it in midstream. The king supplanted it in 1963 with a new National Development Plan for 1964–67. The new plan abandoned industrial development goals, and, in so doing, forswore the urban middle class that had called for a constitutional monarchy, where Hassan II's role would be become increasingly symbolic. Instead, it mandated the development of large-scale commercial agriculture, reviving the California model of agricultural production and reinstating with it the network of political allegiances and patronage between the caïds and the ruler—now Hassan II instead of the French. The plan allocated significant state resources to the construction of vast irrigation systems and completely skirted the question of land redistribution, which the urban middle class opposition had supported.

Poverty Effects

In a revival of colonial land policies, the crown actively fostered the consolidation and expansion of the estates owned by rural elites as well as those that were royal property. After France quit its protectorate, colonists, fleeing a political situation they viewed as unpredictable, sold 400,000 hectares of prime agricultural land at bargain prices to the crown and rural elites, and the Moroccan state confiscated much of the remainder (Clement and Paul 1986). Over the next two decades, the state would redistribute less than a tenth of that land to small-scale farmers. The remaining tracts were either maintained as state or royal property or were granted to rural notables in exchange for their allegiance (Entelis 1980; Dalle 2001).

As a result of the crown's policies, the distribution of land that, under the protectorate, was already the most unequal in all of North Africa, became even more inequitable after independence (Ashford 1969). Between 1961 and 1963, 3.5 percent of landowners held 33 percent of the available land, while the poorest 60 percent of the population shared 7 percent. By 1974, distribution had become even more polarized: the number of large landowners grew slightly, with 6 percent of landowners laying claim to 50 percent of available land, at the expense of the poorest 60 percent, who were reduced to sharing barely 4 percent of the cultivable area (Safi 1990; Daoud 1981).

Predictably, the endorsement by the crown and the Moroccan government—for all practical purposes, one and the same after 1965—of a version of the California model of agriculture had significant economic consequences for both rural and urban areas. The consolidation of land, compounded by rapid population growth through increased life expectancy and high birth rates, aggravated rural poverty. In 1960, a full three-fourths of the Moroccan population lived in rural areas; according to a household consumption survey conducted by the state in 1959–60, over 80 percent of people who lived outside cities endured moderate to extreme poverty (World Bank 1981: 224). By 1970, after a decade of healthy agricultural growth at close to 4 percent per annum, the percentage of rural households classed as living in extreme poverty had nearly doubled from 9 percent to 17 percent (World Bank 1981: 224). Not only did poverty increase, but the distribution of wealth became markedly more inequitable: the percentage of overall expenditures by rural households in the two lowest income deciles fell by half, from 8 percent to 4 percent. The moderately poor were also affected: the proportion of expenditures represented by the poorest 40 percent of the population shrank from 20 percent in 1960 to 14 percent a decade later. Meanwhile, the richest fifth of the rural population expanded their expenditures by almost 20 percent (World Bank 1981: 223).[7]

The rural poor fled to Morocco's cities in unprecedented numbers, at a rate of almost 100,000 a year between 1960 and 1970, at a time when the kingdom's total population was a little over 11 million and its urban population just over 3 million. Due in large part to the migration of working-age peasants, Morocco's cities grew at a rate of almost 6 percent a year, a rate that would double the population of urban areas every decade (Safi 1990). The employment-generating capacities of the kingdom's urban economies were overwhelmed.[8] The unemployment rate for urban areas during the 1960s has been estimated at anywhere between 30 and 50 percent, with an equally large proportion of those holding jobs underemployed or employed in the informal sector (Garson and Tapinos 1981; World Bank 1966).

Exporting Labor

To address the labor surpluses in both rural and urban areas, the crown drew on the colonial strategy of precision-targeted emigration policy. According to the text of the guest worker accords signed with European countries, the Moroccan Ministry of Labor maintained the discretion to organize recruitment of Moroccan workers by foreign firms or governments as it saw fit (Morocco, Ministry of Labor 1963a, 1963b, 1964, and 1969). Morocco drew on this authority and used the guest worker programs strategically to reduce pressure on

TABLE 2.1
Cumulative Moroccan Worker Emigration, 1915–76

Year	Emigrant workers (cumulative)	Year	Emigrant workers (cumulative)	Year	Emigrant workers (cumulative)
1915	700	1945	44,000	1966	102,193
1918	13,121	1949	17,000	1967	112,479
1919	3,000	1950	16,000	1968	119,521
1920	7,000	1951	18,000	1969	143,397
1920	9,000	1955	11,368	1970	170,835
1921	10,000	1956	14,200	1971	194,296
1924	15,000	1957	23,290	1972	218,146
1929	21,000	1958	31,296	1973	269,680
1936	10,000	1959	23,125	1974	302,295
1938	13,000	1960	29,718	1975	322,067
1940	40,000	1961	36,957	1976	347,984

Source: Moroccan Ministry of Employment, in Safi 1990.

rural labor markets, to divert migration away from Morocco's cities, and to assert political control.

Under the guest worker conventions, the Moroccan state exported a significant portion of its workforce in the late 1960s and early 1970s—in effect 13 percent, or 1 in 8 of the nation's workers, between 1963 and 1974 (CERED 1991: 72). In order to micromanage the effects of emigration so as to benefit large-scale commercial agriculture, the government drew on data that the reformist parliament, displaced by Hassan II had, ironically, collected in order to dismantle the latifundiary system and alleviate the rural poverty it perpetuated. The abandoned 1960–64 National Development Plan, which recorded a wide array of data on the rural population in anticipation of land redistribution, documented the rural population. The plan also contained estimates of agricultural unemployment and underemployment, disaggregated by geographical location, age, and skill level, among other variables. It also noted how many laborers were employed per hectare, classified the intensity of labor usage by region, and forecast future supplies of agricultural labor for production (CERED 1991: 21–32).

That emigration under the guest worker accords showed significant regional differentiation, with a clear bias toward rural areas, and to specific rural areas in particular, suggests that the state drew heavily on the data in the discarded 1960–64 plan as well as the data it collected for the duration of the accords. The Moroccan government directed guest worker recruitment to rural areas, and rural laborers represented anywhere between 69 and 75 percent of all workers who emigrated under the terms of the worker agreements (Belguendouz 1987). Areas with larger labor surpluses were specifically targeted for emigration: the provinces of Meknes, Oujda, and Taza experienced proportional emigration rates between 1969 and 1971 that were higher than the national average, and all had official unemployment rates that were well above the national average, with Meknes and Oujda in particular registering rates that were almost double the national rate (Belguendouz 1987; World Bank 1981: Statistical Annex, 8).

Furthermore, in a reprise of the colonial tactic of using emigration as a means to weaken opposition to rule and to "pacify" areas in active rebellion, the Moroccan government directed recruiters to areas of the kingdom that it viewed as restive and as a potential threat to stability because of political activity. The Ministry of Labor sent European recruiters, especially those from Belgium and Germany, to the Rif region in Morocco's mountainous north. The Rif had been the base of the Armed Liberation Movement, the guerilla army of Berber tribes whose activities in rural areas helped drive the French out. After independence, it reemerged as a popular movement calling for free and fair elections and a representative national government that took Berber concerns and identity seriously. In 1958, Hassan II, then crown prince, accompanied by 30,000 soldiers, went personally to the Rif to subjugate the movement by force. In his wake, he left 3,000 dead and a region that would remain politically marginalized throughout his reign.[9] Not coincidentally, the region would be strongly represented among Moroccan emigrants. Emigrant worker recruitment between 1969 and 1972 showed a glaringly disproportionate reliance on the Rif Mountains and surrounding areas: according to data collected by the Moroccan Ministry of Labor, the Rif and al-Hoceima administrative regions experienced labor emigration rates of 26 persons per thousand inhabitants and 19 persons per thousand inhabitants respectively, whereas the corresponding rate for the rest of Morocco averaged below 10 persons per thousand inhabitants (Belguendouz 1987: 24). By 1974, the main administrative province of the Rif, Nador Province, would account for 18 percent of all migration from the kingdom, even though it represented only 3 percent of the country's total population (Bossard 1979). So satisfied was the Moroccan government with the results of its emigration policy that it featured emigration in the five-year National Development Plans of both 1968–72 and 1973–77, in which the Ministry of Planning called for the significant expansion of labor emigration. Both plans also forecast the positive effects of labor export for the Moroccan economy and mandated the creation of institutions to foster the virtuous impacts of emigration.

As the scale of emigration increased and the government became interested in capturing the resources it was perceived to generate, the state determined that the close monitoring of emigration implied close monitoring of emigrants. To keep emigrants in Europe within its sight, it engaged intensively with them throughout their stay abroad, and its style of interaction, complete with a repertoire of reinvented colonial practices to track and control them, would shape its interpretive exchanges with Moroccan workers abroad and the kinds of innovations it would eventually produce.

Mexico: Discretionary Optics

Whereas Morocco kept its attention trained on emigrants, Mexico averted its gaze. When its emigration policy changed in 1963, the Mexican government disengaged from practices that would have made emigrants visible to the state. The main reason for this change lay in Mexico's asymmetrical relationship with the United States. Once the United States outlawed much of Mexican immigration, Mexico had a vested interest in concealing migration from its powerful northern neighbor. In a strategy based on the understanding that the movement of people who cannot be tracked cannot be regulated or stopped, the shift in Mexican state practices shielded Mexican emigration from U.S. control.

On December 4, 1963, the U.S. Congress extended the bracero program, a large-scale guest worker agreement with Mexico, for one final year. Since its inception in 1942, close to 5 million labor contracts had been issued to Mexican workers. The United States–Mexico bilateral recruitment scheme was the largest guest worker program in either country's history, and indeed in the world to date. The name of the program, derived from *brazo*, the Spanish word for "arm," evoked the role that Mexican workers were to play in the U.S. economy: the immigrant contract workers filled the most arduous and difficult jobs in the industries to which they were assigned, and yet they were treated as "arms" to which the host society had few, if any, obligations (Calavita 1992: 1). The overwhelming majority were dispatched to agribusiness growers in California and throughout the Southwest, but during World War II significant numbers were also sent north to work on railroad tracks and to man heavy industry production lines (Calavita 1992; Driscoll 1999; Galarza 1964).

The bracero program was not, strictly speaking, a program at all. Instead, it was a series of policy measures which U.S. government agencies, after conferring with Mexican authorities, instated by administrative fiat. The agreements were ratified and periodically extended by the U.S. Congress, and rescued through executive branch intervention when domestic or international political pressure called for their repeal (Calavita 1992: 2). With each legislative iteration, the terms of the program were renegotiated. For most of its duration, U.S. agribusiness lobbied Congress successfully to lower wage and housing requirements for the braceros, regularly persuading lawmakers to abrogate the baseline conditions Mexico had set for its participation (Galarza 1964; J. R. Garcia 1980; Calavita 1992).

In the late 1950s and early 1960s, however, opposition to the program began to mount. Organized labor and church groups mobilized, arguing that the braceros were exploited and that their presence depressed agricultural wages and working conditions for domestic workers (Galarza 1964). In the early 1960s, after a series of newspaper articles and a widely viewed film documentary exposed the poverty and abysmal living conditions of Mexican immigrants hired under the program (Calavita 1992: 143),[10] broad public outcry lent support to the union-led campaign. When President Kennedy signed a two-year extension for the bracero program in 1961, he did so only reluctantly, stating that he could no longer ignore the grievances of domestic agricultural workers: "The adverse effect of the Mexican farm labor program as it has operated in recent years on the wage and employment conditions of domestic workers is clear and cumulative in its impact. We cannot afford to disregard it" (Cross and Sandos 1981: 41). The ambivalent president also qualified his assent to the program's renewal by arguing that its abrupt termination would have a detrimental effect on the neighboring country's economy: "I am aware . . . of the serious impact in Mexico if many thousands of workers employed in this country were summarily deprived of much needed employment" (as quoted in Craig 1971: 173).

By 1963, however, opposition to the program had grown so formidable that even staunch allies of agribusiness judged the political costs of extending it too steep. Representative Sisk of California, a longtime supporter, summed up the situation: "The time has come to serve notice on the American farmer that he and we must come up with an alternative program. . . . This is the last time I shall enter the well for an extension. . . . We have come to the end of the line" (as quoted in Rosenberg 1993: 3). Agribusiness issued predictably dire warnings about the ruinous effect labor shortages would have, but under an administration that had passed the Civil Rights Act and launched the War on Poverty, well-worn threats of crops rotting in the fields for lack of workers simply did not hold the sway they once had (Martin 2001; Calavita 1992; R. Craig 1971).

The Mexican government, faced with the specter of hundreds of thousands of newly unemployed Mexican laborers crossing back across its border, lobbied vigorously for the program's extension, or at the very least a staged phaseout (Creagan 1965; R. Craig 1971: 185; Calavita 1992: 208). The Mexican ambassador Carillo Flores pleaded for "an attempt [to] be made to make the decrease gradually, in order to give Mexico an opportunity to reabsorb the workers who have habitually been working in the United States and thus stave off the sudden crisis that would come from an increase in national unemployment" (as quoted in Creagan 1965: 548). But the U.S. Congress, faced with rising domestic pressure, was unmoved. On December 31, 1964, the bracero program was quietly allowed to expire. As the New Year dawned, braceros began returning to Mexico by the thousands (Salazar 1998b).

For Mexico, the program ended in the same manner that it had begun. The colossus to the north had set the terms virtually by fiat, with scant attention to the impact on Mexico. Throughout the program, the U.S. government had defined how many workers it would need, what work it would need them for, and what remuneration they would receive. Unlike Morocco, Mexico was only a reluctant participant in the recruitment of its nationals. As U.S. negotiators and government agencies made clear on several occasions throughout years of the program, the United States was prepared to run it unilaterally if necessary, and with a largely unguarded border 3,000 miles long, there would be little Mexico could do about it. The United States involved Mexico in the management of the bracero program only as a matter of diplomatic courtesy and bureaucratic convenience (Galarza 1964; Calavita 1992; Driscoll 1999).

The Mexican government spent the duration of the bracero program trying to contain its effects. Through a series of administrative and diplomatic agreements with its northern counterpart, the Mexican state strove to manage the significant repercussions that aggressive U.S. recruitment of Mexican labor had on Mexican national economic growth policy and political stability. While Mexico certainly enjoyed benefits from the guest worker program, the negative effects were by no means insignificant. The program caused shortages in strategic labor markets, particularly in those that supplied agricultural production in northern Mexico, a sector in direct competition with agribusiness on the other side of the border; it generated considerable political fallout as segments of the Mexican public were incensed at the treatment of their compatriots working on American farms; and it hardened into a symbol of subordination to the United States. Every time Mexico drew a line in the sand over the manner in which its nationals were recruited and used, the U.S. government, with agribusiness generally goading it on, scuffed it out.

When the bracero program expired in 1964, the informal system of labor emigration that replaced it, with vast numbers of Mexicans migrating illegally, arguably served Mexico's interests much better. With close to 5 percent of Mexico's population in 1960 having labored under a bracero contract at some point since 1942 (Cross and Sandos 1981), the program fostered structural dependencies of local economies on emigration. It also created durable social networks through which Mexican emigrants were able to enter the United States and then find work. Together, these two factors would ensure that labor emigration from Mexico would continue apace, irrespective of whether a formal recruitment program was in place.

Furthermore, over the two decades of the bracero program, Mexico's economic policy underwent a shift that transformed its attitude toward emigration: from a drain on strategic labor pools, large-scale emigration evolved into a safety valve that reduced political pressure generated by a sharp rise in rural poverty. As industrial policy went from one that supported agriculture both as an export commodity and as a source of food for Mexico's growing urban proletariat, to one that favored industrial development to the serious detriment of agricultural production, emigration became an outlet for growing numbers of unemployed and underemployed in increasingly depressed rural areas, and a check on exponentially intensifying rural-to-urban migration. However, with no organized demand for Mexican workers from a politically consolidated industry base—such as agribusiness—the likelihood that the U.S. government would instate a new guest worker program was slim.

Undocumented labor emigration emerged as the only viable means for Mexico to rely on U.S. labor markets as economic cushion and political buffer. The

Mexican government explicitly disavowed undocumented emigration as a matter of state policy but quietly tolerated, even facilitated, the migration of Mexican workers north. The Mexican government's treatment of Mexican emigrants in the United States, both legal and illegal, reflected its "policy of having no policy" (J. A. Garcia 1987). For close to two decades after the end of the bracero program, the state essentially refused to recognize the vast numbers of Mexicans living and working in the United States. It engaged with emigrants only with the greatest political reluctance, preferring to deal only with groups that identified themselves as representing Americans of Mexican origin. Even as the numbers of Mexican workers north of the border grew rapidly, they became their nation's phantom citizens. Mexico's "policy of having no policy" toward emigration had deep historical roots, all of them gnarled by interaction with the United States in the joint management of the bracero program. Over the course of the program, the United States had gradually turned the optics that the Mexican government had instituted to regulate worker emigration into tools to undercut Mexican demands and undermine Mexican interests.

The Emergence of the Bracero Program

In May 1942, the Mexican embassy in Washington and the U.S. government began preliminary negotiations for the creation of a contract labor program that would allow the large-scale employment of Mexicans in U.S. agriculture (Galarza 1964: 47; Driscoll 1999: 54). Growers in California and throughout the Southwest had been pressing for such a program since the outbreak of World War II. Mobilization had suddenly revved up industrial growth in U.S. cities, drawing unskilled farm workers to production lines in the nation's rapidly expanding heavy industries, especially those critical for national defense. As a result, U.S. agribusiness faced an increasingly acute labor shortage, even as the demand for grains and vegetables soared because of the war effort. Stopgap measures—including shortening the school year, recruiting the mentally ill, closing businesses during harvest periods, and after April 1942, conscripting Japanese and Japanese American workers held in U.S. internment camps—proved insufficient (Gamboa 1990; Driscoll 1999: 52; Galarza 1964). Growers lobbied the U.S. government hard, threatening food scarcity as crops went unharvested and demanding relief from labor shortages they viewed as generated by the United States' decision to enter the war. For several years, the U.S. government had resisted such pressure out of concern that the introduction of temporary foreign labor would undermine working conditions for domestic farmhands. But early in 1942, the government yielded and created a commission to explore the possibility (Calavita 1992; Galarza 1964).

In response to United States overtures about a guest worker program, Mexican president Avila Camacho set up an interdepartmental committee which he directed "to study the various aspects of the migration of braceros" (secretary of labor, Mexico, 1946, as quoted in Galarza 1964: 47). The Mexican government had a series of grave reservations about entering into such a program with the United States, based on experience with an informal bracero program at the close of the First World War (J. R. Garcia 1980; Driscoll 1999). In 1917, the Wilson administration, faced with shortages in the U.S. agriculture sector, unilaterally repealed portions of the restrictive Immigration Act then in effect to allow for the large-scale immigration of Mexicans, many of whom headed north fleeing the violence of the Mexican Revolution and, later, of the Cristero Wars. U.S. growers, along with railroad, mining, and other industrial sectors, sent legions of labor recruiters south to Mexico to try and fill their labor needs. Large-scale recruitment depleted labor markets in key sectors of Mexico's economy, most notably agriculture and mining. The Mexican government, newly installed and ill prepared for such a mass exodus of labor, attempted unsuccessfully to control emigration. Even before Wilson's secretary of labor exempted Mexican braceros from immigration controls, the agricultural labor pools were affected by the illegal emigration of Mexican workers. Beginning with the Madero administration in 1910, the Mexican national government had instated various programs to attract braceros back and integrate them into programs for agricultural development (Alanís Enciso 2004; Driscoll 1999: 41–46). Mexican state and municipal governments, as well as consulates in the United States, had also tried myriad strategies to slow or reverse emigration, ranging from a requirement—unheeded—that labor recruiters post a $1,000 bond for each worker contracted in the state of Sonora, to a patriotic plea published in a Spanish-language newspaper in El Paso urging miners to return to their jobs in northern Mexico (Driscoll 1999: 43–44). But the labor shortfalls that the bracero program caused in Mexico were injurious, and the Mexican government tried to limit large-scale emigration by passing a law in 1917 that made it illegal for Mexicans to emigrate without a contract in hand that guaranteed certain wage levels and working conditions (Driscoll 1999: 41–46; Alanís Enciso 1999). The law was widely disregarded, and Mexico continued to hemorrhage workers until the Great Depression (Alanís Enciso 1999; J. R. Garcia 1980).

After 1929, agricultural and mining output in the United States fell drastically (by more than 50 percent by some accounts; see Cross and Sandos 1981: 13), and the United States' aggressive poaching of Mexican workers was completely reversed. Nativist opposition flared,[11] and Mexico was soon dealing with a massive influx of returning migrants. Mexican authorities recorded the return of 400,000 braceros and their families between 1929 and 1937 (Driscoll 1999: 48). The return of many others went undocumented by the state. As a rule, the migrants returned under very difficult conditions, often penniless, many having been subjected to zealous and bruising deportation sweeps. The Mexican government was saddled with the costs of transporting tens of thousands of indigent workers from the border back to their communities of origin in northern and central Mexico. In the core migrant-sending region, labor markets swelled by 10 percent in a few short years. Many returning migrants, faced with worsening economic conditions in their rural areas, continued on to urban centers, contributing to a growing underclass bloating the already ruthless urban labor markets: between 1930 and 1940, for example, 250,000 emigrants settled permanently in Mexico City (Cross and Sandos 1981: 14; Alanís Enciso 1999; Driscoll 1999: 46–48; J. R. Garcia 1980: 20–23; González Gutiérrez 1999: 78–83; Lipshultz 1962).

As negotiations to reinstate the bracero program as a formal labor agreement proceeded, several departments in the Mexican government added concerns that a large-scale guest worker program with the United States would undermine the Camacho administration's plans for agricultural expansion. In the early 1930s, the government had begun to make significant investment in agriculture. Until 1940, however, the costs of implementing large-scale land reform and the *ejido* system of communal landholding represented the lion's share of these expenditures, although the state also established institutions tailored to agricultural production (like agricultural development banks). With Camacho's accession to the presidency, the emphasis shifted from land redistribution to the development of large-scale commercial agriculture. Rather than a means of providing large numbers of Mexicans with basic livelihoods, agricultural production came to be viewed as a strategy to subsidize industrial modernization. Large-scale agribusiness would supply new urban industrial centers with low-priced staples, but more important, agricultural exports would provide Mexico with the foreign exchange required to import necessary inputs for industrialization. In keeping with this new vision, the state made important capital investments, primarily in irrigation and related infrastructure, which would benefit large landowners, concentrated in the north of the country. It also promulgated a variety of advancements in seeds and fertilizers, focusing extension services and agricultural credit on border enterprise agriculture (Levy and Székely 1983: 139–42; Cárdenas 1996: 23–85; Cross and Sandos 1981; World Bank 1953: 19–37).

Given the strategic importance planned for agriculture in Mexico, Camacho's secretary of agriculture, Marte Rodolfo Gómez, was staunchly against a bracero program. A quorum of officials in other departments allied themselves with him, among them Miguel Aleman, secretary of government, who had stated that "the rightful place for Mexican labor is at home" (as quoted in J. R. Garcia 1980: 22). This remark caused a stalemate that obstructed negotiations over the guest worker agreement for a while and made U.S.-Mexican relations dangerously tense at a time of world war. According to a dispatch from the U.S. ambassador in Mexico at the time, Camacho was forced to intervene and impress upon Gómez just how critical cooperation with the United States was to Mexican security (Driscoll 1999: 68; J. R. Garcia 1980: 20–23).

Faced with the prospect of a second bracero program, the Mexican government sought both to prevent the problems caused by the first one and to protect domestic agribusiness. The state tried to codify a series of legal mechanisms that would enable it to monitor—to "see"—labor migration so that it could regulate it. Its goal was to develop policy tools both to limit the flow of workers northward and to anticipate the repatriation of workers no longer needed, in order to mitigate effects on local labor markets. At the close of deliberations with the Americans in June 1942, the measures negotiated to make emigration visible and subject to Mexican management, if not control, were twofold: government-to-government labor contracts and bracero permits allocated by the Mexican government. The labor contract for each and every Mexican worker was to be a clear, legally binding agreement between the federal governments of Mexico and the United States, and explicitly not between the worker and the employer. Moreover, each contract had to meet three main conditions: first, the Mexican worker would be hired only to supplement and not to replace domestic labor; second, he would be paid prevailing wages, and working conditions would be equal to those of domestic workers and backed by a written contract; and third, the United States would pay round-trip costs between the recruitment center in Mexico and the migrant's place of employment. Additionally, the Mexican government insisted that Texas growers be excluded from the guest worker program because of egregious mistreatment of Mexican workers in the Lone Star state during the first bracero program. The Mexican government viewed the U.S. government as guarantor of all of these conditions, even when it was not the direct employer of the braceros,[12] and made clear to the Americans that it was within its rights to abrogate the contracts if they did not meet the stipulated standards (Calavita 1992; Galarza 1964; Driscoll 1999; J. R. Garcia 1980). The labor contracts kept the employment of Mexican workers in the United States highly visible to Mexican authorities. In principle, the contracts would make it possible for the Mexican government to track the distribution of Mexican workers in U.S. agriculture, the level of demand for braceros, and the labor conditions, and to calibrate the number of contracts it would ratify in response.

The bracero permits were designed to enable the Mexican government to retain administrative control over recruitment and, more pointedly, to export labor from areas with more workers than local markets could absorb. The Ministry of Interior identified regions with surplus labor, designating central western Mexico as a priority recruitment zone. For a series of geographical and political reasons, the effect of the Mexican Revolution and the Cristero Wars was particularly brutal in this region. They decimated profitable agricultural production, reducing the impoverished and traumatized residents who chose to stay to subsistence farming and sending thousands of others to urban centers in search of employment. Accordingly, the Mexican government allotted more than 50 percent of its bracero permits to the states of Durango, Guanajuato, Jalisco, Michoacán, San Luis Potosi, and Zacatecas, which together comprised only 25 percent of Mexico's total population (Sandos and Cross 1983: 44). The Ministry of Interior assigned quotas to the state governments, which would then parcel them out to municipalities. Local magistrates then issued *permisos*—emigration permits—to potential braceros, certifying that the laborers met the necessary requirements to qualify: they were unskilled, landless, and performed no vital function in the local economy (Driscoll 1999: 85; Cross and Sandos 1981: 37; J. R. Garcia 1980: 18–63).

The Mexican government also insisted that recruitment centers be located near the braceros' current places of residence in the center and center-west of the country. Not only would this placement mitigate the disruption caused by large numbers of aspiring braceros traveling to centers far from their homes; it would also ensure that U.S. recruiters were actually drawing on the labor pools that the Mexican government designated as able to withstand the loss. U.S. growers, responsible under the agreement for the costs of transporting workers from the recruitment centers to their farms and back, resisted these demands. A compromise was reached during the initial bilateral negotiations over the program design; it allowed for recruitment centers in northwestern as well as central Mexico. Over the duration of the bracero program, this compromise, along with numerous other provisions in the agreement, would be revised several times, each time drawing the staging arena for recruitment closer to the border, each time favoring U.S. agribusiness and industry over the interests of Mexico and its workers (Calavita 1992; J. R. Garcia 1980: 18–63; Galarza 1964).

Problems with the Bracero Program

The guarantees that Mexico negotiated and the administrative controls it maintained over recruitment proved insufficient right from the start of the guest worker program. Mexico quickly was confronted with the same labor shortages and social dislocations that had been caused by the first program. As early as 1944, Mexico was struggling to fill demands from the United States that in a year and a half had already amounted to well over 100,000 workers for agriculture and railroads.[13] Local labor markets in the states to which the Mexican government directed recruiters were rapidly depleted, and offices of the U.S. War Manpower Commission in Mexico reported that they were falling far short of their targets. In January 1945, for instance, the commission noted that in the state of Zacatecas alone, 6,000 slots for the railroad bracero program had gone unfilled (Driscoll 1999: 82). The United States government's unilateral decision to include Texas agribusiness in the bracero program in 1943 exacerbated Mexican labor shortages: after California growers, those in Texas registered the largest demand for Mexican labor (Calavita 1992).

During World War II, the United States negotiated with the Mexican government to address the latter's concerns about labor shortages, recruitment centers, and working conditions on U.S. farms, suggesting all the while that the bracero program be viewed not just as a vehicle for labor exchange but also as a concrete symbol of Mexico's allegiance to the Allies (Driscoll 1999). After the war ended and with it the labor emergency, the U.S. government, under formidable pressure from an increasingly powerful agribusiness lobby, not only extended the bracero program but significantly augmented the number of workers contracted under its terms. Yearly bracero recruits went from 50,000 in 1945 to 110,000 in 1949 to 310,000 in 1954 to almost 500,000 at its peak in 1956 (Congressional Research Service, 1980, as quoted in Calavita 1992: 218; see table 2.2 for more detailed information on numbers of braceros contracted yearly from 1942 to 1964).

Furthermore, various departments in the U.S. government made it unambiguously clear that the United States was prepared to conduct the bracero program unilaterally if Mexico refused to cooperate. In 1947, the U.S. government, summarily and without warning, changed the contracts from government-to-government agreements to contracts between growers and workers. Mexico perceived this move as a grave affront, but the political costs of withdrawing from the program were too steep. The change in contract structure severely curtailed the Mexican government's ability to control the numbers, skill level, and geographic origin of the workers recruited. In 1952, the United States added insult to injury: even as Mexico was complaining vociferously that Texas growers were employing Mexican workers illegally, outside the scope of the bracero program, and at wages significantly below the agreed minimum, the U.S. Congress included the so-called Texas Proviso in the Immigration and Naturalization Act passed that year. The addition made it clear that hiring an undocumented immigrant did not constitute harboring an illegal alien, and thus no penalties would be applied. Texas growers could go on hiring Mexican workers, in a clear violation of the bracero agreement, with impunity.

Moreover, on two infamous occasions, in 1947 and again in 1954, when Mexico suspended its participation in the program because it objected to U.S. recruitment practices and falling wage rates, the U.S. Immigration and Naturalization Service, in clear violation of the terms of agreement, unilaterally opened the border to thousands of Mexican workers who had massed at checkpoints in response to advertisement of the event. A mere five months after the 1954 incident, the U.S. Attorney General's Office launched Operation Wetback, a massive deportation sweep of undocumented immigrants, tens of thousands of whom U.S. agriculture had employed with impunity; the operation, by the INS's own estimate, sent over a million Mexicans back over the border within a matter of months (see J. R. Garcia 1980 for a detailed account of Operation Wetback; Calavita 1992; Galarza 1964).

As the bracero program evolved, the United States turned the measures that the Mexican government had demanded to keep emigration visible on their head and used them for its own benefit. It added a series of bureaucratic optics to the bracero contracts that made Mexican workers with certain attributes both apparent to U.S. growers and increasingly subject to their control. It inserted provisions designed to attract and capture skilled Mexican laborers for U.S. growers, the two most significant of which were the I-100 card and the Specials permit issued to braceros. The I-100 card, instituted in 1954 after Operation Wetback, certified that the bracero was skilled or performed his job in

TABLE 2.2
Mexican Workers Admitted under the Bracero Program, 1942–64

Year	Number admitted	Year	Number admitted
1942	4,203	1954	309,033
1943	52,098	1955	398,650
1944	62,170	1956	445,197
1945	49,454	1957	436,049
1946	32,043	1958	432,857
1947	19,632	1959	437,643
1948	35,345	1960	315,846
1949	107,000	1961	391,240
1950	67,600	1962	194,978
1951	192,000	1963	186,865
1952	197,100	1964	177,736
1953	201,380		

Source: Congressional Research Service, 1980, in Calavita 1992: 218.

a manner that was "satisfactory," meaning that he had completed his contract without deserting, without "agitating," and in a manner that the employer considered adequate. The Specials cards were versions of the I-100 that indicated that the worker had a special skill. The Mexican government viewed the new measures as aggressive poaching of its most experienced agricultural workers at a time when it needed their skills. In response, it resisted the new policies at various levels of its bureaucracy. When the central government was unable to achieve the repeal of the card system, it responded by creating disruptive delays at recruitment centers (Calavita 1992: 94).

In addition to abrogating agreements with Mexico, the U.S. government also undermined the bargaining power of Mexican workers. Over time, the card system evolved to permit growers to submit lists of workers they wanted to rehire, a move in violation of the bracero agreements that undermined the Mexican government's desire that braceros should work in the United States for only one turn. Workers perceived as troublemakers or who had deserted were not issued I-100s, effectively blacklisting them and making their return to the United States under the bracero system almost impossible. This measure tied workers contractually to their employers. Growers' main complaint about undocumented immigrants was that they would desert their jobs if the conditions were too arduous or the pay insufficient. Combined with an INS campaign to arrest, deport, and blacklist "skips"—workers who left the farm to which they were contracted—this system reduced braceros to the status of bonded workers who could not even "vote with their feet" (Calavita 1992: 87–100). Constantly at risk of deportation either because of work permit inconsistencies or because of accusations that they were agitators in a climate of anticommunist hysteria, workers were unable to challenge falling wage rates already well below those paid to domestic workers (especially in Texas; see Galarza 1964). One midwestern grower in 1960 summed up the position to which the bracero program had reduced Mexico and Mexican workers: "We used to buy our slaves," he said; "now we rent them from the government" (as quoted in J. R. Garcia 1980: 230; Calavita 1992; Galarza 1964).

The "Mexican Miracle" in Agriculture and Its Undoing

As Camacho's secretary of agriculture had predicted at the start of the bracero program, large-scale labor recruitment by U.S. growers eventually undermined agribusiness south of the border. This effect was not straightforward or immediate, however. For a time, unprecedented levels of public investment in irrigation and new technologies throughout the 1940s and early 1950s paid off handsomely. Mexico experienced a Green Revolution so remarkable that it set the standard for developing countries. From 1947 through 1958, its agricultural production registered growth rates between 7 and 10 percent, equal to the highest in the world (Cross and Sandos 1981: 18). The production of Mexico's main staple—maize—increased by over 500 percent between 1940 and 1970 (Cross and Sandos 1981: 18). Agricultural exports also soared, growing at a rate of 9.7 percent between 1951 and 1956, and constituting a full 50 percent of all Mexican exports for 1956 (Cárdenas 1996: 74). Outside observers labeled the geometric growth in output "the Mexican Miracle" (Cross and Sandos 1981: 20).

The policies that spurred such impressive rates of growth allowed Mexico to maintain them despite intensive U.S. recruitment of Mexican labor because the policies favored large landowners at the border at the expense of the rural areas in the center and center-west, the regions that the Mexican state had designated as the source for the bracero program (Levy and Székely. 1983: 139–43). In fact, the central band of Mexico was subject to significant policy neglect and mismanagement, compounding the economic dislocation and low agricultural productivity that were already the region's legacy (Cross and Sandos 1981). With economic prospects poor in the migrant-sending area and population growth rapid—Mexico's population more than doubled between 1940 and 1970 (Cross and Sandos 1981)—large numbers of laborers from the region migrated to border states in search of work, often as a first stage in a journey to cross into the U.S. illegally. For at least three out of the six states the Mexican government had privileged in the allocation of bracero permits, migration to the border region rivaled or surpassed migration across the border (Cross and Sandos 1981: 33). Many of the migrants traveled to work in the north of Mexico as an intermediate stage on their way to U.S. farms (see Zabin and Hughes 1995 for a contemporary analysis of "stage migration"), and the Mexican authorities struggled to contain the exodus of skilled laborers across the border.

The downturn for Mexico began when technological improvements coupled with heavy reliance on cheap labor on both sides of the border raised production to levels so high that agricultural markets were periodically glutted. This overproduction by U.S. and Mexican growers, who were in direct competition with each other for certain goods, helped bring an end to the Mexican miracle. In 1958, U.S. cotton growers, who ranked a close second in the use of bracero labor after tomato growers, experienced a banner year. They flooded international markets with their products, causing prices to plummet, while at the same time they successfully lobbied the U.S. government to institute protective trade barriers to safeguard the U.S. market from foreign competition. Mexican growers, who also did well that year, suffered badly from the international drop in prices and their exclusion from U.S. markets. The turn of events that hobbled Mexican cotton production for export was repeated for other agricultural products, although in less dramatic form, that year and in the years immediately following. The cumulative impact was disastrous. The rate of annual agricultural growth dropped from almost 10 percent in 1958 to a little over 2 percent in 1959, a rate Mexico was unable to rise above for the next decade. By 1961 Mexico's agricultural exports had dropped by half; they would never recover (Nacional Financiera and Banco de México, as cited in Cárdenas 1996: 33, 73–77) and could no longer be relied on as a lucrative source of foreign exchange (Cárdenas 1996; Cross and Sandos 1981).

Mexico's agricultural crisis caused the trajectories of Mexico and U.S. agribusiness to diverge such that within a short time they were no longer competing directly. Mexico's economic planners modified their growth policy to favor industry more heavily, and the state diverted funds and resources away from agribusiness while at the same time imposing a series of price-distorting controls on growers (Cárdenas 1996: 23–85). In one indication of this policy shift, the proportion of direct state investment in agriculture dropped from 23 percent in 1949 to less than 10 percent in the early 1960s (Nacional Financiera, as cited in Cárdenas 1996: 68). As a result, Mexican agriculture began a steady decline that ultimately transformed Mexico from a net exporter of food to a significant importer of agricultural products, especially staples like maize and beans (Cross and Sandos 1981; Cárdenas 1996).

Meanwhile, U.S. growers embarked on the aggressive mechanization of agricultural production. In 1951 only 8 percent of cotton, for example, was harvested by machine, but by 1964 a full 78 percent was mechanically harvested, producing a "radical transformation," as one analyst termed it, in the agricultural system of production and the organization of farm labor (Calavita 1992: 143).

The transformation of both U.S. and Mexican agribusiness changed the function of braceros on both sides of the border and revised the significance of the program for the Mexican economy more generally. No matter how low bracero wages were, U.S. growers found machines to be more cost effective, and once they had mechanized important aspects of agricultural production, their demand for bracero workers dropped. As their dependence on braceros declined, so did their willingness to expend the rising political capital necessary to get the program renewed in the face of mounting opposition (Calavita 1992: 1943–44; Cross and Sandos 1981: 52–59).

In Mexico, the program came to represent an increasingly vital safety valve. From a concern that it would siphon off critical labor supplies, the Mexican government came to rely on it as a source of livelihood for hundreds of thousands of rural residents and a source of political stability for a regime struggling to cope with rapid rural-to-urban migration and the sharp rise in urban poverty that it presaged (Creagan 1965). Increasingly invested in the program's continuation, the Mexican government could only look on helplessly as the U.S. government dismantled it (Cross and Sandos 1981: 59–73).

From Bracero Program to Bracero Networks

Mexican emigration dropped after the termination of the bracero program, but only for a very short while. By the end of the 1960s, it had already rebounded to previous levels (Calavita 1992; Cross and Sandos 1981; Samora 1969). Thanks in part to U.S. growers' consistent disregard of the rules, the end of the bracero program had had little impact on migration flows from Mexico, with one important caveat. Mexican workers now entered the United States of their own accord, both with and without documentation.

Those who entered with documentation did so as so-called commuter aliens—immigrants who had at one point in time received a permanent residence card but lived in Mexico and commuted to the United States on a seasonal basis. The U.S. Department of Labor estimated in 1969 that commuter aliens represented a significant portion of the agricultural labor force in California and the Southwest, filling 85 percent of the agricultural jobs in California's Imperial Valley alone (as cited in Calavita 1992: 154). Yet however large the numbers of commuter aliens were by the late 1960s, they were far surpassed by the numbers who entered the United States illegally (Valdes 1995). Although it is, by definition, impossible to accurately tabulate undocumented migration, all observers agree that illegal entry into the United States rose dramatically after the end of the bracero program and that the total number of Mexican immigrants in the United States (including permanent and seasonal) actually increased (Valdes 1995; Cross and Sandos 1981; Calavita 1992; Samora 1969).

During the two decades of the bracero program's existence, local economies in Mexico's sending regions organized themselves around the seasonal migration of a large segment of their workforce (Mines 1981). Cross and Sandos's survey of ethnographic case studies of villages in the center west of Mexico provides a powerful, if impressionistic, view of just how deeply the program had penetrated rural economies:

> In Tzintzuntzan, Michoacán, 50 percent of the adult males had been to the U.S. by 1960, many of them on 10 or more occasions. Other village studies yielded similar results: "most able-bodied village men" from Las Animas, Zacatecas, participated; San José de Gracia in Michoacán frequently sent 20 percent of its workforce in a given year; by 1962 Huecorio, Michoacán had seen a third of its

adult male population obtain work experience in "the North"; an anonymous village in West Central Mexico had sent 53 percent of its male laborers, and 34 percent of the households in another unnamed community in Michoacán had a family member who had worked as a bracero. A field study of nine villages in Jalisco found that "just about everybody went." (Cross and Sandos 1981: 43)

Braceros had acquired information about how to cross the border, about labor markets and job opportunities, and about how to cope with U.S. employment arrangements (Mines 1981; Cross and Sandos 1981; Calavita 1992; Samora 1969). They could access social networks that facilitated entry into the United States, into specific labor markets, and often into specific farms or firms. Through community networks and family ties, this knowledge and social capital quickly became communal property (Mines 1981; Samora 1969). Thus, even after the bracero program had ended, it continued to provide the framework for Mexican emigration. Sampling studies of undocumented migration conducted between 1969 and 1978 consistently bear this out: an average of 50 percent of the undocumented migrants surveyed came from the six states that the Mexican government had designated as priority sending areas during the bracero program—and to which it had allocated 50 percent of all bracero contracts (as cited in Cross and Sandos 1981: 59; Sandos and Cross 1983).

For the Mexican government, this informal dynamic of labor migration offered several advantages over the formal guest worker program. Under the economic conditions emerging in Mexico in the late 1960s, emigration became an important strategy for managing economic downturns (Cárdenas 1996). Under the informal system, it did more than merely continue apace: it increased dramatically. Over the next thirty years, Mexican migrants to the United States would increase steadily from the equivalent of just under 2 percent of the population in 1970 to over 8 percent in 2000 (Fitzgerald 2006). The practice of seasonal and personal migration provided employment and income to communities in some of Mexico's poorest rural areas, and it curbed the rural-to-urban migration that was still swelling the urban centers (Cross and Sandos 1981).[14]

Released from administrative engagement with the United States over bracero labor, the Mexican government was no longer subject to the capricious strong-arm tactics of its northern neighbor, and with the decline of Mexican agribusiness, the government no longer needed to protect its labor pools. Furthermore, with U.S. agriculture, and to a growing extent U.S. industry, dependent on migrant labor, the Mexican government could rest easy that a large-scale deportation operation like Operation Wetback, which had imposed significant economic costs and political disruption on Mexico, was unlikely (Calavita 1992; Jenkins 1978).

The perpetuation of this informal system of labor export depended on its administrative invisibility. For almost two decades after the formal termination of the bracero program, the Mexican government purposefully avoided addressing the considerable emigration of its citizens north (Santamaría Gómez

1994). The laws Mexico did have on the books to limit undocumented emigration were rarely, if ever, enforced (Samora 1969). Furthermore, the government
periodically reiterated that Mexicans were free to circulate within their own
country, including up to its very border (A. Craig 1981). Furthermore, in a tacit
agreement that suited both the Mexican authorities and U.S. business interests,
rarely did either government bring up the subject of migration—particularly
undocumented migration—in bilateral negotiations (A. Craig 1981; Santamaría Gómez 1994). When pressed by U.S. organized labor as well as Chicano
groups to address the question of large-scale Mexican emigration, the Mexican government stalled by ordering a series of studies on the question, beginning in the late 1970s (A. Craig 1981). Last, it avoided engaging with Mexican
migrant organizations, which were generally weak and informal anyway, for
years after the end of the bracero program. For the informal Mexican emigration dynamic to continue and thrive, Mexican authorities kept it invisible:
through their administrative actions, they acted as if Mexican emigrants did
not exist.

3

Reaching Out

Beginning a Conversation with Moroccan Emigrants, 1963–1973

In 1963, Morocco began ratifying migrant worker agreements with several European countries and soon began exporting labor en masse. To send labor, however, the Moroccan state first had to produce it. In conjunction with European labor recruiters, it set about transforming largely non-Arab Berber peasants who were firmly rooted in their communities into Moroccan workers for export. Drawing heavily on areas that presented the twin challenges of high unemployment and political opposition to the king's often tenuous but brutal rule, the state divorced landless peasants from their communities and remade them into a homogenized migrant workforce. Workers selected to man Europe's Taylorist production lines, descend into its mines, and harvest its crops had to be young, strong, healthy, and docile. At recruiting centers set up in the country's rural areas, candidates were subjected to invasive and dehumanizing medical exams—"they treated us like livestock"—tagged and identified with a contract—"I could barely read, I wasn't even sure what I was signing, they told me, just hold on to it, and follow instructions, and there will be work"—transported to Casablanca or Tangier for final clearance, and shipped directly to their place of employment in Europe ("I was sick the whole way, but there was no rest. Bus, boat, cattle car, bus. . . . [When we arrived], they threw us out in front of the factory barracks in the middle of the night" (interview, Paris, February 2004). On European soil, the transformation was complete: men from villages in the Moroccan Souss, from the Rif Mountains, and from the plains near Meknes had become Moroccan labor—undifferentiated from the rest of the immigrant proletariat hailing from Algeria to Poland in all respects except one. European employers singled out Morocco as a source of manpower they "appreciate[d] very much" (*Le Soir*, January 1964, as quoted in Belguendouz

1999: 47) for being "just as capable but more malleable" than migrant labor from other sources (Belgian consul general in Casablanca, 1963, as quoted in Frennet–De Keyser 2004: 220).

In severing migrant workers' ties to their communities, the Moroccan state was also creating a resource for its own economy. As the Ministry of Planning specified in its National Development Plan for 1973–77, state-assisted Moroccan labor emigration was "the equivalent, in economic terms, of the export of a product produced in Morocco" (as quoted in Belguendouz 1999: 39). Moroccan workers provided foreign currency and investment capital through their remittances, and with their eventual return, anticipated in government economic projections, they would contribute to "the constitution of a larger group of nationals having acquired the professional qualifications and attitudes favorable to entrepreneurship and economic development" (National Development Plan, 1968–72, as quoted in Belguendouz 1999: 34).

Because of the role it envisioned migration playing in the economy, the Moroccan state monitored emigration fastidiously, tracking migrant recruitment, calibrating migrant employment and wages, and counting migrants who had returned down to a man. It quickly discovered, however, that "seeing" was not the same as "apprehending." Meticulous accounting was not sufficient to keep emigrants tethered to the Moroccan economy. To capture the capital the emigrants could provide for the kingdom's development, the state had to create institutions to do so. What remained frustratingly unclear was the shape those institutions should take and how to build them.

To determine how to enforce emigrant participation in the economy, the Moroccan government approached emigrants for information. Particularly keen to collect data on financial practices, it began to query migrants in the late 1960s about the remittances they sent home. Although the government's market research yielded no useful information, its survey unwittingly began an interpretive conversation. The conversation opened a space in which state bureaucrats and emigrants together interpreted the lived experience of emigration, and it evolved in ways that neither side could have imagined. Bureaucrats and migrants together generated a series of mutually intelligible—although not always mutually agreed upon—insights about what it meant to be a Moroccan emigrant working in Europe to collect a paycheck on which a family in Morocco depended. The conversation enabled Moroccan migrants to articulate for the first time the kind of financial services they would like and to identify the obstacles that had made access to formal banking services unimaginable. Likewise, the conversation provided the state with the space to create services that addressed the financial needs migrants expressed.

Another interpretive conversation arose at the same time—between the Moroccan leftists who fled to Europe to escape repression and Moroccan migrant workers. In the mid-1960s, the opposition in exile reached out to workers in an effort to broaden its political base. Moroccan workers were skeptical at first, tending to view the leftists as troublemakers and agitators. As a result, the exchanges began very tentatively. Over time, however, they grew into rich conversations that provided migrants with the interpretive space to reinvent themselves from faceless laborers to workers with rights that they could and would defend. Soon they were at the forefront of the immigrant labor mobilization that took France and its European neighbors by surprise in the early 1970s.

These two interpretive conversations shared a pervasive and sometimes uncomfortable ambiguity, in terms of both content and process. It was precisely that ambiguity that made them generative (Fonseca 2002; Lester and Piore 2004; Lakoff 1987). The dissonance among the distinct and often mutually unintelligible meanings and perspectives participants brought to the conversation created misunderstanding, confusion, and mistrust. Because both bureaucrats and leftist activists had a vested interest in continuing the conversations they had initiated, they strained to understand what migrants were saying. At first, they construed migrants' comments through the prism of their own worldviews and experiences (Lakoff 1987). For the conversation to function as a real exchange, however, they had to make the beliefs and contexts that they used to interpret the meanings they encountered visible to themselves—meanings so taken for granted that they appeared natural, and so dominant that it was virtually impossible to imagine that things might be otherwise. So too did the migrants. Once drawn into the conversations, they were drawn also into the process of reflecting on why they understood their experience in a certain way. Once participants unearthed the meanings they used to understand themselves and each other, they could blend them in new ways, bringing together previously unconnected fields of meaning and using the new meanings as the inspiration for bold imaginative leaps.

Both the Moroccan government and the Moroccan left in exile focused most intently on emigrants in France, and so does this chapter. The conversations that began there, however, generated concepts that would guide Moroccan government policy toward its emigrants, and identities that would shape emigrants' sense of themselves, wherever they were in Europe

Initiating Conversations, 1963–74

By the end of February 1964, the era of state-managed export of Moroccan workers was in full swing. Morocco had ratified labor export agreements with France, Belgium, and West Germany. Even as the North African kingdom struggled to establish a modern economy, it sent legions of workers to staff the production lines of French and German heavy industry, and to labor in the coal mines of Belgium and northern France. The flow of workers sputtered at first, as Morocco and the receiving countries set up institutions to recruit and transport them: "the efficiency of the Moroccan authorities [in the matter of recruitment] is not quite up to speed," complained the Belgian ambassador to

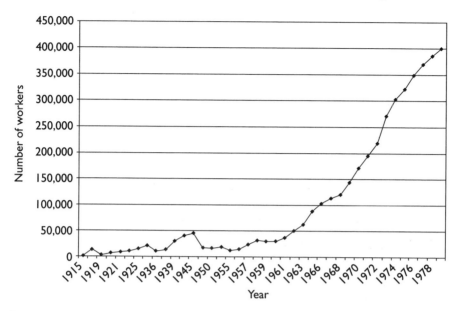

Figure 3.1. Cumulative number of Moroccan registered emigrant workers sent abroad, 1915–78 (Morocco, Ministry of Employment n.d.).

Morocco in 1963 (as quoted in Frennet–De Keyser 2004: 227). By the late 1960s, however, Moroccan registered-worker emigration began to pick up momentum. Between 1969 and 1974, the stock of workers that the Moroccan authorities sent abroad grew by almost 20 percent annually (Belguendouz 1987; Frennet–De Keyser 2004; see fig. 3.1). The lion's share went to France: between 1968 and 1974, France's share hovered at about 65 percent, with Belgium a distant second with about 15 percent (Groupe d'Études et de Recherches Appliquées [GERA] 1992: 18; see table 4.1).

The unregulated emigration of Moroccan "tourists," who traveled to Europe on temporary visas and stayed to work, augmented state-managed labor export. Although definitive numbers of Moroccan workers who emigrated on their own initiative are unavailable, the evidence suggests that they were substantial. In France, the National Office of Immigration was granting far more immigrant worker contracts to "tourists" who had been hired on-site by local enterprises than to immigrants recruited in their countries of origin; by the early 1970s, the proportion of immigrant worker contracts that the French authorities rubber-stamped after the applicants were already working for French employers mushroomed to 80 percent (Tapinos 1975: 65). Similar trends were observed in Belgium and Germany (Frennet–De Keyser 2004).

The Moroccan government looked to emigrant workers as a potential source of national income even before the ink on the labor accords had dried. Indeed, the accord Morocco signed with France specified that "Moroccan workers shall be able to transfer their savings to Morocco in compliance with existing legislation and regulations" (Morocco, Ministry of Labor 1963b, article 13), and the accords with Belgium, Holland, and West Germany echoed that language. With informal emigration adding to formal labor export and the number of Moroccan workers in Europe rising exponentially, the Moroccan government looked increasingly to emigrants as geese who could lay golden eggs. And Morocco, in the 1960s, was badly in need of gold.

Capturing Water and Remittances

During the 1960s, the Moroccan government doggedly pursued the ambitious latifundiary agricultural development policy Hassan II had promoted to secure the support of rural elites. Even though agricultural investment already represented approximately 60 percent of all investment in the national economy in the early 1960s, the government laid out a strategy to increase that share in the 1965–67 and 1968–72 National Development Plans and pledged huge sums to foster the productivity of large-scale commercial farming. With no river running through Moroccan territory, however, return on the government's investment depended on the fickle rains that fell across the kingdom's valleys. As insurance against erratic rainfall, in 1968 the government launched a project to build twenty new dams to irrigate an additional one million hectares (2.5 million acres) by the end of the millennium. The high dams would reliably supply large estates with water and finally make the colonial vision of Morocco as the California of Africa into a reality (Swearingen 1985; White 2001). Hassan II officially declared the high dams project a national objective, asserting that if Morocco could "stop precious rainfall from rushing into the Mediterranean Sea, the Atlantic Ocean, or the Sahara desert," the kingdom would become "an enormous reserve of food, a veritable granary" (Hassan II, as quoted in Hughes 1968). The much-touted *politique des barrages* quickly attained "mythic proportions" (Swearingen 1987) with the king personally orchestrating public events to promote it (White 2001: 125).

Despite the regime's economic grandstanding, however, the government did not even have the funds to support existing investment. Capital flight after former colonists quit the country, the costs of waging a border skirmish with Algeria that escalated into a war, and the outlay of rebuilding Agadir, a southern port destroyed by an earthquake, had already emptied the state coffers. By 1964, the state was running a deficit that amounted to about a third of its operating expenditures, and its shortfall continued to grow throughout the decade (World Bank 1966, 1981). To close this gap, the government launched a public relations campaign in the midsixties to promote private savings and investment, and to press citizens to deposit their money in bank accounts. To direct the newly available funds to the state, it also compelled banks to purchase treasury bonds equivalent to no less than 30 percent of their deposits (Banque Centrale Populaire du Maroc [BCP] 1987; World Bank 1981). This two-pronged initiative was successful, doubling domestic savings in six years, between 1968 and 1974, and increasing the number of treasury bonds purchased in equal measure (World Bank 1981).

To the Ministry of Finance, extending this initiative to Morocco's migrant workers seemed promising. When aggregated, the monies that emigrants sent home were already substantial enough by the mid-1960s to catch the Treasury's attention. In 1964, migrants remitted an estimated 93 million dirhams; by 1967, that sum had doubled to 208 million dirhams, or a little over 1.3 percent of the country's GDP (Bossard 1979; World Bank 1966, 1981). Although remittances padded national income nicely, the government could not leverage them for any of its development schemes because emigrants sent their money home informally. They rarely used postal money orders, to which the state had access, and almost never entered a bank. As a result, remittance flows bypassed the formal banking system that the government had strong-armed into loaning it money.

For the most part, emigrants either brought their earnings back in cash when they returned or sent their money home through couriers. Trusted representatives of Moroccan rural communities, or of Berber tribes, would travel to industrial centers or agricultural areas in Europe where members of their villages or tribes worked, collect a portion of their wages, and hand-carry the cash back to the migrants' families for a fee (BCP interview, Paris delegation, February 2004). Ethnographer Bossard observed this arrangement in the Moroccan Rif:

"They are playing postmen—*Ils font de la poste*" people in the villages would say. One man, [for example], a former emigrant from a prestigious and well-off family, dedicated himself to that occupation, traveling through a number of European countries. He would bring back the amounts necessary to support migrants' families during their stay in Europe. . . . These people enjoyed the trust of the migrant workers but also of the local authorities, and earned a certain profit from the services they rendered. (Bossard 1979: 127)

Recalls one "postman," a former migrant himself, interviewed in the mid-1970s:

I know Europe like the back of my hand because I worked there for 20 years . . . in France for 10 years, and then in Belgium, Holland, and Germany. That's why I speak five languages, along with Arabic and Berber, and a couple of local dialects like Alsatian. I decided to stop working for others and start working for my relatives (tribe) by offering my services. I started by helping them get jobs in Europe; at the beginning, in 1967, it was easy, now it's harder. I make two trips a year, two months each. Once before crops are sowed and once before the harvest. (As quoted in Charef 1981: 221)

In addition to carrying money, "postmen" acted as quasi–social workers to the migrants they took on: they helped them find jobs in Europe, they gave them moral support, they offered financial advice, and they provided loans, which were later deducted from remittances if the migrant or his family faced an emergency, such as an illness or a crop failure (Charef 1981: 221). "I take care of the business and family affairs of my relatives," explains a postman from the Moroccan province of Taza. "The money repatriated varies by year, you know, there are illnesses, ups and downs. I take care of twenty-seven workers (eleven in Germany, seven in Holland, five in Belgium, and four in France), and even if they are hardworking, sometimes there is nothing you can do about destiny" (Charef 1981: 221). "Postmen" also facilitated communication between migrants and families: given the low levels of literacy, the well-traveled postman provided migrants with an indispensable source of oral information about their families, their harvests, Moroccan provincial politics, and employment in factories throughout Europe. For migrants' waiting families, postmen brought news, sometimes embellished, about migrants, their jobs, and their lives in Europe (Charef 1981: 220–21).

For emigrant workers, these informal arrangements were invaluable but costly. Because postal money orders were not accessible to the majority of these workers, the "postmen" could extract the equivalent of monopoly rents: "I keep a tithe of the transfers for myself," specified one (Charef 1981: 221). Authorities also took a cut of the remittances sent back to communities of origin (BCP interview, Paris delegation, February 2004). The monies migrants sent home through couriers were not infrequently lost in transit: couriers often claimed, sometimes truthfully, that they had been robbed. Other times they insisted that migrants misremembered the amount of money they had sent, and with no written documentation of the transfers, to say nothing of formal contracts, migrants had little basis to challenge the couriers' recollections (BCP interviews, Paris delegation, February 2004; interviews, Taroudant, January 2004; Charef 1981).

After remittances arrived, migrant workers and their families again paid a premium when they exchanged them for Moroccan currency (Bossard 1979). Most migrants and their families changed their European currencies on the black market, rarely using formal banks, even when the official exchange rates were more favorable than those they received in informal exchanges. Moroccan government policy to control the value of the dirham deterred emigrants from using formal exchange channels: through its National Office of Exchange, the government jealously regulated currency exchange, requiring written authorization for the conversion of more than 200 dirhams (or DH200, about 20 dollars) into foreign currency (Charef 1981: 218). Even if migrants wanted to use the government-sanctioned services, bank branches in rural Morocco were scarce, and when they were available, migrants and their families found them less than welcoming. In small-town branch banks, migrants reported being treated with disdain by tellers, who dismissed them as rough peasants (interviews, Paris, February 2004). The lobbies of local hostels and the back rooms of general stores where francs were exchanged for dirhams were ubiquitous and welcoming (Bossard 1979).

Banking for the Masses: La Banque Centrale Populaire

To bring migrant remittances into the national banking system, the Ministry of Finance selected the Banque Centrale Populaire du Maroc (BCP), a state-owned bank that was already the main implementing institution of the government's private savings and investment initiative. In 1968, the minister of finance directed the bank to complete "the elaboration of a very refined system such that the repatriation of savings by the workers [abroad] no longer escape state control" (as quoted in Laftasse et al. 1992: 39).

The Ministry of Finance chose the BCP for this mission because it could compel the bank to carry out its orders; the BCP had little autonomy and was, in effect, an arm of the Moroccan bureaucracy. The ministry, however, also selected the BCP for its expertise in introducing people to financial services: the BCP specialized in bringing Morocco's burgeoning middle class into the banking system so that its savings could be used as capital for economic development. As the meticulous files the government kept on migrant labor contracts made clear to accountants in the Ministry of Finance, emigration had projected the poorest rural laborers into a new rural middle class.

Created by the colonial administration in 1926 as a network of state-supported credit unions, the institution that would become the BCP began by providing loans to agriculturalists who deposited enough to become full members of the union, but membership was restricted to French colonists. After independence, the credit unions were ceded to the Moroccan state and consolidated into the BCP by royal decree in 1961. When it appropriated the credit unions, the government also adopted their rhetoric, defining the institution as a renewed expression of "a banking model . . . based on conceptions of mutuality and cooperation" (BCP 1986) suited to the economic needs and political identity of a newly independent Morocco. The BCP continued to serve the well-established landowners who had been the credit unions' main constituency, but it also began targeting an emergent class of smaller farmers, many of whom had purchased land from French colonists when they made their hurried departure from a newly independent Morocco.

Once the national savings drive was launched in 1964, the government recast the bank's mission: its new purpose, populist and pragmatic, was "to bring banking to the masses" (interview, January 2004). The bank expanded its client base to include the middle and lower-middle classes in urban areas, placing special emphasis on small business owners and artisans. It tailored its services to that clientele, often offering a "hands-on" introduction to banking for clients using a bank for the first time. It extended its network of branches, already the largest in the kingdom when the bank was incorporated, and deployed several mobile branches—called *camion-guichets* or "van branches" because they operated out of refurbished Volkswagen vans—to regional centers that did not yet have a branch or to areas where clientele was insufficient to support a permanent office. The BCP van branches would roll into small towns on the day the weekly market was held. People from surrounding villages who had come to sell or buy at the market could also deposit their earnings or withdraw funds from the BCP account that the bank staff had helped them open on one of its previous trips to the town, after having painstakingly convinced skeptics of the advantages of having a formal bank account. To handle the large volume of small transactions that this implied, the BCP also developed a specialized information system, based on the telex and streamlined bookkeeping, that made it possible to keep track of countless deposits and withdrawals of very modest sums, while at the same time reducing the costs associated with processing them (BCP interviews, Paris and Casablanca, January–March 2004; BCP 1986; Morocco 1961).

Because the BCP was already experienced in "bancarizing" new clients—introducing them to formal banking—incorporating emigrants into the BCP's drive to increase domestic savings and bank use seemed consistent with its mission. The emigrants, predominantly rural in origin, fit the bank's client profile on several counts. First, they were an extension of the rural sphere that the bank had traditionally targeted; second, the wages they earned in Europe propelled them into Morocco's middle- and lower-middle classes; and third, they were already engaging in the small financial transactions, albeit informally, that the bank had made it its specialty to manage.

Nevertheless, many at the bank viewed the project as outlandish, even ludicrously impractical. Despite its rhetoric about "bancarizing the masses," the BCP would never have extended its services to emigrants had they remained in Morocco. Before their departure, they were poor, illiterate or marginally literate laborers who earned subsistence wages. According to one state-sponsored study, almost 80 percent of emigrants fit this profile: a household survey of three migrant-sending regions found that only 23 percent of migrants who had left Morocco between 1965 and 1975 had any formal schooling, and only 7 percent were more than marginally literate (Hamdouch et al. 1979: 79). The bank would not have considered them bankable, not only because their incomes were too low to make extending services worthwhile, but also because they were viewed as coarse peasants without even the basic level of actual and cultural literacy necessary to use a bank. More important, the BCP had absolutely no understanding of what it meant to offer financial services to people whose everyday financial practices were stretched across national borders—people who worked in Europe but whose family lives and, more important, family expenditures were in Morocco—and knew of no templates. With the exception of one bank in Portugal that was just beginning to experiment with offering banking services to its migrants in Europe (Ribeiro et al. 2005), no other banks worldwide were providing systematic services for emigrant populations in the 1960s. As one veteran BCP director recalled, when the minister of finance charged the bank with serving emigrants, "everyone thought he was crazy! No one—no one!—at the bank or anywhere else—thought it could be done. People said the minister was out of his mind" (BCP interviews, Paris, February 2004).

Initiating a Conversation: Bringing the Bank to Emigrants

Compelled to comply with the minister of finance's order despite its reservations, the BCP dispatched an exploratory delegation to Paris in late 1968 to investigate the possibility of providing services to emigrants and, if possible, to come up with a prototype of financial tools to capture remittances. The bank staff opened provisional offices in the Moroccan embassy and in the city's suburban consulates, and set out to discover how emigrants' informal networks for money transfer operated. As former members of the BCP staff in Paris described it, the BCP set out to "map out the circuits" through which migrants moved their money from Europe to Morocco (interview, Casablanca, March 2004). The institution also wanted to identify what dissuaded emigrants from using the formal channels of money transfer that did exist. In the 1960s, formal channels generally meant postal money orders, which, according to Moroccan authorities, accounted for almost 80 percent of formal transfers in 1969 (Morocco, Office des Changes 1982).

The BCP delegates tried to ask emigrants about their remittance practices but were brusquely rebuffed by migrants who were extremely suspicious of the Moroccan government officials' sudden interest in their financial affairs. In the face of such a cool reception, the BCP staff abandoned this direct line of questioning and under pressure from Casablanca, intensively reassessed their strategy. Soon, they changed tactics and began simply trying to forge relationships with Moroccan workers in Paris.

BCP staff spent time attempting to earn the trust necessary for workers to feel comfortable discussing financial issues with them. They visited migrants at the worker dorms and factory trailers where they lived; they went to the barber in the *bidonvilles*—shantytowns—at the edges of the city to which Moroccan workers were relegated and spent time chatting with those who had come for a shave or a haircut; they prayed with them in "basement" mosques and prayer rooms; they had lunch with them outside the factories where they worked and relaxed with them in Arab teahouses where migrants gathered to socialize after their shifts. Officials at the BCP in Paris recall stories told by senior colleagues who had participated in that initial mission: "They had running competitions over who had drunk the most glasses of Moroccan tea during the course of the day" (BCP interviews, Paris, February 2004).

In the process of forging solid social relationships, BCP staff opened up a space for an interpretive conversation about Moroccan emigrants' social and financial needs, and eventually about how to create a transnational banking system that would respond to those needs. Initially, conversations revolved around the families and villages that migrants had left, but they also touched on the conditions under which Moroccans worked and lived in France. Workers talked with BCP staff about the difficult living conditions in shantytowns or workers' barracks, where they often had only sporadic access to electricity, and indoor plumbing was a rarity. They also talked about the hostility and bewilderment they felt on the rare occasions that they ventured into other Paris neighborhoods. (Although few of the emigrants that the BCP engaged with had been in France in 1961, the bodies of dozens of Algerians thrown into the Seine after being gunned down by the police during peaceful demonstrations to protest the draconian curfew the French government had imposed on Arabs in the city still haunted its Arab residents well into the next decade.) Sometimes, but very circumspectly, the emigrants also mentioned the difficulties they faced at work with supervisors or with unfair treatment.

Eventually the conversations expanded to include discussions about the complications of sending money home. Migrants described the role that "postmen" played in their lives, extending them support that ranged from help finding a job to caring for a sick relative. They also began to express the frustrations of discovering that money sent through informal couriers was not received, and of paying a pretty penny for services that "postmen" cloaked in the altruistic language of family obligation.

The BCP staff and the Moroccan emigrants brought very different questions to the interpretive engagement that was growing out of these everyday conversations, but the questions were interconnected in ways both groups would only come to understand after they had answered them. Ultimately, rather than providing a means of gleaning existing information—of discovery—the interpretive exchange produced *new* understandings both about why Moroccan emigrants used informal networks for money transfer, and about how those choices were related to the constraints they faced because of their status. Specifically, the conversations brought to the surface three barriers to entry that kept migrants from using formal money transfer channels in particular, but also prevented them from accessing government institutions—both in Morocco and in France—more generally. These were low levels of literacy, a disconnect between Moroccan government regulations and the new service needs that Moroccan workers had as emigrants, and racist and cultural attitudes that made French government offices inaccessible to them. The BCP had previously recognized some of these obstacles in the provision of banking services to emigrants, but only vaguely. Through the interpretive conversations between migrants and staff, these obstacles now became clear to the BCP—and they also became clear to the migrants who articulated them for the first time, not merely as personal problems they faced as individuals but as challenges they faced collectively.

Collaborative Articulation: Specifying Challenges to Formal Remittance Transfer

The problem of literacy had to do primarily with illiteracy in French, or rather in the Latin alphabet. Although data on migrant levels of literacy and education are not available through the Moroccan Ministry of Labor, composite data from a variety of surveys conducted from the mid-1970s through the early 1990s indicate that almost half of all Moroccan workers who migrated to Europe before 1974 had received minimal or no schooling (Institut National de Statistique et d'Économie Appliquée [INSEA], 1976, as quoted in GERA 1992; Hamdouch et al. 1979; Garson and Tapinos 1981). Among those who had received schooling, it is likely that only a small proportion, less than 20 percent (Courbage 1996; INSEA, 1976, as quoted in GERA 1992), would have been functionally literate in French, or in the Latin alphabet. Sending money via a postal money order required that the postal form be completed in the language of the country in which it was issued, generally French in the 1960s and 1970s, and that the address of the recipient be written correctly and in a fashion intelligible in the host country and in Morocco. Because a vast majority of Moroccan migrants were from isolated rural communities, this last detail itself posed significant problems: addresses in rural Morocco were often approximate, and even if the postal workers in the area were literate in French and Arabic and could decipher them, it is not clear that they would have been able to pinpoint the exact physical places or households indicated. Bossard confirmed the obstacle that this represented for money transfers: "errors in the addresses were frequent and it created great inconveniences" (1979: 126; Monnard 1998; BCP interviews, Paris and Casablanca, January–March 2004).

Even if the money reached the correct post office in Morocco and the correct household could be contacted to collect the funds, government regulations confounded migrant families' attempts to cash the postal orders. Postal workers refused to disburse funds for myriad reasons: the absence of government-issued identification, a signature deemed illegible, or an attempt to collect funds after the deadline for doing so had passed (Charef 1981: 221–22). Compounding these administrative hurdles was the dissonance between government regulations and social norms in rural areas. Most migrants named their father or brother as the recipient–an arrangement that often produced conflict between the father or brother and the migrant's wife over how to manage the household budget (Charef 1981: 217–18). To resolve the tension and clarify who would determine how income would be allocated, some migrants named their wives as the recipients on the postal form. At that time, however, gender norms in many parts of rural Morocco made it difficult, if not impossible, for a woman to leave the house, even if accompanied by a male relative, to go to the post office in regional centers, which were often some distance from the village. Save a legal procurator or power of attorney, the postal worker could disburse the funds only to the person named on the form. Furthermore, the administrative processes for establishing someone, a male relative acceptable to the migrant's wife, as a legal substitute were prohibitively convoluted. Migrants' attempts to resolve family disputes got caught up in the Moroccan government's administrative web, and postal money orders were returned without ever being disbursed (Bossard 1979; Benguigui 1997; Bennoune 1975; BCP interviews, Paris and Casablanca, January–March 2004).

The third factor that hampered formal money transfer was the fact that French post offices, like French government offices more generally, were less than welcoming to Arab workers. Moroccan workers who braved them reported that they were treated dismissively and received exceedingly poor service, if they were served at all (BCP interviews, Paris, January 2004). Moreover, workers from the Maghreb were systematically segregated from other workers—including other migrant workers—and the larger community, housed in dedicated lodging, and subject to various forms of racial discrimination (Valabrègue 1973; Granotier 1970; Benguigui 1997). Entering a French government institution at a time when North African workers were often barred from grocery stores was daunting for many Moroccan migrants (interviews, Casablanca and Paris, January–March 2004).

The interpretive engagement that allowed these three main obstacles to be articulated soon came to embody the means of overcoming them. During the everyday interactions that made up the engagement, it became clear that the government bureaucrats could provide Moroccan workers with access to information and institutions simply by being with them. The BCP staff could read and translate for emigrants with limited literacy, and could make everything from newspaper articles to documents related to migrants' employment newly available and intelligible to them. Similarly, the presence of BCP staff could make it possible for Moroccan workers to enter spaces, especially government offices, which had been inaccessible to them: places ranging from doctors' offices to certain neighborhoods in Paris became less inhospitable when workers brought BCP staff along. This observation, and the relationships on which it rested, grew into the framework through which the BCP sought to address the barriers that kept emigrants from using a formal bank. The BCP staff devised a series of formal solutions to the problems migrants faced in using formal transfer mechanisms, but those solutions were effective only because the BCP embedded them in the relationships its staff had forged with workers. The way the BCP conceptualized banking services was revolutionized: banking the unbankable was less about banking than it was about engaging.

Institutionalizing the Conversation: *Stratégie d'Accompagnement*

At the core of BCP's response was an approach built around assisting migrant workers with the transfer of money through the postal system in what the bank termed *une stratégie d'accompagnement*—"a strategy of accompaniment." Formally launched in 1969 as Operation Moroccan Workers Abroad (Opération Travailleurs Marocains à l'Étranger, also called Opération TME), the financial service the bank offered basically consisted of going to the post office with migrant workers and filling out money order forms for them. When accompanied by a Moroccan professional who was fluent in French and could advocate for their rights, Moroccan workers received better service than if they went alone. "Postal clerks became much more patient with Moroccan workers when they saw us with them," remembered one veteran BCP staff member (interview, Paris, February 2004).

Once the staff member completed the form, migrants with rudimentary literacy only had to sign their name: "In the early years, sometimes they just signed with an 'x' or a thumbprint," explained a BCP staff member in the Paris office (interviews, Paris, February 2004). Instead of going to a specific person at a specific address, the money was wired to a general BCP account in Casablanca. The funds were then transferred to individual migrants' personal accounts at BCP, which they or whoever else was a signatory on the account could access at will. Wives or relatives could withdraw funds at the BCP's extensive network of branches in regional centers or from any of its mobile van branches that circulated through small rural towns. The entire transfer took only a couple of days, which, given the technology available at the time, was considered extremely efficient. The BCP's innovative strategy addressed the specific literacy and institutional constraints that deterred migrants from using formal financial channels; it also enabled the Moroccan government to capture migrant remittances. By linking transfers to deposits, the bank fulfilled the mandate of the minister of finance to ensure that those migrant funds that passed through the institution "no longer escape[d] state control."

The success of the BCP's strategy depended on the quality of the engagement it maintained with emigrants, and the bank went to great lengths to foster the relationships on which that relied. Extension officers continued outreach efforts, visiting migrants at their homes and workplaces, and traveling throughout France and Belgium to meet groups of them. Building on the mobile branch model developed in Morocco, BCP outreach staff "carried a branch in their briefcase" (BCP interviews, Paris, January 2004), with all the necessary materials to open accounts for migrant workers on the spot. Much like the informal couriers who were their antecedents, the staff also acted as quasi–social workers: they helped workers with day-to-day tasks, like going to the doctor, reading or writing letters, or filling out administrative forms related to their employment. BCP staff became the "postmen" of their day, and their engaged style of banking outreach became a mainstay of the bank's approach, even as the services it offered evolved over time. As late as the midnineties, a BCP delegate general remarked that the functions that BCP staff performed were "not exclusively commercial. They are often called upon to provide a whole menu of other services. They are called upon to write a letter or resolve an administrative problem" (A. Belqziz, as quoted in Monnard 1998). Benaces Lahlou, director of the bank's department for emigrant services, added: "We are not satisfied with opening branches. We bring the bank to the emigrants. We follow them all the way to their homes" (as quoted in Ikram and Jouhari 1997; BCP interviews, Paris and Casablanca, January–March 2004, Monnard 1998; Garson and Tapinos 1981; Association des Travailleurs Marocains en France [ATMF] 1984: 63–65).

The BCP cemented its informal rapport and cultivated trust with emigrant clients using formal documentation of their banking services. The bank provided emigrants with evidence of the institution's credibility in order to cultivate the trust required to maintain the relationship on which the BCP's strategy of accompaniment hinged. "The migrants were extremely distrustful of this system at first . . . suspicious of anyone who wanted to handle their money," recalled one officer at the Paris offices. "We were as much in the business of building trust as in the business of banking—*c'était un travail de confiance*." Before relying on the BCP postal transfer system, migrants would test it with a token amount of money. "They would send just 100 dirhams at first and they'd have their wife or another co-signatory on the account check to make sure that the money actually went through, that it was there and that they could withdraw it." To demonstrate its probity, the bank provided emigrant clients with one receipt per transaction, regardless of the number of transactions completed—a practice that it still maintains. The receipts also served as a tangible symbol of the BCP's relationship to individual clients, and bank officers often delivered them to emigrants'. homes, or stopped by to check that emigrants had indeed received the receipts that had been mailed to them. The bank statements documented the tie—and the interpretive exchange that it held—in a practice that both confirmed it and reified it (BCP interviews, Paris and Casablanca, January–March 2004).

Doing the Unimaginable: Results of the Strategy of Accompaniment

The strategy of accompaniment showed remarkable results in a short time. By the end of 1969, within less than a year of the launch of Operation Moroccan Workers Abroad, transfers through the BCP reached 13 million Moroccan dirhams a month and amounted annually to almost a quarter of all remittance transfers to the kingdom. Moreover, an impressive 16,550 migrants had opened accounts at the BCP in the initiative's first year, and those accounts represented 9 percent of the bank's deposits. Over the next several years, the expansion of Opération TME continued apace: by 1970, the number of migrants among the institution's clients had doubled to 35,000 and by 1975 had increased fivefold to 159,000 at a time when the total population of Moroccan workers in Europe was estimated at only slightly more than 300,000. By 1976, the BCP was handling 50 percent of all remittance transfers to Morocco. With remittances as a whole representing close to 5 percent of the GDP, the BCP was bringing in about 2 percent of GDP by banking on those previously considered unbankable (see table 3.1). Although data on the exact sum of monies that that emigrants held in BCP accounts before 1977, as opposed to amounts transferred, are not publicly available, the fact that emigrants were transferring money via BCP deposit accounts suggests that the amount was significant. Only four years after the BCP staff began to strike up conversations in emigrant barracks and coffee shops, migrant deposits in the BCP possibly represented a full percentage point of the national income. So successful were the BCP's efforts in France that by early 1974 the bank had extended its activities into Belgium, with a planned expansion into the Netherlands and Germany (BCP 1986, 2003; Safi 1990).

TABLE 3.1
Remittances and BCP Results, 1969–76

	1969	1970	1971	1972	1973	1974	1975	1976
Remittances (in millions of DH)	302	316	480	640	1,020	1,557	2,159	2,417
Percent of GDP	1.6	1.6	2.2	2.8	4.0	4.6	6.1	4.7
Proportion of transfers through BCP (%)		22.3				49.0		72.0
Number of BCP migrant-held accounts	16,550	35,000					159,000	
Number of Moroccan migrant workers in Europe	143,397	170,835	194,296	218,146	269,680	302,294	322,067	347,984

Sources: Bossard 1979; World Bank 1966, 1981; BCP 1986.

Over time, the formal banking services held more of the relationship between migrants and the bank; the tie between migrants and staff did not require the same level of intensive social support. In fact, soon after the BCP's program of accompanying migrants to the post office became widespread, discussion between staff and migrants revealed that the extension officers could not keep pace with demand. BCP staffing constraints were creating a bottleneck for remittance transfer that was frustrating, even alienating, for the bank's migrant clientele. To respond to their concerns, the bank negotiated an agreement with the French postal service in 1972 that allowed the bank to provide migrants with money orders preprinted with the necessary information, save for the amount to be sent and the migrant's signature. This practice allowed migrants to go to the post office alone to send money using the BCP system if they chose (BCP interviews, Paris and Casablanca, January–March 2004).

Although the relationship between the BCP and its emigrant clients became more institutionalized over the course of Operation Moroccan Workers Abroad, the quality of the rapport continued to determine the success of the BCP's initiatives. Innovations that did not grow out of conversations with migrants fell flat and were discontinued. In the early 1970s, for example, the BCP began a policy of opening branches in various cities throughout France, incorporated under the name Banque Achaabi, in a strategy that was an extension of the bank's actions in Morocco. The European branches were not popular with migrants, who preferred to use post offices, which were conveniently local and were places where migrants had come to feel at ease, and indeed received significantly more respect than when the BCP first began its initiative. The effort to open European branches was abandoned in 1976, and all but three of the eight or more that were set up have since been closed (BCP interviews, Paris and Casablanca, January–March 2004; BCP *Rapports annuels* 1979–2002).

Emigrants and Exiles: Conversations for Political Interpretation

Most of the scores of leftists who fled to Europe during the political retrenchment and roundups of opposition activists that began in Morocco in 1963 landed in Paris, which quickly emerged as a center for the Moroccan opposition. Mehdi Ben Barka, the exiled leader of the Union Nationale du Front Populaire (UNFP), the main opposition party in Morocco, founded the Association of Moroccans in France (AMF) as a clearinghouse for activists. Moroccan university students became active in the association, congregating at its headquarters in a tiny apartment in the Latin Quarter. Some had been members of the left-leaning and soon-to-be-outlawed National Union of Moroccan Students in Morocco and had left to avoid being harassed by the government, arrested, or worse. Others had come to France to study and joined the opposition movement in Paris and other large French cities as they observed their nation's disturbing lurch toward absolute monarchy. The students were not represented in the leadership of the opposition movement, made up of seasoned Moroccan politicians who had fought for independence from the French but had then been squeezed out of government as the king tightened his grip on power. They were, however, the energy of the movement, doing the day-to-day organizing needed to keep it alive, uprooted as it was from its native soil (Daoud 2004; Diouri 1992).

The students, many of them former members of the outlawed Moroccan Communist Party, began to take note of the conditions under which Moroccan workers, arriving in growing numbers, labored and lived. "In Paris," writes Daoud in her monograph on Moroccan labor activism in France, "they discovered those people that called themselves 'the tunnel people,' those that never see the light of day" because they were already at their posts on assembly lines before daybreak and finished their shift after dark (Daoud 2004: 15). Over the next decade, student engagement with the workers would transform how the Moroccan Left conceived of its resistance to Hassan II's rule. From an association of exiled political parties determined to dislodge the king's authoritarian chokehold on the government, the opposition movement began to consider, albeit somewhat dismissively at first, the needs of Moroccan emigrant workers as part of its agenda. The engagement between migrants and activist students also transformed the workers' view of themselves and their possibilities for collective action. From "tunnel people," they became workers with legal rights who could mobilize "in the light of day" to demand them.

Reaching Out to Emigrant Workers

Moroccan student concerns about the situation of their compatriots were well founded. Firm and industry studies from the period indicate that Arab workers in France, and Moroccan workers in particular, were assigned tasks generally below their skill level. Furthermore, they were promoted at a much slower pace than their French counterparts: French sociologist Granges surveyed the automaker Renault's employment practices during the 1960s and early 1970s, and found, for example, that it took twice as long for equally qualified Moroccan workers to receive a promotion as their French counterparts, and also as their Spanish and Portuguese colleagues (Talha 1983). The wage discrepancy between Arab and French workers in the same job classification was also significant, although studies disagree about how significant, with some analyses noting that wages for Arab workers were on average no more than 60 percent of those of French workers (Granotier 1970).

Historical accounts also observe that Arab, and more pertinently Moroccan, workers were assigned the most physically trying and dangerous jobs, both in factories and in mines, leading to a disproportionately high rate of occupational injury (Blanchard et al. 2003; Daoud 2004; Gharbaoui 1971). One of the workers at the Simca factory at Poissy, which turned out Fiat cars, recalled conditions on the assembly line manned by Arab workers: "Because of all the sparks that would fly, we used to call it Vietnam" (as quoted in Daoud 2004: 30). Arab workers were often paid below the contract wage, and charges were routinely deducted from their paychecks, but because of the workers' limited literacy, they were often unable to fully decipher their pay receipts. Numerous instances of intimidation and degrading and racist treatment were also recorded (ATMF 1984; Daoud 2004; Granotier 1970). Because the workers' right to stay on French territory was based on their employment contracts, underreporting of mistreatment and injury was chronic, as workers feared discharge and deportation. Employers also compelled them to join "house unions" under management control, and workers reported seeing Moroccan authorities—"a kind of Moroccan police" (Daoud 2004: 17)—providing employers with guidance on what Moroccan workers and activists would term a "colonial" style of labor control (Vidal 2005; Daoud 2004). The substandard lodging provided—barracks often lacking in basic amenities such as running water and heat[1]—also served to segregate migrants from the French population and, more important, from their French co-workers (Derderian 2004; Malet and Simon 1996; Dubet and Lapeyronnie 1992).

Student activists, most of them members of the National Union of Moroccan Students (Union National des Étudiants Marocains, or UNEM) and of the exiled branch of the Moroccan Communist Party, broke that isolation. "The student members of the ex-communist party of Morocco wanted to breathe new life into the worker question which did not seem to be receiving sufficient attention from party leadership," recalled Raymond Benaim, a former Moroccan student activist in Paris (as quoted in Daoud 2004: 12). "The question was whether Moroccan workers could join the French labor movement, whether they could be unionized," he added (Daoud 2004: 18). To try and organize Moroccan workers, the students used a strategy of social outreach that was more proactive and directed than BCP's open-ended approach. They organized literacy classes in French and Arabic. In an embryonic version of a Popular University that they set up at Genvilliers, an industrial suburb with a high concentration of Moroccan workers, they also provided courses in economics, history, and politics. They spent time in worker hostels, celebrating traditional feasts and holidays with the laborers. They also managed to enter factories on several occasions and document some of the transgressions of French labor law that workers endured (Daoud 2004; interviews, Paris, February 2004).[2]

The reception the students received from emigrant workers was mixed at best. Some workers appreciated the political education they felt they were acquiring through the contacts: "We were fascinated," recalls Saïd Tahri, who came to France at the age of sixteen in the 1960s to work alongside his father on construction sites. "We were far from understanding everything, but we learned a lot" (as quoted in Daoud 2004: 20). Many others, however, viewed the students as upper-class troublemakers who were jeopardizing workers' jobs for their naïve political ideals. Student activists recall being chased out of worker gatherings and factory dorms with insults and, on occasion, with blows (Daoud 2004: 19). The leadership of the Moroccan leftist opposition-in-exile was equally ambivalent about the student initiative, but for different reasons. They considered the needs of Moroccan emigrant workers a distraction from their goal of creating regime change in Morocco. This attitude became even more pointed after 1965, when Mehdi Ben Barka, de facto leader of the Moroccan opposition in France, was kidnapped and assassinated. The Moroccan opposition was under attack, and all energies had to be refocused on changing the increasingly autocratic monarchy in the homeland (Daoud 2004; interviews, Paris, February 2004). French unions were also disdainful of the student activists' attempts to organize a worker population they had little interest in. Not only were Arab workers not a priority for French unions, but even sympathetic union leadership viewed them as impossible to organize, undisciplined and hotheaded, prone to wildcat strikes that threatened to undermine long-term bargaining strategies (Blanchard et al. 2003; Daoud 2004; Zancarini-Fournel 2002; interviews, Paris, February 2004). The National Union of Moroccan Students was nevertheless able to break through this reticence and forge a tentative but thorny working alliance with the General Confederation of Workers (CGT), a French socialist union. However, when, at the national conference of the Association of Moroccans in 1967, the students proposed the creation of a "Committee for the Defense of Moroccan Workers in France" as a joint initiative between the French union and Moroccan leftist movement, they were sidelined by UNFP leaders (Daoud 2004: 18). The student efforts to organize Moroccan workers, rebuffed by the workers themselves and embargoed by French and Moroccan leftist leadership, seemed to hold little promise.

May 1968 changed the situation dramatically. That spring, French student protests over the lack of adequate educational funding quickly snowballed into a nationwide movement after the de Gaulle government tried to stamp out student strikes with police force. The students were joined by unions, leftist political groups, and high-profile poets and philosophers, and soon France saw massive demonstrations, with over a million people marching through Paris on May 13. By month's end, roughly ten million French workers, about two-thirds of the national workforce, had gone on strike to demand pay raises and better working conditions (Touraine 1968; Singer 2002). Immigrant workers, who represented a full 20 percent of France's workforce, were underrepresented among the strikers to the point of being almost completely absent, but the mobilization nevertheless sparked a debate among student and worker leaders about the role of immigrant workers in the revolution they foresaw (Gastaut 1994).

The movement that shook France to its political core also opened up space for Moroccan students, Moroccan leftist exiles, and Moroccan workers to enter into an interpretive conversation about the events and their significance. During the explosive protests that May, Moroccan students occupied a pavilion at University City in Paris, formerly named after a Moroccan colonial industrialist, and proudly renamed it the Morocco House. They set up a committee of Moroccan activists in France and appointed philosopher-activist Jean-Paul Sartre as president.[3] The heart of Moroccan leftist organizing shifted from a small apartment in the Latin Quarter to the Morocco House, and UNFP leaders, students, and workers all gathered there, holding assemblies and meetings, and planning discussions. Additionally, students on modest scholarships and workers temporarily homeless for a host of reasons spent nights there, sleeping on the dilapidated sofas and floors. The interactions, even the collisions, within this chaotic space created new bridges between the exiled leftist opposition, the students, and the workers (Daoud 2004).

The conversations, the joint activism, and social exchanges opened an interpretive space in which Moroccan leftists and workers developed new ways of understanding themselves and each other. Leftists began to view their solidarity with workers in France as an extension of their struggle against the Moroccan regime. "Very focused on Morocco in its work, [the AMF] in its structure began to defend the interests [of workers] in addition to its pursuing its political positions" recalls one activist of this period (Daoud 2004: 32). In the heady days of May, they saw the mass worker mobilization as a prelude to a revolution that would spread from France to Morocco: "We, the Moroccan workers, have chosen revolution," read a broadsheet published by student activists. "The victory of the French proletariat is ours as well. Our support and our solidarity are a step toward revolution in our own country" (partisans, May–June 1968, 84–85, as quoted in Gastaut 1994). Moroccan workers began to interpret their situation differently as well, as one worker's memory of this period illustrates:

> I was dazzled, overwhelmed, I went to meetings, I didn't understand anything, but the activists spoke well, they analyzed the events. We had good times, it was convivial, we organized together, we distributed tracts, we hung posters, we spent time together in cafes, we cruised women together. I owe everything to the [AMF]. I was born in it, I was educated in it. I learned everything I know through it. [The AMF] opened my eyes to the world. . . . I learned how to think. (As quoted in Daoud 2004: 52)

Many others echoed this sentiment (Daoud 2004; ATMF interviews, Paris, February 2004). For Moroccan emigrant workers, the space and the discussions that took place there fostered the beginning of their labor mobilization. Under the roof of the Morocco House, workers and leftist activists together established embryonic worker committees; within a few short months, the collectives would serve as the organizational backbone for strikes by Moroccan emigrants that would jolt French employers and the Moroccan state (ATMF interviews, Paris, February 2004).

Largely excluded from the large-scale labor mobilization during France's hot summer of 1968 by French unions, which, despite their rhetoric, gave immigrants the cold shoulder, Moroccan migrant workers actively participated in the migrant labor protests that swept through France in the early 1970s. With their grievances sidelined by French unions, migrants staged wildcat strikes in factories throughout the republic and drove home the point that they too could force production to grind to a halt. Although Moroccans made up a relatively small proportion of immigrant workers in France—less than 15 percent of new entrants during 1966–74 (Tapinos 1975)[4]—they were disproportionately represented in the protests that stunned both the French establishment and French unions. At many work sites, Moroccans were the driving force behind the work stoppages and plant takeovers (Lloyd 2000; Zancarini-Fournel 2002; Dumont 2008). Daoud, in her monograph, chronicles the sweep of Moroccan involvement: "The protest movement involved 52 Moroccan immigrants in the recycling factory in Nanterres, then moved to the line workers at Girosbell at Bourgets, all the plants belonging to the Pennaroya group, and then one after the other, the automobile plants in the Paris metropolitan region, the Chasson at Montbéliard, those at Carbonne Lorraine, at Marjolaine, at Câbles de Lyon, as well as a number of smaller firms mostly in the Paris region" (2004: 33). In all of these strikes, Moroccan workers asserted their entitlement to rights that French unions had demanded for their members only months before; they wanted wages, contractual benefits, and protections equal to those of their French co-workers. They also demanded that their living accommodations meet minimum standards, and they participated in hunger strikes organized by immigrants from a variety of backgrounds to demand lodging that complied with France's housing code.

The AMF's relationship to Moroccan worker mobilization shifted as radically. The AMF went from reluctantly tolerating the Moroccan students organizing efforts among workers to wholeheartedly backing the workers in their labor mobilizations. AMF activists camped outside the factories; they walked picket lines; they provided strikers with logistical aid as well as food and blankets; they organized collections of donations for the workers; and they acted as a relay between Moroccan workers and French left-of-center unions that, belatedly, offered migrants their backing (Daoud 2004; ATMF interviews, Paris, February 2004).

Of all the strikes that seemed, at least to the French public, to explode out of nowhere, those at the Pennaroya foundries in Lyon and Saint Denis, a satellite city just north of Paris, were the most searing. These would come to represent the social problems that the French increasingly felt they had unknowingly imported along with the strong arms that powered their factories. The strikes began in late January 1971 in Saint Denis: a group of Moroccan workers were joined by Algerian, Tunisian, Malian, and Senegalese co-workers in a wildcat strike to protest low wages and dangerous working conditions. The workers, 120 strong, struck for seventeen days. The strike failed to win them any improvements, largely because the French, Spanish, and Portuguese workers, who received higher wages than their North African counterparts, refused to stand with them. The protest was enough, however, to draw the attention of the labor inspectorate, which then issued a series of damning reports on the Pennaroya group, listing violations of safety codes, especially the high risk of lead poisoning, and the deplorable conditions in the barracks where immigrants were housed. In particular, the inspectorate noted the lack of sanitary facilities and the segregation of workers depending on whether they were of European or non-European origin (Zancarini-Fournel 2002; *Sans Frontière* 1980).

On December 19, 1971, Mohamed Saleh, a Tunisian worker in the Pennaroya Lyon lead foundry, was crushed by the lid of the smelting oven. The lid, weighing 1,500 kilograms, had been suspended seven feet in the air by an old chain that had rusted through; the lid then fell onto Saleh, mangling his body beyond recognition. After the accident, the factory manager replaced all the chains in the plant and ordered workers to keep quiet about the incident if they wanted to keep their jobs: "If you are asked what happened here today, you say that you were working and saw nothing," he told them (*Rebellyon* 2008). Incensed, immigrant workers at the plant, with Moroccans leading the effort, formally submitted two well-documented portfolios of legal violations and grievances to their employer and to the French government. The portfolios recorded numerous burn injuries, broken bones, bruises, and cases of lead poisoning (*Rebellyon* 2008). The workers received support from a committee made up of the AMF and the short-lived Movement of Arab Workers (Mouvement des Travailleurs Arabes, or MTA), composed primarily of Algerian activists, and a group of volunteer French doctors and lawyers who joined them, and together they publicized the grievances widely through the media. When their complaints received no response either from the government or from Pennaroya, five hundred immigrant workers, predominantly Moroccan and Algerian, began a strike on February 9, 1972, in the foundry's two largest outfits, Lyon and Saint Denis. The strike lasted thirty-three days and received media coverage unprecedented for an immigrant labor protest. It ended with workers securing all of the concessions they had demanded to improve safety and living conditions, with the exception of a raise. A documentary about the victorious strike was screened at union locals throughout the country, and immigrant workers in factories throughout France were inspired by the strikes at Pennaroya to create informal worker collectives and submit formal dossiers of grievances to their employers and the French authorities (Zancarini-Fournel 2002; *Sans Frontière* 1980).

Emigrant Labor Protests: The View from Morocco

The Moroccan state regarded the spreading worker protests with alarm. The incipient alliance between the Moroccan left and the Moroccan workers who were largely of rural origin, from areas that the crown had still not fully subjugated, was a particular source of concern for a regime once again in crisis. The king had just barely survived two successive coups in 1971 and 1972. In 1971, a thousand cadets from a supposedly loyal army descended on the summer palace. After the king narrowly escaped with his life, he conducted a purge of the armed forces so sweeping that they were "rendered virtually leaderless by firing squads" (Giniger 1972). The second attempt was initiated thirteen months later by General Oufkir, the king's trusted minister of interior defense. He ordered the king's plane shot down, and Hassan II survived only through a ruse: he grabbed the radio, saying, "This is the mechanic speaking," and told the attackers that the king had been mortally wounded and to hold their fire to spare the lives of the other passengers (Giniger 1972). The two coup attempts bookended a series of labor and student protests that swept through the country. In late 1971, a miners' strike in Khouribga proved to be the opening gambit in a wave of factory protests in Casablanca, Rabat, and Fes, especially in the textile factories that were at the forefront of the country's push toward industrialization. The worker mobilizations were followed by high school and university student protests in early 1972. Demonstrations, arrests, and counterdemonstrations shook Morocco's major cities, and in March the government expelled 8,500 of the 13,000 students enrolled in the national university system (Diouri 1992: 30–41).

Shaken by the attempts on his life and the protests that were their backdrop, the king ordered indiscriminate roundups of all potential opposition, including leftist leaders, student activists, and state-controlled union leaders and labor organizers. As he made explicit in a 1972 speech to the Moroccan public, he considered few measures too extreme to preserve his seat on the throne: "God has placed the king on his throne to safeguard the monarchy and to do this the Maliki school of Islam stipulates that he must not hesitate, if necessary, to eliminate the third of the population infected by evil ideas to protect the two-thirds not so infected" (as quoted in White 2001).

Within the year, an armed uprising in the rural mountainous areas in the center and southwest of the kingdom challenged the regime once again (Diouri 1992: 38). In response, the crown ramped up its offensive against the political opposition in all forms. The press was further censored; political parties, including the relatively conservative Istiqlal Party, were reined in, and their space for legal activity drastically reduced. Police tactics such as house-to-house searches and identity checkpoints became widespread. The crown's harshest measures were reserved for the Moroccan left, however. The rural unrest was pinned on the leftist UNFP, which was outlawed in March 1973. Over the next few years, hundreds associated with the party or with underground Marxist-Leninist organizations were tried for sedition. Many who had fled to Europe were tried in absentia. Furthermore, student unions, perceived as possible advocates of leftist positions, were banned, and as the Middle East Research and Information Project reported, "repression against students [was] extremely brutal, as schools [were] summarily closed, students beaten and arrested" (*MERIP Reports* 1977: 24).

In this context, the militancy of Moroccan student leftists in exile and migrant workers in Europe was viewed as an extension of the unrest the regime faced domestically and, as such, a potential threat (Belguendouz 1999; Daoud 2004; el-Houdaigui 2003). The regime's preoccupation with the mobilization of Moroccans abroad was augmented by a concern with "political contagion" (Belguendouz 1999). As observers of the Moroccan political economy during this period have stated, Hassan II's government was anxious that political mobilization would spread back to Morocco, specifically that leftist views, especially those critical of the government, would spread from emigrant workers to the larger Moroccan labor pool once those workers returned (Belguendouz 1987, 1999; Baroudi, in Berwart 2004; ATMF interviews, Paris, February 2004). Although emigration was projected to continue for an extended period, individual emigrants were expected to return to Morocco permanently after some years in Europe. This pattern had in fact been in place for much of the 1960s: migrants worked in Europe for several years and then came home, with another male family member taking the relay (Garson and Bennabou 1981; Garson and Tapinos 1981). Indeed, the state counted on workers' return as a part of its long-term development strategy; as specified in the 1968–72 National Development Plan, migrants were to come back after a period abroad "having acquired the professional qualifications and attitudes favorable to entrepreneurship" (as quoted in Belguendouz 1999: 34) to act as agents of economic modernization. The specter of large numbers of workers returning to take their place at the vanguard of a push toward industrial modernization, but bringing with them not only notions about fair working conditions but experience in labor organizing, was too much for Hassan II's increasingly paranoid regime to bear.

More concretely, the crown was concerned that emigrant worker protests threatened the system of labor export on which the government had come to depend as a major source of capital for national development. The regime worried that Moroccan workers spouting revolutionary rhetoric and the wildcat labor activism spreading through France's factories would belie the Moroccan government's representation of its workers as "docile" labor inputs and would dry up Europe's demand for Moroccan brawn, in which the Moroccan government had invested heavily for turning into a resource for Moroccan national development.

Emerging political reactions to immigration in France seemed to lend credence to the Moroccan government's concern that migrant workers' protests in French factories might jeopardize the kingdom's labor export arrangements. In 1972, the French government instituted new regulations designed to curtail the steady influx of illegal migrants. The postwar economic expansion seemed to be cooling, with unemployment on the rise since 1968, and the political resentment that immigrant strikes caused among French workers, who felt immigrants were vying for their jobs, lent a sharp edge to a growing public debate about how many foreign workers France could continue to absorb. These new regulations released in response, called the Marcellin-Fontanet circulars after the ministers of interior and labor who issued them, tightened France's laws regarding work and residency permits. Specifically, the circulars ended the practice of "regularization" whereby immigrants who came to France illegally, often as "tourists," were issued work and residency permits as soon as they found employment. The new regulations required that all employers seeking to hire an immigrant first petition the National Employment Agency of the French government. Work permits could be denied for a host of reasons, including the availability of French workers or legal immigrants to fill the position, a surplus of immigrant workers in that sector, or the employer's failure to provide adequate housing for immigrant employees. The government allowed for no appeal, and immigrants denied regularization were to be summarily expelled from French territory (Garson and Bennabou 1981; Togman 2002). The circulars were met with heated protests from employers and immigrants alike. Prolonged hunger strikes by groups of immigrants facing expulsion added intensity to the immigrant labor protests that continued unabated in industrial centers throughout France (Garson and Bennabou 1981; Zancarini-Fournel 2002). Although Moroccan emigrants rarely participated in the hunger strikes, they remained well represented at the wildcat strikes that periodically closed down France's automobile factories, foundries, and shipyards, and they continued to distinguish themselves as skillful labor organizers (*Sans Frontière* 1980).

As Moroccan government planners, as well as the increasingly nervous Hassan II, surveyed the protests exploding in one European factory after another, with workers they had marketed as diligent and docile at the forefront, they began to explore ways to bring Moroccan workers to heel. With Germany, Belgium, and the Netherlands all considering or implementing immigration controls similar to the Marcellin-Fontanet circulars by 1973, engaging with its emigrants to discover how to control them was a priority that took on new urgency for the Moroccan state.

4

Relational Awareness
and Controlling Relationships

*Moroccan State Engagement with Moroccan
Emigrants, 1974–1990*

On July 4, 1974, the French government announced that in order to preserve employment for French workers during the recession that was looming,
foreign workers would no longer be allowed into the country. André Postel-
Vinay, head of the newly created Secretariat for Immigrant Affairs, specified
that the ban would remain in place until October, "when the situation will be
reviewed" (as quoted in *New York Times* 1974). By October, however, France
was reporting its highest level of joblessness since the end of World War II, and
unions were staging strikes and demonstrations as determined as anything the
nation had ever seen (Farnsworth 1974). France's president, Valéry Giscard
d'Estaing, spoke of France entering an economic period of "enduring crisis"
and pronounced gloomily that, "Europe is in decline. . . . The Europe we have
to build now is a Europe of penury" (as quoted in F. Lewis 1974: 1, 8). France's
decision to close its borders was never reassessed. Nor were the similar decisions of its neighbors, from West Germany to Britain: by the end of 1974, every European country that had had a guest worker program in the postwar
period had suspended it (Cornelius et al. 1994; Garson and Tapinos 1981).
The change in European policy had an immediate effect on Morocco. All the
countries with which it had signed labor conventions stopped issuing contracts, and the annual number of Moroccan workers who departed for Europe
plummeted from 30,500 in 1974 to a mere 9,000 in 1975 (GERA 1992: 13;
see fig. 4.1).

European countries closed their borders in response to the economic contraction caused by the 1973 oil embargo. In the 1970s, Europe received between 80 and 90 percent of its oil from Arab countries, and when the price of
petroleum skyrocketed due to the embargo, European heavy industry was

brought to its knees. The embargo lasted only a few months, however, with Arab countries returning their exports to normal levels by March 1974, and an economic rebound was widely hoped for. Unfortunately, the oil crisis unleashed a series of shocks that ricocheted through European economies, and their industries, organized around rigid Taylorist production systems and fixed wage structures, were pummeled. It would be close to two decades before Europe recovered. As European economies imploded, their governments imposed stricter immigration controls, including limits on family reunification and some of the most forceful measures against undocumented immigration since the Great Depression (Garson and Tapinos 1981; Basfao and Taarji 1994; Cornelius et al. 1994). They erected barriers that would turn once avid importers of foreign labor into fervent defenders of a new "Fortress Europe."

In this new era, Morocco became preoccupied with how to keep migrant remittances flowing into the kingdom. By 1974, these represented 5 percent of the national income. And thanks to banking services that the government had developed in concert with emigrants in the early 1970s, almost half of those remittances had been deposited in accounts at the Banque Centrale Populaire (BCP), from which the government could draw virtually at will. The Moroccan government had come to rely on remittances as an important source of capital for national development projects. To ensure that emigrants kept sending their wages to their country and, more pointedly, into state coffers, the Moroccan government recommitted itself to the conversation with them begun in 1969. Then, it had focused on creating financial tools that would make remittances available at once to the families of migrants and to the government for national development investment. From 1974 onward, the conversation would address how to draw emigrants more deeply and permanently into Morocco's financial system. The state began to engage with migrants as more than mere purveyors of capital; it began to approach them as an emerging market for new financial products that it planned to sell, just as soon as it managed to develop them.

Alongside this engagement, the Moroccan government started another more pernicious one to ensure that migrants continued to earn the wages it eyed. In the wake of the oil shock of 1973, European employers began shedding a workforce that had, almost overnight, become redundant. Moroccan emigrants drew on their experience in the labor mobilizations of the early 1970s and fought the layoffs tooth and nail. They organized prolonged strikes, which they backed with forceful public relations campaigns challenging the prevailing view that they were expendable workers to whom neither their employers nor the governments of the countries in which they labored had any responsibility. Their actions flew in the face of their own government's strenuous representation of Moroccan workers as not only as capable and strong as those from other countries but also more docile. Overnight, it seemed to the Moroccan government, the workers whom it had marketed as compliant and submissive were becoming instigators of labor unrest, troublemakers who companies would only be too happy to be rid of. Alarmed, it tried to intimidate Moroccan workers abroad into obedience, doing everything from negotiating with the strikers to physically brutalizing them. Although its contact with emigrants around the issue of their rights as workers was repressive, through it the Moroccan government unwittingly opened up an interpretive space in which emigrants and government staff could tease out and elaborate the meanings and identities associated with emigrant activities. Steeped in conflict and mistrust, the interpretive engagement nevertheless allowed for the emergence of new understandings about emigrant workers' potential to act as powerful political agents. The government reluctantly began to recognize the individual and collective ability of Moroccan emigrants to effect change in the economic and political spheres in which they participated, whether in Europe or in Morocco. Once the Moroccan government recognized that ability, it actively schemed to destroy it where possible and to contain it elsewhere.

This chapter examines the evolution of these two streams of interpretive engagements until 1990, with the first stream centered on remittances and emigrants' economic participation in Morocco, and the second concerned with emigrants' status and rights as workers. It traces the twists and turns in each of these interpretive conversations, and it shows how profoundly the course they charted and the meanings they yielded were informed by political and economic events in Morocco and Europe. Both conversational streams were deeply situated in historical moments and contexts. Periodic rebellions against Hassan II's regime and the kingdom's vertiginous cycles of boom and bust shaped the tenor of the government's interaction with its workers abroad. Likewise, the gradual breakdown of Europe's system of Taylorist production and the new immigration restrictions that accompanied it made certain areas of discussion more urgent. The events in Europe that most resoundingly reverberated through the engagement occurred in France, and thus this chapter focuses there.

In one conversational stream, the Moroccan state and Moroccan emigrants collaboratively interpreted migrant financial participation in the economic life of the kingdom. They developed institutions that enabled emigrants to participate in the Moroccan economy as suppliers of capital, as consumers, and eventually as investors. The insights that emerged compelled the state to address emigrants' increasingly diverse and sophisticated financial needs. Through the second stream of engagement, the state tried to circumscribe emigrants' identity as workers and to contain their mobilization. The Moroccan state aimed to acquire understandings about its émigré workers, who were changing during their stay in Europe, so that it could better control them. In the process, however, the interpretive engagement redefined state conceptions of worker identities and their political role in Morocco, and it reshaped emigrants' political relationship to their country of origin.

These two streams were characterized by different processes. In the conversations focused on financial issues, the state, and especially the government staff fostering the engagement on its behalf, became adept at what Judith Jordan calls "relational awareness" (2004). Eager to glean new ideas about how to better transfer migrant resources back into the Moroccan economy, bureaucrats developed the relational skills to keep interpretive conversations vital and to push them forward in new directions. They cultivated their own capacity, as well as that of the government department they represented, to hold the ambiguity necessary for interpretive conversations to yield insights, and to sustain that ambiguity long enough for the engagement to offer up new understandings. Moreover, they developed a heightened sensitivity to relational patterns, noticing when the engagement began to break down and sensing when the conversation held the potential for new insight. Furthermore, they acquired the ability, often tacit, to identify when a new concept had become robust enough to scale up into a new policy or institution. The interpretive conversations in this stream continued seamlessly through repeated cycles of engagement, exchange, insight, and institutionalization in a very collaborative fashion.

In sharp contrast, the conversations over the status of emigrants as workers were marked by a chronic lag between the generation of insights and their institutionalization. Contrary to the assertion that, to be generative of insight, interpretive conversation requires a friendly receptiveness on both sides (Lester and Piore 2004), the conversations about emigrants' political rights as workers were highly adversarial. The antagonistic but intensive exchange of meaning generated new perspectives about emigrants' function in Morocco's economic development, and about its relationship to the political power they could exercise in Morocco and in Europe. Because many of these insights posed fundamental challenges to the monarchy, however, the state displayed a pointed reluctance to transform them into policy, only doing so when government recalcitrance caused workers to threaten to disengage completely.

Although very different in tenor, these two conversational streams were deeply intertwined. The creative potential of one stream of interpretive engagement was contingent on the richness of the exchange in the other. The conversations were connected in what organizational theorist Thompson (2007: 54) has called "pooled interdependence": a situation in which branches of an organization or their actions do not interact in an obvious way but are interdependent in the sense that the failure of one can threaten the survival of the other. They drew on a common source for their meanings: the lived experiences of migrant workers in Europe. As we shall see, this lesson is one that the Moroccan state discovered only after it was too late.

Relational Awareness: Interpreting Money

The timing of Europe's change in immigration policy could not have been worse for Morocco. The closure of Europe's borders coincided disastrously with Morocco's spectacular bust of the mid-1970s, which followed directly on the heels of an equally spectacular boom. Thanks to a surge in worldwide phosphate prices in the early 1970s, the kingdom had found itself temporarily flush with cash and ramped up its public spending dramatically. As prices for the mineral peaked in 1974, quintupling from $14 to $68 a ton in a matter of months (Lalutte 1976: 8), the government revised its 1973–77 five-year plan to treble public expenditures in capital-intensive parastatals and basic infrastructure. The state also increased financing for its new "Moroccanization" campaign, launched in 1973 ostensibly to promote majority Moroccan ownership in major enterprises and agribusiness outfits, but designed primarily to placate urban industrialists and large commercial growers who were emboldened in their resistance to the regime by the successive coup attempts in the early 1970s.

The rise in state spending on the economy was matched, and at times even surpassed, by a sharp escalation in military spending. In 1975, the state initiated a military operation to lay claim to the Western Sahara, an area to the south of Morocco that the Spanish considered their protectorate and the Moroccan crown viewed as part of the kingdom that Spain had refused to return. The campaign to annex the phosphate-rich territory began with an unarmed expedition—the highly symbolic Green March in which 350,000 Moroccan conscripts and volunteers crossed into the Western Sahara armed only with Korans—but the action quickly escalated into a war with the Polisario independence army. This guerilla force, native to the Western Sahara and backed by the Algerians, had organized originally to expel the Spanish, who claimed the territory as their colony. Although Saudi Arabia bankrolled a large proportion of the expense, the military engagement cost the kingdom between 20 and 30 percent of its annual budget for the duration of the hostilities, which lasted well into the 1980s (World Bank 1981; Layachi 1998).[1]

Within a couple of years of their dizzying rise, phosphate prices underwent a radical correction. By 1976, Morocco's receipts from phosphate exports had fallen by half and thereafter saw a gradual decline. As its income from phosphate exports dropped, the cost of the petroleum it imported quadrupled after the 1974 oil shocks. Faced with a serious liquidity crisis, the government borrowed unprecedented sums, both domestically and internationally, to complete the economic and military projects that it had started. State borrowing skyrocketed from DH516 million in 1973 to almost DH8 billion only five years later, in 1978, with two-thirds of the funds sourced from abroad (World Bank 1981). Morocco became so overstretched that the World Bank and the International Monetary Fund (IMF) required the country to embark on a structural adjustment program as a condition for any further loans. The program was highly unpopular and widened already stark economic inequalities (Layachi 1998).

The combination of Europe's change in immigration policy and the kingdom's liquidity crisis posed a serious challenge to a state that had grown increasingly dependent on financial transfers from migrants. In the mid-1970s, Mo-

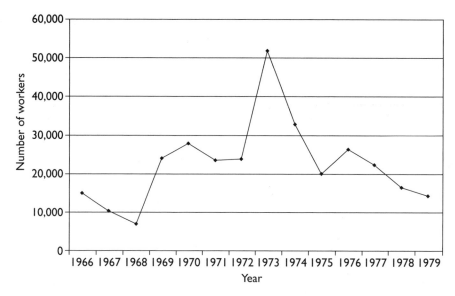

Figure 4.1. Number of registered Moroccan workers per year, 1966–79 (Morocco, Ministry of Employment 1966–79).

rocco could not afford to see the 5 percent of GDP that migrants sent home or the third of national savings that they represented reduced in any way.

Interpreting the Changing Profile of Moroccan Emigrants

The Moroccan government responded to this liquidity crisis by turning once again to remittances as a source of cash. Migrant remittances were a resource the government believed it was in a good position to tap. However, the Moroccan population that the government, and especially the BCP, thought it knew so well had changed as a result of the immigration restrictions passed in 1974. And it would continue to change as European countries that were the main receivers of Moroccan emigrants passed new policies controlling immigration and regulating employment.

When those European countries that were importers of Moroccan labor discontinued their large-scale worker immigration policies in 1974, Moroccan workers stopped returning to the kingdom for fear that they would not be able to secure another emigration contract. The circular pattern of migration ended; migration that Moroccan emigrants and the Moroccan state viewed as temporary became permanent. Workers began to bring their families to join them under European family reunification policies, and the importers of Moroccan labor were mandated by the terms of the labor conventions they had ratified to allow migrants to do so (Khachani 2004; Morocco, Ministry of Labor 1963a, 1963b, 1964, and 1969).[2] European governments initially expressed some reticence at systematic family reunification, with France and Belgium in particular erecting legal barriers to the immigration of family members, including minimum income and housing requirements. After domestic political pressure from migrant advocates and migrant employers, however, all the major importers of Moroccan labor eventually yielded, permitting wives and children to join husbands, and siblings to join brothers (Garson and Tapinos 1981; Khachani 2004). The profile of Moroccans living abroad went from that of an unaccompanied male, working temporarily to send money home, to a family that needed the income earned to raise children on site, in a host country that many would adopt as their own.

The demographic profile of Moroccan communities in countries that were former importers of Moroccan labor illustrates the magnitude of this transformation. Data from France, host to three-quarters of Moroccan emigrants throughout the 1970s and 1980s, convey the significance of this change most distinctly: in 1975, 73 percent of Moroccans living in France were male. By 1984, that share had dropped to 61 percent, and it fell even farther to 55 percent in 1990, as female migration from Morocco increased. The change in absolute numbers of Moroccan women living in France is even more striking: 69,000 lived in France in 1975. By 1984 that number had nearly tripled to 194,500, and by 1990 it had reached 290,000 (el-Mansouri 1996: 86, based on data from the French National Institute of Statistics and Economic Studies, 1990, and the Ministry for the Moroccan Community Abroad, 1990). Couples and the children who lived with them represented over 60 percent of all Moroccans in France (Courbage 1996). Similar trends were observed elsewhere: the proportion of men among Moroccan migrants dropped from almost 70 percent in 1971 to 55 percent in 1981 in Belgium (National Institute of Statistics, Belgium, in Morelli 2004), and from about 80 percent in the mid-1970s to 45 percent in the mid-1980s in Germany (Moroccan consulates in Germany, in Berriane 2003).

The Moroccan government and the BCP found themselves once again confronted with a migrant population that they did not understand. The client base the BCP carefully cultivated had changed so dramatically that it was as if the bank that marketed itself as the "bank of Moroccan workers abroad" no longer spoke their language. The BCP had to return to the interpretive conversation it had opened in 1969 to try and understand the new aspirations migrants had and the new challenges they faced—aspirations and challenges that migrants were only beginning to articulate to themselves. Furthermore, the bank had once again to work collaboratively with emigrants to create financial tools that addressed their new economic difficulties, new anxieties, and new desires.

Over the next two decades, the government, primarily through the BCP, would redevelop a compendium of products to capture migrant remittances and draw migrants deeper into the financial system of their homeland. The new products fit into one of two broad categories: products developed using knowledge about migrant financial practices that was gained pre-1974 and refined afterward using a set of analytic tools rather than consultation with migrants,

TABLE 4.1
Number of Moroccans Living Abroad as Recorded by the Moroccan Government, 1968–2002
(in thousands)

	1968	1975	1984	1987	1993	1997	2002
France	84	260	500	615	690	722	1,024
Belgium	21	65.9	119	120	172	199	214
Germany	18	25.7	46	50	78	104	99
Holland	12	32.2	106	117	157	274	276
Italy			15	30	96	146	287
Spain			32	70	115	119	222
Total EU	135	383.3	818	1,002	1,308	1,564	2,122
Middle East and North Africa			248	NA	206	219	197
Americas			40	NA	37	84	159
Sub-Saharan Africa			10	NA	2	3	6
Asia			0	NA	0	1	4
Total	270	767.1	1,934		2,861	3,435	4,610

Sources: Morocco, Ministry of Foreign Affairs 1968–2002; GERA 1992.

and products developed based on insights that emerged from the interpretive conversations that the BCP continued to have with the changing migrant population after 1974. Monetary incentives to entice Moroccan emigrants to remit their earnings were the main intervention in the first category, and to calibrate them, the BCP methodically analyzed variations in remittance deposits, using bank balance sheets rather than migrant perspectives for information. In the second category were new products that addressed not only the emerging financial needs of workers and the families that had joined them in Europe, but also their social and cultural needs. How the bank, and the state on whose behalf it acted, "saw" emigrant remittance practices shaped how they tried to manipulate them.

Cash for Cash: Analyzing Remittance Transfers

The BCP's success in drawing Moroccan emigrants into the formal banking system made their remittance practices conspicuous to the state, and in great detail. With the numbers of emigrants using the BCP to send their wages to Morocco growing so fast between 1969 and 1974 as to afford it a virtual monopoly over formal remittance transfers, the bank was able to compile hundreds of thousands of data points documenting emigrant transfer and deposit behavior and to gauge with a high level of validity the factors that affected emigrants' propensity to transfer earnings to Morocco. A straightforward statistical analysis of the data indicated that emigrants were extremely cost sensitive. They responded rapidly and significantly to shifts in the price of sending money home, regardless of whether those increases were produced by fluctuations in exchange rates or by the costs of the transactions involved. With the causal relationship between costs and transfers unequivocal—"We discovered a correlation coefficient very close to 1," remembered a BCP director (BCP interview, Paris, 2004)—the government, through the BCP, was able to design instruments to manipulate it.

The government began issuing incentives and reducing costs as early as 1973, when the regime upped its public investment and needed cash. That year the Moroccan treasury offered a 5 percent bonus on all emigrant transfers. The policy had an immediate effect: emigrant remittances doubled between 1973 and 1974, from DH640 million to DH1.02 billion. In late 1974, the government supplemented the bonus with a 3 percent interest rate on all savings kept in Moroccan banks, which at the time meant the BCP almost exclusively. Emigrant savings also responded quickly to the measure: migrant deposits as a proportion of GDP jumped from 2.8 percent in 1972 to 5.7 percent in 1975.

The state complemented these incentives with compensation for variable gaps between European currencies and the Moroccan dirham. When the French franc began to slip in relation to the dirham in 1978, the Moroccan treasury stepped in to cover the difference and mandated banks, primarily the BCP, to extend a 3 percent "fidelity bonus" to emigrant clients. It also softened the impact of fluctuations in exchange rates between the dirham and other European currencies. In 1981, struggling with a serious budget deficit, the Moroccan government rescinded the 5 percent bonus on transfers but maintained parity with the French franc. Remittances in currencies other than the French franc dropped precipitously the following year. The Moroccan state engaged in a complex balancing act between its budget constraints, the value of the dirham relative to other currencies, and its need to increase its currency reserves. It raised and then rescinded bonuses, then offered them again. At times it compensated for shifts in exchange rates; at others, it let the disparity between currencies stand.

Additionally, the BCP implemented measures to reduce transaction costs for emigrants: the bank shaved a day or two off of the financial transfer time; it allowed workers, for example, to have their European pensions and social security allocations for family members direct deposited in their accounts in Morocco; and it multiplied its branches throughout rural and urban Morocco, doubling them from 100 to 200 between 1977 and 1987 (Morocco, Office des Changes 2004; GERA 1992; Garson and Bennabou 1981; Garson 1986; BCP *Rapports annuels* 1978–88).

By coupling financial incentives to real-time information that BCP produced on remittance transfers and by improving the BCP's transfer and deposit services, the government, through the Moroccan treasury and the BCP, managed to keep remittances steady from 1975 through the late 1980s (see fig. 4.2), a turbulent time during which Europe fundamentally redefined its immigration policy, and migrant employment underwent radical shifts. As we shall see, remittance flows would remain constant until the Moroccan government's attempts to suppress migrant workers' activism alienated so many that they adopted Europe as their home and stopped sending money back to their communities of origin.

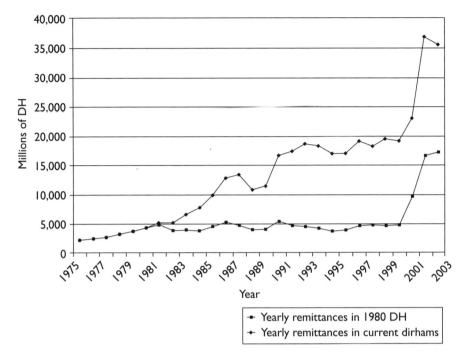

Figure 4.2. Annual recorded remittances to Morocco, 1975–2003 (Morocco, Office des Changes 1963–2006, IMF country statistics).

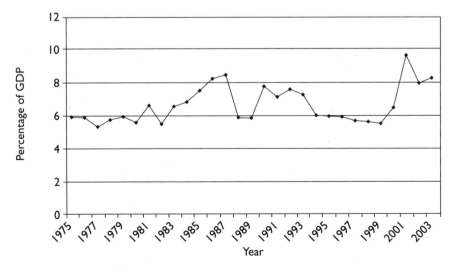

Figure 4.3. Annual recorded remittances to Morocco as a percentage of GDP, 1975–2003 (Morocco, Office des Changes 1963–2006, IMF country statistics).

The BCP's Renewed Interpretive Engagement

Alongside the incentives the Moroccan treasury offered migrants to continue using the services it had already developed, the government, primarily through the BCP, tried to develop new services to draw emigrants deeper into its financial system and tap a greater portion of their earning. With little sense of the financial needs of migrants and the families that had joined them beyond basic deposit and transfer services, the BCP returned to the interpretive conversations that it had begun some five years before, moving on to consider how it could be a truly transnational bank, serving clients who were putting down roots in Europe. As the BCP wrestled with the question of how it could be a bank that straddled "here" and "there"—*une banque d'ici et d'ailleurs*—it was confronted with the fact that emigrants were also trying to figure out how to live at once both here and there.

The experience the state institution had acquired in fostering and sustaining interpretive conversation with emigrants produced what can most closely be described as "relational awareness" (Jordan 2004). Through engagement with migrants, BCP staff developed a capacity—often tacit—to sense where the conversations were charged and generative, and where they might lead to new insight. That is not to say that they could perceive the direction in which the conversations were heading or predict the new understandings they would produce. The conversations were as ambiguous and murky as they had ever been: with the profile of Moroccan emigrants changing so radically after 1974, neither who the participants were nor what priorities they had were at all clear. Nevertheless, the BCP, with the Moroccan state in tow, developed a "hunch" about where to linger in the process, and what areas to explore with greater commitment. Moroccan emigrants, through their engagement with the BCP, also developed a heightened sense of when to compel the bank staff to pay more attention to what they were trying to articulate, when to introduce new concerns that may not have seemed related to financial services at all, and when to protect the ambiguity that this generated against the BCP's overzealous attempts to turn insights into policy prematurely.

The BCP's "emigrant mortgages" program exemplifies the policies produced thanks to this relational awareness and the kind of interpretive engagement that it supported. Moroccan emigrants tended to invest heavily in housing in their communities of origin: a study conducted in 1975 indicated that 71 percent of those surveyed had used income they earned abroad to build housing for their immediate families (Hamdouch et al. 1979: 102). Emigrants mostly built the homes themselves, with the help of brothers, uncles, and cousins, during periods of return to Morocco. They constructed these dwellings in stages, adding rooms and amenities as they could afford to; in this, they were no different than their non-emigrant neighbors (particularly in rural areas but also in urban centers), who also built their houses in phases. They treated their homes as changing spaces, almost like living organisms that could expand or contract depending on a family's means and needs. New rooms could be tacked on the main structure to reflect an increase in wealth or to accommodate new members of the family, or they could be torn down once adult children married, or when a room built in better days had become too expensive to maintain (Berriane 1998; Mohamed 1998; interviews, Taroudant, January 2004).

In conversations between the BCP and emigrants in Europe, the construction of housing in communities of origin emerged as a compelling topic. Emigrants' aspirations to build a family home pulled the conversation in that direction, and the BCP's "relational awareness" kept it there. BCP staff returned to the theme of housing over and over again, in a kind of organizational hunch that the area represented an opportunity for the bank. Out of those conversations, new trends in emigrant housing preferences began to emerge, trends that emigrants had observed during their trips home but that coalesced into new patterns only during discussions with BCP staff. Emigrants were building houses closer to basic infrastructure: water, electricity, and roads. Many were moving to new urban areas in regions of heavy emigration, like Nador and Agadir, purchasing either plots or small houses that they planned to expand in the rapidly urbanizing suburbs where land was still cheap. In rural areas, migrants were moving down from the rugged mountainsides, resettling on the more accessible plains that had traditionally been reserved for agriculture. Emigrant remittances were often not sufficient to purchase outright land for a house, or the shell of a new home, and emigrants were often compelled to borrow from family members or to sell other assets, such as land in the villages they were abandoning, to raise the necessary capital (BCP interviews, Paris, February 2004; and Casablanca, January 2004; Charef 1995; Berriane 1995; Lazaar 1995).

Accordingly, the BCP launched a program in 1978 to offer Moroccans living abroad subsidized mortgages to construct or purchase housing in Morocco. The bank used emigrants' current deposits as collateral and their history of transfers as a means to predict creditworthiness. The program empowered migrants to make housing investments without the approval of family members whom they would have otherwise pressed for a loan, and it allowed them to keep their land in their villages, with all the social standing that came with it. It represented a significant departure from the way emigrant workers had typically conceived of housing investment and the way they thought of their homes. Instead of incremental investments constructed over several years, the mortgages allowed migrants to acquire houses immediately or borrow the money to build the entire structure all in one go. The product was an instant hit; within a couple of years, the bank had provided close to 8,000 emigrant mortgages, a number that corresponded to 85 percent of the loans the bank made for real estate investments (BCP 1979, 1980, 1981, 1982). The program's success surprised even the BCP staff that had helped design it. They concluded that their conversations had begun to change the Moroccan workers' views of housing and real estate investments (BCP interviews, Paris, February 2004). The BCP had cultivated a need among emigrants for mortgages, a need that had not existed in an articulated form before the bank engaged the emigrants. As one director of the bank put it, "we created that market out of nothing. Nobody [none of the emigrants living in Europe] was interested in mortgages or in houses that had already been built until we got involved. There was no market before us" (BCP interview, Paris, February 2004).

Emboldened by the warm reception BCP emigrant mortgages received, the Moroccan Ministry of Housing, confronted with grave housing shortages in urban areas, joined forces with the BCP in 1978 to draw migrant investors into state schemes for housing construction. The emigrants, however, appropriated the state programs by reinterpreting them to meet their own needs, even when those were at cross-purposes with government priorities. The government plan focused on the kingdom's large metropolitan areas, like Casablanca, where slums were increasingly crowded. From the late 1970s through the late 1980s, representatives from the ministries of Housing, Finance, Labor, and Foreign Affairs, as well as from regional planning and construction offices, traveled to Europe a couple of times a year to meet with emigrants (GERA 1992). In conjunction with the BCP, they promoted low-cost housing packages: homes and business locales constructed by Morocco's semipublic Regional Planning and Construction Agencies (Établissements Régionaux d'Aménagement et de Construction, or ERACs), affiliated with the Ministry of Housing, were offered almost at cost, and rebates on any interest paid on mortgages provided by BCP were extended to sweeten the deal. Referring to the houses constructed by the state in Morocco, a BCP director described the collaboration as follows: "The state built it and we sold it" (BCP interview, Paris, February 2004). The Ministry of Housing reserved 20 percent of all lodging built by the ERACs for emigrant clients.

Emigrants, however, were on the whole not interested in buying public housing in Morocco's large littoral cities. Because many were still keen on buying or building housing in their communities of origin, they deflected the program to small emerging semi-urban centers in predominantly rural areas, marshaling the program to accelerate the transformation of the agricultural fields they appropriated for construction into vibrant souks surrounding their new houses. Migrant investment and the micro-urbanization that it caused pressed the state to extend basic infrastructure services to the nascent towns, and the shops that sprang up seemingly overnight provided migrants with opportunities for investment and their relatives in the village with job opportunities (GERA 1992: 94–100; Berriane 1995). As a result, the effect of migrant participation in the initiative was geographically concentrated in emigrant-sending areas, far removed from the kingdom's large coastal cities. In migrant-sending regions, emigrant clients represented a respectable 15 percent of all participants in public housing programs (Charef 1995; GERA 1992: 89–91).

Banking on Cultural Identity

Over time, emigrants became skilled at cultivating and directing their interpretive engagement with the BCP. Their adeptness is best illustrated by the way they reinvented BCP attempts to cast banking with the institution as an expression of Moroccan identity, and a specific state-sanctioned version of Moroccan identity at that. Migrants subverted the bank's efforts and turned the bank into a space where they could express their experience as people who lived and worked on both shores of the Mediterranean.

When BCP staff first tried to start conversations with migrants, they used the cultural background they claimed to share with the workers as part of their opening gambit. Although in actuality the social and cultural distance between well-heeled urban BCP extension officers and the working-class emigrants was large, BCP staff spoke with their emigrant clients in Moroccan Arabic and invoked common cultural and religious points of reference; they engaged in practices that were manifestly, even stereotypically, Moroccan, like drinking Moroccan tea or using their hands to eat a Moroccan meal from a common plate (BCP interviews, Paris, Casablanca, and Brussels, January–March 2004).

From the mid-1970s onward, as the state became more determined to augment the flow of remittances, the cultural allusions evolved into a deliberate, if heavy-handed, marketing strategy that equated banking with the BCP with preserving a Moroccan identity. The BCP began to distribute marketing materials that explicitly evoked themes of national belonging: on BCP posters, for example, people were drawn wearing Moroccan traditional dress, and images of people holding trees with pronounced roots appeared over and over again, in a clear trope, reinforced by captions like "my future, my roots, my bank," which likened banking with the BCP to returning to one's cultural and national roots. Similarly, the BCP extended various forms of insurance that cemented migrant ties to Morocco, including insurance for travel between Morocco and Europe, to cover the costs of emergency trips home should a relative fall ill, and for the repatriation of bodies. "Even if the emigrants are less certain about returning home to live, many, instead, want to be buried in the region of origin. A new demand emerges, therefore, for repatriation of the body in case of death," reflected a former BCP delegate general for Moroccans living abroad (as quoted in Monnard 1998). The BCP also funded regular Moroccan cultural events in Europe, including the annual Fête du Trône to celebrate the anniversary of the king's ascension to power, and established a foundation dedicated to supporting the lived cultural identity of Moroccan emigrants and their children. The foundation's first large project was to open a school in 1984 in Agadir, a major port city in the Moroccan Souss, for the children of emigrants who had decided to return to Morocco, a project it later duplicated in Tangier (BCP 1986, 2003; BCP *Rapports annuels* 1979–90; BCP and ATMF [Association des Travailleurs Marocains en France] interviews, Paris, February 2004; Garson and Tapinos 1981)

The type of national and cultural identity that the BCP promoted was politically loaded, however. It was a direct expression of state policy. It endorsed a form of patriotism that was based on the *beia*, an expression of individual allegiance to the king and to the kingdom as a whole of which Hassan II was the steward. The cultural identity the BCP promoted was a deterritorialized version of Moroccan subjectivity, explicitly delinked from any sense of belonging to regions within Morocco and from the political claims on behalf of those areas that a regional identity might support, even though emigrant origins were still regionally concentrated, with an overrepresentation from the south and north of the country. The identity fostered was also Arab, as opposed to Berber. In keeping with a state policy to repress expression of Amazigh, or Berber, identity and to suppress the use of Tamazight, the language of Amazigh peoples, BCP materials were presented either in Arabic or in the language of the European migrant host country, even though emigration from Berber regions was particularly strong and many migrants spoke Arabic only as a second language (BCP 1986, 1991, and 2003; Ennaji 2005; interviews, Brussels and Paris, February 2004).

Just as with "emigrant mortgages," however, migrants refashioned that cardboard cutout version of Moroccan identity. Appropriating the spaces and services that the BCP provided, in both Europe and Morocco, they used them to create profoundly transnational expressions of identities and lyrically interwove their experiences as migrants and as workers in Europe with their deep roots in their communities of origin and in specific regions of Morocco. For example, during the summer, when emigrants returned for vacation, they turned the BCP bank branches located in rural centers throughout Morocco into gathering areas. Migrants converted bald rural offices, some of which were set up temporarily, into festive places, where they not only completed bank transactions but caught up with friends and neighbors from the region who had also migrated to Europe and who were also there doing their banking. Bank branches became as intimate as living rooms, where emigrants could show off the economic fruit of their hard work, and where the price they paid for it with their pride, their health, and their abandoned dreams was understood by friends and kinfolk who had also migrated. An anecdote recounted by a BCP director who in the mid-1980s supervised several rural branch offices illustrates this phenomenon well:

> The lines were always really long during the summer. The branches would be full of migrants who had returned home for the *vacances*. The lines were out the door. Migrants brought their kids—kids would be screaming and playing as their fathers stood in line. And you know, people would catch up, talk about what they had been doing, how things were going for them in France, in Belgium, or wherever they had gone. At a certain point [in the mid-1980s], other banks started to try and penetrate the MRE [Marocains Résident à l'Étranger—Moroccans Living Abroad] market. [One of our competitors] opened a branch right next door to

ours, and they had this guy standing right in front of our entrance. The guy spent the whole day trying to poach our clients, telling them that service with him was better, faster, cheaper; that the lines were shorter. Finally, he convinces one of our clients to follow him. When the man walks into [our competitor's] branch, he turns right around and leaves. And I overhear him yelling back at the [other bank's] guy that he's not banking there, that the place is empty, there's no one there, and that he's no fool, he's not going someplace where he's the only one. (BCP interview, Casablanca, January 2004)

The director's description expresses the understanding the BCP developed over the course of the 1980s that not only had emigrants made BCP spaces their own, but also that this process had served the bank's business interests. The bank realized that emigrants viewed it as one of the few places in Morocco and Europe where they were seen and understood, where their struggle to negotiate a life that unfolded "on both shores" was respected, and where the financial and social needs that grew out of that transnational existence were addressed. Marketing material from the 1980s promoted the sense of "being seen" by the bank: "Our long experience serving Moroccan workers abroad is the strength that allows us to execute your banking operations better and help you realize your dreams," read a poster distributed in the 1980s (BCP 1991: 21). "We want Moroccans living abroad to know that the bank is theirs," added the director later in the interview (BCP interview, Casablanca, January 2004).

Seeing Results: Interpretation and Liquidity

The efforts of the BCP, and of the state to which it belonged, to promote and expand emigrant banking after Europe closed its borders showed results that were outstanding by any measure. Through straightforward financial incentives combined with a host of services tailored to emigrants' socioeconomic needs, the BCP and the state extended the Moroccan national economy into Europe. The BCP brought huge numbers of Moroccan emigrants into the kingdom's banking system, even as many were settling permanently in Europe. In 1990, when the total population of Moroccans living in Europe was estimated at one million—men, women, and children—the BCP had an astounding 400,000 emigrant clients. The bank continued to handle most remittance transfers that, to its credit, remained steady in real terms through the 1980s, even after migrants brought their families to live with them. This accomplishment seems all the more remarkable when considered in the light of prevailing theories on remittance behavior, which predict that as emigrants settle abroad, and especially after their families join them, remittances drop off precipitously. Remittance transfers grew as a proportion of GDP, expanding from 5 percent in 1975 to somewhere between 6 and 8 percent throughout the 1980s. Even more significant were the deposits that migrants held in the Moroccan banking system. During the 1980s, the emigrants' deposits that the BCP held represented

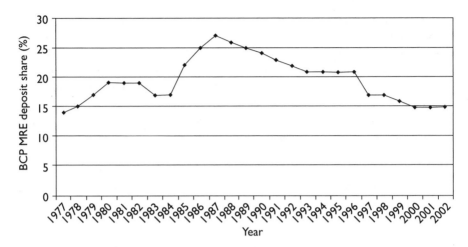

Figure 4.4. BCP Moroccan emigrant deposits as a share of total national deposits, 1977–2002 (BCP *Rapports annuels* 1978–2002; IMF *Balance of Payments Statistics Yearbooks* 1977–2002).

an average of 20 percent of the total deposits in Moroccan banks, peaking at close to 30 percent in 1987 (see fig. 4.4) (BCP *Rapports annuels* 1978–2002; IMF 2005; Morocco, Office des Changes 2004).

Another indicator of the effectiveness of Moroccan state policy and of the BCP's success with the emigrant market is the high proportion of Moroccans who used formal channels for remittance transfer. In 1981, the French National Foundation for Political Science published a survey on immigrants' financial behavior, with a particular focus on remittances to countries of origin. The study found that not only did Moroccan emigrants as a group transfer significantly more money than any other migrant group surveyed (which included those from Portugal, Italy, Spain, Tunisia, and Algeria), sending an average of 20 percent more money than the Tunisians, who came in second, but also that more Moroccans remitted their earnings than any other immigrant group, with a low 14 percent transferring none of their income compared to an average of 31 percent for all groups surveyed. Moroccans were also twice as likely as any other immigrant group to be aware of financial institutions that enabled them to place their savings in accounts in their country of origin (Garson and Bennabou 1981).

In and of themselves, the vast sums of money migrants sent home would have had an important impact on the Moroccan economy, particularly at a time when the kingdom was in desperate need of foreign currency. The BCP, however, representing at least one-third of the nation's financial sector in the 1970s and 1980s, was also one of the Moroccan state's main financiers. By extension, so were the migrants who held the lion's share of the bank's deposits. Although definitive data on exactly where and to whom the BCP tendered its funds are impossible to obtain, press reports suggest that the BCP played a dominant role in the kingdom's "Moroccanization" program, launched in 1973 and lasting through the 1970s, to buy majority Moroccan ownership in all the country's dominant firms (Clément and Paul 1986), and that it underwrote the war in Western Sahara. It was also a main financier for capital-intensive investment in public, semipublic, and to a lesser extent, private enterprises in coastal cities (Claisse 1987; A.D.N. 1993; Banque al-Maghrib interviews, March 2004). In addition to supporting their families, emigrant workers bankrolled the development of heavy industry and agribusiness—development that for the most part bypassed the communities from which most migrants came. Thus, although their engagement with the BCP redefined the bank as a bridge between "here" and "there," it also contributed to exacerbating the inequality that had caused migrants to leave Morocco to begin with. The products the BCP elaborated based on the insights that emerged in the interpretive conversations addressed the financial needs as well as the social and cultural anxieties of migrants and their families. Those same products, however, widened the economic gap that separated the booming cities on Morocco's coast and industrial farms in its midlands from the impoverished rural areas in the south and north.

Controlling Relationships: Interpretation in Conflict

Even as the Moroccan government built more institutions to extend the nation's economic space past its frontiers and include emigrants settling abroad, the regime also tried to extend its political control to Moroccans who looked increasingly likely to remain in Europe indefinitely. From 1974 onward, it attempted to exert the same political dominion over Moroccan economic and social spaces abroad as it did at home. Over the fifteen years that elapsed after Europe closed its borders to labor immigration, the regime's approach to Moroccans living abroad changed significantly. The state went from the crude application of violence, to more nuanced and insidious forms of intimidation that played on nationalist themes, to attempts to co-opt Moroccan emigrant labor movements that had grown increasingly organized and sophisticated in their political analysis.

The evolution of state tactics to control the political activities of Moroccans living abroad grew directly out of engagement with emigrants. Through its interactions with emigrant workers, the Moroccan government opened up interpretive conversations that, over time, transformed state perceptions of who Moroccan emigrants were and what their capacities for collective political action meant for the regime. Through those same interactions, emigrant workers and organizers developed new critiques of the Moroccan regime: they linked their exploitation as workers in Europe to the government's active collusion with their employers and adopted the political vocabulary of human rights to challenge Moroccan state attempts to control their activities.

The conversations were riddled with confrontation and bitter recriminations, and the state's bruising attempts to silence emigrant activists made them all the more jagged. Nevertheless, they remained a durable source of new understandings about the relationship between the communities abroad and the country of origin, because the Moroccan state and emigrant activists had little option but to remain engaged in order to achieve their respective political goals. For the government, losing political control over a segment of the population that pumped a hefty portion of the national income into the kingdom each year was a political and economic outcome too devastating to allow. Emigrants were forced to engage with the state in order to resist its maneuvers to defeat their labor mobilization and to suppress their criticism of the regime, and of the king in particular.

The conversations were fitful, stalling and starting, because there was a lag between the emergence of the insights the engagement produced and the state's implementation of them. The new understandings about political and cultural changes in the emigrant population that emerged out of that engagement contained implicit challenges to the monarchical hegemony in Morocco and to the methods the crown used to enforce it. As a result, the state resisted acting on those insights as long as possible, responding only when not acting would have severed its engagement with the emigrants.

In a reflection of this uneven pattern, the relationship shifted abruptly and divides into three historical phases. The first was during the mid-1970s, which saw a resurgence of Moroccan labor protests, a last fulmination of the labor mobilization over working conditions that began in the early 1970s. Hassan II's regime viewed worker activism as part of a larger subversive movement to dislodge the king from his throne and deployed various measures to stamp out what it considered seditious behavior, whether it occurred in Morocco or in Europe. Moroccan workers, meanwhile, began to differentiate their needs and political aspirations from those of the Moroccan leftists in exile. The second phase began in the early 1980s, when the regime began to view emigrant labor protest as a separate political movement that posed its own unique threats to the kingdom, and the kingdom's access to remittances. The government acted aggressively to prevent immigrant workers from organizing, even as their mobilizations against massive layoffs by European heavy industry became more forceful and their ability to resist Moroccan government intimidation more savvy. The third phase took place during emigrant strikes of the late 1980s, as Moroccan workers protested the conditions under which they were discharged when Europe closed down many of its primary resource extraction industries, mostly coal mines. The Moroccan government, realizing that it could not effectively suppress worker mobilization, switched strategies and moved to co-opt the leaders of the migrant movement. Many emigrant workers viewed this strategy as cynical and underhanded, and those who had been active in the worker protests as well as those who had been spectators began to disengage from the Moroccan state. The conversation that had lasted for over two decades seemed to have come to an end.

Although these three moments of intense labor mobilization were roughly synchronous in the four major countries that used Moroccan labor, their correlation with the articulation of new understandings about the relationship of emigrants to the political and economic trajectory of the kingdom was clearest in France, and thus, the description of the evolution of the interpretive engagement also centers there.

Controlling Labor: Moroccan State Tactics

In the mid-1970s, the wave of immigrant labor protest that followed on the labor unrest of 1968 picked up new momentum, once again sweeping through France's industrial areas in response to widespread layoffs. As in the strikes of the early 1970s, Moroccan workers figured prominently and were often at their vanguard. The Moroccan government viewed these protests with consternation and would begin to take action to stamp them out.

By 1974, the Moroccan government was essentially controlled by Hassan II. The political repression that the crown applied in the wake of 1971 and 1972 coup attempts wiped out all opposition parties and brought even fervent monarchists to heel. "Like it or not, the monarchy is the only remaining political institution left intact," lamented one political observer quoted in a *Washington Post* profile of the country (Randal 1974: A13). The crown's attitude toward the labor movement within Morocco was no different from its attitude toward any group that voiced political dissent. It tightened its control over organized labor and destroyed any elements that it could not control. It would extend to Moroccan workers in Europe the same repression it applied to labor organizers within the kingdom.

For a brief period in the early 1970s, the crown had afforded the Moroccan trade union movement, led by the Moroccan Workers' Union (Union des Travailleurs Marocains, or UMT), some latitude for action to counterbalance the urban bourgeoisie's protests against the monarchy and armed rebellions mounted by dispossessed peasants in the rural hinterlands. Although kept on a tight leash by the state, the UMT was able to lead several hundred strikes in 1971 and 1973, virtually all of them defensive, and its membership grew by a fifth between 1970 and 1973, swelling to about 20 percent of workers in the formal private and public sectors (Clément and Paul 1984). By the end of 1973, however, the effort to co-opt segments of the opposition through minimal concession and drive a wedge between peasants and urban workers was abandoned; the iron fist of the sultanate came down hard on Morocco's organized labor. By the time the kingdom had embarked on its Western Sahara campaign in 1975, labor protests were deemed a form of treason. As an observer of Moroccan politics, Jean-François Clément, remarked: "Beginning in 1975, the country was sunk in a state of hysteria and war. At a time when strikers were condemned as traitors, neither workers nor unions could risk a militant stance" (Clément and Paul 1984: 24). In its determination to snuff out labor protest, the crown made no distinction between Moroccan workers in Morocco and those in Europe; a Middle East Research and Information Project dispatch from 1977 reported, "Moroccan workers are subject to arrest for even restricted expressions of militancy and those who emigrate to France are regularly turned over by the French to the Moroccan police for political or trade union activity" (*MERIP Reports* 1977: 18; Clément and Paul 1984).

To control Moroccan workers in Europe, the regime built on the shadowy "management consultants" it had sent to European enterprises in the 1960s to keep Moroccan labor docile with a network of so-called friendship societies or *amicales*. The first Friendship Society of Moroccan Workers and Traders was established in Paris in 1973, but others quickly cropped up in cities throughout Europe that had large concentrations of Moroccan workers. Their official mandate was to "establish contacts with the consulates, with the administration of both countries [i.e., Morocco and the migrant-receiving country], and in a more general fashion, with all the organizations that were concerned with the situation of Moroccan workers and traders and their families" (Belbahri 1994: 306). Their unofficial role was far less communitarian. The friendship societies were set up as extensions of Moroccan embassies and consulates (as well as, some argue, of the Moroccan secret police) and acted as agents of the government in labor disputes. At their worst, the members, generally migrants recruited by the consulate, were state-sponsored thugs, physically intimidating workers who engaged in any sort of labor mobilization, from distributing pro-labor and pro-union literature to participating in work slowdowns ("working to rule") or strikes (Daoud 2004; Baroudi 2005; ATMF 1984; ATMF interviews, Paris, February 2004).

Their primary function, however, was to serve as informers, providing the government and employers with lists of workers who either were labor organizers or had simply refused to join "house"—or management-sponsored—unions. Workers identified as labor agitators were routinely fired. Either they were dismissed directly by employers, or the government revoked their passports and national identification—legal documents they needed to have their labor contracts renewed. The government also confiscated passports of suspected labor organizers at the Moroccan border, which made their return to Europe impossible. In a number of cases, the Moroccan authorities resorted to more drastic measures, taking organizers into custody. Throughout the 1970s and 1980s, literally hundreds of labor organizers were arrested, or they disappeared when they returned to Morocco during their vacations. "The Moroccan authorities wanted to rope in the Moroccan community abroad, which is why they created the Friendship Societies, [which were] directed by the Moroccan police," remembered Mohamed el-Baroudi, a Moroccan leftist activist in Belgium, in an interview. "[These were] associations that terrorized, informed on Moroccan activists. . . . [They] waited for them at customs to denounce them as labor agitators! Also worth noting is the disappearance of Moroccan activists at that time" (Baroudi 2005; Daoud 2004; ATMF interviews, Paris, February 2004; ATMF 1984; Belguendouz 1999).

The 1975 strike at the Chausson automobile factory near Paris was, as one labor organizer put it, Moroccan workers' "first real response" to the Moroccan government's tactics (Vidal 2005). Moroccan workers had been organizing at the Chausson factory under the guidance of the General Confederation of Labor (CGT) and with the help of the leftist Association of Moroccans in France (AMF; see chap. 3) since 1971, but in 1975 they joined forces with co-workers from Italy, Spain, North Africa, and sub-Saharan Africa to stage a major labor protest that brought production at the large plant to a halt for several months that spring (Traversian 2004). As part of the mobilization, the Moroccan workers, in conjunction with the AMF, ran a campaign to have representatives of the local friendship society—"pigs in the plant, *des flics dans l'entreprise*," who were "connected to the embassy" (Massera, as quoted in Traversian 2004)—excluded from worker meetings and expelled from the plant premises. Labor activists uncovered documentation proving the working relationship between the friendship societies, the Moroccan embassy and consulates, and the secret police apparatus of the Ministry of the Interior. The strikers named names (ATMF 1984: 10). In response, the Moroccan authorities orchestrated an aggressive roundup during the summer, incarcerating 105 emigrants who had participated in the protests. At summer's end, the CGT organized a rally at Saint-Ouen near Paris for the missing Moroccans. With the French national press reporting on the event, thousands demanded their release. The prisoners were eventually freed and allowed to return to France, but all of them, without exception, found that they had been laid off during their enforced absence (Daoud 2004; ATMF 1984; Vidal 2005; Traversian 2004; ATMF interviews, Paris, February 2004).[3]

Emigrants: "The King Is Complicit"

The Moroccan state's crude repression of Moroccan labor activists in Europe continued and, over time, changed emigrant workers' analysis of the factors that led to their exploitation as immigrant labor.[4] The government's tactics reopened old fissures in the alliance between emigrant workers and the Moroccan leftist opposition in exile. In France, emigrant workers began to feel that the Moroccan opposition's attention was trained principally on events in the homeland, often at the expense of the concerns of Moroccan workers in Europe. This difference in priorities began to widen into an estrangement during Hassan II's Green March into Western Sahara in 1975: for many leftists, maintaining an appearance of national unity overrode the defense of emigrant workers against repression at the hands of their home government. Many Moroccan workers in the AMF experienced this as a profound betrayal: "To see comrades marching alongside those that cried 'Long live the King!' and alongside the Friendship Societies disturbed me deeply. It's one of my worst memories," recalled one (as quoted in Daoud 2004: 43).

The divide between the leftists and the workers became definitive in 1981, after an uprising in Casablanca. In May, the Moroccan government announced rollbacks on subsidies of basic foodstuffs, as mandated by the terms of its loan agreement with the IMF. In response, the UMT called for a general strike in Casablanca on June 18; two days later, the enormously successful strike exploded into a mass popular uprising against a regime perceived as authoritarian and corrupt. The Moroccan army advanced on Casablanca and other cities to which unrest had spread (Paul 1981). By the time the military had put down the rebellion, over 600 protesters were dead, thousands more wounded, and reports of between 2,000 and 5,000 arrested, among them at least 200 prominent union and political leaders, were issued by the palace and by opposition groups (Slyomovics 2005: 109–13; Paul 1981). Leftist opposition groups in Europe, the AMF among them, organized widespread demonstrations against the Moroccan government's violent actions. Those protests, however, never made the link between the monarchy's harsh measures against labor leaders and workers in Morocco and disturbingly similar tactics that it deployed in Europe (Daoud 2004).

Frustrated with the leftist opposition's singular concern with political events in Morocco, workers in the AMF split off from the mother organization in 1982 to form the ATMF—Association des *Travailleurs* Marocains en France, the Association of Moroccan *Workers* in France. One of the founders of the new organization explained: "We felt there needed to be coherence between what we defended, what we fought for and the realities that we faced as immigrants, and for us, those realities were primordial" (ATMF interview, Paris, February 2004). The new organization made explicit workers' new perceptions of the Moroccan government, articulating the connections they saw between Moroccan state repression of labor activism in Morocco and in Europe, and between state actions against workers and the exploitative conditions under which they worked. The founding platform of the ATMF codified these new understandings as the raison d'être of the organization: "As immigrant workers, we are the victims of capitalist exploitation by our country [Morocco] and of the collaboration of the reactionary Moroccan regime with imperialist interests . . . in France; we are the scapegoats; since the 1970s, over and above [the] exploitation [of our labor], we have lived under repression and under conditions of constant insecurity" (as quoted in Daoud 2004: 53).

Escalating Engagement: Moroccan Government Repression and the Citroën Strikes

During the protests against layoffs in European heavy industry in the early 1980s, the Moroccan government proved the emigrants' analysis correct by ratcheting up its stratagems against Moroccan labor mobilization in Europe. It intensified its practices of nullifying passports and national identification documents and of taking emigrants into state custody upon their return to Morocco for family visits. Moreover, the regime also added to its arsenal myriad new forms of bullying and intimidation, most of them applied through the increasingly infamous friendship societies. These displayed two new traits: first, they used more intimate forms of persuasion, engaging with emigrants in an intensive style reminiscent of the BCP, lacing the social niceties of everyday interactions with chilling threats to workers and their families; second, they played on notions of cultural belonging, stressing that participating in labor protests ran counter to emigrants' identity as Moroccans. Both of these features emerged prominently in the Moroccan government's attempt to smother strikes in the French auto industry in the early 1980s. These strikes were unprecedented in their magnitude, and the sight of tens of thousands of immigrant workers, Moroccans well represented among them, taking to the streets and occupying the country's larger auto plants profoundly unnerved both the French establishment and the Moroccan regime, which was still trying to reassert control over the kingdom's rebellious poor (Oakes 1984).

The strikes targeted the Citroën group, which after acquiring Peugeot and Talbot, became one of the largest auto producers in the world during the 1980s and a symbol for European heavy industry's use of migrant labor (P. Lewis 1986). The group produced over half the autos turned out in France (ATMF 1984: 58). It was also one of the largest employers of immigrants, especially Moroccans, in the republic: two-thirds of its 12,000-strong workforce was immigrant, and of that group, Moroccans numbered 5,000, followed by other North Africans (primarily Algerian and Tunisian) at a distant 1,300 (ATMF 1984: 58). Immigrant workers called Citroën "the factory of fear—*l'usine de la peur*" (ATMF 1984: 59; Daoud 2004: 61; ATMF interviews, Paris, February 2004). They drew a strong analogy between the conditions they faced there and those in force in Morocco: "At Citroën, there's repression, just like in Morocco," commented one (as quoted in Daoud 2004: 48). Workers compared Citroën factories to prisons, complaining that they were shuttled by company vans directly from the plants to worker dormitories; unauthorized visits were not permitted, and workers were fired for any suspected labor mobilization activity (ATMF 1984).

The working conditions were becoming intolerable. Labor leaders claimed that the company engineered line speedups, with cadences that were impossible to maintain, as a pretext for firing workers—in essence, a way to get around some of the French state regulations that tempered, if only slightly, the massive layoffs of immigrant labor as the auto industry underwent a profound restructuring (Marie 1996; Grason and Massera 2004; Kutschera 1984). ("You have to pick up a piece that weighs up to 6 kilos, put it down, press it, pick it up again; the cadence varies from 500 to 550 an hour . . . you just can't finish," recalled one worker, Abdel Razzak [as quoted in Kutschera 1984].) In April 1982, 1,500 workers at a Citroën plant staged a slowdown and then a strike to protest the increase in line speed. Within a week, the strike spread to other plants and mushroomed to close to 10,000 workers. Over the next two years, the Citroën group saw repeated labor unrest and strikes disrupt production: the strikes that began at Citroën plants spread to the Talbot factories it had acquired (Bernstein 1984; ATMF 1987). Moroccan workers, with the ATMF at their side, were leaders of the mobilization (Daoud 2004).

Faced with actions by its nationals that were shutting down production in major segments of the French automobile industry, the Moroccan government took strong measures. It resorted to the usual physical intimidation—workers reported the torching of cars and homes (Daoud 2004)—and bureaucratic harassment through the confiscation of passports. In an advance over the tactics of the 1975 strike, however, the Moroccan government blended persuasion with duress. Consulates dispatched members of friendship societies to talk workers out of participating in the strikes. The diplomatic service funded a host of cultural and social events nominally sponsored by the friendship societies, and at these barbecues, concerts, and prayer sessions, emigrant workers were informally advised against striking. In particular, workers reported that they were told that the labor conflict was a French problem that did not concern Moroccans ("*ça nous regarde pas*" was the refrain they heard), and in a misinformation campaign, they were assured that participating also invariably resulted in deportation (ATMF interviews, Paris, February 2004; and Rabat, March 2004; Kutschera 1984). Workers also remember visits to their homes when they were told to stay out of the labor struggles; the exhortations followed a common refrain: "You came here to work, not to do politics. . . . You should be satisfied with what you have and thank God for what he has given you. What would happen to your family if you lost your job? Citroën can replace you at a moment's notice, there are millions of 'arms' waiting for the opportunity. . . . And don't forget how we deal with hotheads at home" (ATMF 1984: 63).

These chats not infrequently closed with a recommendation that workers "think of [their] family back in Morocco" (as quoted in *Le Canard Enchaîné*, in ATMF 1984: 103), a thinly veiled threat. Friendship society members also offered to facilitate loans from the BCP (they also threatened to impede loans as well as access to personal funds), suggesting a less than ethical affiliation between the BCP and the friendship societies, and by extension, between the BCP and the Moroccan Ministry of Interior's police services (Kutschera 1984; ATMF interviews, Paris, February 2004; Daoud 2004).

The Moroccan government backed up these informal "social calls" with consular visits to factories and worker meetings. The consular officials stressed repeatedly that participation in the strikes was un-Moroccan. During the strike at the Talbot subsidiary of Citroën, for example, the ambassador and the social affairs counselor at the Moroccan embassy in Paris summoned migrant workers in small groups to "give them a lesson." As workers reported, the ambassador attacked them, saying, "for two years [the duration of the labor mobilization leading up to the Talbot strike], we knew the socialists and the communists would lead you to this point where you are today. . . . A Moroccan worker worthy of his nation knows how to fight [such pressures]" (*Le Canard Enchaîné*, January 25, 1984, as reprinted in ATMF 1984). Workers were also informed that the dues they were paying to French unions were "destined to finance the enemies of [their] country in the Western Sahara," and that the Moroccan government was "concerned about their future," insinuating that their participation in a strike might be considered a form of treason, with all the ensuing consequences, which, under the repression that earned that period of Moroccan history the moniker "the leaden years," were predictably dire. The consular messages were reinforced with royal admonitions in which the king counseled them to "remain Moroccan, remain Moroccan always," and ready to obey the political mandates of their homeland (Belguendouz 1999).[5] The king's directives were reiterated through numerous letters that workers received at their lodgings or in their factory lockers, from groups such as Africa Express (Afrique Express) and the Association of the Green Star (Association de l'Étoile Verte), the symbol of Islam and Morocco, urging them to preserve the reputation of Moroccan workers, to refrain from labor unrest in the name of their faith, and to send any "confidential" information they wished to an address in Casablanca (*Sans Frontière* 1981–1983, in ATMF 1984).

Identifying Oppression and Moroccan Identities of Resistance

Moroccan workers responded in two ways to this escalation of state pressure. First, they organized. To break the intimacy of the state's style of intimidation, the ATMF began to document the practices of the government and its affiliates systematically. The goal was to make the seemingly "social" practices transparent as political bullying and strikebreaking, and therefore subject to organized challenge. The organization compiled lists of people whose travel documents had been docked or who had been arrested. It recorded incidents of intimidation by friendship societies and the consular staff. It collected accounts of the rhetoric with which members of friendship societies plied workers, and it tallied instances of implied threat, such as receiving suspicious correspondence or being followed. The information was then passed on to French unions that supported workers in their strikes and to the French press. In Belgium, Holland, and Germany, the chief labor-supporting Moroccan organizations carried out similar resistance activities (Ouali 2004; Van der Valk 2004; Daoud 2004).[6] In the early 1980s, they finalized a compact—the Common Charter for the Coordination of Moroccan Democratic Associations in Europe—to share information and synchronize efforts to "confront the repression imposed on Moroccan communities abroad and on Moroccans as a whole by the repressive apparatus of the Moroccan regime" (ATMF 1984: 16; ATMF Archives 1982–85, correspondence; ATMF interviews, Paris, 2004; interviews, Brussels, February 2004).

Second, workers and labor activists asserted their identities as Moroccans, independent of Moroccan state approbation. They did this in the context of both their labor protests and their communities. Even though the workers on strike were not exclusively Moroccan, the Citroën/Talbot strikes took on a distinctly Moroccan flavor. The recollections of an ATMF organizer who joined the workers at the Aulney Citroën factory in a 1982 strike illustrate this well:

The workers from the Atlas Mountains and from the Souss, from the extreme south, with their Sahroui turbans, turned to their old guerilla reflexes: . . . workers threw hot oil on the doors to close them off, machine tools were used to fight management militias, helicopters flew over [the] Aulney [Citroën factory] to bombard the occupants. . . . Deprived of food, the workers had to rely on the factory cafeteria. Some Soussis worried, "is it *alouf* [meat not slaughtered according to the precepts of the Koran and therefore forbidden]? Others answered, "Say *bismillah* [in the name of God] and eat!" . . . [The workers] invented a language made up of a mix of French, Arabic, [and] Berber. Those were very important and meaningful times—*des moments très forts.* (As quoted in Daoud 2004: 62)

Outside the factories, the ATMF organized cultural activities that expressed Moroccan identities and art forms. The most important of these were the yearly *moussems*, days-long festivals that the ATMF produced with other Moroccan organizations throughout Europe. These "grand festivals of humanity," as one organizer called them, were held yearly in different cities and invited performance groups from Morocco to participate. They also served as a means to publicize Moroccan emigrant labor strikes throughout Europe. In 1982, at the height of the Citroën strike, the *moussem* was held in Amsterdam, and over a thousand Moroccans from France traveled north to join the festivities but also to broadcast information about the workers' struggle with the auto manufacturer and the Moroccan government (Daoud 2004: 64; ATMF interviews, Paris, February 2004; ATMF Archives, 1980–90).

By the end of 1984, it became clear that the Moroccan workers had lost their fight against Citroën. The strikers were forced to accept massive layoffs: over the next several years, the Citroën group, facing chronic profit shortfalls, would dismiss over half of its immigrant workforce (Daoud 2004; ATMF 1984; P. Lewis 1986; Bernstein 1984). The message of the strike's denouement was clear: immigrant layoffs would continue despite workers' protests. "We were defeated," concluded an ATMF organizer (interview, Paris, February 2004).

The Moroccan state, however, profoundly unsettled by the sheer magnitude of emigrant worker protests, was not reassured by this outcome. The capacity to mobilize toward an end that the government viewed as seditious was deeply unnerving (Mohammed V University interviews, Rabat, March 2003). The wave of popular uprising that swept through Morocco in 1984, after the state announced yet another rollback of subsidies for food and other services, undoubtedly made the regime more sensitive to the threat that emigrant worker mobilization might represent. On January 5, a protest by high school students in Marrakech over a hike in school fees turned violent as the students clashed with police, and scores of youngsters were injured and taken into custody. Months later, the prosecutor in Marrakech would tell the parents of the teenagers still languishing in jail: "Your children have declared war on the state, we declare war on them" (as quoted in Demir 1990). With food prices having jumped 70 percent the previous year even before the removal of subsidies, the unrest quickly escalated and spread, and by month's end the government had dispatched the armed forces to quell large-scale rebellions in cities throughout Morocco, including Rabat, Casablanca, Tetouan, and El Hoceima. In rural areas in the northern Rif region, protestors stormed police stations and seized arms to defend themselves against the regime. In towns throughout the north, slogans and wall signs railed against the king, targeting his person with their critiques, an act that in Morocco was—and still is—considered a crime of treason punishable with a long prison sentence. Army troops airlifted in to put an end to the unrest themselves pillaged local food stores before angrily and indiscriminately firing into the crowds. When the smoke cleared at the end of the month, hundreds were dead and well over 10,000 Moroccans had been taken into custody. Hassan II was forced to cede to public will and reinstate the subsidies (Seddon 1984; Paul 1984; Clement 1984; Oakes 1984).

The government saw disturbing connections between the mobilization of emigrant workers in Europe and the popular rebellion at home. The king identified their source as the same: the regime blamed the Moroccan labor protests in France on "Marxist agitators" (ATMF 1984), and when calm had been restored in Morocco after the turbulent January of 1984, the king appeared on television and declared that the uprising had been instigated by "the Marxists," who in this case were in cahoots with "Iran and the Zionists" (Paul 1984). More troubling to the regime was the fact that the rebellion against the state had been boldest in the areas from which emigrant workers disproportionately hailed: the semirural and rural regions of the Rif and the Souss. This conclusion was no coincidence. The closure of Europe's border to labor migration in 1974, and with it the elimination of the only real alternative for employment and income, had begun to weigh heavily on these areas in the early 1980s. A combination of factors, including a severe drought in 1980–81 and a drop in already pitiful levels of state investment, economically devastated the poor in those regions and heightened dramatic income inequalities (Seddon 1984; Paul 1984; Clement 1984). The specter of Moroccan emigrants, whose political ties to their communities of origin the state had taken pains to sever (see chaps. 2 and 3), supporting rural mobilizations against the crown was not one the state was willing to tolerate.

From Conversation to Co-optation

The Moroccan state, viewing the increasingly organized emigrant workers as a clear threat to national security, changed its strategy for dealing with them. To its practices of intimidation it added a concerted effort to co-opt emigrants and channel their political mobilization into an institutional vehicle that it could control. This shift in approach was an extension of the strategy of political normalization that the regime deployed internally to reclaim sufficient legitimacy and therefore avoid a revolution. The broadening of its political intervention to include its emigrant communities was consistent with the fact that the state continued to view Moroccan migrants as a branch of its national economic system. The specific way in which it applied attempts at co-optation, however, was built on the familiarity the regime had developed with emigrants by engaging with them.

The centerpiece of the crown's strategies for political normalization after the riots of the early 1980s was to allow parliamentary elections in 1984, for the first time in almost a decade. In an unprecedented move, the king reserved five seats for representatives of the Moroccan community abroad. The constituencies the delegates were to represent were nonsensically broad and geographically dispersed: although two delegates were allotted to France, a third represented Moroccans in Belgium, the Netherlands, Germany, and the Soviet Union, a fourth Moroccans living anywhere in the entire Arab world, and a fifth delegate those living in Spain, Portugal, England, Italy, the Americas, and sub-Saharan Africa (Belguendouz 1999). In theory, the delegates were to be elected, with voting held at the consulates. In practice, however, with serious irregularities characterizing elections already problematic in design, the consular authorities handpicked the delegates (Belguendouz 2003; interviews, Paris and Belgium, February 2004).

In general, the Moroccan government chose emigrants who assumed leadership roles in labor movements of the 1980s, but whose politics were relatively moderate and who thus could be brought around to the regime's position on emigrant labor mobilization (Belguendouz 1999; AMTF interviews, Paris, 2004; Espace Memorial de l'Immigration Marocaine interviews, Brussels, 2004). A prime example was Akka al-Ghazi, chosen as one of the two delegates to represent Moroccans living in France. During the Citroën strike, al-Ghazi had been a major leader, representing the CGT at the Aulney factory and encouraging workers to strike because it was the "only way to break the chains of oppression" (as quoted in Kutschera 1984). Soon after he was instated as a delegate in 1985, he began to parrot the regime's line on emigrant activism and was dispatched to labor disputes in which Moroccan workers were heavily represented to check the protests.

In 1987, al-Ghazi was sent to Nord-Pas-de-Calais in France to meet with Moroccan miners who had gone on strike to protest the conditions under which they were being laid off. The mines in which the miners had worked, many for over fifteen years, were slated to close in 1992. The miners had labored under temporary contracts that were periodically renewed. Charbonnage de France was simply going to refrain from renewing their contract, depriving them, by the same token, of the legal right to remain in France. The workers demanded severance packages on a par with those of French workers, including full medical care to treat the silicosis that many had incurred on the job, and the right to remain in France if they so chose. The strike, which lasted over eight weeks, made the headlines of major papers for much of its duration and drew attention to the difficult conditions under which immigrant, and especially Moroccan, workers had labored (Confédération Française Démocratique du Travail) that represented phosphate miners (*Voix du Nord*, October–November 1987; *L'Humanité*, October–November 1987; *Libération*, November 1987; ATMF Archives 1986–88). It also caught the attention of members of the state-supervised, if not completely state-dominated, Moroccan union. A high-ranking member of the union traveled to France in a show of support for the Moroccan coal miners: "We follow this strike very closely in Morocco. All of the opposition papers are writing about this strike" (as quoted in *Voix du Nord*, October 18, 1987). To defuse a situation the government perceived as a threat to its control both in France and in Morocco, Akka al-Ghazi was charged with making it clear to the Moroccan strikers that their action had no legal basis. "My mission is to explain to my compatriots who are miners, regardless of whether they are members of the CGT, the terms of their contract, because most of them don't know what the terms are" (as quoted in *Libération*, November 18, 1987).

From Co-optation to the End of a Conversation

The government's co-optation of someone who had represented the struggles of Moroccan workers, who had become a public symbol of their fight and even a martyr for their cause when he was beaten by antilabor thugs, was perceived as an insult that debased workers and their concerns (ATMF interviews, Paris, February 2004). Strike organizers responded forcefully to al-Ghazi's visit, accusing him of "having applied intolerable pressures on the strikers . . . designed to break the unity of the movement" (as quoted in *Libération*, November 18, 1987). Additionally, the ATMF filed formal complaints with the French ministries of Foreign Affairs and Labor about the tactics of the friendship societies. The missives detailed the actions of the associations and cautioned the French authorities that if they wished to obviate "disturbances that [were] likely to have grave consequences," they should "dissolve" the friendship societies and put an end to the "dangerous and systematic practice" of labor repression that they embodied (ATMF 1987). The engagement between Moroccan labor activists and the Moroccan government that had lasted for fifteen years, even though defined by conflict and power struggle, finally broke down. The space for interpretative exchange, even if contested and acrimonious, had closed.

Moroccan labor activists remembered that period as a time when they "grieved for [their] country and let it go—*on a fait le deuil de notre pays*" (ATMF interviews, Paris and Brussels, February 2004; Interviews, Paris, February 2004; interviews, Brussels, February 2004). "In the 1970s, we thought that if democracy came to Morocco, everything else would follow," remembered one worker. "But as time passed, we saw that nothing was changing, that there was no real hope" (Daoud 2004: 76). "The hand of the government was too heavy . . . we knew we would not return," reflected another (ATMF interviews, Paris, February 2004). After years of eschewing the adoption of French citizenship, the ATMF began to advocate naturalization. It also began to work on questions of bicultural identity, supporting antiracist activism and the Mouvement Beur, a movement that asserted the cultural, religious, and political rights of first-, second-, and third-generation Arab immigrants (Derderian 2004). The ATMF sister organizations in Belgium, Holland, and Germany made similar shifts, turning away from engagement with the Moroccan government and looking instead to issues of political and religious rights and cultural identity of Moroccan immigrants and their descendants (Daoud 2004; Ouali 2004; Van der Valk 2004; M'hammed 2004).

The state was gradually beginning to note this effect. As early as December 1985, Hassan II remarked that he was "disappointed" by the friendship societies because of their lack of inclusiveness (Belguendouz 1999: 260). He added that it was time to reestablish them "on a base that [was] truly democratic," calling for the creation of a congress that would "define this democratic base in keeping with the free will expressed by Moroccan workers in France, taking into consideration only their interests and the interest of each individual worker" (discours et interventions de S. M. Hassan II, 1985, as quoted in Belguendouz 1999: 260). The congress was organized by the Ministry of Labor the following year in Rabat. By all accounts, it was a huge disappointment because of a lack of transparency, credibility, and organizational effort (Belguendouz 1999: 260). The palace, however, combined these sheepish acknowledgments that its strategy to control emigrant workers' political activity may have been ill judged with strident condemnations of emigrant integration of any sort in receiving countries. Hassan II pronounced stern critiques of the movement for naturalization and electoral rights, in what seemed almost a panicked effort to retether Moroccan emigrants to the kingdom.[7] In an interview broadcast on French television in 1989, for example, he was forceful in his condemnation of emigrant integration into receiving countries, unequivocally answering: "I am against it . . . for the simple reason that for me, there is no distinction between a Moroccan born in Morocco and raised in Morocco and a Moroccan born in France and raised in France. I told them [Moroccan emigrants]: you shouldn't fill your head and your spirit, at night before going to bed, with electoral problems that do not concern you, that are not yours. Because you are definitely not French. . . . I know the Moroccans, they are very humble and modest [*pudique*]. They won't even go ask for the few crumbs that are due them the next day" (Morocco, Ministère de l'Information 1990).

Moroccan emigrants were not listening, however. They either simply disregarded the monarch, dismissing him as increasingly irrelevant to their lives in Europe, or they sharply challenged the right of the Moroccan government, and of the king, to intervene in their affairs in any way. As one labor organizer summed up at a plenary meeting of Moroccan workers and community organizations in 1989:

The maneuvers of the Moroccan authorities weigh heavily on us. They don't help us. . . . They isolate the Moroccan community in France by trying to prevent it from organizing and integrating in France. By compelling us to work here and not return to Morocco, they want us, oblige us to remain more than loyal; a complete loyalty to the Moroccan regime. I think that everyone feels that. It weighs heavily on us and we need to make an effort to free ourselves from it. (Mohamed, as quoted in ATMF 1989: 68)

More tangibly, naturalization rates of Moroccan emigrants for all the major receiving countries, already on the rise, picked up noticeably at the end of the 1980s (Fondation Hassan II 2003). Acquisition of French nationality quadrupled in four years, rising abruptly from around 3,000 in 1988, a number that had stayed steady throughout the 1980s, to 12,000 per year in 1992. Moreover, Moroccan emigrants and their children were increasingly creating institutions based on their Moroccan heritage, developing and celebrating their identities as Beurs—French citizens of North African origin, and advocating for their cultural and political rights in the European countries where they had begun to claim political and social membership. These associations were completely independent of the Moroccan state and did not identify in the least with the Moroccan regime, even oppositionally (Bousetta et al. 2005 Charef 2003; Dumont 2008).

The breakdown in the engagement between the Moroccan state and Moroccans living abroad began to show in remittance transfer levels. Yearly levels (adjusted for inflation) dropped 20 percent between 1986 and 1988 (Morocco, Office des Changes 1977–2003). Furthermore, emigrants' deposits in the BCP as a percentage of national deposits fell steadily after 1987 and would never recover their previous levels (BCP *Rapports annuels* 1978–2003; IMF 1977–2003). Coupled with a reduction in bonuses on transfers, Moroccan state policy toward emigrant workers had, in effect, begun to undermine the BCP's long-standing strategy of accompaniment. The collapse of one area of interpretive engagement was eroding the other. The government's drive to keep emigrants from becoming enfranchised workers was undermining its ambition to turn Moroccan labor into capital for the kingdom's economy.

5

Practice and Power

Emigrants and Development in the Moroccan Souss

Morocco's development strategy from the mid-1960s onward reflected a cynical economic and political cartography which carved out *le Maroc utile*—the useful Morocco—of the kingdom's littoral cities from the rest of the country. Initially drafted by the French colonialists, this exclusionary map was embraced by Moroccan policymakers, who favored industrial projects in burgeoning urban areas and large agribusiness outfits in the fertile plains of the central north, and directed any resources left over after military expenditures for the border skirmish with Algeria and later Western Sahara to these endeavors. The jagged Atlas Mountain chains running in parallel across the south, the desert in the far east, and the Rif Mountains butting up against the Mediterranean coast were cast as backward, resistant to development, and irrelevant to the nation's future, as were the Berber tribes that lived there. Other than interventions to extract natural resources, especially phosphates, the government ignored rural areas it viewed as useless, and it failed to provide them with even the most basic infrastructure and services.

Thanks to the government's vigorous directing of European labor recruiters to the rural backlands, emigration was disproportionate from regions located outside *le Maroc utile*. In the nation's parade of five-year economic plans, emigrants were rapidly transformed into one of the resources that the government extracted from the countryside to support development on the Atlantic coast. As soon as they were placed in European factories, mines, and fields, the government worked assiduously to turn them into a source of capital for development, and once it captured their remittances, it channeled them toward government initiatives that benefited industry and agribusiness. Meanwhile, emigrants' communities of origin suffered egregious neglect: they remained poor, abandoned, and lacking in even the most basic amenities.

The Moroccan Souss, a narrow band of steppes pinched between the two chains of Atlas Mountains, had been subjected to this pattern of state treatment since independence in 1957. For decades, this region was sidelined in a policy framework that dismissed the subsistence agriculture of the kingdom's Amazigh heartlands and marginalized its independent rural peasantry, which from time to time leveled serious challenges at the monarchy (White 2001). Compounded by geographical isolation, a highly inequitable land tenure system, and a drought that was becoming endemic, the Souss's predicament had produced some of the worst human development indicators in the Arab world. Dismal economic prospects, combined with the strong and long-standing presence of European labor recruiters, made out-migration a structural feature of the local economy. Soussis emigrated to Morocco's burgeoning cities as well as to Europe's industrial areas in numbers so large that political commentators in the 1970s and 1980s warned that entire swathes of the region risked being depopulated (Daoud 1990).

Beginning in the mid-1980s, the same emigration that was once viewed as proof of the Souss's economic distress began to challenge the crown's political cartography. In the wake of French industry's massive layoffs of Maghrebi workers, a group of emigrants from the Souss, dismissed from jobs at an aluminum smelting plant in the south of France, began to discuss the possibility of returning to their villages of origin and opening up small businesses. They determined they could not survive economically in their isolated hamlets unless they took it upon themselves to equip the villages with at least the very basics in infrastructure—electric power, water and sanitation, and roads—and their deliberations quickly turned to how they might supply these public works. In concert with their communities of origin, they came up with new ways of providing the villages with essential amenities: they erected community-managed electricity networks; they revived traditional strategies for the collection, purification, and distribution of rain and spring water; and they built roads to link isolated hamlets to rural centers, using funds they had raised, dirham by painstaking dirham, from Soussi emigrants laboring in France and in Morocco's coastal cities. They devised solutions, both technological and organizational, to the obstacles that the state had claimed made it plainly unfeasible to provide basic amenities to those villages. In doing so, they turned their craggy, barren mountainside into a fountainhead of innovative approaches to economic development. More subversively, however, the Soussis belied state claims about the difficulties of serving the area and implicitly called into question the state's prima facie justification of topographical constraints and technical difficulties for its policy dereliction toward the region.

Instead of confronting the government's neglect of their valley head on, the Soussis drew the state into the processes of innovation. They involved government employees in the local, day-to-day practices through which they built electricity networks, dug out reservoirs and water channels, and mapped out roads. "We want to take the state by the hand and bring it here," explained one Soussi migrant. "We don't have the resources the state does; we can never accomplish what the state can. What we want is for the state to do the work of the state *here*" (interview, January 2004, emphasis in original). As the state's engagement with the Soussis grew, the Moroccan government began to rely on the region as an incubator for new ideas, to appropriate the creative approaches for infrastructure and service provision that it observed there. Slowly it applied the lessons learned there to select rural areas throughout Morocco, well beyond the confines of the valley. As it did so, the state gradually but irrevocably amended its own conceptualization of development, especially the brutal cleavage of Morocco on which it was based. No longer was a seemingly technological and apolitical pretext for the neglect of large areas of the countryside easily available. By the late 1990s, the state found itself compelled to begin connecting rural Morocco to baseline infrastructure services, and it built on the models elaborated in the Souss as the basis for remarkably successful large-scale programs.

How did a conversation that a group of migrants started with the state about rural infrastructure transform the way Morocco's authoritarian government provided services to hundreds of thousands of its citizens? How did a few innovative community-based experiments for infrastructure delivery compel the state to erase the thick line it had drawn across the Moroccan territory to demarcate the areas worth tending to? This chapter argues that the answer lies in the way that interpretation mediates the relationship between practice and power. The power structures that divided Morocco into useful and useless halves depended on certain meanings to legitimate them—to make that division seem not just reasonable but natural. Those meanings, however, existed only in the practices through which they were enacted; they came into being, in a sense, only when people acted or experienced their world in ways that reflected their understanding of Morocco as divided into regions that were "useful" and regions that were "useless." The practices, especially the government practices, that expressed that partition of Morocco were routine and well established, repeated over and over again, in large part because the meanings they enacted make other practices seem unimaginable. With their repetition, those practices reinforced the notion that Morocco was made of two kinds of lands and people, that it had always been thus, and that it would always be so.

Interpretation focuses attention on the meanings in everyday practices. It teases them out from the fiber of action, turns them over, reconsiders them, and reinvents them. And thereby it opens up new possibilities for action. The Soussi communities' ability to reshape the government's approach to rural development shows that interpretive processes have the capacity to alter entrenched power structures. But the Soussis' experiences also show that interpretation is stealthily transgressive: the practices that interpretation imagines erode the riverbank of hard-baked meanings and progressively change the flow of practice. In their interpretive conversation with the state, Soussi migrants and their communities focused on specific development practices. Yet the practices they debated and enacted embodied nascent understandings about community, development, and political identity, all of which contested, to varying degrees, the meanings that had previously made categorizing the Souss as part of the *Maroc inutile* seem reasonable and irreversible. Once the state engaged in the new practices, it unwittingly joined in displacing the old meanings. Practice by practice, the meanings that divided Morocco in two were eroded away.

Getting Power

Since the 1930s, French employers had looked to the Souss for manpower for their factories and fields, so it was no accident that the changes that migrants would spearhead in their native Souss in the 1980s and 1990s began in a mining town in the south of France where Soussis had for years labored to extract and process aluminum. Argentière-la-Bessée, in the shadow of the French Alps, grew up around a plant set up by Péchiney, one of France's largest aluminum processing outfits and major recruiter of immigrant labor during the *trentes glorieuses* of France's postwar expansion. Péchiney preferred workers from the Souss over migrant labor from other places: in internal correspondence, company managers specified that Soussis were favored because they were "quick-witted, rarely fell ill, and compliant" (J. Lahoussain, as quoted in Cans 2005). Throughout the 1960s and 1970s, company recruiters traveled regularly to the Souss, selecting workers from the men they had strip to the waist and file in front of them, and they prevailed on their Soussi employees to refer friends and relatives (Cans 2005).

By the 1980s, however, after several decades of headlong growth, the town's main employer began to show signs of trouble. The economic crisis in the wake of the oil shocks of 1974 had hit Péchiney hard. Stuck in a pattern of overproduction for a European economy that had slowed to a crawl, the company tried, and failed, to cope with its major financial losses by increasingly radical waves of downsizing (*New York Times* 1984). Péchiney was lurching toward collapse. The French socialist government finally stepped in and nationalized the company in 1982, and began restructuring. As part of the reorganization, sixteen Péchiney plants were slated for closure, and the Argentière plant was among the first to go. To cushion the massive layoffs this entailed, Péchiney—now a quickly shrinking but politically accountable parastatal—extended start-up funds to former employees so that they could establish small firms in the region. The idea was to rescue the town from economic disaster and to create an economy that might become as vital as that created by the clusters of small firms across the border in northern Italy, which were receiving much press at the time (Corrado 2003). French government planners hyped a vision of vibrant businesses that would produce high-end products for niche markets, with unemployed workers turned entrepreneurs at the helm. Through Péchiney, they offered workers business development assistance to set up forty firms (Daoud 1997: 16–17).

Among the workers who were laid off were 54 North African immigrants: 26 Moroccans, 20 Algerians, and 8 Tunisians (Daoud 1997: 17). When they lost the jobs that had kept them in France, they decided to return home rather than try to rebuild their lives in Argentière. The migrants nonetheless appropriated the notion of small firms leading to an economic revival and began to view firm clusters as the economic strategy that could heave their regions out of chronic poverty, as well as ensure them a solid income.

When they approached Péchiney for funds to start up small businesses in their communities of origin, the firm refused, insisting that the funds were tagged for the development of the Argentière valley. The migrants countered that they had equal rights to the aid since the award was in fact a form of severance pay. With the backing of the Confédération Française Démocratique du Travail (CFDT), a federation of labor unions that had locked horns with Péchiney when the company downsized, the immigrants organized and took Péchiney to court. After a protracted legal battle, Péchiney was forced to disburse the same funds to the immigrant plaintiffs as it had to the rest of its workforce. The North Africans began planning for their return (Daoud 1997; Mernissi 1998; Migrations et Développement [M/D] interviews, 2004).

The migrants' plans were modest: making marginal agricultural improvements to family landholdings, opening grocery stores and gas stations, and setting up small agro-processing firms that would produce for local markets. Although small in scale, the projects nevertheless were impossibly ambitious. Most of the migrants would be returning to hamlets that lacked electricity, running water, passable roads, or telephone lines. The disconnect between their plans and the infrastructure available was glaring (Daoud 1997).

To address these obstacles, the returning migrants formed an association under French law. They called it Retour et Développement—Return and Development. All of them had long contributed to community projects in their villages, sending money for the renovation of the village mosque or the digging of a new well. This time, however, they turned their attention to the structural obstacles that would prevent them from establishing businesses. Specifically, they wanted to pave the roads, set up the electricity networks, build the wells, and erect the telephone lines that would turn their plans for return from pipe dreams into projects (Daoud 1997; M/D interviews, 2004).

Retour et Développement served as an interpretive space where possible approaches would become clear. The members of the group deliberated extensively about how to build the infrastructure they wanted without government support. In the end, they decided to pool a portion of the start-up funds they received from Péchiney to fund these infrastructure and service projects. As they traveled back and forth from Argentière to their villages, both to scope out possible business opportunities and to hone in on the exact infrastructure needed, the migrant activists began to draw the villagers into their conversations about how to obtain basic services in the face of what the migrants complained was "total abandonment by the state—*la démission totale de l'état.*"

Jamal Lahoussain, the group's founder, remembers urging villagers to join them: "You have to get involved, the state won't do anything for you. Let's take the initiative ourselves. With your participation and ours, we can breathe life back into our villages" (as quoted in Daoud 1997: 20; Mernissi 1998; M/D interviews, 2004).

Because the majority of the members of Retour et Développement were from the province of Taroudant, they decided to launch their experiment there. Imgoun, a small village hugging the slope where the Souss valley rises to meet the Atlas Mountains and Jamal Lahoussain's birthplace, was chosen as the first project site. The fact that well over half of the village's thirty-six emigrants had worked in Argentière-la-Bessée cemented the choice (Missaoui 1996: 115). The association—renamed Migrations et Développement (M/D) after it became clear that the obstacles to setting up a profitable enterprise were more intractable than at first thought—conducted an informal assessment of village needs. The migrants congregated in Imgoun, going house to house and visiting with villagers. They asked about the problems the villagers faced and found that these were many, each compounding the last: overgrazing and deforestation, which led to desertification; the serious disrepair of retaining walls for cultivated terraces, as a result of which the eroded steppes were being washed away in the rains and the clay beneath was impermeable to the fast running waters; and the overuse of wells, which rendered them briny and dry. Villagers' answers also revealed that their top priority was getting electricity. As an M/D activist recalls, "the villagers told us: without electricity, we can't do anything" (as quoted in Daoud 1997: 19).

The reason was motor pumps. For villagers, motor pumps meant sure access to water. The machines could siphon water from the rapidly falling underground water tables and rescue parched fields during drought years. Buying a pump represented a significant outlay, however, and even more costly than the machinery itself was the benzene required to run it. The fuel had to be hauled in on four-wheel-drive vehicles able to negotiate dirt roads, and a hefty transport surcharge was tacked on to the already elevated price it garnered at regional markets. In Imgoun, as in villages throughout the Souss, motorized water pumps were a popular investment among international migrants. Because of the costs of purchasing and operating them, the noisy contraptions became a symbol for some of the socioeconomic changes migration had wrought in the village: the remittances that migrants sent home not only dramatically widened disparities of wealth, but also modified the opportunity structure. The ability to invest in land and cultivate agricultural plots in an ongoing fashion became contingent on international migration. Migrant families purchased water pumps and the benzene to power them with income earned abroad and could thus irrigate their crops with enough regularity to turn a profit. Their neighbors without motorized access to water, by contrast, had to rely on fickle seasonal rains and communal wells that the nearby motorized pumps had drained through indiscriminate water use. During years when rainfall was scarce, many of these farmers had to abandon their plots and seek work as day laborers tending fields that their migrant neighbors, absent landlords as they themselves toiled in Europe, irrigated with motorized pumps. For many of these villagers, electric power would put pumps within reach. After an initial capital investment, they could use cheaper electricity instead of benzene to run them and could cross over the economic divide that migration had opened in the village.

Migrants shared the villagers' desire for electricity but for different reasons. The value of electricity to migrants—the meaning it had for them—had more to do with the dislocation they experienced as migrant workers in European industrial settings. They also saw electricity as a means to cross over a divide. Lack of it was the main barrier that separated them from the prosperity available to their French co-workers-turned-entrepreneurs in Argentière. From a more personal perspective, many migrants I spoke with recounted that they experienced the lack of electricity in their village of origin as symbolic of the divide that had opened between themselves and their children, a chasm they felt helpless to close. They explained that when they had returned home for vacations, their children, raised in European cities, rebelled at the prospect of spending weeks in an isolated hamlet without electricity, and thus without the easy entertainment (televisions, stereos, and so forth) they were used to. For many migrant families from the Souss, the *vacances* became the cause of a fight, replayed year after year, in which the lack of electricity became a lightning rod for cultural and generational differences. For migrants who remembered the promise the Moroccan state had seemed to hold for all its citizens in the years after independence, being unable to refute their children's portrayal of their villages as "backward" and "poor" was a betrayal that cut to the quick (interviews, Taroudant, December 2003–January 2004).

Imgoun was not alone in its predicament, and the Moroccan government's track record on rural electrification lent credence to the migrants' sense of having been abandoned. At the time that Migrations et Développement began its work in the late 1980s, close to 70 percent of Morocco's population was rural, and no more than a fraction had access to electric power. Although data for the 1980s are sketchy at best, they indicate that rates of electrification were abysmally low, estimated at anywhere between 4 and 18 percent. The data from the 1990s are more reliable, having been drawn from a series of government and aid agency studies. Although they still display some variation, with the Moroccan National Office of Electricity estimating that only 21 percent of rural Morocco was connected to electricity in 1994, and the World Bank measuring that access as somewhat higher at 25 percent, they clearly indicate that the rates of electrification for rural Morocco lagged far behind those for countries of similar income in the region (Office Nationale de l'Électricité [ONE] 1999; World Bank 1990). By 1990, Algeria had achieved 70 percent rural electricity coverage and Tunisia was close behind with 60 percent. The Moroccan government explained away its poor performance by noting that its administrative structure made the provision of electricity dependent on local revenues (World Bank 1990).

In the early 1980s, prodded by the World Bank, the central government embarked on a rural electrification program, but by all accounts it was a Potemkin village of a scheme, a halfhearted effort with little impact: between 1982 and 1996, the state hooked up a mere 70 villages to electricity per year on average (ONE 1999). At that rate, it would have taken Morocco over three hundred years to provide electricity to its 34,000 villages (V. Butin, pers. comm., 2004). As the former director of the National Office of Electricity, Driss Benhima, tersely conceded, "between 1960 and 1990, it [rural electrification] was not a priority" (Daoud 1997: 40).[1]

The approach that Migrations et Développement took to supplying Imgoun with electric power in the face of this state abandonment was both experimental and experiential. At its core was a highly participatory process of interpretive engagement that involved M/D, the organization's migrant constituents, and villagers, as well as the European funders and collaborators that M/D recruited for the project. The discussions that M/D sparked were lengthy, and sometimes heated, verbal affairs between all these actors. Language, however, was only one idiom in which interpretative conversation occurred: in Imgoun, practice emerged as a central vehicle for collaborative interpretation. As the migrants of M/D, Imgounis, and the French electricians they enlisted attempted to envision and build a working electricity network, they explored new means of using the funds, the technology, and the contacts that migrants channeled back to the village. When they ran into stumbling blocks, when they found that the technological blueprints sketched out for the project were ill suited to village needs, and when they realized that the village needed to create a local organization to manage the network's construction and maintenance, they improvised. They remolded existing practices and tried out new ways of applying the resources migration made available. In the process, they engaged with the meanings vested in those resources. Their nascent, often not fully coherent, practices were new interpretations of meanings attached to remittances, to migration, to local development, and, of course, to electricity.

As Imgoun's experience shows, those meanings were not neutral. They reflected the power relations that structured life there: they conveyed the tensions between traditional village elites and migrants, relatively wealthy thanks to their European wages, who were displacing them; they captured the unspoken social distance that separated migrants and villagers from the French consultants who assisted on the electricity project; and most poignantly, they rendered visible the state's neglect of rural communities. As the meanings were transformed through interpretation, the power structures they legitimated were also changed. When the migrants of M/D, the villagers of Imgoun, and the French consultants improvised new practices and reinterpreted the meanings held within them, they did more than just influence the effect the resources generated by migration would have. Drawing intensively on local assets, they molded what the resources themselves would in fact be; they used local materials, local knowledge, local forms of social organization, even local conflicts, to determine what form the resources would take. However, the technological model for electricity provision and the social institutions to support it that emerged were not strictly local: these innovations were situated in the practices that created them—practices that would span regions, countries, technologies, languages, and ultimately, the boundary between state and society.

The innovations produced in Imgoun were radical in that they paved the way for other villages to erect similar electricity networks. However, not the migrants, nor the villagers, nor the French consultants could have imagined the outcome of their efforts when they began. Out of the ambiguity that saturated their interpretive conversations—in language and in practice—emerged a model for electricity provision, as well as for community development initiatives more generally, that none of those involved could have anticipated. To set it in motion, the migrants reached back into the social networks they had established during their struggle against Péchiney.

Poles and Wires: Technology in Practice

In 1986, M/D contacted the Agence Française pour la Maîtrise de l'Énergie (AFME) about the possibility of setting up solar-powered water pumps in Imgoun. The leadership of the AFME—a French governmental agency for energy management now called the Agence de l'Environment et de la Maîtrise d'Énergie (ADEME)—had ties to the Confédération Française Démocratique du Travail (CFDT), the federation of labor unions that had locked horns with Péchiney. Members of M/D had been involved in union organizing during the prolonged battle with the aluminum magnate. By the time the migrants of M/D had lost their jobs and had begun exploring energy options for the village, the union boss of the CFDT, Michel Roland, had been named president of the AFME.

The migrants' project piqued the AFME's interest because the agency had already been commissioned by the Moroccan National Office of Electricity to study the provision of decentralized solar power to rural areas. Imgoun represented a potential site for a pilot project. In the AFME, the migrants of M/D found an experienced partner to help them capture the energy they needed (Missaoui 1996, Daoud 1997; V. Butin, pers. comm., 2004).

To investigate the feasibility of a solar project, M/D and AFME conducted an extensive diagnostic survey of energy usage in Imgoun in 1987. In the intimate setting of the village, the survey, formal in design, was casual and interpretive in its process. The people conducting it were mostly emigrants from the village, and they went house to house, chatting about how the villagers used energy. They talked with people about how they prioritized energy expenditure, how much money families actually spent on energy, how much time the women spent collecting firewood, and how families would imagine themselves using energy if it were readily and cheaply available. Through these conversations, household members reflected on their actual practices, some for the first time. They articulated patterns of energy usage; in particular, they made connections between the different types of energy they used and expenditures to light their homes, cook their food, and in some cases, irrigate their fields (M/D interviews, January 2004).

The study, and the interpretative conversations that underpinned it, yielded two unexpected findings. First, gas-fueled mechanical pumps did not represent Imgoun's greatest energy consumption by any stretch. The noisy machines were not the energy gluttons that they were widely maligned as being. Instead, to the migrants' and residents' surprise, the M/D-AFME study found that the village's largest energy consumption was at the household level: butane gas and candles for lighting, batteries for radios and portable televisions, and wood for cooking. Wood was the most exploited source of energy by far: it represented 80 percent of household energy consumption. Most families purchased wood from vendors who made deliveries to their homes, but more than a third of the wood used by Imgouni households was scavenged from the communal, and rapidly thinning, nearby forests. The two poorest income deciles of the village relied much more heavily than others on found wood, using it for over 50 percent of their energy consumption. They also used the wood in much less energy efficient ways than wealthier households, owing to the poorer quality of their housing and in particular of their ovens (Missaoui 1996: 123–33). The second unanticipated finding was that households were spending a large portion of their incomes on energy, an average of 30 percent. Moreover, the wealthiest fourth of the village was spending about five times as much on energy as the poorest (Missaoui 1996: 130–36; Association pour la Valorisation des Echanges par la Coopération [AVEC] 1992).

The study showed that providing Imgoun with electricity was both more viable and more urgent than anyone had thought. With households already devoting so much of their income to buying energy, more in fact than urban residents, the villagers could afford most of the costs involved in setting up and maintaining a local electricity network (J. Lahoussain, e-mail correspondence, May 2004). More important, hooking households up to alternate sources of energy for cooking was the only way to prevent the rapid deforestation that was turning the surrounding landscape into a bald wasteland. All households would have to have access to the network, regardless of their ability to contribute to the costs of building it; otherwise, the poor would continue to collect wood, denuding the mountainsides even further (J. Lahoussain, e-mail correspondence, May 2004; Missaoui 1996: 134–41). Deforestation was perilous for the whole village, not just because it reduced access to wood and to the almonds and argan nuts that grew on the trees. The overharvesting of communal orchards led to soil erosion that made the slopes around the village slick, and water from the occasional rains would pour down the mountainside instead of being absorbed into the earth to refill underground aquifers. Through the interpretive conversations occasioned by the migrant-led study, Imgounis made the conceptual connection between electricity and the availability of water. The provision of electricity for all was the only way to protect water, the communal resource on which the survival of the village depended. As a result, energy, once thought of as a good that people could access according to their financial means, came to be interpreted as a communal resource as well.

The next step was to create an electricity network to make the resource available to every household, regardless of income. Other villages had done it. *Douars*—as Moroccan villages are called—throughout the Moroccan countryside had patched together networks based on local generators. In fact, external consultants working for the National Office of Electricity estimated that in 1993, about 2,000 villages had set up informal electrification schemes (Berdai and Butin 1993). Those networks, however, suffered from two serious shortcomings. First, the community-funded systems used equipment of a quality so poor that electricity provision was sporadic and eventually broke down permanently. Low-hanging cables, too weak to carry the voltage that passed through them, along with faulty connections and no circuit breakers, created dangerous conditions that were not infrequently fatal. Second, informal electricity networks tended only to serve those who had contributed funds for their construction—between 20 and 50 percent of residents by most estimates (Butin and M/D 1993). As Imgounis had intuited, poorer families, excluded from service, continued to forage for wood with the same intensity, aggravating already rapid deforestation (Berdai and Butin 1993; Butin and M/D 1993).[2] For M/D and Imgoun, the challenge, therefore, was twofold: to create a network that was affordable, reliable, and safe, and to ensure that all villagers had access to it.

M/D's contacts with French electricity providers enabled Imgoun to overcome the technological hurdles involved. Through the AFME, M/D forged a relationship with Électricité de France (EDF) and with a nonprofit set up by EDF employees, called Codev and later renamed Électriciens sans Frontières. EDF provided extensive technological know-how. M/D so captivated Codev with the project and the technological puzzle it represented that the organization sent thirty-seven volunteers to the village to build the network (Daoud 1997; interviews, Taroudant, January 2004). The idea was that they would donate the knowledge acquired through years of experience to come up with a solution that would fit Imgoun's specific constraints. That, however, is not quite what happened. Knowledge was not simply transferred to the village. Instead, Imgoun actively helped to constitute the knowledge the French technicians brought with them. Through its topography, its people, and its bold resistance to state norms, the village shaped and reformulated the technological expertise and concepts of Codev. In concert with the EDF electricians, they arrived at a technological solution that fit the needs of a small hamlet huddling on an arid slope rising to the Atlas Mountains.

Even before the EDF technicians arrived, conversations with M/D ruled out a number of technological options. For the M/D-AFME study, villagers identified not only their current uses but also how they would consume electricity were it to be made readily available, making clear that household appliances would represent an ever-greater share of consumption. After consultation with Codev, Imgoun abandoned the idea of capturing solar or wind energy, opting instead to rely on a generator, which, unlike the more environmentally sound solutions, could provide an alternating current better suited to household electronics. Once the village had committed to a technological course, an iterative exchange between technicians and villagers determined what form the technology would take locally. The conversations occurred in the planning phases: EDF electricians brought blueprints for the network with them, but as the migrants of M/D commented on the plans, the drawings were redrafted several times. The interpretative conversation continued all through the construction, as the villagers sweated alongside EDF electricians to erect the distribution network, and in the evenings, when the visitors stayed in villagers' houses, shared their meals, and followed their daily rhythms (M/D, e-mail correspondence, 2004; interviews, Taroudant, January 2004). Together, they brainstormed and improvised to solve obstacles. When materials specified in the plans were impossible to find in regional markets or were prohibitively expensive, they experimented with more affordable materials available locally. When the mountainous terrain or the layout of village houses created unexpected challenges, they tried out different construction techniques until they found a way to get the pole network to stand erect. And when, in the course of the evening exchanges between EDF technicians and Imgounis, needs for electricity that had remained implicit or unclear were articulated, the network was modified to address them.

The exchange was powerful for all involved. It reached beyond technological conversations to transform the preconceptions that the French and the Moroccans had of one another. As Jamal Lahoussain, M/D's director, recounts: "At the end of the project, two EDF employees came to see me. They said that, as members of the National Front [a French far-right party with a forcefully anti-immigrant platform], they had joined the project to mock it and show it up. But they were so impressed with the reception that the villagers had given them, and they understood just how much local families relied on immigrants for their livelihood. [After their stay], they decided to tear up their [party-membership] cards" (Daoud 1997: 24). He also recalled that migrants from the village who had spent over two decades abroad without ever entering a non-immigrant household also crossed new thresholds when they returned to France and were invited to the homes of the EDF volunteers (Daoud 1997; Mernissi 1998).

Ultimately, the electricity network diverged significantly from standards set both by the Moroccan National Office of Electricity and by the EDF itself. Through the interpretive conversations that Imgounis had with the EDF, they brought the logic that underpinned the standards—the meanings embedded in them—to the surface. Once they did that, they were able to create a network that adhered to the principles of safety and reliability expressed in the standards without complying with their literal requirements. The dimensions of the network and of the physical structures to support it were based on the real and projected electricity use in Imgoun, a tiny village made up of squat houses, and were therefore smaller than the norms based on urban usage. Thinner-than-usual cables were strung on poles that were only six meters tall instead of the required ten. The poles, stripped eucalyptus trunks, were bought locally and substituted for the mandated concrete columns. Electricity was transmitted along this network at a frequency one-third the intensity of the industry standard (Missaoui 1996: 141). After the project, Lahoussain reflected on how the perception of what technological options were viable shifted with the Imgoun project: "The standards of the National Office of Electricity were too draconian. They imposed them on the villages. In the end, even EDF found that they were excessive and that they did not take technological evolution into account. Certain technicians argue that poles can be as short as 4 meters, that you can reuse old materials, reduce the size of the transformers, introduce new technical options that are more adapted to a rural setting" (as quoted in Daoud 1997: 37). The rough poles and slack wires that now wove through the village, rudimentary though they appeared, represented a significant technological advance. They embodied a new way of thinking about rural electricity provision.

In late 1988, the generator was powered up at last and the lights in Imgoun were turned on for the first time. In her monograph on M/D, Daoud describes the scene: "children ran every which way, women let out ululations of joy, the men took on an indifferent air that reflected their status, but their gaze was illuminated with a different light, with pride: at long last they feel connected to the rest of the world, they have become full citizens of the world" (1997: 36). For the migrants and for the villagers who had never left Imgoun, electricity shed new light on their hamlet and its connection to world beyond.

Organizing Development

Although the design of such a functioning electricity network was an impressive feat in itself, the social institutions that migrants and villagers established to carry out the project had a far greater impact for long-term economic development. Like the poles and wires that ran among the squat houses, the social institutions were themselves the product of interpretive conversations between migrants and villagers, and would keep those interpretive exchanges alive.

In the initial planning phase of the project, before it was fully conceptualized, M/D organized a village association in Imgoun. Made up of local villagers and Imgouni emigrants, the association played a dual role: it managed the logistical tasks necessary for construction and maintenance of a network, but it also opened up an interpretive space that supported ongoing innovation. The new conceptual connections and the possible futures that they made imaginable ensured that Imgoun's electricity network would only be the first in a series of creative efforts to promote economic development.

The logistics that the association managed were extensive. It participated intensively in the pre-project surveys; it organized the reception and lodging of the French volunteers; and it managed the budget for the construction and operation of the generator-powered network. It raised 60 percent of the funds needed for the project from sources outside Imgoun: the EDF and AFME each contributed sizable amounts, but migrants also donated a respectable sum. The association collected the remaining 40 percent of the cost from village householders, many of whom used remittances from migrant members in Europe and Morocco's coastal cities to cover their contribution. To accommodate households that did not have the means to make the suggested donation, the association set up a sliding scale and a subsidized loan scheme through which wealthier families covered the participation costs of poorer households, which would repay them at no interest. The association also valued the sweat equity that households contributed; it determined how much the labor of the men who helped build the network and of the women who cooked and laundered for the French volunteers was worth, and how much to discount from poorer households' share of the costs as a result. After the network was in place, the association also took charge of maintaining it and collecting fees, which—in keeping with the principle that all families should have access to electricity, regardless of income—were based on ability to pay. Additionally, the association sent ten semiskilled, literate young people to France for training at the EDF's vocation program (Missaoui 1996: 142). When they returned, the association formally employed two of them to run the generator, to make sure that the network remained functional and safe, and to manage the budgetary aspects of electricity production, including calculating and collecting monthly service dues (Butin and M/D 1993; Daoud 1997: 44; interviews, Taroudant, January 2004).

The results of M/D's electricity project depended on the competent logistical management that the village association provided, and they were impressive. The electrification of Imgoun cost half of what it cost the Moroccan government to provide electricity to villages in rural areas: whereas the government spent a minimum of 10,000 dirhams per household, M/D's outlay was an average of 5,500 dirhams (Missaoui 1996: 136; World Bank 1988). The network also achieved the village's goal of protecting surrounding forests by reducing wood use: the energy supplied by wood fell by a third in five years after the network was set up, from nine gigajoules per household per year in 1988 to six gigajoules in 1994 (Missaoui 1996: 133). Two changes in household energy consumption caused this drop: first, with electricity readily accessible, families no longer spent money on the candles and batteries they used for lighting and to power their home appliances. Second, because electricity was priced on a sliding scale in the village, using it instead of wood or benzene to power certain cooking appliances, such as kettles, became an attractive option even for households of limited means. As a result, households rich and poor used the income that was freed up by the availability of electricity to purchase butane gas, which they used to replace wood for cooking and heating. Gas ovens replaced the traditional wood ovens buried underground; gas heaters replaced charcoal furnaces; electric lamps replaced gas-powered lamps, and so on (Missaoui 1996: 136; Daoud 1997: 37). Because gas was more efficient than wood for cooking and heating, and electricity more efficient than candles and batteries, household energy consumption dropped by 20 percent between 1988 and 1994, even though the use of energy-consuming appliances grew. For women, this shift was especially significant. The task of collecting wood traditionally fell to them, and before Imgoun set up its electricity network, it was not uncommon for women to spend two to three hours a day gathering firewood, returning home with their backs bent under the 30- to 50-kilogram (approx. 65–110 pounds) load necessary for a family's daily heating and cooking needs. Moreover, women suffered disproportionately from eye and lung complaints because they spent large parts of the day in smoke-filled kitchens. "Gas relieves us from the chore of gathering wood and from the smoke that choked us and irritated our eyes all day," observed one Imgouni woman (as quoted in Missaoui 1996: 139; Daoud 1997: 36–39).

Migrants and the local villagers reported that the social dynamic the association had set in motion was even more significant than the advent of electricity itself. The association became an institutional space where villagers could take stock of their needs, together imagine a different future for themselves, and then articulate the concrete steps they had to take to get there. In effect, the village association provided a setting where villagers and migrants could come together and have the interpretive conversation necessary to create new avenues for development. As the founder of M/D reflected, "It's by acting that we build a pedagogy of development, starting from the motivations of the villagers and not imposing it from outside. Right from the first project, a participatory dynamic is set in motion with the creation of a village association" (Daoud 1997: 26).

Over time, the association became a place where Imgounis could explore the meanings that their new energy practice brought to the surface. It became a conversational space where they could reinterpret meanings and forge new connections between them, creating new understandings that could become the basis for the next generation of innovation. In Imgoun, conversations about the electricity network led to the envisioning and then planning of a new irrigation system powered by electricity that was much more efficient than traditional systems that functioned through gravity and water pressure. The conversations changed the understanding of water management from an activity that had always been done a certain way to an area that could be improved through technological innovation. As the new irrigation system turned fields that had oscillated from waterlogged plots to arid patches into tracts that were reliably lush, conversations in the association explored the possibility of cultivating high-value-added crops for sale. The definition of agriculture shifted from a family subsistence activity to a commercial practice. This shift led in turn to the idea of increasing the cultivation of saffron, a crop traditionally grown in the area, and as participants in the association considered the corner grocery stores many emigrants had established in Europe after being laid off from assembly lines, they contemplated exporting saffron through migrant networks. A cooperative for the export of high-quality organic saffron was created, and in the process of interpretation that produced it, commercial agriculture was transformed into a communal activity, no different than the collective management of natural resources in the village. Harvesting saffron is a labor-intensive activity traditionally done by women, and women in the cooperative were responsible for collecting, sorting, weighing, and packaging the delicate pistils. Not only did they have to comply with European Union standards when they performed these tasks, but they had to keep accounts of how much saffron they were processing. Literacy rates for women in Imgoun were even lower than the national average of 10 percent—estimates suggest that only 7 percent could read or write (CERED 1999: 137)—and keeping even rudimentary accounts was impossible. Discussions about the cooperative turned the villagers' attention to women's low literacy levels, and out of that exchange, the idea of founding an informal school for adults, primarily for women, surfaced—another plan that previously would have seemed unimaginable (interviews, Taroudaut, January 2004, Paris, February 2004; Daoud, 2004).

Related to its function as a forum for interpretative exchange and for creative envisioning, the association became a tool of self-government through which the village set up the additional institutional mechanisms it needed to carry out the projects it planned. It took the logistical steps to ground the ideas that emerged through interpretation and turn them into real interventions for economic development. For example, to collect funds for future projects, the village association levied a tax on each household based on the amount of electricity the household consumed. The funds were then deposited in an account that the association would draw on for larger development projects (either with M/D or independently), but also for smaller community expenses, like celebrations on feast days.

The village association was itself a reinvention of a very local practice. It was, in essence, a new take on the *jema'a* (pl., *jema'at*), a traditional council of elders that had for centuries governed the management of communal resources in Amazigh villages in the Souss region. Often celebrated as an indigenous form of proto-democracy, the jema'a elected its leader each year, and most decisions were made by consensus (Gellner 1983; Mernissi 1998; Haas 2003). Vested with the legitimacy that the participatory process afforded, the jema'a had also acted as the representative of the village as a whole in its dealings with the central authorities. Historically, Morocco's Berber tribes had always enjoyed a high degree of autonomy from the central sultanic state, which could never bring them fully under its control despite repeated and often famously murderous raids. Outside the kingdom's imperial cities, the rule of the sultan had to be secured through negotiation rather than by force. In the central High

Atlas region and the Souss valley at its heart, the sultan bargained with jema'at for the allegiance of those they represented, offering self-government, an exemption from tribute, and other concessions in exchange for provisional loyalty (Haas 2003; Mernissi 1998). In pre-colonial Morocco, this "domestic diplomacy," as one scholar of Morocco's political history has dubbed it (A. Radi, as quoted in Mernissi 1998: 55), afforded Amazigh villages wide latitude in the government of their own affairs. In the more laudatory accounts of the jema'a, this local and independent form of self-government is what allowed the Amazigh tribes to survive and profit in a harshly austere natural environment, maintaining a strong cultural and political identity despite centuries of efforts by the central authorities to "Arabize" them (Mernissi 1998).

By the time M/D began its work in the Souss, however, the jema'at of the valley seemed fated to become relics of the past. Socioeconomic changes had seriously eroded their husbandry of natural resources in their villages. In an irony that was not lost on many of the migrants I spoke with, most of these changes were due to the intensive migration from the regions since the 1960s. The remittances migrants sent home, substantial by local standards, upset the local socioeconomic hierarchy. The local distribution of wealth, especially in the form of land ownership, was one of the central principles around which the jema'a was organized. Although participatory in its process, the jema'a was not egalitarian in its makeup. Its membership was restricted to male members of land- or water-owning clans, and the council was often dominated by the wealthier families represented (Haas 2003). The decisions the jema'a made regarding water and land use, as well as the assignment of community labor, tended to impose on landless sharecroppers a disproportionate share of the burden of maintaining terraces, irrigation canals, wells, and so on, without affording them corresponding usage rights (Haas 2003; Missaoui 1996).

Starting in the late 1970s, families that had been landless and marginalized for generations began buying land with the income that migration earned them. As new landowners, they pressured resistant jema'at for membership, and the ensuing contests damaged the legitimacy of the traditional councils. Migrants complained that the institutions were "undemocratic" and nonegalitarian, and that they favored a historically landed elite; the new landowners began to challenge the jema'at's authority in ways large and small, through direct confrontation as well as through quiet disregard for their edicts. Migrants circumvented community rules about water use in particular, investing in motorized pumps to irrigate their lands, many of the tracts newly purchased. They refused to contribute labor to maintain community infrastructure such as retaining walls and irrigation canals, paying others to sweat in their place. Unheeded, the jema'at, vital community institutions for centuries, fell into disrepair, and with their decline, the delicate ecological equilibrium they orchestrated was thrown off balance. In Imgoun, by the late 1980s, hills covered in dense forests existed only in the memories of elders, and with surface streams and irrigation canals parched by the advancing desert, water could be found only deep underground for years at a stretch (Daoud 1997; Haas 2003; interviews, Imgoun, January 2004).

In addition to the economic upheavals caused by migration, a series of political events in Morocco's modern history seemed to presage the end of the jema'at's role. After the French brutally defeated the Amazigh resistance to their rule in the 1930s, the colonists brought Amazigh tribes firmly to heel, incorporating them into colonial administrative structures, dividing up their lands into rural municipalities, and taking over the management of some communal resources, especially water. The Alawite king inherited the French colonial governance structures after independence and deployed them to govern Berber regions with as firm a hand as possible. However, the Moroccan tradition of domestic diplomacy between Amazigh tribes and the sultanate eventually resurfaced, only in a more provincial and clientelistic form. Negotiations with the central government were replaced, at least in part, with negotiations with local representatives of the central authority, and domestic diplomacy veered precipitously toward the reinforcement of self-interested alliances between local elites and municipal bureaucrats. No longer was the jema'a representing the interests of the village to government; it was representing the interests of notables who sat on the council and cementing their clientelistic ties with government. The moral authority that gave the council's decisions binding weight in the villages was squandered in enough cases to make the jema'at of the Souss valley generally suspect (see chap. 2; Haas 2003; Mernissi 1998).

The migrants of M/D resuscitated Imgoun's jema'a by reimagining it. In several important respects, the village association was closely patterned on the jema'a. It reproduced the participatory decision-making processes and the practice of reaching conclusions by consensus. It fulfilled the jema'a's traditional function of communal resource management, which quickly grew to include those resources created through migrant initiatives, and it served as the village's interlocutor and negotiator with the state in matters pertaining to village development projects.

The migrants modified the institution in important ways, however. Membership in the association was extended to all villagers, regardless of wealth, land ownership, social status, or age.[3] Migrants and locals were invited to participate in meetings and in decision making, and the association set its meeting schedule around migrants' yearly return. As M/D's description of village associations in an internal evaluation of its rural electrification projects—that of Imgoun and the several dozen that followed—reveals, toppling locally entrenched socioeconomic hierarchies was now an integral part of the association's role in community development:

> Associations allow for the management of collectively owned equipment and for the envisioning of future projects while, at the same time, balancing the power between the young and old. In the traditional system [the jema'a], village elders, strong because of their experience, had the power to decide what should be done

in the village, and the younger villagers had to obey those decisions even if they did not seem adapted to reality or to current needs. . . . The association enables everyone to get involved in the development of the village, and reduces the hierarchical inequalities between rich and poor, between young and old. (M/D 1993: 5)

The interpretive conversations that had always taken place in the traditional councils were opened to include a more diverse set of voices and wider range of perspectives. This change did not happen without struggle, however. Some village elites who had sat on the jema'a and felt that their rightful place as community leaders was being usurped by the new association, so prosaic in its membership, and by the migrants that initiated it, resisted. "There were always tensions between the notables and those that turned the order of things on its head because of the economic resources (remittances) that they injected into the village" (J. Lahoussain, e-mail correspondence, May 2004). But whereas tensions ran high at various times during the electricity project and the development projects that followed, the interpretive exchange and the new practices to which it gave rise drew traditional village elites into the conversation and dissolved their opposition to the new institutions. In Imgoun, interest in having electricity was stronger than attachment to a social status in the village that migrant remittances were undermining anyway.

A similar dynamic surrounded the participation of women. Although formally invited to join the association, women rarely attended meetings when the association was still new to Imgoun. Gender norms in the rural Souss discouraged women from taking part in public deliberations. When the cooperative to cultivate saffron for export was set up, however, women's perspectives became indispensable to the discussions, and women were actively encouraged to attend meetings and voice their views. Once they began participating, their perspectives continued to inform the imagination and definition of development projects that followed. The innovative practices that the association created, and the interpretive process that fed them, transformed well-entrenched gender relations within the community, but they did so without challenging the gender norms head on. Rather, the new practices changed the way women's participation was viewed; it slowly amended the meaning attached to women's entrance into public forums (interviews, Taroudant, January 2004).

Occasionally, migrants in the village refused to pay their service fees, claiming that they had already contributed so much to the construction of the network that they should be exempted from the cost of using the electricity. The village association had no punitive authority. Moreover, because electricity was viewed as a resource that had to remain communal to have the desired ecological benefits, it never cut off service to households for any reason. The process of interpretation and of creating new development projects, however, vested the association with moral authority. Because this process made electricity the first step in a long journey of economic transformation, migrants who did not pay their service dues and thus jeopardized the network's financial viability were undermining the village's development prospects. Their position became morally impossible to defend.

In addition to opening membership to all villagers, the migrants formalized the association, registering it as a legal entity. In 1989, Imgoun incorporated its village association under a *dahir*—or law—passed in 1957. In doing so, migrants and villagers made their association both visible and legible to the government. They made the state formally aware of their activities, officially notifying it of the social mobilization on which their electricity network was built. In doing so, they implicitly resuscitated the principle of domestic diplomacy: by creating an entity that would, just as the jema'a had, represent the village in dealings with the state, they signaled that they were demarcating an area not fully subject to state control. Their action also implied that the state would have to negotiate with the association to govern the village, and that the village would no longer be caught up in the web of clientelistic ties between village elites and local government. And they did so using an institutional design that the state had, in fact, codified and sanctioned with the passage of the 1957 dahir.

The year 1957 seemed very distant in 1989, however, when the country was groaning under the weight of Hassan II's dictatorship. After the political unrest of the mid-1970s and early 1980s, the central government eviscerated opposition parties and press, and tightened the vise around the nongovernment organizations that managed to survive during *les années de plomb*—the leaden years—of absolute monarchy. For Imgoun, and for the villages that followed, to register their village association with the state at that historical moment was nothing short of a bold affront to state authority.

Their audacity was met with determined state resistance, but not with outright refusal or even targeted repression, because the villagers had clear legal ground for their action. "It filed all its paperwork, did things by the book," remembers a French electrical engineer involved with M/D. "For that reason, it encountered a lot of political opposition from the local government at first." Municipal authorities attempted, in the case of Imgoun and later several other villages, to intimidate them instead into dissolving their association. The villagers' response was that they were not responsible for the association—that it was a migrant initiative. "We told them, 'the migrants set it up. They're in France now. You'll have to go talk with them.'" Their strategy drew on the profound ways that emigration, encouraged by the state through direct and indirect policies, had altered village life as a source of resistance to state control: although the association was registered in Morocco, the villagers placed it symbolically outside the government's reach.

Harassing migrants was not outside the repertoire of state strategies to maintain control. By all accounts, the Moroccan government had an elaborate surveillance network in receiving countries, especially France and Belgium, and resorted to myriad tactics of intimidation, including, but not limited to, confiscation of passports when migrants returned for the yearly vacation (which made it impossible for them to return to their jobs in Europe legally), targeted auditing of migrants at customs and with respect to land ownership and tax issues, and on a few occasions, arrest and disappearance (ATMF Archives 1981–85). However, persecuting migrants for organizing to provide basic infrastructure that the state itself had so far been unable or unwilling to provide, and for notifying the state formally of the association that they set up, in keeping with Moroccan law, to manage the new service, was too flimsy a charge on which to base direct action, even for a government as insecure as Hassan II's. Such action would have ultimately undermined the state's legitimacy in the valley, still frail after the riots of the early 1980s. As a result, the local government tolerated Imgoun's village association, although it maintained a watchful eye over its activities (interviews, Taroudant, December–January 2003–4).

Thanks to migrant efforts, 126 households were connected to electricity in Imgoun. As a technical evaluation of the project stated, "electrification was a mobilizing project that catalyzed a veritable social dynamic, the only real guarantee for success for any and all development projects" (Missaoui 1996: 148). That social dynamic was the process of interpretation through which the community imagined new possibilities for economic action, envisioned new patterns of social interaction in the village, and created the practices to carry them out. It was also, however, the process through which migrants and their communities reinterpreted state-defined practices and used them to shield their experiments from state repression. Soon the protected space they opened would extend past the modest hamlet of Imgoun to include large swathes of the Souss.

Tâche d'Huile: Spreading Innovation

The technological model that the migration communities developed for energy provision as well as the social model of the village association spread like wildfire among the villages. An elder from a village not far from Imgoun explained: "Imgoun is across the way, just there. We saw that they had electricity. At night, it was all lit up. We went to Migrations et Développement and told them come bring us electricity too" (interview, December 2004). M/D members use an analogy to describe the spread of the technological and social models: they say it works like a drop of oil on a piece of paper—une tâche d'huile—which quickly widens far beyond its initial circumference.

The oil stain soon became an oil slick. By 1996, M/D had worked with over 70 villages to set up electricity networks and had a waiting list double that number. Thanks to its efforts, over 2,000 households could switch to electricity for household appliances and use the money they had spent on candles and batteries to buy butane gas for cooking and heating, replacing the firewood that was growing ever scarcer. When night fell on New Year's Eve in 1995, close to 19,000 people could turn on the lights. Between 1989 and 1996, the migrant organization was providing electricity to an average of 10 villages per year at a time when the Moroccan government was hooking only up 70 villages a year in all of rural Morocco (M/D Note de présentation 1994–97; Daoud 1997).

M/D worked with villages to tailor the networks to topographical and usage needs. In each case, the organization launched informal needs assessment surveys to identify patterns of energy use but also to start discussions among inhabitants about the significance of electricity in the village. Although EDF was no longer directly involved in translating the needs articulated into the network design, M/D was able to supply villages with the technical assistance they needed: M/D retained the help of French engineers specializing in rural electricity, and it brought several literate young men from each village to Imgoun to learn from its EDF-trained electricians how to manage a network. Moreover, although M/D had to do without the small army of EDF volunteers who had labored alongside Imgounis, it was nevertheless able to channel funds it had raised from EDF and other French development organizations to villages it worked with, subsidizing the electricity networks it established throughout the Souss by about 50 percent (Daoud 1997: 42; M/D Note de présentation 1994–97; M/D interviews, 2004; M/D, e-mail correspondence, 2004).

M/D did impose a series of conditions on each village for participation, the most important of which was that they create and legally register a village association. The association had to be inclusive and function according to a participatory decision-making process; it had to collect a minimum of 40 percent of the cost of building the network from local residents and from migrants;[4] it had to manage the logistics in a manner that ensured that all households got access to electricity regardless of ability to pay; and it had to join the other village associations created as a result of M/D's intervention in a federation. By the mid-1990s, there were close to two hundred federated village associations in the Souss valley, many of them self-taxing, and all of them carrying out development projects ranging from electricity provision to the building of potable water networks to informal schooling (M/D, Note de présentation 1994–97; M/D, interviews, 2004; M/D, e-mail correspondence, 2004).

The oil stain not only spread throughout the valley but also leaked into the state's approach to rural electricity provision. During the early 1990s the state, in a discreet and sometimes indirect exchange with migration communities in the Souss, observed how the technological and social models they had developed functioned in practice. Soon afterward, it would appropriate many of their innovations, reinventing them all, much as the migration communities had reinvented the jema'a, and apply them to a massive national rural electrification program launched in 1996.

Innovating the State

In 1988, even as M/D was working hard in Imgoun to set up an electricity network, the Moroccan government program for rural electricity was sputtering to an ignominious end. The National Program for Rural Electricity (Programme Nationale pour l'Électrification Rurale, or PNER), bankrolled and supervised by the World Bank, was formally launched in 1982 but was mired in a bureaucratic quagmire that caused a two-year delay before electrification could begin. It was, by all accounts, a disappointing attempt: over six years, the National Office of Electricity (Office Nationale de l'Électricité, or ONE) connected only 286 villages to the national grid, the overwhelming majority of which were already on the verge of being swallowed up by urban centers where the network was already well established (World Bank 1988: 6; ONE 1999). Under PNER, the average annual rate of rural electrification dropped from 70 villages per year to about 50. The World Bank program evaluation, though written in the bureaucratic language typical of such reports, positively seethed with frustration at the execution of the project: "The Government's performance was weak. . . . The loan typifies an all too common case where Government decisions and actions may delay a project which is technically implemented satisfactorily" (World Bank 1988: 17). The Moroccan government's foot-dragging stemmed from the high cost of the project: under the PNER, the cost was 17,000 dirhams per customer to connect rural households to the national grid, almost double the cost before the program was launched (World Bank 1988: 11, 21; Missaoui 1996: 136). Coupled with a brutal devaluation of the dirham halfway through a project funded by a loan taken out in U.S. dollars, the outlay required made the program too expensive for the government to envision on a grand scale, especially if it were to include villages at some distance from existing networks.

In search of other options, the Moroccan government commissioned the French Agence Française pour la Maîtrise de l'Énergie and the Directorate of Technical and Scientific Cooperation and Development, another agency housed in the French Ministry of Foreign Affairs in 1987, to create what would become the PPER—Program for Rural Pre-Electrification (Programme pour la Pre-Électrification Rurale): a pilot program to experiment with energy strategies that did not require villages to be linked to the state network. At a time when the consensus among multilateral development agencies was that the most efficient and reliable strategy for electricity provision was through connection to a national grid (Gulyani 1999), the PPER was viewed as a maverick approach with little chance of success at best and a stalling tactic at worst (World Bank 1990, 1998; ONE interviews, Rabat, 2004; EDF interviews, Casablanca, 2004). Wearied by the World Bank's assertive guidance, the Moroccan government decided to strike out on its own and pursue the unorthodox program anyway. In 1993, the government would nevertheless reluctantly implement a second phase of the PNER at the World Bank's behest—PNER 2—but its performance was dismal and its dedication halfhearted. Rural electrification rates under PNER 2 dropped to between 30 and 50 villages a year (ONE 1999),[5] and the World Bank complained again of the Moroccan government's "hesitant commitment" to the project and judged the borrower's performance "very slow and considered as deficient" (World Bank 1998: ix, 14). Whatever interest the Moroccan government did have in rural electrification, it directed to the PPER. The program was placed under the supervision of the Ministry of the Interior, the most powerful ministry in the government and the only one with the clout to shift national policy meaningfully. The government viewed the PPER as a vehicle that would provide it with cheaper alternatives to complete a task that was not high on its list of priorities anyway (interviews, Rabat, 2004).

The PPER, however, rapidly became a venue through which the migrants of M/D, authors of a working model of an independent electricity network, could talk with the state about rural electricity provision. As we shall see, the PPER opened a conversational space that crossed the political boundary dividing state and society at a moment in Morocco's history when the crown's policies made that boundary extremely charged. Although the exchanges among migrants, their communities, and the state were political, in terms of both what was communicated and the form that the conversations took, they were never overtly confrontational. The focus on supplying electricity to rural villages, mandated by the frame of the PPER, gave sensitive political issues a technical gloss: for example, although the subtext of conversations about rural households' unmet electricity needs was certainly the government's pattern of policy neglect, the exchange concentrated on how to discern current and future usage patterns among rural customers. Moreover, the conversations held under the rubric of the PPER, a program explicitly created to develop new approaches to electricity provision, were steeped in ambiguity. Because the subject explored was how to design energy solutions for a whole swath of Morocco that the government had ignored for decades, the problems to be solved were still only vaguely understood. Into the morass of views, the migrants of M/D and their communities were able to interject critiques of the method that the government, and the ONE in particular, had until that point adopted for rural electricity provision without their suggestions being perceived as a clear affront. The ambiguity also made the authorship of the ideas impossible to identify and afforded the state enough political leeway to integrate those ideas into policy without appearing to capitulate to political pressure. Through the PPER, the migrants were able to "bring the state by the hand" into the interpretive conversations they had started in their communities, and the state could claim any ideas that emerged from them as its own.

Conversations-in-Practice

The migrants of M/D were initially brought into the government's deliberations by the French electrical engineers retained for the PPER. Consultants from the AFME were the first to serve as a conversational bridge between M/D and the state. In 1987, at the same time that the AFME was working with the government to design the PPER, it was also helping M/D and Imgounis interpret the results of their informal survey and brokering M/D's relationship with the philanthropic branch of Électricité de France, which was laying out the blueprint for the village's electricity network and would later send volunteers to help build a much amended version of it. AFME consultants invited representatives from M/D to meetings with the Moroccan bureaucrats, but they also brought the insights that had emerged from AFME's work in Imgoun to the drawing board where the PPER was being laid out. Soon, the migrants of M/D would also bring the French consultants collaborating on the PPER into the interpretive exchanges they had in their villages. As the French engineers began to participate in the community conversations, they brought their Moroccan colleagues in tow. So dense did these interactions become that at one point in the early 1990s, the leading French consultant for the PPER, seconded to the Moroccan Ministry of Interior for the duration of the pilot program, also served as the director of one of M/D's local offices (M/D, Note de presentation 1993). The exchange of ideas was substantial, and it would amend both M/D strategies for building and running local electricity networks and the Moroccan government's approach to rural electricity provision. The contact between M/D and Morocco's Ministry of the Interior, the executing agency of the PPER, remained ad hoc and unofficial, however. As a consultant who worked with both sides recalls, the exchange of ideas "was informal, indirect. It's difficult to establish a formal link. The information passed through people rather than through institutions" (interview, Rabat, August 2004; AFME, e-mail correspondence, 2004; EDF interviews, January–March 2004).

Although the exchange may have been informal, its impact was tangible right from start. So impressed were the consultants from the AFME with M/D's project in Imgoun that they overrode any objections from the Moroccan government about bringing the director of M/D, Jamal Lahoussain, into high-level discussions about how to design the PPER. Including a representative from a nongovernmental organization at a time when the Ministry of the Interior was actively suppressing civil society mobilization of any kind was an exceptional move, and indeed, the M/D director was the only Moroccan present who was not affiliated with the government in any way. The PPER planning document issued at the close of that meeting displays evidence that M/D's participation informed program design. Specifically, it suggests that the experiment in Imgoun, still under way at the time, influenced the strategic priorities of the pilot program. For example, the program document includes detailed blueprints for rural energy systems, complete with meticulous calculations of how much the networks, with their various hardware components, would cost. Alongside the down-to-dirham budgets, however, the report also states the importance of conducting a careful microstudy of household electricity consumption and constructing a network using technology that reflects the village's particular needs—a conclusion that, if not drawn straight from Imgoun's experience, must have been informed by it. The provinces that were named as pilot sites for the program also indicate that M/D left its mark on the proceedings. Errachidia, Safi, and Azilal were all selected, but the province of Taroudant, recommended in the meeting as an ideal locale for the program, was eliminated. "Taroudant was rejected for political reasons," according to a source close to the PPER planners. "There was political opposition behind the scenes" (interview, August 2004). Including Taroudant, the province where M/D was active, in the PPER would have given the migrant organization too much direct influence in structuring a rural electrification initiative for which there was only lukewarm enthusiasm, and that possibility was presumably disturbing enough to some in government that it had to be closed off (AFME et al. 1988; V. Butin, pers. comm., 2004; A. De Gromard, pers. comm., 2004).

Although the exchange through direct conversation between the state and M/D ended with the design phase of the program, conversation through practice continued for almost a decade. The institutional design of the PPER drew the state into the innovative practices that migration communities in the Souss were developing for electricity provision. In what would grow to over two hundred PPER pilot sites, the Ministry of the Interior, in partnership with French consultants, tried out many of the same strategies—the same practices—that the Soussi communities had developed, often with the help of the same consultants who worked with the government. They conducted household surveys, used nonstandard technological solutions, and relied on community management of networks. In the process of using those practices, however, they also transformed and elaborated on them. For example, they applied M/D's approach of using locally sourced material for electricity systems that were based on solar, hydro, and wind power instead of the generator used in M/D villages.

The modified practices for electricity provision and management were then reintroduced into the Soussi migration communities. The French consultants and their Moroccan colleagues relied on M/D villages to try out technological solutions before they introduced them into PPER pilot sites. According to the consultants, the M/D villages were useful laboratories because they had independent networks that, by the standards of rural Morocco, were already mature. They wanted to test whether the electricity networks had the carrying capacity and appropriate electrical current for technologies ranging from lightbulbs to alternators. They also believed that M/D villages could serve as examples to other communities considering the new technologies, an idea in which M/D was an enthusiastic partner: "M/D has offered to integrate these innovations in their projects and in this manner to show their usefulness and to have a training effect for villages already electrified through the organization, and to show the viability of this new model for those that are planning an electricity project" (Butin and M/D 1993).

M/D villages were particularly appealing because they all had a village association that provided a space for residents to react to the new technology. Village associations were interlocutors for the PPER electricians: through the community groups, they could join the process of reflection about the practices the new technologies made possible and the new meanings they revealed. As one of the directors of the PPER observed: "The difficulty of introducing these innovations resides less in their technical aspects than in their social dimension. This is especially true for [introducing novelty] into projects started by local initiatives: novelty causes worry, requires numerous explications, as well as a relationship based on daily contact and trust with those actors who suggest the innovations. This attitude of trust favorable to the introduction and assimilation of an innovation is more likely when the project takes place in the context of an initiative led by a [village] association than in the context of a state program" (Butin and M/D 1993: 2).

A 1993 project to replace incandescent with fluorescent lighting in the homes and streets of Imgoun is one example of these initiatives (M/D, Note de presentation, 1993). PPER engineers had planned to introduce the low-watt fluorescent lightbulbs right from the start of the PPER but had no sense of whether they would be accepted by users, or even how to persuade them to try the strange-looking tubes (Morocco, Ministry of the Interior 1988). The M/D villages of Imgoun, Tinfate, and Imi N'Wassif provided the ideal setting to try out the technology: all three had networks that had been running uninterrupted for at least a year. M/D secured funding to purchase 1,200 fluorescent lightbulbs for 420 households in the three villages, and PPER engineers partnered with the migrant organization to install them. What M/D and the PPER staff discovered was that although the fluorescent light used 80 percent less energy than incandescent and drew much less electricity from the low-capacity networks, users found it a less than ideal solution. If tension in the current dropped by more than 10 percent, the fluorescent tubes turned black. Because they were powered by generators that roared into action when they were refilled with benzene and sputtered when their tanks ran low, the electric current in village networks fluctuated constantly. Villagers found that the newfangled bulbs burned out quickly, and as there were no affordable replacements for them in local markets, users switched back to incandescent bulbs and refused to retry the fragile tubes. PPER engineers learned that they had to invest in high-quality cables to regulate the electricity current if they wanted any chance of introducing fluorescent bulbs to skeptical villagers, who were likely to try a new technology only once before dismissing it (Berdai and Butin 1994: 46–47).

Through these exchanges, the PPER provided an institutional structure for the conversation about rural electricity that would continue for several years between the state and migration communities. As government engineers and M/D staff together experimented with different electricity practices, they improvised new solutions to the technical challenges and explored the meanings attached to the networks and to the social practices that surrounded them. So close was their partnership that the insights and innovations they produced could be traced to neither. Practices so collaborative began to erase the line that distinguished engineers on the government's payroll from amateur electricians. The interpretation in practice that the PPER supported had begun to blur the boundary between state and society.

The Ministry of the Interior retained several important lessons from these conversations-in-practice, all of which echoed but did not duplicate the insights that M/D had gleaned. First, the state recognized that it could use technology that was more adapted to rural topography and less expensive without compromising service or safety—whether in expanses of desert in the Moroccan south, the jagged Rif Mountains, or the stately mountain chains of the central High Atlas.

Second, energy needs were different in each village, and a participatory needs assessment had to be conducted in each one. The assessment had to consider local energy resources, household usage patterns, and the appropriateness of technological options for electricity delivery, but it also had to explore the local social and economic significance of electricity. The directors of the PPER would conclude unequivocally that "numerous missions to the field, regular dialogue with the households affected in the context of village meetings, are indispensable for defining the process and adapting and improving the solutions (technical, financial, organizational) envisioned" (Berdai and Butin 1994: 4).

Third, because communities already spent a significant portion of their income on energy, buying everything from candles to wood, they were able and willing to contribute funds for the construction of networks. Furthermore, the contribution that communities could make was calculated as high enough to make rural electricity provision profitable for the government if the market were big enough to create economies of scale (V. Butin, pers. comm., 2004). The state, however, recognized that households' ability to share in the costs of electricity provision was limited by the nonnegotiable threshold of their income (Kingdom of Morocco, Ministry of the Interior 2003; Mossadaq 1996a).

Fourth, the state acknowledged that supporting electricity networks with some sort of social organization was essential for those networks to function properly and cost-effectively, especially over the long term. In fact, the directors of the PPER did not just appropriate the idea that local associations were indispensable for the management of the networks; they went so far as to promote it within the Ministry of the Interior as well as in other ministries and levels of government. Furthermore, through the PPER, the Ministry of the Interior recognized that local associations established to support electricity networks also served as catalysts for local economic development more generally. At a meeting of several ministries in 1994, the PPER directors spoke of the relationship: "The provision of rural electricity should be seen as a stage in a broader strategy of rural development. . . . Because it depends on local autonomous organization for its use, management, and for its funding, decentralized electricity builds an institutional motor to drive other developmental actions. Local associations are the PPER's choice for this function . . . because they are totally autonomous and legally/judicially well equipped" (Berdai and Butin 1993: 25). Not only did they identify local village associations as the most appropriate institutional form for this local social organization, precisely because they could acquire a formal legal status affording them a degree of autonomy from local state control; they went further and suggested that the goal of the program should be to foster "highly developed local dynamics" in addition to providing electricity. (Berdai and Butin 1993)

For a division of the Ministry of the Interior—the ministry that had enforced Hassan II's autocratic reign over the kingdom for close to two decades and had actively sought to snuff out citizen organizing efforts—to advance a perspective that favored independent social mobilization represented a significant break with the prevailing political culture. It also represented an implicit acknowledgment that rural communities were vital settings where economic growth and development could occur; it suggested that a redrawing of Morocco's political cartography and redefining of le Maroc utile was called for. The conversations-in-practice between migration communities and the state had shaken entrenched government views on rural communities, on local activism, and on development. Not only had the government practiced new ways of providing rural electricity and fostering rural development through the PPER; it also had identified the concepts those practices embodied as lessons of the program. Once those lessons had been articulated, they could not be unsaid, regardless how profound their challenge to the long-standing policy of marginalizing rural areas. In short order, moreover, the Moroccan power sector would enter a crisis so severe that the government became desperate for any way to resolve it. As the government scrambled for a solution, the political ramifications of the lessons would come to matter much less than the lessons themselves.

Institutionalizing Practice

In the mid-1990s, the Moroccan energy sector was in dire straits. Since the mid-1970s, the National Office of Electricity (ONE) had generated the kingdom's electricity in its plants and supplied it to cities and a smattering of villages.[6] Years of underinvestment, in both capital and maintenance, led to the slow-motion breakdown of the machinery that the producer depended on, so that by the 1990s, the ONE's production and distribution started to drop. The drought that Morocco suffered throughout the 1980s and into the 1990s compounded this situation: for several years, no rains supplemented the water supply at the hydraulic power plants that represented about 30 percent of the ONE's production capacity. With the economy growing at a clip, urban, and particularly industrial demand was rising, and the ONE simply could not deliver the electricity required. After the ONE failed to manage the shortage with scheduled blackouts and brownouts, after the so-called vigilance committees it dispatched to the industrial centers near Casablanca and Rabat to pressure firms to ration their energy usage met with fierce opposition, and after the ONE began to default on its petroleum bills, it became clear that the power producer was beyond repair.[7] The state was forced to privatize energy production. The government also sold the concession for a significant portion of urban electricity distribution (World Bank 1998; *L'Économiste* 1996; Mossadaq 1996b, Triki 1994).

After privatization sheared off its main functions of energy production and distribution for the kingdom, the ONE lost its raison d'être.[8] The public-sector utility employed close to 10,000 people, however, and dismantling it out of hand was not a political option (World Bank 1998). Even downsizing was delicate: the ONE could not lay off its workers without breaking its contractual agreement with the public-sector employees. To find a new rationale for its existence, it had to develop new markets for its services—now limited to electricity distribution. To stay afloat, the ONE adopted rural electricity as its new mission. Rural distribution had always been part of its charge, but its commitment to the task had been "tepid," in the World Bank's characterization (World Bank 1998: 11); now the ONE turned to it with wholehearted gusto (World Bank 1998; V. Butin, pers. comm., 2004; Bentaleb 2004).

In 1995, the ONE announced the beginning of a massive rural electricity initiative and committed itself to linking 90 percent of rural households to the national network by 2010. To meet its target, it dedicated significant financial and institutional resources to the program—called Programme d'Électrification Rurale Globale (PERG) or the Total Program for Rural Electrification. It restructured its bureaucracy and shifted the majority of its employees to the newly created Directorate of Rural Electrification. It jealously brought distribution functions (especially the procurement of equipment) previously contracted out to rural townships back into its own shop, banking on economies of scale as it prepared to ramp up its activities. Additionally, the ONE folded the PNER 2, as well as all the monies borrowed from the World Bank that had gone unspent under the mediocre program, into its outfit (ONE 1999, 2006; ONE interviews, Rural Electricity Division, 2004).

The ambitious new program had clear objectives: the ONE would expand the geographic territory that it served; it would use new technology in rural areas; and it would come up with a system for financing the program that would allow it to remain solvent (ONE interviews, Casablanca, March 2004). How to meet those goals was far from clear, however, and the ONE's declaration that it would produce a study evaluating the effectiveness of the first few years of the PERG did not seem promising. Under pressure to make rural electricity a workable proposition, however, the ONE looked to previous rural electricity initiatives for guidance. The PERG drew on lessons from all of Morocco's electricity programs, but it relied most heavily on the PPER because the PNER, in both of its incarnations (PNER I during 1982–86 and PNER 2 during 1991–96), had failed miserably. "The PERG was the culmination of Morocco's experience with rural electrification, of which the PPER and the PNERs, to a lesser extent, were a part," explained a director of the PPER (interview, August 2004).

In its design, PERG differed significantly from the lackluster rural electricity programs of the past. It adopted several of the strategies that the government had come to recognize as valuable through the PPER, but it modified them to fit the political and institutional concerns of the ONE and the Moroccan state more generally. Three of the most important lessons from the PPER—about technology, cost sharing, and social organization—defined the broad lines of the program's structure. The ONE, however, reinterpreted each of these findings to glean insights about how it could provide electricity to rural households more cheaply, without catalyzing a wave of community mobilization in rural areas.

The ONE deployed a series of "low-tech" technologies to connect villages to the national grid. It revised its standards for equipment, used materials that were less expensive and more readily available locally, and reviewed its administrative and training procedures in view of more accessible technologies. As a ONE description of the program explains, "before the PERG, the installations and equipment for rural electricity provision were too luxurious, even compared to rich countries like Canada. . . . As a result, the ONE has adopted a cost-reduction strategy for rural electricity provision based on the realistic concept of 'electricity provision for a poor country' and translated into a search for economies at every level," including "standards," "technology," and "investment in human capital and materials" (ONE 1999: 9). Driss Benhima, director of the ONE at the time, clarified what some of those amendments to technological practices might entail and mentioned that technological solutions could be tailored to specific village requests: "If we worry less about esthetics, we can quarter the costs. If people want poles that are 9 meters tall, instead of 10.5 meters high, we can satisfy them, we can even go down to 6 meters" (Daoud 1997: 36). Tailoring, however, had its limits under the PERG. The ONE explicitly decided not to conduct the village-by-village needs assessments forcefully advocated by the electrical engineers of the PPER. It insisted that the technology and materials that it used remain standardized enough so that the program could be rolled out on a large scale. To make the PERG cost-effective, the government needed to buy in bulk (ONE 1999; ONE interviews, Casablanca, March 2004; PPER interviews, Rabat, January and March 2004).

The ONE incorporated insights from previous programs about how to make providing rural electricity affordable, and the insight that rural households were willing and able to contribute financially to the construction of a network became an organizing principle. The ONE developed a cost-sharing scheme that required individual households to contribute. The utility bore 55 percent of the cost of hooking up each village, the local township 20 percent, and the consumer the remaining 25 percent, with the specification that for 70 percent of the villages concerned, that amount should not exceed a threshold of 14,000 dirhams (approximately 2002 US$1,400) to be paid over seven years.

In a remarkable break from past practice, the ONE also levied a tax on urban consumers to fund the program. In doing so, it symbolically knitted the "useful" and "useless" areas of Morocco—back together, making the well-being of each dependent on that of the other. Just as had happened in M/D villages, electricity became a public good that all Moroccans needed to access for the development of the nation.

Finally, the PERG reflected an acknowledgment, although limited, that community management of local electricity networks was important to keeping them functional and cost-effective over the long term. The program mandated some degree of community management, mostly in the form of fee collection from households, which would then be remitted to the ONE. In cases where the village in question was too isolated to be efficiently connected to the national network and the ONE provided access to autonomous sources (such as hydroelectric or solar power), the PERG envisioned a much larger role for local social organizations. In fact, the program design document calls for a partnership with local groups, among them "associations or federations of associations that have as their goal the support of rural households, the most active of which is Migrations et Développement" (ONE 1999: 16).

While the ONE and other segments of the government, the Ministry of the Interior among them, admitted the valuable role that village associations could play in electricity management and, by extension, in development, it was an observation that did not sit comfortably with the regime. Although the Moroccan state was willing to let the lines it had drawn across its territory fade away, it was not prepared to have its rural areas organize in ways that made them self-governing or to have Berber groups mobilizing to assert their autonomy.

The movement of organized, federated, and in many cases self-taxing Soussi village associations which gained momentum in the early 1990s continued to grow: by 2000, not only had close to three hundred village associations joined the M/D federation, but new (sometimes overlapping) federations were also emerging. To neutralize this trend, the Moroccan state, in partnership with the World Bank, in 1999 created the Agence de Développement Sociale (ADS), a semi-autonomous government agency to funnel grants from foreign donors—mostly the EU and the World Bank—to local nongovernmental organizations, including associations. Essentially, this agency enabled the state to control the type and amount of funding to which associations, and federations of associations, had access (World Bank 2002). Furthermore, the ADS conducted outreach in local communities, encouraging them to form associations and apply for funds, thus bringing new associations directly under the state's tutelage. The government brought in a former director of a local branch of M/D as executive director of the new agency (ADS interviews, 2001).

The PERG was the end of a long stream of interpretation. Lessons that first emerged in Imgoun were translated and reinterpreted when they spread to neighboring villages; they were again appropriated, enacted through practice, and adapted when M/D drew the government into its interpretive process through the PPER; those amended findings then percolated upward to PERG, where they were again modified and reinvented. This extended process of interpretation and learning led to a new model of service delivery, and something that for decades had been viewed as impossible became feasible. The results were extraordinary. As a director of a rural electricity program sidelined by the new initiative put it, "the PERG revolutionized rural electricity provision in Morocco" (interview, March 2004). After more than a decade of providing electricity to a paltry 50 villages a year, the ONE connected 500 villages in its first year of operation, 1996. Five years later, it was linking 2,000 villages a year to the national network. As 2005 drew to a close, the government had provided electricity to 21,689 villages under the PERG program—a little over 2,100 villages on average for every year it had been in operation. Rural electricity coverage in the kingdom rose from 21 percent to 81 percent in just under a decade (ONE 2005, 2006).

Coda

The process of interpretive exchange between migration communities and the state, which had produced such dramatic effects in rural electricity provision, was repeated in other policy areas, leading to considerable amendments as to where and how major state agencies carried out their functions. Like variations on a melodic theme, the exchanges all supported a vital process of policy innovation, but in each case in a slightly different manner. The interpretive conversations sparked changes in state practices and in the structure of state institutions relating to fields from education to technical support for agricultural production. Their effects, however, were most significant in the areas of water and road construction.

Water: Resuscitating Villages

When I visited the village of Ifri in the Soussi heartland of Morocco in the winter of 2004, I was stunned by its beauty. Ifri sat at the base of a spectacular cliff, into which the village's ancestors had carved an *agadir*, a fortified communal granary with storerooms for each family's grain. In the shadow of the agadir, with its lattice-like network of nooks and small wooden doors with intricate ancient locks, the village spread out in a patchwork of lush olive and almond orchards, blanketed in delicate white blossoms in January, and stone houses atop parcels of packed earth, knitted together by irrigation canals that directed water to the fields and the community cistern, at which young women did their families' washing. New cement buildings crowned with large satellite dishes stood out, their boxy modern-looking structures advertising the financial success of emigrants from the community. A modest hostel for European ecotourists was under construction and had already received several dozen visitors, even though its toilet facilities were not finished.

Ten years earlier, in 1995, Ifri's situation had been radically different. The nearby spring that was the only source of water had been completely exhausted. The parched village was dying because the people were unable to withstand yet another of the droughts that were visited upon the province of Taroudant with increasing frequency. Residents abandoned their dried up fields, and soon there were only eight families in a village that had once been several hundred families strong. Ifri was not unique. The surrounding foothills were dotted with villages that had been abandoned to droughts, their adobe structures beginning to crumble and their orchards dried into eerie rows of black stumps. In fact, according to Moroccan state estimates in 1995, only 13 percent of rural residents in the kingdom had reliable access to water, for either irrigation or household consumption, compared to 82 percent in urban areas. Additionally, the state estimated, with a range so broad that in and of itself it reflected the level of state neglect, that one water pump was available for every 250–1,000 rural residents. It was a situation likely to get much worse, with underground water tables falling approximately 1.5–2 meters per year (National Office of Potable Water, as quoted in Daoud 2005).

The remaining villagers of Ifri approached the state for help. Village elders remembered a spring that used to gurgle up seasonally, but that now was permanently dried up, and they asked the state to dig a well there. State technicians ignored their local knowledge and picked a spot thirty-five meters away, which predictably yielded only stone. The desperate and frustrated villagers contacted M/D, with which they had already collaborated on an independent electricity network. Working through the village association that M/D had set up, the village organized to dig a well where the elders had indicated—and found water. In much the same improvised fashion that they erected electricity networks, M/D and the village association drew on the hydraulic expertise of a French consultant (and former labor organizer), combined it with traditional water preservation techniques, and began constructing concrete walls around the well to protect the new water source and direct overflow into the fields. Just as it had done for electricity distribution, the village association set up a system of tariffs that enabled everyone in the village to access the water, regardless of income, but also levied a small tax that would provide resources for further projects: an irrigation network, a saffron cooperative, a cistern, and finally, a hostel. Former residents quickly began returning, and the village eventually grew larger than it had ever been (Daoud 2005; interviews, Taroudant, January 2004).

As other villages took note of Ifri's renaissance and the water collected in puddles in its orchards, they approached M/D for help with their own water shortages. In each village, the emigrants of M/D set up a village association, if one did not already exist, and brought in expert consultants. Interpretive conversations, promoted by emigrants and hosted by the associations throughout the process of construction, generated innovative hydraulic solutions that combined local knowledge with the latest technologies to produce a bricolage that none of the participants could have imagined on their own.

In Imgoun, when the underground water tables seemed to drop in a free fall, the villagers worked with M/D to build retaining walls into the surrounding foothills to hold back rainwater, allowing it to sink into the earth and feed the underground lakes that had dried up. During construction, village elders offered their suggestions for how the walls should be placed. They based their comments on intuition, unable to explain why they felt that the builders should proceed in a certain way, but their guidance was nevertheless included in the ongoing conversations that accompanied construction. As the retaining walls were built, using the elders' advice and the consultants' knowledge of the structural elements that had to be incorporated to prevent soil erosion, the villagers uncovered similar walls, ancient and made out of stone, that even the elders had forgotten, retaining them only as images they hardly believed in. In Anighd, villagers worked with M/D to build an artificial lake using a network of minidams that directed rainwater to a tub they surrounded with concrete walls. They insisted on setting the lake on the exact spot where the state had, in 1957, agreed to build a dam for the village, but never fulfilled the contract it had signed with so much fanfare. The consultants advised against it, but the villagers, unable to give solid reasons, nevertheless insisted, and the artificial lake was built on that site. During the next wet season, rain, directed by the minidams, flowed easily into the mold that quickly grew into an emerald lake; the place was a natural basin for rainwater, but before the dams were built, it had been absorbed by the parched ground on its path down the mountain. In the village of Tinfat, with M/D's help, Anighd's artificial lake was reinvented as a series of *tanoutfis*, traditional rain reservoirs built with cement instead of the traditional stone, and flanked with the customary wall of porous rock, reinforced this time with rust-resistant metal netting, to filter the water.

By year's end, the nearby villages of Tilfou, Timsarit, Tidnas, and many others had approached M/D for help in building hydraulic interventions. The collaborations generated new solutions for each case. M/D's resources were stretched to their limit, however, and the organization appealed to the Moroccan government for assistance. It asked the Taroudant Regional Agricultural Development Office (Office Régional de Mise en Valeur Agricole, or ORMVA), to contribute some of the building materials, and to verify the constructions to ensure that they complied with state norms. The partnership was a tense one, with the state attempting to standardize the projects and to use inappropriate and expensive equipment (Daoud 2005).

In 1998, the Moroccan state shifted from a reluctant collaboration on M/D hydraulic projects to a careful examination of the solutions those initiatives represented. That year, the government, pressured by foreign donors who were alarmed at the ravages of droughts in the countryside, signed into law a mandate for a rural water program. The Program for the Collective Provision of Water in Rural Areas (Programme d'Approvisionnement Groupé en Eau Rurale, or PAGER), along with a subprogram for drought prevention (PNLCES), underwritten by the World Bank, the EU, the UNDP, and others, aimed to increase water coverage for rural Morocco from 13 to 80 percent. PAGER directors drew on emigrant-fostered hydraulic solutions, and the social organization on which they rested, in designing the program. PAGER director for research and water management wrote the EU office in Rabat that "the hydraulic projects of M/D should rank as priorities of the government," adding that "[village] associations are better performers, more dynamic" in their elaboration of hydraulic interventions (as quoted in Daoud 2005: 89). The state organized PAGER around a partnership between village associations, requiring them to contribute 10 percent of project costs and to participate in design and upkeep. As corroborated by the World Bank, "villagers determined the facilities they needed, participated in project construction, and received training in water-system management" (World Bank 2003). By 2005, PAGER, in collaboration with village associations and M/D, had provided water to 140,000 residents, extending basic coverage to almost 50 percent of rural villages in Taroudant (Daoud 2005).

As the World Bank's evaluation of PAGER noted, the program had effects that went far beyond simply making water available for agricultural and household use. The government's partnership with village associations increased the villages' political ability to define priorities for their own economic development. "Each association's decision-making capacity enhanced rural political voice," concluded the World Bank summary. It also quoted the institution's Moroccan evaluator, who observed that "it is a social revolution and an extraordinary change PAGER has introduced into Morocco's countryside. Thanks to these associations, a new vision is growing for local development and democracy" (World Bank 2003).

Roads: Paving the Way Out of Isolation

The Moroccan state's record on road building until the mid-1990s was abysmal. In 1994, according to the World Bank, less than 40 percent of the rural population had access to roads, paved or unpaved, on a consistent basis, and in some of the more isolated regions that percentage dipped under 20 percent (Levy 2004). The Moroccan government focused its resources on the construction and upgrade of highways between cities. It added only an estimated 280 kilometers to its national network per year between 1988 and 1994, with most construction occurring in urban areas (World Bank 2004). In Taroudant province, fewer than 500 kilometers of roads had been built, less than a third of that required for minimal, basic coverage (Daoud 2005). At least 2,000 villages were completely cut off from reliable road service, with many having access to roads only seasonally (Daoud 2005). This isolation made it impossible for children to attend schools, for residents, especially women, to seek health care, and for farmers to transport their goods to markets outside their village, confining them to subsistence agriculture (Levy 2004).

As early as 1985, villagers and their emigrants began to take matters into their own hands. Largely using remittances, they funded the construction and pavement of roads, prioritizing many paths viewed as essential for otherwise isolated villages accessible only by donkey or on foot. Over the next ten years, they would pave or upgrade almost 80 kilometers of roads—a heroic achievement for the rural farmers and emigrant laborers who bankrolled the public works with their own savings, but far from enough to pierce the geographic and social isolation exacerbating severe rural poverty (Daoud 2005).

In 1995, the Moroccan government, pressed and funded by the World Bank, launched its first National Rural Roads Program (Programme Nationale de Construction de Routes Rurales, or PNCRR). The program was designed to upgrade a select group of already existing roads to all-weather conditions and aimed to improve 11,000 kilometers—or 20 percent of the national network—by 2005. The Moroccan government revised laws to allow the Ministry of Infrastructure to extend loans for road construction to provincial governments and local collectivities (roughly equivalent to municipalities) that represented groups of villages (World Bank 2004).

During the elections that accompanied the political reforms—*l'alternance*—of 1997, Mohammed Sajid was elected parliamentary deputy for Taroudant. A Casablanca native but the son of a wealthy industrialist from the province, Sajid set foot in Taroudant for the first time during his campaign. He held a series of town meetings during his visit and learned of the village associations created by M/D, as well as by other emigrants who had followed M/D's lead. Intrigued, he later met with M/D staff in the province and asked in particular about how their system for electricity provision was adapted by the state, focusing especially on community contribution to the construction of networks linking villages to the national grid. The interest of a government official with easy access to the Ministry of Infrastructure sparked an intensive deliberation between M/D, village associations in Taroudant, and emigrant associations in France about how to get the state to devote more of its resources to rural road construction in the province under the auspices of the PNCRR (Daoud 2005; interviews, Taroudant, January 2005).

Recognizing that road construction was too large a project for a village association to undertake on its own, they created a federation of associations to allow them to pool their resources. The federation elected Sajid its president, and he presented a proposal to the Ministry of Infrastructure on its behalf: in collaboration with the local collectivities, some of which were receiving PNCRR funds, the federation would contribute 30 percent of the cost of building or paving new roads, with emigrants covering about 10 percent. In exchange, the federation wanted to select the location of the roads, direct the project studies for the routes, and supervise their construction. The ministry was generally agreeable, largely, according to Sajid, because of the federation's financial contribution, but insisted on final review of construction plans. If there was a difference of opinion about location or design, they would return the plans to the federation to devise a solution that addressed the ministry's concerns. The central government signed a convention with the federation in 1998, pledging to construct 600 kilometers of roads over the next seven years (Daoud 2005; M/D 2002b; interviews, Taroudant, January 2005).

As the first roads were constructed under the agreement, it became clear that in both planning and supervision, community involvement, through the federation, was decisive. Roads chosen and managed by the federation cost significantly less than the PNCRR average, sometimes 50 percent less than state estimates. Furthermore, the federation's roads tended to have greater social and economic impact on villages. In particular, they resulted in noticeably higher school enrollment, especially for girls, and in the increased use of butane for cooking, which protected the soil from erosion caused by overharvesting of firewood (Daoud 2005; interviews, Taroudant, January 2005).

Significantly, the Ministry of Infrastructure's participation in the federation's matching-funds scheme contributed to its revision of the criteria it used to select roads and evaluate their impact. The ministry revised its targets from the number of kilometers constructed to the number of people who would benefit from improved access. Additionally, an amended version of the program strengthened the involvement of local collectivities, and village associations through them, in the selection, planning, and maintenance of roads (World Bank 2004).

Reflecting on Practice

A group of migrant workers, laid off from aluminum smelting jobs in France, built a rudimentary electricity network in an isolated hamlet in the folds of the Atlas Mountains and changed the way a nation provided electricity to hundreds of thousands of its citizens. Then, through the same small-scale innovation-in-practice and the same tactic of drawing the government into interpretive conversations, they went on to change the way the state supplied water to rural villages and the way it planned road networks and rolled out pavement to link isolated areas to urban centers. By the late 1990s, migrants had contributed to the conceptual understandings and had amended the practices of three major state initiatives launched at the behest of donor institutions to alleviate rural poverty (van de Walle 2004). They had engaged the state in the process of interpretation, which caused the reinvention of three programs that had combined yearly operating budgets totaling several hundred million dollars (World Bank 2001).

By involving the state in these interpretive conversations, migrants and their communities of origin changed state practices and institutions in fundamental and unprecedented ways. In particular, they challenged the premise that some areas were inherently resistant to development, and brought the state in as a participant in a movement that belied the politically motivated division of Morocco into useful and useless areas. In their version of the map, rural areas were not only part of *le Maroc utile*, they were some of its most dynamic locations.

Migration communities—migrants and the villagers who never left— engaged with their resources actively and intensively, and in the process cast themselves as protagonists of their own history and their own local processes of development, in ways that were far more profound than simply migrants bankrolling community projects or villagers spending the money that migrants sent home. As the director of Migrations et Développement explained in a moving reflection, migrants reclaimed a sense of themselves as members of their communities and recognized the agency that they could exercise to envision and create their futures:

> The act of doing local development work, that's something very important. Important not only for the village, through what emigrants do and what comes into being in the village, but also for emigrants' concept of themselves, their personality. Because these emigrants, they are uneasy in France, they feel they have a debt, they feel they are responsible, even guilty of something. When they are over there, they feel like returning, and when they are here, they feel like going back there. They are always in that tension and always between two places. Doing development work, it's revealed to them that they are, that they can be actors. This is over and above the money that they bring, over and above what they can do, the skills that they have and that they can bring back. (J. Lahoussain, as quoted in M/D 2002b).

Through the interpretive practices that they authored and engaged in, they could share in the transformation of their communities, they could catalyze the reform of state bureaucracies that affected their personal fate and the socioeconomic lot of their villages, and they could redefine prevailing definitions of national development, bringing them down to the level of interpretive practice.

6

Process as Resource

Two Kings and the Politics of Rural Development

In the late 1980s, the approach Morocco had used to engage with emigrants for more than two decades began to fail. The government's treatment of emigrant workers as a commodity began to alienate Moroccans abroad, crushing their increasingly tenuous connection to their country, and emigrants and their families began to view Europe as their home. In 1987, for the first time since Morocco had begun its labor export program in 1963, remittances stopped rising steadily, and they dipped worryingly the following year. The share of national deposits represented by emigrants' accounts in the BCP began declining in 1988, a trend that would never be reversed. Naturalization rates for Moroccan emigrants skyrocketed in the late 1980s, as unprecedented numbers of them took European nationalities, despite the king's increasingly strident exhortations against it.

In an effort to revive emigrants' connection to the kingdom, Hassan II personally launched a bold new strategy in 1990 to engage with them. By royal decree, he created three new institutions: a royal foundation to serve emigrants, a ministry for Moroccans living abroad, and an investment bank for emigrant entrepreneurs. These were designed to capture the resources that emigrants could provide for development, and this time around the Moroccan government trained its sights on the skills emigrants had acquired abroad as well as on their remittances. Just as in the late 1960s, the government reached out to emigrants in Europe and began a series of interpretive conversations. The breadth of the conversations was encouraging, and the insights they generated were promising. Yet despite their potential, the government shut down the conversations almost as quickly as it had initiated them. Within five years, the institutions created to renew the engagement with migrants had been either dismantled or eviscerated. The reason for the abrupt reversal was that among the many ideas that the exchanges produced were critiques of government policy. Especially troubling to the crown were emigrants' demands for greater political voice.

Hassan II's successor, Mohammed VI, reversed this approach. After the new king acceded to the throne in 1999, the Moroccan government began to see emigrants as the authors of innovative solutions for rural development. The self-styled King of the Poor made alleviation of poverty in Morocco's rural areas a national priority, and as his government put rural development at the top of the agenda, it reappraised the interpretive conversations that emigrants had started about how to supply rural villages with basic infrastructure and began to perceive such conversations as important to the kingdom's economic development. Not only did the government revive the conversations, but they sustained them even when the conversations generated critiques of Mohammed VI's policies.

The two kings' approaches stemmed from the role they viewed emigrants as playing in Morocco's economic development. Hassan II, and the government he led, saw emigrants primarily as producers of inputs into the economy: first and foremost, a source of cash, and later a possible source of skill as well. The resources migrants generated were applied to a national economy whose direction they were given no latitude to influence. Hassan II's government engaged with them so that the capital, both financial and human, that they represented would not escape the state's control. In its approach, Hassan II's government was not unlike those firms that draw on "user-driven innovation," a term that refers to products or services improved or designed by the people who ultimately use them, rather than by the firms that produce them (von Hippel 2005; Lakhani 2005; Shah 2000; Dalpé et al. 1992; Danish Enterprise and Construction Authority 2007). Advocates of user-driven innovation posit that organizations are most able to incorporate the new ideas developed by users when they limit the range of innovations that users can produce. By keeping the spectrum of possible innovation narrow, limited to what observers of this process have called a "solution space" (von Hippel and Katz 2002), an organization can absorb the new ideas that users may generate without having to redesign its base product, to say nothing of the system of production required to manufacture it. The Moroccan state actively encouraged the articulation of new ideas for capturing migrant capital, and within the confines of that "solution space" it was even receptive to ideas that at first seemed outlandish or impractical. The state's engagement, however, was instrumental: it was interested in harvesting ideas that could help it achieve the goal that drove its exchanges with emigrants, and even caused it to acquiesce, from time to time, to emigrant demands for political and cultural recognition. Ideas that fell outside the tightly drawn boundaries of that "solution space" were discouraged and, if they were perceived to threaten the crown in any way, ruthlessly crushed. The course that the government charted for national development, articulated once every five years in Morocco's steady stream of National Development Plans, was never up for renegotiation.

Mohammed VI had a more ambitious view of emigrants' role in development and of the transformative potential of innovation. The new king, and by extension his government, saw emigrants as actors who could identify creative development strategies, especially for areas long viewed as inherently resistant to economic change. The resource that emigrants could provide was not primarily capital. It was the ideas they could help generate for doing things in new and better ways: for supplying infrastructure, providing education, and stimulating domestic and international trade. Emigrants went from being regarded as a source of cash to a source of creativity. Under Hassan II, the government viewed interpretation as a means to an end: it used it to glean insights that would allow it to achieve goals it had already set for itself. Under Hassan's son, the government came to appreciate the process of interpretation for its own sake, valuing it as a process that supported ongoing innovation in government policy.

As a result, Mohammed VI's government came to value interpretive processes for their own sake, it did not police the borders of some predefined "solution space." Indeed, shutting down interpretive conversations that strayed beyond borders the regime had drawn would have deprived the government of a resource it desperately needed to supplement its anemic understanding of how to promote rural development. It needed migrant-generated perspectives on what it considered a particularly frustrating problem, one that produced inequalities too politically charged to ignore. Still a top-down monarchy, the government developed more subtle strategies of control and worked to refocus conversations when they began to levy challenges against state policy. Although gentler than Hassan II's repressive tactics, government attempts to steer interpretation diminished the richness of the creative process. When emigrants believed they were being manipulated, however deftly, they retreated from the conversations and, emboldened under the new king, established preconditions for resuming the interpretive exchange. The resulting tensions affected how the processes of interpretation unfolded and how they traveled across institutions, across political settings, and most importantly, across emergent and fluid thematic—or "solution"—spaces.

Hassan II: Collecting Ideas, Crushing Dissent

On July 13, 1990, Hassan II placed his seal on the royal decree creating the Hassan II Foundation for Moroccans Living Abroad. As specified in the royal order that mandated it, the mission of the foundation was to "preserve the fundamental ties that [Moroccans living abroad] maintain with their homeland and to help them overcome the difficulties they encounter as a result of their emigration." The institution was charged with tending to relationships with emigrants in "the cultural, religious and social domains" in a manner that was "in keeping with the orientation of the government and His Majesty the King" (Morocco 1990, article 2). More specifically, the foundation was tasked with organizing and financing social and cultural activities for Moroccan emigrants, offering national, religious, and language education to second-generation emigrants, and providing emergency social services and financial assistance to emigrants in need (Morocco 1990; Brand 2002; Belguendouz 1999).

Hassan II had alluded to the need to create an institution to strengthen the connection between Moroccans living abroad and the kingdom a few years earlier. In December 1986, during a visit to France, he announced that he planned to create a Solidarity Fund to aid Moroccan workers abroad (Belguendouz 2006: 7). He explained that he envisioned the fund as a means to "ensure the permanence of the ties between you and your country and especially between your children and your country" (as quoted in Belguendouz 1999: 151). In a startling break with past declarations, he also added that emigrants should benefit from the resources—the monetary remittances in particular—that they sent back to Morocco: "It is inadmissible that you are not involved in the way that a part of the capital that you send to the country thanks to your labor, minimal though that part may be, is spent. . . . With a very small portion of that capital, it is possible for us to double, even triple, the number of educational establishments, of Koranic schools, and of government employees that can protect the constancy of the connection between you and your country" (as quoted in Belguendouz 1999: 151).

Although the foundation was established to revive emigrants' tie to their country, its organization reflected the government's decades-old instinct to control the shape and tenor of that connection. The state named all twenty-seven members of the executive committee, which by law had to have at least thirteen representatives from friendship societies as well as at least one delegate from the Professional Association of Moroccan Banks (Belguendouz 1999; Brand 2002: 12). Funding for the institution, estimated at around US$15 million a year (Boukhima 2000), was generated through a diversion of the bonuses on deposits that had previously been offered to emigrants (Berrissoule 1998).[1] (A leader of the ATMF called the move "the biggest hold-up in history" [interviews, Paris, February 2004].) The foundation was exempt from all government audits of its activities and was ultimately answerable only to the king (Morocco 1990; Brand 2002; Belguendouz 1999; Fondation Hassan II interviews, September 2003, December 2003–February 2004).

Two weeks after Hassan II established the foundation, he created a special ministry to cultivate the kingdom's political relationship with Moroccan communities abroad, and named Rafik Haddaoui as minister-delegate to the prime minister, charged with the portfolio. In his speech nominating Haddaoui, Hassan II declared that the regime could not safeguard emigrants' loyalty to their country of origin simply by managing their contractual relationship with their employers in Europe:

> The representatives of the Moroccan community asked us to put in place a governmental institution or organ charged with dealing with their affairs outside the realm of employment. Given that the problems of Our Moroccan communities have nothing to do with the Ministry of Labor [which had until then managed emigrant labor contracts], that We are bound by the act of allegiance to Our subjects abroad in the same way as We are to their brothers in Morocco, that We have a paternal, religious and moral responsibility to them—Our subjects abroad deserve more attention than their fellow citizens living in Morocco whose needs are looked into day and night—We charge you with these sons that are Ours. . . . The objective of this mission is to safeguard this bond and the act of allegiance. (Morocco, Ministère de l'Information 1991, July 31)

The Ministry for the Moroccan Community Abroad was charged with cultivating an intensive engagement with emigrants and their families in order to "safeguard" their bond of allegiance to their country. In this sense, the ministry was tasked with rolling out a political version of the strategy of accompaniment that the BCP had launched to woo emigrant clients. Moreover, just as the government had ordered the BCP to ensure that migrant remittances "no longer escaped state control," it directed the ministry to reinforce emigrants' loyalty to the kingdom so that they themselves did not "escape state control."

Also in 1990, the government finally launched Bank al-Amal, a new bank for emigrants nominally created in 1989. Bank al-Amal (roughly translated as "bank of work") was established as a vehicle to encourage emigrant investment in the kingdom. In actuality an organization that managed a fund pooled from a consortium of Moroccan banks rather than a traditional bank, the financial establishment offered subsidized interest rates on long-term loans as well as equity participation for emigrant investment projects. The bank embodied a significant shift in the state's view of emigrants, casting them as economic actors who could have a transformative impact. Indeed, the king had grand aspirations for the bank and for the emigrant investment it would draw into the country. In his nomination speech for Haddaoui, he made explicit his ambitions for the bank and the view of emigrants on which it rested:

> Every Moroccan working abroad should return to his country as a professional so that he may transmit what he has learned to others.
>
> If he has saved an amount of money and wishes to invest it or build a house, he has every right to do so because those are legitimate aspirations. We now have a new vehicle [for this], Bank al-Amal, which, if it functions in accordance with the way We have conceived of it, will become the largest bank in Morocco within two years. . . . [The bank] is a means for our citizens to act, even those that have

settled as far away as Australia or other far off regions. (Morocco, Ministère de l'Information 1991, July 31)

The bank also epitomized the government's new combination of economic and political policies toward emigrants, in this case to an ultimately unhealthy effect: Bank al-Amal's board of directors was stacked with friendship society presidents (Belguendouz 1999; Kaioua 1999; Bank al-Amal interviews, Casablanca, March 2004).

Although the three institutions were formally established as separate organizations, they functioned in practice as one. Haddaoui, minister for Moroccan Community Abroad, was also president of the Hassan II Foundation. The ministry and the foundation were housed in the same building, used the same amenities, and with no government oversight of the foundation's expenditures, their budgets tended to merge (Brand 2002; Hassan II Foundation interviews, Rabat, December–March 2003–4).[2] As one employee at the foundation noted, *"le ministère pense, la fondation dépense*—the Ministry thinks, the Foundation spends" (as quoted in Brand 2002: 13). Furthermore, during the multiple outreach visits of its directors, the foundation/ministry recruited (and vetted) potential emigrant investors for Bank al-Amal, suggesting investment projects to Moroccans living abroad and directing them to the banking institution for funds and guidance (Bank al-Amal interviews, Casablanca, July 2002 and March 2004). The three institutions-in-one further blurred the distinction between the political, economic, and cultural aspects of emigrants' lives, in both Europe and Morocco, which the kingdom had maintained in the past. "Our objective," said Haddaoui, "is to create a synergy amongst all of the forces that act, from close up or from afar, to foster relationships with Moroccans living abroad" (as quoted in Berhoumi 1993: 7). The coordinated institutions brought together the two streams of conversations that the Moroccan state had worked so hard to keep separate (Morocco, Ministère de la Communauté Marocaine à l'Étranger, lettre d'information, October 1992–September 1995).

Talking with Everyone: Interpretation Revived

Under the charismatic leadership of Haddaoui, the state organizations reopened a space for interpretive exchange with emigrants, one that re-created the two conditions that had enabled previous conversations to generate new insights and was pioneering in its inclusiveness. First, they made the changes that emigrant communities had undergone visible to the state. By the 1990s, the Moroccan population in Europe had grown more diverse than ever. The children of emigrants began to come of age, and the government began to talk about outreach to large numbers of the second and third generation, whom the state considered Moroccan regardless of where they had been born and raised. Additionally, Moroccans began migrating to new destinations, primarily Spain and Italy, in flows unregulated by the Moroccan state in which undocumented immigrants were heavily represented. In Spain the documented Moroccan population alone rose from a little over 15,000 in 1990 to about 200,000 in 2000 (Khaldi 2003), and in Italy the number underwent a similar expansion, from a little under 15,000 in 1987 to almost 160,000 in 2000 (Schmidt de Friedberg 1994; M'Barki 2003). Furthermore, the profile of emigrants from Morocco was changing: more and more were of urban origin; their educational levels were significantly higher than those of emigrants from the 1960s (60 percent had completed secondary education or higher compared to less than 20 percent of emigrants from the 1960s and 1970s); and a growing proportion were women who were migrating in search of work rather than primarily to join spouses (AMERM 2000; INSEA 2000).

The new institutions began an energetic effort to collect data that would enable the state to "see" who its emigrants were in the 1990s and where an engagement with them might lead. The ministry and foundation commissioned a number of studies on Moroccan communities abroad. Beginning in 1993, the foundation published a series of reports that addressed everything from the demographic profile of emigrants, including down-to-the-person counts of Moroccans in various European cities, to the challenges of maintaining a Moroccan identity in a European context, with special attention paid to the identity crises that were leading to delinquency among Moroccan youth abroad (*Rivages*, April–October 1993). The research focused in particular on gathering information about Moroccans in new destination countries such as Italy (*Rivages*, May 1993) and Spain (*Rivages*, Summer 1994). In 1994, the foundation released *L'annuaire de l'emigration*, a 600-page volume that compiled the latest information on Moroccan emigrants in Belgium, Canada, Spain, France, Germany, and Holland, with an additional section detailing the economic impact of emigrants on Morocco itself (Basfao and Taarji 1994). Over and above these initiatives, the foundation forged a working partnership with the International Organization of Migration (IOM) in 1992 to create a Moroccan Observatory of Emigration (Observatoire Marocain de l'Emigration) (Morocco, Ministère de la Communauté Marocaine à l'Étranger, lettre d'information, November 1992). As part of this collaboration, the IOM trained foundation staff to conduct research on emigrant communities and assisted the foundation in setting up a library that grew into a modest clearinghouse of data on Moroccans living abroad (Fondation Hassan II interviews, September 2003).

The new organizations engaged without defining all the terms of the engagement. This was especially true of the Ministry for the Moroccan Community Abroad. Within the first three years of his appointment, Haddaoui and his senior staff made dozens of trips to Europe. "I can't remember a time under Haddaoui when we didn't have someone in Europe. Someone was always traveling" (Fondation Hassan II interviews, November 2003). There they met with representatives of emigrant communities and displayed a degree of attentiveness and openness that many of them found to be unprecedented.

"Haddaoui met with everyone," recalled an activist with ATMF. "He met with the friendship societies, he met with the associations that supported Morocco's actions in the Western Sahara, he met with associations of Sahraouis that were against Morocco's action in the Sahara, he met with associations of young people, he met with associations of women. He even met with us, even after we had a demonstration where we burned a photo of the king" (ATMF interviews, Paris, February 2004). "Haddaoui was the era of openness of the Moroccan state," remembered another worker activist. "He didn't just want to hear prayers for the health of the king, and speeches of allegiance. He wanted to hear what your concerns were" (ATMF interviews, Paris, February 2004). Haddaoui himself confirmed this perception, observing, "as soon as we said 'we're here'—*nous voici*—it was as if the floodgates had opened. We got so many comments, so many complaints. . . . I think our most important accomplishment was to build a capacity for dialogue and for listening" (interview, Rabat, March 2004).

The ministry and foundation also organized a series of conferences in Morocco and Europe on emigrant concerns. Although these addressed a wide range of issues, they tended to focus on ways to involve emigrants more directly in initiatives that would support the nation's economic development. In 1993, for example, the ministry and foundation organized a conference on the participation of emigrant researchers and scientists in Morocco's technological advancement. The conference, underwritten by the United Nations Development Program (UNDP) under the rubric of its Transfer of Knowledge through Expatriate Nationals or TOKTEN program, was the first of its kind in Morocco. The meeting was well attended, with almost two hundred prominent emigrant scientists and scholars traveling to Rabat to reflect on the possibilities for knowledge transfer back to the kingdom (*Rivages*, September 1993). The institutions also organized events in cities throughout Europe on emigrant investment in Morocco both in housing and in the state's massive privatization drive of the early 1990s. Explaining the need for these conferences, Haddaoui affirmed that promoting investment would "require a dialogue that [was] more direct and more intense" than the Moroccan government had previously supported (as quoted in Morocco, Ministère de la Communauté Marocaine à l'Étranger, lettre d'information, November 1992: 4; October 1992–September 1995).

The ministry and the foundation also produced multiple publications to sustain their engagement with emigrant community. About once a month, the foundation published a glossy magazine titled *Rivages*—"Shores"—referring to both shores of the Mediterranean. The first issue stated explicitly that it had been launched by the foundation to serve as a venue for dialogue. "The need for a medium that serves as a tie between all Moroccans is not recent," reads the opening editorial: "*Rivages* was born in response to this call; it brings a long wait to an end. But it was not sufficient to hear—belatedly—the call. It was necessary to decipher, to understand, and even at times to interpret it. That is what we have done. . . . Our mission: to serve, in all senses of the term, men and women that have faith in exchange and believe in dialogue" (*Rivages*, January 1993: 3).

For a time at least, *Rivages* lived up to its goal, covering aspects of emigrant life ranging from relationships with communities of origin to the education of Moroccan children in Europe. On a regular basis, it also included contributions from emigrant authors. The ministry's more businesslike newsletters complemented the polished feature stories in *Rivages*. The newsletters chronicled meetings that Haddaoui and his staff held abroad and reproduced press interviews that he conducted in Morocco and in Europe (Morocco, Ministère de la Communauté Marocaine à l'Étranger, lettre d'information, October 1992–September 1993).

The ministry and foundation backed this intensive communication with concrete action to strengthen the engagement. The foundation funded cultural events and trips to Morocco for emigrant social groups; although friendship societies benefited handsomely from this type of support, the foundation extended grants to many other organizations. It also funded Arabic lessons for the children of emigrants in Europe and supported Koranic instruction. In 1994–95, for example, the foundation paid for close to 500 teachers of Arabic and Moroccan culture to give lessons to 70,600 children of emigrants, 41,500 of whom were in France. Sixty-three imams were sent to Europe for Ramadan, along with boxes of traditional Moroccan sweets. Additionally, the foundation created summer camps where the children of emigrants participated in activities designed to deepen their connection with their Moroccan heritage (Morocco, Ministère de la Communauté Marocaine à l'Étranger, lettre d'information, February 1992–October 1994; Brand 2002; Belguendouz 2006).

The foundation and ministry's most visible form of outreach was its massive logistical support for emigrants who returned during the summer months. Every year, over half of Morocco's emigrant population—by that time 2 million strong—passed through the kingdom's two main ports in the space of the few days in July and August that framed their month-long vacations. Tangier in particular was swamped, with lines of cars miles long and passengers waiting literally days to board the ferry to cross the Strait of Gibraltar to the equally overwhelmed Spanish port of Algeciras. The Hassan II Foundation, in cooperation with the Royal Armed Forces and the Spanish, orchestrated a yearly Operation Transit, trying to speed its nationals through the bottleneck of customs checks and ferries straining at capacity. Initiated in 1988 as a trial in cooperation with the Spanish government, which had complained of highways choked with returning Moroccans during the first week of July and the last week of August, the foundation formally adopted Operation Transit in 1991. It quickly became the most tangible expression of the fact that the government was listening to emigrant concerns. In the short time since the foundation and ministry had been created, complaints about the adverse conditions that emigrants faced when returning in the summer, including several days' wait to board the ferry and their (mal)treatment by the Spanish authorities as they sat parked in Algeciras, had featured prominently in conversations with the government. Emigrant reaction to Operation Transit was overwhelmingly positive, although many pointed to wait times that were still long, petty crime, and the arbitrary behavior of customs officers: "Clearly a big effort was made," observed one emigrant interviewed in 1994. She added, "We no longer feel like second class citizens. We feel really touched, this goes straight to our hearts" (as quoted in Chaoui 1994: 38; Fondation Hassan II interviews, July 2001 and September 2003; Tangier and Algeciras, July 2001, August 2003; Ministry of Foreign Affairs interviews, Tangier and Algeciras, July 2001 and August 2003; Morocco, Ministère de la Communauté Marocaine à l'Étranger, lettre d'information, November 1992, May 1993–August 1993; Chaoui 1994; Brand 2002).

The Emergence of Critical Insight

The interpretive engagement that the ministry and foundation fostered allowed for the emergence of new conceptual links, many of them extremely controversial in the Moroccan political context. The critiques of the regime that surfaced were trenchant, and as the ministry's and the foundation's engagement with emigrants progressed, these escalated into bold challenges to government legitimacy. "It's true, some of the grievances were very deep," recalled a former employee of the ministry (interview, Rabat, November 2003; interviews, Paris and Brussels, February 2004; and Rabat, September 2003 and March 2004).

In the spirit of dialogue, the ministry and the foundation published muted versions of these criticisms, primary in *Rivages*. Coverage of the TOKTEN conference, for example, reveals that the meeting produced a clear articulation of the relationship between knowledge transfer and the promotion of research centers in the kingdom and free speech. "I've chosen to stay in Canada because there I find there is a respect for the individual, a principle of the open door, and the autonomy of the researcher," declared one scientist at the gathering (as quoted in Mana 1993: 24). *Rivages* also published a truncated version of the resolution that the researchers in attendance had drafted which outlined measures to promote research in Morocco; in particular, they urged the government to "relax state management of research in order to favor the creativity and autonomy that go hand in hand with scientific production" (*Rivages*, September 1993, 28). The king apparently had a different view: speaking to the assembled scientists, he proclaimed that science alone "is not sufficient. It must be accompanied by the correct consciousness, by exemplary behavior, by an attachment to the teachings of Islam and by a love for one's country . . . that borders on idolatry" (Morocco, Ministère de l'Information 1993). Interestingly, his perspective was not represented in the foundation's coverage of the event.

Several features in *Rivages* also echo emigrants' complaints about how bureaucratic red tape and corruption discouraged Moroccans living abroad from investing at home (*Rivages*, June–July and October 1993, Winter 1994). A special issue on emigrant investment in real estate published in winter 1994 refers to the cumbersome and costly procedures required for everything from acquiring building permits to paying property taxes, to say nothing of the interminable legal proceedings necessary to evict illegal squatters (Jibril 1994: 24–28). Even more disquieting to government authorities, perhaps, was the connection that surfaced between emigrant-sponsored rural development projects for the provision of basic amenities and the state neglect of rural areas that generated the need for them in the first place. The June–July 1993 issue of *Rivages* ran a profile of Migrations et Développement, noting that in Imgoun, where the organization began its work, "each emigrant worker spent a significant portion of his salary for the electrification [of the village]" and that the emigrants then spent their own funds to build a clinic and a school (*Rivages*, June–July1993, 33). *Rivages*, a government publication, was essentially pointing out how neglectful the government had been of those communities that the migrants it was celebrating were from.

The conversations also generated nuanced but sharp critiques of government policy toward emigrants themselves. To the extent possible, Haddaoui chose not to deal with friendship societies; in the new era of openness he was working to create, they had outlived their usefulness: "Friendship societies, and their methods of actions . . . are no longer adapted to the [current] situation," he would announce in 1991 (as quoted in *Le Matin du Sahara et du Maghreb*, March 21, 1991, in Belguendouz 2006: 9), and he later characterized them as "empty shells" not representative of Moroccan communities abroad and made up of a handful of people more interested in cultivating patronage than in serving their communities (interview, Rabat, March 2004). Furthermore, Haddaoui and the institutions he headed broke with royal policy on undocumented immigration. Whereas the king reiterated his categorical opposition to undocumented immigration of any kind, Haddaoui made a subtle but important distinction between recent illegal emigrants, whose choice to break the law to emigrate he deplored, and Moroccans who had worked in Europe without proper documentation for some time, often with their families, whose plight he felt deserved fair attention (Berhoumi 1993). Referring to those who had lived abroad for "sometimes ten or fifteen years," Haddaoui hazarded that "it would be good to perhaps consider the situation of these people, case by case, to see how their situation could be resolved" (as quoted in Berhoumi 1993: 24). The foundation also published oblique critiques of the harsh conditions that Moroccans faced when they emigrated illegally (*Rivages*, April 1993).

Disengaging and Dismantling

The conceptual links and challenges to government policy articulated through these interpretive exchanges ultimately led the Moroccan government to narrow the scope of engagement. Although the regime had been making strides

toward political openness in the early 1990s, the memory of the riots that began in Fez on December 14, 1990, and then spread to the cities of Rabat,
Tangier, Agadir, and Kenitry, still smarted. They grew out of a strike called by
the country's two biggest trade unions to demand an increase in the national
minimum wage, and by the time the armed forces had crushed the uprising, at
least a hundred protestors lay dead (Bouzerda 1990; *Economist* 1990). The
use of deadly force, unremarkable in the Morocco of the 1970s and 1980s, had
become a high-stakes political gamble by the 1990s. As the war in the Western
Sahara began to abate and the heavy hand of monarchy began to chafe, opposition parties became more assertive, going so far as to propose motions of no
confidence in the government. Human rights groups also became emboldened
and mounted a vocal campaign for the release of political prisoners and the end
of torture (*Economist* 1990; Slyomovics 2005). The set of conversations with
emigrants had spun off into critiques of government that Hassan II's regime
viewed as dangerous, even seditious.

As early as 1992, even as Haddaoui claimed that the ministry and the foundation were still ramping up their activities, the government was already taking issues off the table. All formal venues for emigrants to voice their demands
other than the foundation and the ministry were being closed off. Although
there had been much criticism of the five parliamentary representatives elected
in 1984 to represent emigrants in the Moroccan legislature, and much debate
about the fairness of the elections that won them their seats, the representatives, all from different parties, had joined together and lobbied as a group for
emigrant demands (Belguendouz 1999; interview, Ghazi and Rabat, March
2004). Once the foundation and the ministry were set up in 1990, the five representatives pushed hard for more transparency and accountability in the two
institutions, calling for a report on their activities and an evaluation in particular of Operation Transit, which left much to be desired during its first few
years (Fondation Hassan II interviews, Rabat, March–April 2004). When the
parliament's powers were expanded under the 1992 constitution, the five seats
reserved for emigrant representatives were abolished. Haddaoui, addressing
this change in interviews, became an apologist for government policy. In one
interview, for example, he claimed that the parliamentarians could not represent emigrant interests effectively for the simple reason that they had to be in
Morocco twice a year for the three-month sessions of parliament. During that
time, he asserted, they were "separated from the lived reality of immigration,"
and thus "their representation did not correspond to the nature of the presence
of Moroccans throughout the world" (as quoted in Berhoumi 1993: 24).

Furthermore, the veneer that had been applied to the foundation's and ministry's eager outreach to emigrant organizations of all persuasions, and not just
those that toed the regime's political line, began to wear thin. The foundation
worked to create a roster of all emigrant groups abroad—a list that would allow the Moroccan government to "see" them and monitor their activities. And
although the foundation was liberal with its backing at first, it began to be

more selective of the groups it chose to support, both financially and politically. Haddaoui's discussion with high-ranking French officials during a trip to Paris in June 1993 makes this shift explicit. During a meeting with Charles Pasqua, French minister of the interior, the two addressed the proliferation of "unsupervised" Islamic groups and agreed to cooperate "to make the current situation more salubrious—*en vue d'assainir la situation actuelle*" (Morocco, Ministère de la Communauté Marocaine à l'Étranger 1993: 2). In that exchange, Haddaoui noted that many Moroccan associations were engaged in actions that were "extremely positive" and would benefit greatly from the support of the French authorities. Pasqua responded that he would gladly receive representatives from organizations sanctioned by the Moroccan government: as the Moroccan ministry's own report on the encounter describes, Pasqua repeated "several times" during the meeting, "We are very eager" (Morocco, Ministère de la Communauté Marocaine à l'Étranger 1993: 3). In that meeting with French bureaucrats and in others that followed, the ministry and foundation resuscitated the 1970s and 1980s strategy of collaborating with the governments of host countries to control emigrant activism.

Despite these measures, insights critical of the government continued to emerge. Yet with remittance levels back to what they had been in the 1980s and growing steadily (see fig. 4.2), and the regime already being pressed into passing democratizing reforms, the political threat these critiques posed was not as serious. In 1992, to appease an increasingly strong opposition movement, a new constitution was submitted to a national referendum. It passed overwhelmingly, and new protections for human rights as well as new powers for parliament and the prime minister were enshrined in law (Leveau 2000). Emigrant critiques often went far beyond these limited reforms, and the growing sense that the government's engagement was giving those critiques undue importance gave factions unfriendly to the new institutions the leverage they needed to push for their abolition. The Moroccan Ministry of Foreign Affairs, in particular, was jealous of the functions allocated to the Ministry for the Moroccan Community Abroad and the Hassan II Foundation. Senior officials in the Foreign Affairs ministry felt that an overly eager Haddaoui was raiding their portfolio and chafed at his criticism of their friendship societies and the policy approach that they embodied (Brand 2002; Belguendouz 2006; interviews, Rabat, March 2004, and Paris, February 2004). In late 1994, Haddaoui was replaced as minister and president of the Hassan II Foundation by Ahmed el-Ouardi, a much more pliant bureaucrat. A year later, the ministry was downgraded to an undersecretariat attached to the Ministry of Foreign Affairs, and by 1997 the latter had succeeded in its campaign to have the Ministry for the Moroccan Community Abroad abolished. Some of the staff was integrated into the Ministry of Foreign Affairs, as were many of the resources that both the ministry and the foundation had relied on. "They just came and carted off our things, first it was the computers, then the VCR. We thought they would even come for the chairs," complained a person who had been a staff member at the foundation while the ministry was being dissolved (interview, March 2004).

Around this time, the BCP and other banks also began to withhold their contributions to the foundation, depriving the institution of the financial means to continue its outreach and maintain its library and database. Moreover, the BCP, apprehensive about competition in the emigrant market, hobbled Bank al-Amal by delaying disbursement of funds for the loans the "bank of work" had promised for emigrant projects and thereby dealt the king's pet project a fatal blow. The liquidity shortage this created, combined with emigrant complaints that the criteria for selection of projects was not based solely on economic viability, ensured that the bank never became more than a symbolic gesture (AMERM interviews, March 2004; Belguendouz 1999; Brand 2002; Fondation Hassan II interviews, Rabat, December 2003, January 2004, and March 2004; former staff of the Ministry for the Moroccan Community Abroad interviews, March 2004).

In April 1996, in an interview with the conservative French newspaper *Le Figaro*, Hassan II was asked about Moroccan emigration. He answered unequivocally, "I am against it. . . . Moroccans are not emigrants" (as quoted in Morocco, Ministère de l'Information 1997: 63). At a time when close to 10 percent of the Moroccan population was working abroad, the comment signaled a return to a view of emigrants that had shaped government policy in the 1970s and 1980s. The heady period of openness in the early 1990s was over, and out of a constellation of institutions the government had created to engage emigrants, only two were left standing: the BCP and the Hassan II Foundation, and the latter was confined to the task of maintaining emigrants' cultural ties with their country of origin. Moroccan emigrants were stripped of their political personas as emigrants and once again were reclaimed as an arm of the national economy, an integral part of a system that generated resources for national development priorities.

In dismantling or weakening the institutions that promoted interpretive exchange between emigrants and the state, the Moroccan regime divided its policies toward emigrants once again into two familiar streams—one that dealt primarily with emigrants' economic relationship to Morocco and the other that dealt with their political relationship to the kingdom. Just as it had for most of its engagement with emigrants since it began shipping Moroccan workers abroad in the early 1960s, the state sought the conceptual insights necessary to construct institutions to capture emigrant remittances. The government's political engagement with Moroccans living abroad fell back into the restrictive patterns of the 1970s and 1980s. It engaged with migrants in an effort to control them and enforce a contemporary version of the characteristics with which it had initially marketed them to European employers. Instead of "hardworking, strong, and obedient," the Moroccan government now promoted Moroccan emigrants as "well-behaved, moderate, and serious."

In a 1996 speech to representatives of the Moroccan community in France, Hassan II reflected his satisfaction that the state had accomplished its objectives.

He praised emigrants for their hard work and thriftiness, and paternalistically announced that he had received positive reports on their behavior from the French authorities. "My questions [about Moroccans in France] were always the same. . . . How have they behaved? How have they acted with you? The answer to these questions, may God be praised, always filled my heart with joy. . . . The answer was always: we have no complaints, they are excellent" (May 7, 1996, in Morocco, Ministère de l'Information 1996: 116).

The BCP: Reclaiming Interpretive Territory

Just as in the 1970s and 1980s, the conversations about emigrants' economic participation in Morocco were open-ended, offering ample room for interpretive engagement. The BCP reclaimed its position as the main tool through which the state worked to draw emigrants and emigrant money back into the Moroccan economy, extending its tried and true strategy of accompaniment into new markets in Spain and Italy. Just as when it began its operations in France and Belgium, the bank sent staff equipped "with a bank"—and now a laptop—"in their briefcases" to emigrant gathering spaces and places of employment. In teahouses and basement mosques, out of trunks of cars parked in the fields of Andalusia, in the street markets of Sicily and Rome, BCP staff socialized with emigrants and assisted them with nonfinancial needs, such as accessing healthcare or enrolling their children in school, even as they opened bank accounts for them at the state institution. The conversations that bank staff had with the new emigrants produced adaptations of established BCP practices, refashioned to reflect new technologies on which migrants increasingly relied to keep in touch with their families. Chief among these was the cell phone; indeed, according to researchers at the INSEA, emigrant communities consistently ranked connection to a GSM cell phone network as one of their most important—often the most important—infrastructure needs (INSEA interviews, Rabat, March 2004). The bank began to send SMS messages to emigrants confirming their transfers instead of old-fashioned paper receipts, but maintained the practice of sending a receipt for every single transaction, to build a sense among newly "bancarized" migrants that they could trust the BCP with their money. Additionally, the BCP set up dozens of new ATMs every year across Morocco, in the popular neighborhoods of the kingdom's growing cities as well as in rural centers, a choice reflecting its familiarity with the changing profile of Morocco's new emigrants, who were increasingly likely to be of urban origin. The outreach strategy was as effective in the mid-1990s as it had been two decades previously: although the BCP does not publish data about their clients' country of residence when they opened accounts, the banks' directors repeatedly emphasized that Spain and Italy represented significant growth markets and that the bank's performance there was meeting or exceeding expectations (see fig. 6.1). By 2000, this outreach showed clear results: for the first time since the mid-1980s, the number of bank accounts opened by Moroccan

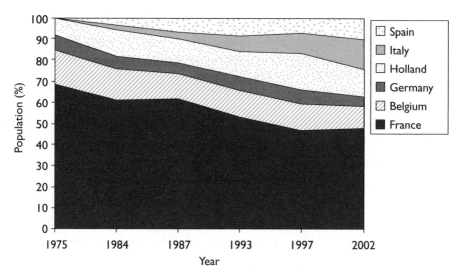

Figure 6.1. Proportion of the Moroccan emigrant population in Europe, by country, 1975–2000 (GERA 1992; Morocco, Ministry of Foreign Affairs 1968–2002).

emigrants jumped significantly, by 15 percent over the previous year (BCP *Rapports annuels*, 1990–2003; BCP interviews, Casablanca and Paris, January–March 2004).

The BCP also strove to reinvent itself as "a bank of the second and third generation," providing a quality of service high enough and a gamut of products innovative enough to appeal to Europeans of Moroccan ancestry (BCP 2003).[3] "The new generations of Moroccans living abroad [MRE] are less and less attached to their country of origin," summarized the BCP's director for investment services. "What counts now is to meet their expectations, which are more and more demanding. These young people have gotten used to the speed of European services. We have to make a significant effort to rise to the standards of international banking services" (J. Sebti, as quoted in Ababou 2002). The bank overhauled its information systems, already the most technologically advanced in Morocco, to meet "international standards," and reduced its fees on a variety of financial services, including premiums on insurance for travel in the case of family emergency and on real estate loans in Morocco.

Concerned, as the director of investment services put it, that the "emotional aspect does not weigh as heavily" (A. Sebti, as quoted in Abadou 2002) in the banking decisions of second- and third-generation Moroccan emigrants, the BCP also began to market itself as a vehicle through which Europeans of Moroccan descent could maintain their Moroccan identity. For example, it issued "vacation passports" to young second- and third-generation Moroccans, which were designed to "show our young *beurs* that their country, Morocco, is culturally rich and that there is so much to see, . . . so many places where all, young and old, can gather and enjoy each other" (BCP 2003).

In an exchange similar to the one experienced by their parents, many young *beurs* appropriated this outreach as a way to assert an oppositional Moroccan-ness, through which they maintained their sense of difference in European countries that were stressing the importance of their integration into national cultures. The comments of Samir, a young Moroccan comedian raised in France, capture this use of the BCP, and its branch in Paris, La Banque Chaabi. When asked in an interview about the connection he maintained to Morocco, the entertainer responded, "My only relationship with my country is with La Banque Achaabi and the Moroccan consulate where I get my national identity card and my passport. . . . I'm 50,000 Euros in debt now because I just bought the Banque Chaabi's white horse [the BCP's trademark] so help me out and come see my show" (Yabiladi 2003). Through this double-edged humor, he emphasized that although he was French, he would always remain Moroccan, so Moroccan that he was willing to purchase the BCP's white horse, but buying the services whose swiftness and sureness over long distances the white horse was supposed to symbolize left him struggling under a mountain of debt.

The BCP also sought to position itself as an institution that managed the transfer of resources other than money, including what it called "immaterial resources [like] brain power, expertise in a variety of domains" (Belqziz, director of BCP Delegations Abroad, as quoted in Foulani 1999). The Moroccan state complemented the BCP's new initiatives with yearly gatherings in Europe—Salons des Marocains Résidents à l'Étranger (1997–2000)—roughly equivalent to trade fairs at which the government (the Ministry of Development, Employment, and Training) presented investment opportunities in Morocco. The fairs' organizer identified one of the main goals of the events as "stimulating the desire to invest through *a direct and constructive dialogue* between Moroccans living abroad and the economic operators of Morocco today" (as quoted in Dades 1998, emphasis mine).

The Hassan II Foundation: Controlling through Culture

After declining in the late 1980s, the level of emigrant labor organizing remained low during the 1990s, as layoffs in heavy industry continued and emigrants either moved to the service sector or retired. Moroccan labor organizations redirected their energies toward promoting cultural activities and extending support toward emigrants' children and grandchildren, many of whom were now young adults. As a result, the Moroccan government similarly shifted its focus from engaging with workers' organizations in order to control their activities to engaging with emigrant families in order to define their cultural relationship to Morocco. It endeavored to tether migrants, new and old, to the Moroccan economy through the cultivation of a particular expression of national identity. And the Hassan II Foundation was charged with promoting that identity.

It was an identity that in several important respects represented a significant departure from the state's established rhetoric. Contrary to what it had been asserting for years, the government suggested that culturally belonging to the kingdom did not depend on returning, or planning to return, nor did it require exclusive allegiance to the Moroccan state. Indeed, the king, and the government following his lead, began to stress that Moroccan nationality was irrevocable: a Moroccan could never lose it, nor could his children, even if they chose to abandon it and adopt another nationality (Fondation Hassan II interviews, Rabat, July 2002, September 2003, January–March 2004). Moreover, in an abrupt about-face from the position the king had maintained vociferously for decades, the director of the foundation, Omar Azziman, appointed a couple of years after Haddoui's dismissal, made it clear in 1998 that the Moroccan regime was no longer against Moroccan emigrants' integration into their host countries:

> On the contrary, we know that their integration in the receiving country is a precondition for their development. . . . It is in this way that our community abroad can become a source of riches that can contribute to the development of the modernization of Morocco. . . . At the Foundation, we are not seeking to influence people's personal decisions or to discourage naturalization because we know that these choices make their lives easier and do not affect either their nationality of origin, or the force, the intensity of their sentimental and affective ties [to Morocco]. (As quoted in Chattou and Belbah 2002: 128)

What the foundation's director implied, the king made explicit. Although national belonging no longer required emigrants to remain exclusively Moroccan and eschew political participation in foreign countries, it depended on their adhesion to a Moroccan national identity, one that the state, through the Hassan II Foundation, would clearly define. In a 1996 interview broadcast on European television, Hassan II made this point emphatically: "This is the message that I send them [Moroccan emigrants]. If you want to become part of Moroccan national life, preserve your identity [as Moroccans]" (as quoted in Morocco, Ministère de l'Information 1996: 203).

A key element of that identity was that it was to rest on a kinder, gentler version of the *beia*, the allegiance to the crown required of Moroccans, defined in terms of friendly kinship as much as the requisite obedience to the monarch. After emigrants unleashed a battery of political challenges to the authoritarian character of the regime in the early 1990s, the crown approached them with a more welcoming gloss on loyalty to neutralize their protests: obedience to the regime was no more onerous than respect for a father. In a reflection of this shift, the king addressed an audience of Moroccan emigrants during his 1995 trip to New York as "My dear sons" instead of the customary "Our loyal subjects." Hassan II went on to explain this startling departure from the traditional designation:

You are indeed my sons. Why? Because the *beia* that binds every Moroccan citizen to the king of Morocco signifies, above all, that a strong familial and religious bond unites every Moroccan to his Sovereign (Morocco, Ministère de l'Information 1996).

He marshaled this new filial interpretation to bolster the stature of the Hassan II Foundation and, through his approbation, strengthened it in the Moroccan political context. In 1996, at a gathering of Moroccan emigrants in France, he announced that the royal foundation would henceforth be a symbol of a relationship between Moroccans and their king that was above all familial:

> To show you, you my children residing in France, how much Our solicitude and care for you is large and Our ties close, We have decided to entrust, as soon as We return, by the grace of God, the presidency of the Hassan II Foundation for Moroccans Living Abroad to Our devoted daughter, Lalla [Princess] Meryem.
>
> Thus, our ties will not be solely those of allegiance, but ties of kinship, since you will be as my sons and my daughters. . . .
>
> In closing, let me offer the prayers that parents address to their children: "May God surround you with his blessings." (Morocco, Ministère de l'Information 1997: 117)

Despite the ostensibly informal nature of this new interpretation, the Hassan II Foundation was domineering in its relationship with emigrants and defined the terms of the Moroccan identity that they were to embrace. The foundation ramped up its linguistic, religious, and cultural program, in particular upping the proportion of its approximately $10 million annual budget allocated to Arabic-language instruction for the children of emigrants to over 70 percent (Fondation Hassan II 1997–2001; Fondation Hassan II interviews, September 2003), Arabic being the officially designated language of Morocco as the regime attempted to suppress Berber and Amazigh identities (Zisenwine 2007). The foundation dictated the content of these programs and did not involve emigrants in their design in any meaningful way. Even when faced with complaints from parents, for example, that the curriculum served up by the 430 instructors the foundation sent to Europe was didactic and disconnected from the realities that their children faced, with some parents even suggesting that it smacked of royalist propaganda in its rosy portrayal of life in Morocco, the foundation did not adjust its strategy, aside from a few slight modifications (interviews, Paris and Brussels, February 2004; Fondation Hassan II interviews, Rabat, March 2004). It truncated its communication with emigrant groups, canceling the publication of *Rivages* and curtailing many of the open-ended forums and other outreach, with the directors traveling to Europe only rarely and engaging only with select groups. As one ATMF activist commented about this shift, "the foundation positioned itself as the mediator between the Moroccan government and Moroccans living abroad . . . but when we would write them, they would never write back" (ATMF interview, Paris, 2004). Furthermore, in a manner reminiscent of the strategy Moroccan consulates had used to maintain their influence over friendship societies, the foundation augmented its registry of Moroccan associations abroad and attempted to tether them to the state by doling out small grants for the narrow range of cultural and social activities that met with the foundation's approval (Belguendouz 1999; Brand 2002). Finally, the Hassan II Foundation continued to research Moroccan emigrants, allowing the state to "see" transformation in Moroccan communities abroad, and released periodic compilations of the data it had collected (Fondation Hassan II 2003).

Scaling Up Operation Transit: *Marhaba fi biladkom*—Welcome to Your Country

In the mid-1990s, the Moroccan government escalated Operation Transit into a logistical operation almost military in scale. The Royal Armed Forces took over the bulk of the work of shuttling Moroccan migrants down Spanish highways to the ports, coordinating the boarding and disembarking of approximately a million people crossing on crowded ferries during a few short days in early July and August. The Hassan II Foundation joined the effort and set up welcome centers, complete with information booths, health services, rest centers, and customs offices, at both Spanish and Moroccan ports and along the European and Moroccan highways that the migrants took to reach them. Additionally, it charged a small legion of outreach officers with personally welcoming returning emigrants. The customs administration was also ordered to improve its treatment of returnees. The BCP joined the effort, underwriting the operation, plastering the ports and welcome centers with marketing materials, and flooding them with BCP staff, who approached emigrants in the idling cars and on picnic benches to explain how to open an account at the state bank and describe the new financial services the BCP launched every year during Operation Transit (Brand 2002; Fondation Hassan II, internal documents on Operation Transit, 1996–2000; Banque Centrale Populaire 1996–2000; Fondation Hassan II interviews, August 2003 and December 2003; site visits, Welcome Center in Tangier and Algeciras, August 2002 and 2003).

Operation Transit became the centerpiece of the government's campaign to reinforce the sense that Moroccan emigrants were welcomed home and should return as often as possible. "Make sure to return to your country . . . to reconnect with your family. . . . That is where the future resides, for you and for the kingdom," exhorted the king (Morocco, Ministère de l'Information 1996). From the perspective of the state, the yearly pilgrimage reinforced the affective, cultural ties to the homeland, but it also reinforced the migrants, belonging to the Moroccan economy. The praise that the president of the National Commission of Agriculture and Economic Affairs showered on the foundation underscored the relationship the state perceived between the reception extended them and their participation in the national economy; in 1998, he praised "the extremely positive role" of the commission that had orchestrated the transit operation, adding, "we can only rejoice at the work accomplished by the Hassan II Foundation" (as quoted in *Al-Bayane* 1998). The enthusiastic state-sponsored reception of emigrants stood in sharp contrast to their exclusion from the political fabric of the country. This contrast would become all the more glaring as Morocco underwent a small but unprecedented movement toward democratic openness.

L'Alternance: Transition and Political Exclusion

In response to international pressure and a growing political malaise that threatened to explode into a widespread uprising—strikes again punctuated the spring of 1996, and Tangier rose up in riot—the ailing Hassan II, eager to push through reforms on his own terms, submitted a series of constitutional amendments to a referendum (Layachi 1998: 97–101). The new constitution reinstated the bicameral system of 1962, in which representatives in the lower chamber were elected by direct universal suffrage (Leveau 2000). The left-of-center Socialist Union of Popular Forces (Union Socialiste de Forces Populaires, or USFP), long in opposition, won the largest number of seats in parliament (14 percent) in the 1997 elections, and Adberrahmane Youssefi, the leader of the USFP, returned from exile in 1998 to help midwife the political change (Layachi 1998: 97–101; Desrues and Moyano 2001). The new transitional government—*gouvernement d'alternance*—reviewed dozens of ministry portfolios and prepared strategic plans for key policy areas. The issues of Moroccan communities abroad, however, were given short shrift (Belguendouz 1999). In fact, they were reduced to a single sentence in the document that outlined the responsibilities of the new department for human rights: "The government will pay particular attention to respecting the rights of our compatriots abroad" (as quoted in Belguendouz 1999: 69).

Emigrants expressed their discontent at this political erasure (*oubli*) in forceful terms. In a manifesto issued by the Forum for Immigrants in the European Union, Moroccan nationals called on the Youssefi government "to repair this neglect by beginning a process of consultation with representatives of Moroccans living abroad in order to elaborate a global vision . . . to give the Moroccan diaspora its rightful place and role in Morocco" (1998, as quoted in Chattou and Belbah 2002). They wanted the new government to engage with them as the short-lived Ministry for the Moroccan Community Abroad had in the early 1990s (Chattou and Belbah 2002). Emigrants, however, continued to be discounted as irrelevant, and their complaints were blatantly ignored (Belguendouz 1999: 68–77). Through the activities of the Hassan II Foundation, and the royal proclamations that steered it, emigrants had been identified as members of the national family, provided, of course, that they adhered to the rules imposed by the patriarch of that family. They were heralded as providers who sent money home and thus supported Morocco, their extended family, in its economic development. They were not, however, considered citizens who could participate in this historic moment of transition. Yet, even as emigrants' right to affect the political process was being dismissed, they were transforming the way major state bureaucracies did business. In concert with their communities of origin, Moroccan emigrants, as described in the preceding chapter, were developing new technological and social models for the provision of basic infrastructure and services and thereby changing the way government agencies conceived of infrastructure provision, rural development, and state priorities about who should receive state services. Once Hassan II died and Mohammed VI ascended the throne, the state's approach to emigrants would change radically. Not only would emigrants' impact on government bureaucracies become visible; they would be courted as important actors and innovators in regional development.

Mohammed VI: Capturing Process

The crowds had been gathering for hours in the hot sun, pressing against police lines and metal barriers for one last glimpse of Hassan II. After the crown prince announced on national television that the king's heart had stopped, tens of thousands of Moroccans left their homes for Rabat, many of them on foot, and two days later, on July 25, 1999, over a million people congregated along the capital's broad tree-lined avenues waiting for the royal funeral procession. As the gun carriage that bore the king's coffin turned the corner, the crowd erupted into wails of grief and deafening chants of "There is only one God, and Mohammed is his prophet." Many waved the Moroccan flag and brandished photos and newspaper images of the man who had cautioned the Moroccan people and their parliament, more than once, that he was the shadow of God on earth. Others flung themselves against the barricades with cries of "He is our father. Our father is dead!" Volunteer teams scrambled to collect the mourners who had fainted from the emotional exertion and the heat. The new young king, Mohammed VI, dressed in the traditional flowing white robes and red fez, walked stoically behind his father's body, with dozens of world leaders, including U.S. president Clinton, French president Chirac, and Israeli prime minister Barak, following several steps behind him on the two-mile route to the royal mausoleum. There, as foreign dignitaries stood at the gates, Hassan II's remains were buried near those of his father in a private ceremony. After thirty-eight years, the rule of the Arab world's longest reigning monarch was finally over (Rosenblum 1999a; Broder and Jehl 1999; MacPherson 1999; Buncombe 1999).

Mohammed VI, still several weeks shy of his thirty-sixth birthday when he ascended the throne, was hailed as a modernizer. Moroccans tentatively began to whisper that it was "time for some new blood" (as quoted in Jehl 1999) and hoped the new monarch would bring change to a country weighed down by an authoritarian bureaucracy and struggling with an unemployment rate of over 30 percent. Part of the so-called Internet generation of new monarchs in the Arab world, which included King Abdullah of Jordan and Sheikh Hamad bin Issa of Bahrain, Mohammed VI pledged to implement democratic reforms and to jumpstart the kingdom's flagging economy. In particular, he advanced a plan for economic development that was regional in focus and placed special emphasis on Morocco's long-neglected rural areas. In doing so, the self-styled King of the Poor broke with the political cartography that had legitimated the exclusion of large portions of the country from Morocco's succession of plans for economic development, and elevated rural development to a national priority.

In October 1999, no more than a couple of months after his accession, Mohammed VI took a trip that encapsulated the sea change his reign would represent (Pelham 1999). He visited the northern Rif Mountains, an area to which Hassan II refused to return after putting down a rebellion there in 1958 while he was crown prince. After he had subdued the area, he reportedly loaded the leaders of the uprising into his helicopter and had them pushed out over the Atlantic on his journey back to the capital. Thousands were left dead. Throughout Hassan II's reign, the people of the Rif Mountains rose up periodically against the regime, and each time their revolt was mercilessly crushed. In retaliation, Hassan II not only swore never to visit the region but also imposed an unofficial state investment embargo to great effect. Thirty miles from Europe, this northern region had not seen a road built since its independence from Spain in 1956. Its human development indicators ranked among Africa's worst, including a 90 percent illiteracy rate among women (Pelham 1999). Hassan II also sent European labor recruiters to the region starting in the mid-1960s, in a ploy to export dissidents, and the Rif Mountains, as late as 1999, still displayed the highest relative rate of emigration of any region in the nation, followed by the Souss (INSEA 2000). When Mohammed VI's plane landed in the region, he became the first monarch to visit in over forty years. Hundreds of thousands of people lined the mountain passes to greet him, and to welcome his apparent desire to heal the bruises left by his father's iron fist (Pelham 1999).

Mohammed VI's visit presaged the shift in economic and political strategy that he would author. He moved from a centralized approach to economic planning, which engineered the development of the national economy as a single whole, to a strategy that favored regional development—of all regions, including the Rif—and delegated important planning functions to the provinces (Brouksy 2002). He also gave legal authority to provincial governors and transferred to them the financial resources needed to carry out their edicts. Governors were nominated by the king under Moroccan law, and Mohammed VI chose them on the basis of their commitment to his decentralized vision for the nation's development. He also broke with the notion of a single Moroccan national identity, Arab and royalist, and began to promote the expression of regional identities and of non-Arab, especially Amazigh, cultures and languages. Before long, he established a Royal Institute of the Amazigh Culture to "protect . . . and consolidate the status of [Amazigh cultures and languages] in cultural, media and educational domains" (Mohammed VI 2002a).

Through his strategy for economic and social development, the young monarch, his hold on the throne still tenuous, followed the pattern that successive sultans and French colonists had used to secure the kingdom: he vested local rulers devoted to his person as monarch with the power to govern regions and keep them loyal. Rather than lash regions to the sultan through control and submission, however, Mohammed VI sought to link them to Rabat via economic growth and prosperity. Emigrants and, more specifically, the interpretive processes that they initiated in their communities of origin would emerge as key resources in his new vision.

Regional Development: A Strategic Choice

Only weeks after his accession, Mohammed VI laid out his plans for the new priorities on which Morocco's economic development was to focus. In his second public speech after his father's death, he promised a developmental strategy that would leave no one out, especially the most needy, toward whom he felt "a special solicitude and care" (Mohammed VI 1999a). Moreover, he placed special emphasis on the needs of the rural poor, who represented over 75 percent of the kingdom's poor (H. Levy 2004), and argued that Morocco could not develop as a nation unless it dealt with the poverty that had settled on it as a permanent scourge:

> How shall we as a nation achieve national development if our rural area struggles with problems that force its inhabitants to abandon their lands . . . because of a lack of strategy of integrated development, based on the organization of agricultural activities and others [in rural areas], because of a lack of interest that should have been devoted to their living conditions and education, to the provision of basic infrastructure, to stemming the exodus [from rural areas] by putting into effect a plan that promotes the participation of local communities, that creates new centers of development . . . and that manages the occasional disasters like drought and others? (Mohammed VI 1999a)

With these words, so unlike those of his father in both tone and content, the new king communicated an unequivocal rejection of the categorization of some regions as resistant to development, and as places where state investment was a futile exercise.

Shortly thereafter, the king sent a letter to the prime minister, el-Youssefi, which outlined the elements he wanted included in the forthcoming Five-Year National Development Plan. He directed the government to draft a plan that would "spread the benefits of prosperity to all of Our subjects" and made clear that his first priority in meeting this goal was rural development: at the top of the king's list, literally, was "the promotion of neglected regions and their integration into the dynamic of economic development, notably by reducing the delay that rural areas suffer in the matter of basic infrastructure and social service provision, and by finding solutions to the drop in income, illiteracy, and the insufficiency of state support" (Mohammed VI 1999c).

Moreover, Mohammed VI specified that he viewed local communities themselves as an important source of the "solutions" he demanded: "Economic and social development is the fruit of the collective effort of the community," he stressed. As such, noted the king, it required the collaboration of "all socioeconomic partners, especially the state, local collectivities, public establishments, the private sector and social organizations." Local collectivities, as the government bodies "closest to the ground," and community associations were to be viewed as privileged actors, and their role as such written into the National Development Plan. In a 2001 speech commemorating the second anniversary of his ascension to the throne, the king would indicate his awareness of the politics of revising entrenched patterns of state neglect in rural, and overwhelmingly Amazigh, areas: "We are convinced of the benefits of local democracy . . . local collectivities are powerful levers for social and economic development" in regions whose "cultural diversity constitutes a source of enrichment for the Moroccan nation" (Mohammed VI 2001).

Infrastructure and Rural Development

To comply with this mandated turn toward rural development, the government initially relied on the infrastructure provision programs it had launched in the last years of Hassan II's rule. Prompted by the World Bank and other donor agencies, including the EU and UNDP, the Moroccan government had, in the late 1990s, instituted several programs to remedy the egregious lack of basic services in rural areas. Three programs stood out because of their size and reach: the PERG, the national program to provide electricity to rural areas; the PAGER, designed to supply them with water; and the PNCRR, developed to construct roads and correct the isolation of hundreds of rural villages. The World Bank alone had provided Morocco with approximately $200 million in loans between 1997 and 2000 for rural infrastructure development under these programs (World Bank 2001). During the first few years, however, under Hassan II, the authorities tasked with their implementation were less than ambitious in their execution. The World Bank's evaluation judged that only 50 percent of nonadjustment loans, a hefty share of which went to the three main rural infrastructure programs, had been satisfactory in their results over the 1997–2000 period (World Bank 2001). Two trends seem to have produced this mixed outcome: initially, the agencies responsible had conducted elaborate surveys and squabbled over program design rather than acting; then, when they did act, they tended to favor the nonpoor and focus resources on easily accessible semirural areas near urban centers (van der Walle 2004; H. Levy 2004).

Once Mohammed VI identified rural development as a national priority, these three infrastructure programs would become the institutional pillars of a new, more assertive approach. They represented, in effect, the only institutional structures in place at the time to address the needs of Morocco's rural population. After the shift articulated by the new monarch, the programs were quickly ramped up in terms of budget and projects executed (H. Levy 2004; van der Walle 2004). The number of villages linked to electricity under the PERG, for example, nearly doubled between the years 2000 and 2003, shooting up from 1,700 to 3,200. Moreover, the National Office of Electricity deviated significantly from its conservative practice of serving villages closest to semi-urban centers, a trend best illustrated by the jump in the number of villages it equipped with solar panels—a technological solution reserved for the most isolated—from 80 in 2000 to 580 in 2003 (ONE 2006).

As the implementing agencies for the PERG, the PAGER, and PNCRR expanded their operations, they spread the techno-social models they used throughout Morocco. In all three, these techno-social approaches had been developed through interpretive engagement with emigrants and their rural communities of origin (see chap. 5). The agencies had modified their methods for infrastructure provision and amended their conceptual approach to one that favored locally generated solutions adapted to specific topographic and social conditions. Most important, through lessons learned in engagement with migrants who stressed that situated interpretive conversations were the basis of development—"they are our treasure" (interview, Taroudant, January 2004)— the programs were revised to build community participation into project design and management. All three programs incorporated an understanding that community involvement was *the* factor that transformed infrastructure into a catalyst for development. As this approach was extended throughout the kingdom, the process that had led to it became visible to state authorities (World Bank 2005). Emigrants began to be recognized officially as important actors in rural development, with Mohammed VI himself acknowledging their transformative role.

Mohammed VI targeted emigrants as a resource from the very beginning. In his first missive to the prime minister on this question, he pointed to emigrants as "dynamic agents" of change and ordered their role factored into the National Development Plan. As his letter underscored, "We would like to praise the laudable efforts of Our loyal subjects living outside the national territory in the matter of investment, and We would like to encourage them to continue in this vein given the numerous and great benefits that they generated for themselves and for Morocco" (Mohammed VI 1999c). In this first statement of his development strategy, however, the king's understanding of precisely how emigrants acted as agents of change was still vague.

As government agencies charged with providing basic infrastructure ramped up their existing programs for rural areas to meet the king's new goals, the role that emigrants had played in shaping how those services were conceived and delivered began to surface. During a visit to France, the king addressed his audience as citizens who "adhere to the French state and the values of its society, without denying your own values and origins" and added that this dual perspective gave them the skills and understanding to foster "cooperation in cultural and economic domains," a cooperation increasingly becoming manifest in rural Morocco:

> The way that you follow the events in your country as well as your determination to contribute to the process of progress and modernization, as is demonstrated by the always increasing number of nongovernmental organizations that you have set up for that purpose, and through which you have contributed to the consideration of urgent questions that demand our concerted attention, like the reduction of the vast poverty and the improvement of basic provision in the rural areas, bring Us great satisfaction.
>
> We would like to express, in relation to this, Our sincere thanks and Our admiration of the community projects that emigrant associations and individuals have undertaken to benefit the poorest of our country. (Mohammed VI 2000a)

The new king's focus on regional rural development, and his growing acknowledgment of the role that emigrants had played in that area, provided tacit support for an "action-study" launched in 2000 by the emigrant association M/D in the province of Taroudant. The study, designed to identify "ways to capitalize on local initiatives to put in place new forms of partnership with public authorities and programs," had the "unconditional support of the Wali [regional governor] of the Souss-Massa-Draa region, . . . as well as the support of the governor of the province of Taroudant" (M/D 2002a: 15). The action-study was based on numerous overlapping rounds of interpretive conversations that included local residents, emigrants, M/D, other nongovernment organizations, and local, provincial, and national state authorities. The discussions addressed activities in the region ranging from electricity provision to the creation of schools for adult women, to the growth of ecotourism, to programs to revitalize Amazigh traditions and languages. More significantly, the conversations addressed head-on how initiatives could be expanded or modified to foster greater state participation, as well as a more meaningful exchange of ideas and practices between government and village associations. So unprecedented were these types of exchanges in the Moroccan context that M/D, in collaboration with the European Union, published not only the findings of its study but also the transcripts of many of the conversations that had produced them (ECIL 2002a; M/D interviews, Taroudant, December 2003–January 2004).

The action-study, the initiatives that it covered, and the avid collaboration of the Wali and the governor, both royal nominees, in an effort that seemed to carry forward his vision, piqued the new monarch's interest. In 2001, Mohammed VI visited M/D's headquarters in Taroudant, toured a number of the projects the association had initiated, and spoke at length with the emigrant organizers who had established over 250 village associations, all self-taxing and part of an M/D federated network. During the annual "Pronouncement from the Throne" that followed his visit, Mohammed VI praised emigrant contributions, stating, "We want to assure them of Our esteem for the efficient contribution that they bring to economic development efforts . . . in Morocco" (Mohammed VI 2002b). The king returned to visit M/D only two years later, in 2003, to inaugurate a road that had been built with the help of the Federation of Villages and Emigrant Associations from Taroudant through the national rural roads program. In the Moroccan political context at the time, such consistent attentiveness from the monarch to what were essentially the activities of an NGO was more than remarkable (interviews, Taroudant, December 2003–January 2004; Daoud 2005).

Mohamed VI: "Democracy is not an end in itself"

Even as the king displayed a growing interest in emigrant development associations, and M/D in particular, he was turning a deaf ear to emigrants' demands that they be allowed to participate in the political transformation that his accession to the throne had seemed to signal. Mohammed VI had been king for less than a month before doubts arose across the Mediterranean. Many emigrants were not placated by his assurances that he would "ponder earnestly on [emigrant] problems and consolidate their ties with their homeland" (as quoted in al-Aly 1999). They demanded that their political rights in Morocco be recognized and that they be given representation in the new administration. "We no longer want to be considered a mere source of hard currency. We want to be fully-fledged citizens and actively contribute to the socioeconomic development of Morocco," said Ahmed M'dini, a Moroccan living in Germany, in a comment that typified the growing frustration of emigrant groups at their political exclusion during this time of change (as quoted in al-Aly 1999). Moreover, emigrants complained bitterly about the paucity of consular services and the lack of protection from—or official condemnation of—the racist attacks that Moroccans were experiencing throughout Europe, especially in Spain. Indeed, in speaking with the Moroccan community in Spain, Mohammed VI referred to the attacks in El Ejido and other areas only obliquely, calling them "regrettable events, limited to certain regions" (Mohammed VI 2000b). Emigrants countered that protection was a "fundamental right that the authorities should guarantee to a community that has so far been like the goose that hatches golden eggs" (as quoted in al-Aly 1999).

The new regime's lack of response to emigrant political demands was consistent with its interpretation of the political rights of Moroccans in general, and of democracy in particular. The parliamentary elections of 2002 were only the second ones held since Hassan II reauthorized them in 1997, after they had been banned for two decades. After the elections the king addressed the new parliament in a nationally broadcast speech in which he told the new representatives that "democracy is not an end in itself." Democracy was useful only insofar as it acted as a tool for economic development, he cautioned sternly, and its exercise must be contingent on whether it served the interests of the nation, a question on which he was—as sovereign—the final arbiter. He condemned what he characterized as the legislators' use of the electoral campaign to make "puerile overstatements and sterile arguments." Cautioning them to refrain from "turning every issue into a priority . . . we should focus our efforts," he said in authoritarian fashion, "with dialogue and unanimity" (as quoted in BBC 2002).

Apart from his interest in emigrants' roles in rural development, his government maintained the practice of dealing with emigrants' participation in the national economy separately from their cultural and political involvement in the country. It was unable to keep emigrants from making connections between the two spheres, however. Thanks to the government's transit operations, migrants grew increasingly reintegrated into their communities of origin and began issuing increasingly vocal and bold critiques. Their challenges were grounded in the relationship between their economic participation in Morocco and their political rights articulated through those previous conversations. Emigrant investors, for example, began to voice critiques in the Moroccan press of cronyism in the financial sector and of a "perpetual harassment for bribes" that was undermining their investment initiatives (*L'Économiste* 2003). "The problem . . . is that [a bank] can reverse its decision [to provide a loan] after a single phone call because you had a disagreement or misunderstanding with your 'connection' [*pistonneur*]. 'Moroccan emigrants need to be respected in administrative transactions as well as in consulates abroad,' " summarized a major glossy in Morocco (Fathallah 2002). Dejected by the poverty in their communities of origin, they began to complain vociferously about "the state's complete abandonment—*la démission totale de l'état*"—of rural Morocco and its role in perpetuating egregious income inequalities (interviews, Paris and Brussels, 2004; Daoud 2003, 2005). Viewing themselves as important contributors to the Moroccan economy, emigrants began to demand institutions that would enable them to shape the nation's political trajectory commensurately. "Moroccans living abroad want the political compensation for their economic contribution," observed one editorial, "not just a warm reception and welcoming billboards on the sides of highways. They want real participation in the management of the country; if not . . . they will shut off the [remittance] faucets" (Économie et Entreprises 2003: 73).

"Keeping the faucets running": Capitalizing on Interpretation

In a bid to "keep the faucets running," Mohammed VI ordered the restructuring of the kingdom's policies and institutions for emigrants. He dictated four major changes in 2002: the improvement of consular support abroad; the redefinition of the Hassan II Foundation as a strictly cultural agency; the transfer of Operation Transit to the Mohammed V Foundation; and most important, the creation of a new set of institutions that would facilitate emigrants' transformative participation in local areas, through investment and community organizing. In essence, he decreed the amelioration of services for emigrants on the one hand, and on the other, the development of policy tools to capture the process of innovation they had sparked in the country (Mohammed VI 2002c). "It is Our firm desire that [emigrants] play an active and effective role in all of the domains of national life," he concluded (Mohammed VI 2002b).

Under this rubric, the government established two new institutions that capitalized on emigrant transformation of local communities. The first were regional investment centers (*centres régionaux d'investissement*) designed to facilitate entrepreneurship in general and emigrant entrepreneurship in particular. The first opened in 2003, and by 2005 sixteen centers were in business. They functioned as "one-stop shops" where investors could set up firms as legal entities within a matter of hours, instead of the days or months it had taken previously. They handled investors' administrative transactions with verifiable and auditable levels of transparency, addressing emigrant complaints of usury and corruption. More important, however, the centers served as mediators between investors and local governments, resolving disputes and facilitating conversations that led investors to amend their projects and local governments to rethink development strategies, planning goals, and infrastructure provision. In sum, the centers provided emigrants with an institutional vehicle enabling them to act as political as well as economic agents (Centre Régional d'Investissement [CRI] interviews, Casablanca, March 2004; Office of the Mayor interviews, Casablanca, January–March 2004; CRI 2004; Lamlili 2004; Jafry 2005).

The second institution created was the Ministry for the Moroccan Community Abroad. Like its shrunken predecessor of the early 1990s, it was a subministry housed in the Ministry of Foreign Affairs. This time around, the new office's portfolio was broader and received the sanction of the Ministry of Foreign Affairs in which it was housed: it was charged with addressing economic, political, and legal issues as they pertained to Moroccan communities abroad. Moreover, like the institution it resurrected, the subministry addressed emigrants' economic and political issues in a single stream of conversations. Emigrants' economic realities and political aspirations were addressed jointly and were not divided, as they had been under Hassan II, into two thematic areas, one that the government explored willingly and the other that it strove to suppress (Ministry for the Moroccan Community Abroad interviews, Rabat, September 2003–March 2004; www.marocainsdumonde.gov.ma).

Moreover, the rationale that inspired its creation in 2003 was different from the logic that gave rise to its predecessor. The new ministry was set up to encourage and direct the interpretive processes that emigrants authored in Morocco—to act in essence as a system of canals and locks channeling processes of innovation to areas that would benefit from them. The ministry strategy documents give, as primary reasons for its creation, "the initiative of the Moroccan community abroad to become involved as a fundamental *human resource in the process of development*; the political dynamic in Morocco that has acknowledged the principles of equality and the citizenship rights of *all its residents*; and the mobilization of the civil society and the private sector *to assist the government in a variety of domains*" (Morocco, Ministry of Foreign Affairs, 2003). In one of her first speeches, the minister for the Moroccan Community Abroad, Nouzha Chekrouni, made this objective even more explicit: "We are witnessing a very active and creative dynamic of local and regional associations, most of them founded and organized by ambitious and entrepreneurial emigrants, that have engaged with determination and success in far-reaching partnership actions, . . . all of them insisting throughout on the endogenous capacities of the associations in Morocco, fostering innovation, and strengthening the actions that support the Moroccan community abroad. These praiseworthy initiatives . . . are what we insist on supporting and saluting" (Chekrouni 2004).

With the creation (or resurrection) of these institutions, the Moroccan government shifted the ways in which all institutions that implemented its policies toward emigrants operated. The state placed a renewed emphasis on creating and maintaining interpretive engagement with Moroccans living abroad around various aspects of their relationship with the kingdom. In fact, the interpretive conversations, and the desire to capture them, that had sparked a renewed wave of policymaking became the heart of the policies themselves. Before defining an agenda for its work, the new ministry began by contacting hundreds of Moroccan associations overseas, asking them to recommend ways it should meet their needs, and following up with outreach to continue the conversation. The ministry also began hosting annual weeklong fairs in cities with large Moroccan populations, like Paris and Brussels. These were not only occasions to celebrate Moroccan culture and interact with Moroccan communities abroad; the ministry also used them to bring emigrants together with government and private real estate developers, the BCP, and regional investment centers and representatives. The fairs—or salons—allowed Moroccans to purchase real estate or to begin investment planning while in Europe, but they also permitted invited institutions and emigrants to engage in conversations about needs and financial aspirations (Ministry for the Moroccan Community Abroad interviews, Rabat, September 2003–March 2004; Morocco, Ministry of Foreign Affairs, correspondence, January 2003–May 2004; Migrant Development Associations interviews, Taroudant, Paris, Brussels, and Rabat, January–April 2004; *Le Matin* 2004a).

In 2002, the Hassan II Foundation for Moroccans Living Abroad began hosting huge annual weeklong fairs for emigrants vacationing in Morocco over the summer. These were expressly designed to create interpretive conversations: the foundation sponsored forums throughout the day on topics of concern to emigrants and their families, covering everything from investing in a summer home in Morocco to negotiating with European school systems; it also laid out areas where emigrants could wander through to meet with financial institutions, publishing houses, traditional artisans, and the like; and it organized cultural events, such as musical performances and caftan fashion shows, that allowed emigrants, their non-emigrant friends and relatives, and government officials to interact informally (on-site visits and interviews, Casablanca, July 2002 and August 2003). Even the reception centers along the route to Morocco were transformed into interpretive spaces, as staff from local consulates, the ministry, state health services and the Hassan II Foundation engaged informally with migrants who stopped there (on-site visits and interviews, Algeciras and Tangier, July 2002 and August 2003). So effective were these in renewing government contact with emigrants that Mohammed VI himself made yearly trips to Tangier to welcome people home.

Co-opting Interpretation

In April 2004, the Ministry for the Moroccan Community Abroad, the regional investment center for Taroudant, and M/D signed a partnership accord to promote local development in the Souss region. That agreement was one of many that emigrant organizations finalized with the ministry, the Mohammed V Foundation, or other government entities. Almost all specified a financial contribution from the state for development projects to be carried out, at least nominally, in partnership. Due to a shift in policy of the European Union and the World Bank, and a change in Moroccan law, the bulk of foreign aid had to be disbursed through Moroccan government institutions, most of it through the semi-autonomous Agence de Développement Sociale (see chap. 5). Soon, however, emigrants soon discovered that, in the majority of cases, government involvement was undermining their efforts. The Moroccan state seemed to be sabotaging emigrant initiatives.

Activists observed that this happened in one of two ways. First, government agencies often tried to supplant emigrant organizations. State agencies either took credit for the actions of emigrant organizations or tried to take over their activities. The ATMF and Immigration, Développement et Démocratie (IDD), a Paris-based organization of former labor organizers turned advocates for community development in Morocco, both complained of this in the aftermath of the 2004 earthquake in Al Hoceima. Both orchestrated a massive drive in the Paris area to collect resources for the earthquake victims, many of them in villages where the organizations were already doing grassroots mobilization to prepare for development projects, and transported these resources down to Morocco in a caravan of trucks. They were blocked at the border and refused passage until they turned over the resources to the Mohammed V Foundation, which later distributed the goods as gifts of the government during widely publicized events that focused on urban centers rather than on the villages the organizations had wanted to help (confidential e-mail correspondence, 2004; Telquel 2003). Other emigrant NGOs found that the state attempted to co-opt the process of community organizing on which they based their development work. As one veteran M/D activist observed, "the state is happy to use [village] associations, but not to work with them; in fact, it doesn't know quite what to do because it's not ready to cede some of its power, it can't engage and imagine solutions with the people. The state tends to kill the initiatives. The populations are treated like supplicants or sub-contractors, and sometimes that's what they become" (as quoted in Daoud 2005: 193).

The second way the state compromised emigrant development work was by withholding funds for the organizing activity on which the projects rested. State agencies, and the Mohammed V Foundation in particular, flatly refused to pay administrative costs and overhead. More significantly, they declined to support financially the mobilization of communities into village associations, which, according to emigrants, was at the heart of their work. "We often spend more time setting up a village organization, building a consensus amongst the old, the young, the local elites, the emigrants, than actually doing the project. But isn't it that organizing work that generates development?" (Daoud 2005: 196). State agencies typically funded only activities for which emigrant organizations could provide receipts of purchase, something impossible to do for community organizing work. Emigrants and the communities they worked with found themselves increasingly compelled to pay for a larger share of projects than they ever had before, contributing to implementation costs as well as the outlays involved in organizing, even as government regulations made those projects more expensive. In a bitter irony not lost on emigrant activists, government attempts to capitalize on the interpretive conversations that emigrants had set in motion and that the state had recognized as invaluable to local development were killing those very processes.

Organizing to Protect Interpretation

In an effort to safeguard community processes of interpretation and innovation, emigrant organizations began to form alliances. By late 2005, Moroccan emigrant development groups had already held several meetings in cities throughout Europe. In part, their goal was to share knowledge about development projects, specifically techno-social innovations. But they aimed also to share information about procedures in various Moroccan state agencies and to create an active network of emigrant development groups. Activists spoke of the need to make the *collective impact* of emigrant initiatives clear as a means to develop political power for negotiations with the state.

In reflecting on their accomplishments, several M/D activists noted that they helped change local communities' relationship to the state. "Before, people didn't even know how to have a conversation [about development issues]. Now, they understand the need to organize, they know how to talk to the state. Now that is progress" (as quoted in Daoud 2005: 197), commented an emigrant who had worked with M/D from the start. "I don't believe in work done by a single administration or organization, because it can only be the reflection of a society, it can't get things moving on its own. The idea is to communicate, to think together," concluded another activist (as quoted in Daoud 2005: 198). As emigrant development associations began to organize to challenge the state and defend the interpretive spaces they viewed as essential to rural development, they were embodying the practices that they had set in motion in their communities of origin, "communicating and thinking together" to generate "new approaches for talking to the state" (interviews, Marrakesh, February 2005; confidential e-mail correspondence, May 2005; www.coordinationsud.org; www.migdev.org).

Forty Years of Engagement

For forty years, beginning in 1963, the Moroccan government engaged with emigrants, consistently and assertively establishing institutions to do so. It opened dedicated spaces for conversations to unfold and charged its agencies with turning the insights those produced into policy. The two banks, the network of friendship societies attached to consular offices, the parliamentary seats, the foundation, and the ministries tasked with sustaining engagement with migrants were only the larger stars in the constellation of institutions that nurtured the conversations.

Emigrants responded to government outreach with a mixture of skepticism and relief. Although some refused to engage with the state altogether, emigrants, on the whole, accepted the invitation to participate in dialogue, but they always made the conversations their own. When, as was all too often the case, an overbearing government interlocutor tried to control what was said and strove to impose meanings onto changing migration dynamics, emigrants resisted by basing their interpretations on their own experiences. They articulated connections and made observations that challenged the government in general, and Hassan II's rule in particular, but that were faithful to their lives.

When the conversations began to produce commentary the Moroccan government viewed as seditious, it shut them down and dismantled the institutions erected to support them. Its aim was to silence political dissent, either by closing off the venue it had offered migrants for expression or by smothering their voices. The callous tactics of intimidation to which Hassan II's regime resorted scarred the exchange between government and migrants, and sometimes the physical bodies of migrants. But the government always reinitiated engagement. Migrants had become too valuable a resource to Moroccan development for the government to turn its back on them. Each time the government recommitted to engagement, its migrant counterparts extracted concessions, insisting on more latitude in the aspects of migration they could interpret and demanding more space to reinvent the institutions the government had created. Each time the government tried to reengage, migrants pushed the exchange further toward a conversation that addressed how development would be defined, and what their role in fostering it would be. By the time Mohammed VI had settled into his reign, the government came to appreciate how profound an effect migrants could have on their country's future.

Just as the government began to recognize the value of interpretation for its own sake, so too did migrants. It became increasingly clear to them that by interpreting their lived experiences in collaboration with officials, they could help shape policy and thus become authors of their future. They attempted to develop new ways of "talking to government" so that they could set the terms of exchange, could protect themselves from being co-opted or silenced, and could safeguard the creativity that comes from "communicating and thinking together."

In Mexico, "talking to government" was all migrants did. For decades, it had been like talking to a brick wall in that their government ignored and rebuffed their overtures. But as Moroccan migrants could testify, talking is powerful. Over time, determined efforts to engage with government chiseled openings, and eventually Mexican migrants too, in collaboration with their government, charted a national future as creative as the one Moroccan emigrants were interpreting an ocean away.

7

The Reluctant Conversationalist

The Mexican Government's Discontinuous
Engagement with Mexican Americans, 1968–2000

With the end of the bracero program in 1964, the Mexican government was finally relieved of the task of managing the emigration of its workers. The termination of the labor export protocols and the formal closure of the United States to all but a trickle of Mexican labor had little effect on the actual number of Mexican workers who crossed the border. Emigration not only continued apace, but it accelerated dramatically as the migration networks and the structural dependence of U.S. production on cheap labor became more entrenched (Piore 1979). Instead of the flow of workers being documented with the allocation of bracero contracts, however, Mexican labor emigration now slipped under the radar, as workers began to cross into the United States illegally or under only marginally legal arrangements. The Mexican authorities, exhausted after two decades of dealing with the strong-arm negotiation tactics of the United States, were only too happy to avert their gaze. More important for the elaboration of policies that linked migration to development, the Mexican government stubbornly refused to engage with Mexican migrants and produced a series of studies arguing that the number of workers emigrating was trivial.

While Mexican and U.S. government policy made Mexican migrants invisible, Mexican Americans (United States citizens of Mexican origin) were bursting onto the public stage. Inspired by the gains that African Americans had wrested through the civil rights movement, incipient Mexican American political activity of the 1950s and early 1960s grew into a full-blown wave of activism that became identified as the Chicano movement. *Chicano* was an in-group term, short for *Mexicano*, which had been used by Mexican Americans to refer to one another since the turn of the twentieth century. In the 1960s, however, *Chicano* and *chicanismo* came to signify the "radically political and ethnic populism" (Gómez-Quiñones 1990: 103) that characterized the Mexican American movement. Chicano activists began to examine how racism and class exploitation reinforced each other to shape Mexican American experiences, and to eschew the assimilationist tendencies of established Mexican American advocacy organizations for increasingly separatist stances. The Chicano movement was a river fed by many streams: it encompassed organizations with agendas as different as those of the United Farm Workers (UFW) union, which focused on the working conditions of agricultural laborers, and the more militant Crusade for Justice and La Raza Unida, which targeted the racist treatment of working-class Mexican Americans; it included a range of student groups from radical to liberal, other intellectuals, and separatists who called for creation of an independent homeland for Mexican Americans, a reinvention of the mythical Aztlán; and it included church groups and Marxist cells. They were all part of the same political current insofar as they couched their vindication of political, economic, and cultural rights for Mexican Americans in a distinct ethnic and historical identity. In sum, the Chicano movement made Mexican Americans visible as a group and demonstrated their growing political power (Gómez-Quiñones 1990).

If the Mexican government acted as though migrants did not exist, it had a more difficult time ignoring Mexican Americans. When Chicano activists approached the Mexican government in the late 1960s, at a moment when it was in the throes of a political crisis, it entered into a dialogue with them. The Mexican authorities hoped that an association with the left-leaning grassroots movement would help to restore the tattered revolutionary credentials of the PRI—the Partido Revolucionario Institucional—which had been in power for decades in what was essentially one-party rule, and thereby help to secure its hold on power. Soon after it began its engagement with Mexican Americans, however, the Mexican government abruptly discontinued the conversation. It found that Chicano leaders, rather than being docile partners, did not refrain from directing bold critiques at the PRI and at its system of governance. Furthermore, the Mexican government quickly discovered that it could not engage with Mexican Americans without addressing the issue of Mexican labor emigration; Chicanos argued that the immigrants undermined Chicanos' already precarious position in U.S. labor markets.

It was a pattern that would be repeated over and over again during the following thirty years. Every time the Mexican government was confronted with a political crisis that its leaders believed they could resolve by drawing on Mexican American political power, it courted Chicanos and renewed its engagement with them. Invariably, the conversations between Chicanos and the Mexican government would raise difficult questions about emigration, PRI hegemony, and later, the quality of economic and political ties between Mexico and the United States; invariably, at that moment, the Mexican government would brusquely curtail its participation in the dialogue. Those repeated, discontinuous cycles of engagement, however, would lay the institutional groundwork for an interpretive conversation that, some thirty years later, would address those same issues head on.

Each round of interpretive conversation produced new insights about the possibilities that a relationship might hold for both parties, and each successive batch of insights built on those produced during previous rounds. Eventually, the insights gave rise to institutions, as both Mexican Americans and the Mexican government created formal structures, short-lived though they often were, to support the new conceptual understandings. With each reconnection, both sides marshaled and manipulated the insights to steer the relationship. In the process, the meanings, deployed so strategically, were reinvented and became distinct in important ways from their previous incarnations.

Although the engagement that produced those insights was suspended again and again, with barren stretches between each conversation's end and the political crisis that would impel the government to entertain the next one, memory became the thread that linked the instances of engagement together. Out of memory, an illusion of continuity between the heady moments of exchange was invented. Jane Jacobs asserts that knowledge is fully held only through practice and being in relationship—in the "countless nuances that are assimilated only through experience" (2004: 5)—and she explores what happens when the practice that holds knowledge is discontinued and recedes into memory. She cautions that the knowledge can only be reconstructed, using artifacts, symbols, and writings; it can never.be revived intact. Its reconstruction is determined by the political, historical, cultural, and intellectual context in which the fragments are painstakingly put together. Present practices fill in the gaps left by the practices that were abandoned and thus remained preserved only in memory (Orlikowski 2002).

The insights produced by successive but discontinuous engagement between Mexican Americans and the Mexican government became depictions of the social processes that sparked them rather than an immediate embodiment of them. In other words, although they were conceptual breakthroughs in their own right, the insights to which Mexican bureaucrats and Chicano leaders held fast were in fact only weathered representations of the original insights, faded records of the conversation that produced them. Each time the government reestablished its interpretive engagement with Mexican Americans, both parties revisited those insights and reinterpreted them based on their current political and economic situation, but also on their recollection of what those insights had meant at the moment they were articulated. It was as if the insights were old photographs that both the government and the Mexican Americans were contemplating. The insight was not just a record—a snapshot—of what had transpired at a particular time; it also became a repository for the meanings that they attached to past events and the ramifications that their interpretation of previous interactions would have for future engagements. In this sense, the Mexican government's interpretive engagement with Mexican Americans was built on the practice of rescuing abandoned insights and reviewing them in the light of contemporary political and economic developments (Jacobs 2004). It was this capacity to resuscitate insights and institutions and reinvent them to meet new conditions that would allow a radically different type of interpretive conversation to emerge after 2000: one that explicitly and forthrightly addressed the relationship between Mexican Americans and Mexican migrants, and between interpretive engagement and the development of new sources of political power beyond the control of the PRI.

Reluctant Engagement

The origins of Mexico's current set of policies toward emigrants can be traced back to October 2, 1968. On that evening, only ten days before Mexico was to host the Olympics, government forces opened fire on student protestors holding a rally in the Tlatelolco neighborhood of Mexico City. In what has come to be known as the Tlatelolco massacre, soldiers and plainclothes policemen shot dead at least 50 students, injured over 500, and took almost 2,000 into custody, as residents and bureaucrats from the Secretariat of Foreign Relations watched from their balconies (Braun 1997: 532–33; Turner 1979).[1]

Despite government efforts to suppress information about the massacre, the shots fired in Tlatelolco's Plaza of the Three Cultures reverberated across the border. Chicano students immediately organized protests at the Mexican consulate in Los Angeles. Participants in the emerging Chicano student movement had been meeting informally and corresponding for months with student organizers in Mexico City. Although their engagement was not structured and had produced no definitive agenda, the students felt an intuitive affinity for one another, with Mexican students looking to their Chicano counterparts as natural allies in their drive for the democratization of Mexico and Chicanos turning to the Mexican student movement as a source of cultural identification (Santamaría Gómez 1994: 30–32). Information and disturbing images from the Tlatelolco massacre, unavailable in the sanitized accounts in both the English- and Spanish-language press, flowed freely through the students' social networks.[2] Chicanos heard jarring accounts of students like themselves shot dead in the street or summarily rounded up for questioning and indefinite detention (Santamaría Gómez 1994: 34–35). When Luis Echeverría Alvarez, then internal security minister (secretario de gobernación), traveled to Los Angeles in 1969, only months after the events, Chicano students demanded an interview in which they held him to account for the actions of government security forces (Santamaría Gómez 1994: 38). During this period, the Los Angeles Mexican consular offices also experienced a number of threats, attributed at the time to supporters of the Mexican student movement (Santamaría Gómez 1994: 30–35).

The Tlatelolco massacre acted as a catalyst that strengthened the political relationship between the Chicano and Mexican student movements. In 1969, a newly formed MECHA (Movimiento Estudiantil Chicano de Aztlán) sent its first delegation to Mexico City to meet with Mexican student activists (G. Orozco et al. 2000: 47; Gómez-Quiñones 1990: 119; Santamaría Gómez 1994: 36–37). The students held meetings and conferences on the campus of the Universidad Nacional Autónoma de México (UNAM), the national public university that had been the nucleus of student organizing, but the Chicanos also visited factories, poor urban neighborhoods, and rural areas. Several other visits followed in quick succession; they were, as one Chicano activist recalled, a source for "important political learning" (as quoted in Santamaría Gómez 1994: 39).

Repeated exchanges and discussions between the movements and activists enabled them to articulate a basis for alliance. The activists' reasoning was expressed in many versions, in many different forums, and by a variety of Chicano and Mexican leftist organizations. The most striking formulation was perhaps the "Letter from Lecumberri," written by Mexican student activists held in the Lecumberri prison outside Mexico City and published in *La Raza* magazine, a broadsheet produced by La Raza Unida Party of San Antonio, Texas, on June 25, 1972. According to the letter, the Chicano and Mexican student movements shared a common history and a common struggle against capitalist imperialism in the United States as well as in Mexico. Moreover, Chicanos were part of larger Mexico, which included the area lost to U.S. aggression in 1848:

> The Rio Grande is just a wound in the heart of our peoples and never a barrier that divides us in our common historical inheritance. . . . Chicano is a word that has come to mean the struggle for auto-determination. It's time that the Chicanos should not have to rely solely on their own strength. And the same is true for us. The next revolution will need conscious individuals that understand the need to transform Mexican society. . . . Chicanos, as the part of the Mexican Nation that lives in the belly of the beast, will be some of the most important allies in the march toward victory. (As quoted in Santamaría Gómez 1994: 41–42)

The logic that the student movements articulated provided Chicano activists with a platform from which to challenge Echeverría during their visit to Mexico City in 1970. When Chicano students confronted him about the Mexican government's treatment of the student movement, those in attendance recalled that the then-candidate for president evaded their questions with diplomatic platitudes (Santamaría Gómez 1994: 39–40). Two years later, when President Echeverría traveled to San Antonio, Chicano activists protested the arrest of Mexican political activists and the murder of eleven students and injury of dozens more by paramilitary thugs during a student demonstration on July 10, 1971. Following the protest, the president met with activists and agreed to allow a delegation of Chicanos to enter and monitor conditions in the Lecumberri prison. When he continued on to Los Angeles, he was again met with crowds of Chicano protestors (Santamaría Gómez 1994: 48).

The rationale for the students' transborder collaboration provided Echeverría and his administration with a discursive bridge that enabled him to engage with and co-opt elements of the Chicano movement as part of a larger strategy to distance himself from the "stigma of Tlatelolco" (Shapira 1977). He won the election in 1970 by an alarmingly low margin: with 34 percent of the voters abstaining, 25 percent of the ballots cast annulled, and another 20 percent going to opposition parties, the PRI candidate won by only 21 percent of the popular vote, arguably the lowest margin since the party had institutionalized the Mexican Revolution (Shapira 1977: 566). As soon as Echeverría took office, he launched a number of initiatives, some substantive but most rhetorical, to neutralize the memory of the bloody events of 1968 and to quell the popular unrest that had continued in their wake, especially the urban guerilla movements. The new president declared that his *sexenio*—his six-year term in office—would be a period of *apertura democratica* (democratic opening), a phrase that quickly became the slogan of his presidency. As part of this democratic opening, he took pains to meet with students, absorbing many key figures into the state bureaucracy and appointing new, more progressive, leadership for the National University of Mexico—Universidad Nacional Autónoma de México(UNAM)—while at the same time weakening the institution's resource base (Shapira 1977; Turner 1979: 252; Braun 1997: 131; Zermeño 1993). His administration supported this message with a marked increase in public spending on infrastructure and social services, designed to defuse rebel activity (Lustig 1998: 18). It complemented its domestic policies with an activist foreign policy, largely, as Shapira (1978) argues, as a substitute for fundamental redistributive and democratizing reforms within Mexico. The backbone of Echeverría's foreign policy was a Third Worldist—Tercermundista—stance, which called for the defense of nations against colonial political and economic exploitation. In this context, Mexico called for the reform of the United Nations and forged stronger ties with leftist governments in Latin America as well as with developing countries beyond the Western Hemisphere that adhered to the Non-Aligned Movement (Shapira 1978). As an extension of his Tercermundista politicking, Echeverría began to offer a warmer reception to Chicano activists, embracing their representation of themselves as part of Mexico—and the Third World—within the United States (Corwin 1978: 197–205; J. Gutiérrez 1986; A. Gutiérrez 1986: 49; de la Garza 1986).

Echeverría's engagement with Chicano leaders was primarily interpretive in its quality, as both the Mexican administration and the Chicano groups sought to develop conceptual bases to support their continued involvement (J. Gutiérrez 1986: 33). The rationale that the Mexican government and Chicanos articulated for their relationship during this early stage provided the logic around which the government would structure its engagement with Chicanos—and, more important, with Mexican migrants—in the decades to come. During the Echeverría administration, however, the government addressed the issue of emigration and emigrant needs with an arm's-length approach in which the state tightly controlled the meanings associated with emigration.

Beginning an Engagement: The Echeverría Administration (1971–76)

The Echeverría administration's engagement with Chicano leaders began in 1971. Late that year, a conference on Chicanos was organized in Mexico, and Echeverría met with a handful of high-profile Chicano leaders, including Reies López Tijerina, who had spearheaded the land-grant struggle in New Mexico; José Angel Gutiérrez, founder of La Raza Unida Party; and the renowned Chicano film director Jesús Salvador Treviño (A. Gutiérrez 1986: 50; Santamaría Gómez 1994: 54).[3] Out of that meeting emerged several tentative efforts at collaboration. The Mexican government pledged funding for the production of two films with strong Chicano content that would target a Mexican audience and educate it about the conditions of Mexican Americans in *México de afuera*. The administration also promised to fund fifty scholarships for Chicano students to study medicine at Mexico's public universities, training them to serve as doctors in Chicano communities, to provide funds for Chicano cultural events and conferences, and to donate Spanish-language books for student libraries in the American Southwest (A. Gutiérrez 1986: 50; Santamaría Gómez 1994: 54; G. Orozco 2001; Bustamante 1986: 16–17). The following year, Echeverría began to formalize the relationship with Chicano groups by naming Jorge Bustamante, then a newly minted Ph.D. who had just completed a dissertation on Mexican migration to the United States, as the official liaison between his administration and Mexican Americans (Bustamante 1986; Mindiola and Martinez 1986; A. Gutiérrez 1986). Over the next several years, Bustamante organized a series of meetings, in Mexico as well as in the United States, between Chicano leaders and intellectuals and Echeverría and his administration (Bustamante 1986; A. Gutiérrez 1986). Echeverría also supported the founding of the Mexican Cultural Institute in San Antonio (Santamaría Gómez 1994: 54).

The engagement was often complicated and delicate, and the conversations fraught with misunderstanding, miscommunication, and confusion. Two main factors contributed to this taxing, but ultimately generative, ambiguity. The first was the social distance between the Mexican government and Chicanos, which made their relations "terra incognita," as Armando Gutiérrez, a Chicano leader who participated in the exchanges, put it (1986: 50). This distance had its roots in the massive repatriation of Mexican workers from the United States during the Depression, which had put an end to the consular activism embraced by the revolutionary Mexican government. In the 1930s, after several decades of advocating for the rights of Mexican workers, intervening in labor disputes, organizing Mexican and Mexican American community groups, and sponsoring cultural events to promote a sense of Mexicanidad (Mexican national identity), "the role of the consulates in defending the interests of Mexican expatriates and in providing limited leadership in the Chicano community was scaled back and forgotten" (Zazueta 1983, as quoted in Sherman 1999: 843). The Mexican state embraced the principle of nonintervention and officially eschewed responsibility for working and living conditions beyond its borders. By the 1970s, after forty years of disengagement, the Mexican government and Mexican Americans had become strangers (A. Gutiérrez 1986; J. Gutiérrez 1968). Mexican bureaucrats displayed a chronic nescience of the conditions under which Mexican Americans lived and worked, of their political aspirations, and of their social and cultural identities. They viewed Chicanos as primarily agricultural workers, due in part to the publicity that César Chávez and the United Farm Workers movement had received, even though an estimated 90 percent of Mexican Americans lived and worked in urban settings (Bustamante 1986: 90). Other misconceptions were more pernicious: as numerous Chicano participants in the conversations with the Mexican state have attested, Mexican Americans were disparaged as lower-class *pachucos* or *ponchos*, who knew only a bastardized version of Mexican culture and had little in common with the elites who staffed the Mexican governmental bureaucracy (Bustamante 1986; de la Garza 1980: 575; A. Gutiérrez 1986; J. Gutiérrez 1968; Shain 1999). A former bureaucrat under Echeverría colorfully summarized the perception of many bureaucrats: "[People thought:] look at him, so Mexican—*con el nopal en la frente*—coming here speaking English in all his conceit" (Fundación Solidaridad Mexicano Americana interview, Mexico City, July 2003).

Chicano leaders and activists brought their own set of misapprehensions to the discussions. Many arrived with only a rudimentary understanding of Mexican politics and the inner workings of the Mexican bureaucracy, to say nothing of the tensions and power struggles within the PRI. Often the activists had only a vague sense of where they and their petitions fit within the Mexican political landscape (Santamaría Gómez 1994: 30–60). Reflecting on the pilgrimages made by Chicano activists during the 1970s, Rodolfo O. de la Garza, a Chicano intellectual who participated in the meetings of that period, observed, "Chicanos often go to Mexico expecting to find themselves but come away instead understanding that being Chicano is not being Mexicano" (de la Garza 1980: 575). A former staffer in Echeverría's Office of the President who was charged with receiving Chicano leaders remembered how this mutual misunderstanding infused the exchanges with confusion and ambiguity, even suspicion.

In the 1970s, after forty years of neglect—*olvido*, the government began to receive Mexican American activists, who, for the most part, came to Mexico without specific proposals or demands, looking instead for a kind of moral support for their struggle in the U.S. for their human rights after the struggle initiated by the African Americans. We forgot them for forty years . . . but [during that time] they didn't come to seek us out either. The 1970s . . . that was the first time that they came to seek us out, the first time Mexican American leaders came to Mexico.

They knocked on doors at Los Pinos, at different offices of the government, and let me repeat, they didn't have a clear proposal. Since there hadn't been this relationship of *acercamiento* [rapprochement], they came with this desire to connect with their roots, to find their homeland. In reality, sometimes all they asked for was a flag—that simple—just a flag. And the authorities at that time, which was when Echeverría was president, well, they viewed them with a lot of surprise and even suspicion, to say the least. "What do they want? How can we possibly help them? Be careful, they are a cell of activists, they could create problems for us with the gringos." And, as you can imagine, that relationship is one that we have to treat with a lot of care. So, we approached them with our claws out, as we say here. And we didn't understand at all what was happening with [the Chicanos], what they were going through. (Fundación Solidaridad Mexicano Americana interview, Mexico City, July 2003)

The lengthy estrangement was not the only factor that fostered misunderstanding. The second cause was the multiplicity of political orientations among Chicano groups. In his dealings with the Chicano movement, the Mexican president showed a marked preference for José Angel Gutiérrez and Reies López Tijerina (Bustamante 1986). Nevertheless, his government received Chicano leaders representing a wide spectrum of political strategies and beliefs, from radical grassroots community organizers with ties to guerrilla movements in Mexico to staid political lobbyists with connections in Washington (Santamaría Gómez 1994: 30–66; Bustamante 1986). This cacophony of voices was matched by the differences of opinion in the Mexican government about the value of extending a warm welcome to Chicano groups. Certainly, there was a quorum of advocates in the government for continued engagement, many of them concentrated in the Office of the President (Bustamante 1986; Fundación Solidaridad Mexicano Americana interview, Mexico City, July 2003). In other parts of the administration, however, especially the Secretariat of Foreign Relations (SRE), officials expressed unequivocal reluctance to engage (de la Garza 1980). As one Mexican academic who had been involved in the implementation of initiatives for Chicanos in 1978 noted, "Mexican officials never thought Chicanos could be important and interesting to Mexico, and there are maybe only five who think so today" (as quoted in de la Garza 1980: 572).

Emerging Insights: Common Cause and Possibilities for Political Collaboration

The ongoing engagement of the Echeverría administration with Chicano groups brought to the surface several insights about areas of common cause. They articulated a mutual recognition of political interrelatedness that embraced Chicano activists' view of themselves as a colonized part of the Third World within the United States, a view that had been formulated in the late 1960s by student activists. The alliance between the Chicano student movement and Mexican leftist activists that the Mexican state had actively repressed had evolved into a political compact between these Chicano groups and the Mexican government itself. *Caracol*, an influential Chicano publication from San Antonio (Palomo Acosta 2005), summarized the emergence of this new relationship: "We have also finally achieved, and this is probably the most important point (declared publicly by the President of Mexico), Mexico's recognition that Chicanos are a colony within the United States and that they are part of the Third World. This has already been published and Echeverría admitted that there is [a people] called Chicano and that we are oppressed" (*Caracol*, November 1975, as quoted in Santamaría Gómez 1994: 60).

Out of this shared understanding, new possibilities for collaboration began to emerge. Chicano activists began to view their involvement with the Mexican government as a source of leverage in their negotiations with the U.S. federal and state governments. Chicano leaders enjoyed unprecedented access to high-level government officials in Mexico, including Echeverría himself, and benefited from ample coverage by the Mexican press of their visits to Mexico and their political endeavors in the United States—access and visibility that they largely lacked at that time in the United States. As José Angel Gutiérrez noted, "Chicanos appear more frequently in the corridors of power in Mexico than they do in the U.S." (J. Gutiérrez 1986: 26). The ease with which Chicano groups could gain audiences with the Echeverría administration gave their agendas a new level of visibility and legitimacy on both sides of the border, an advantage for community organizing as well as for pressing their demands on the U.S. government (J. Gutiérrez 1986: 27; Shain 1999; de la Garza 1986). Gutiérrez offered a succinct but powerful statement on the resource that access to the Mexican government represented for them:

Los chicanos no deberían voltear hacia Wall Street o Washington para encontrar su destino. Nuestro destino es el sur con un pueblo como nosotros. . . . Nosotros somos una familia sin fronteras, somos una familia sin huérfanos. I'll remind you in case you've forgotten que no somos hijos de la Inmaculada Concepción nor of the statue of Liberty. Somos hijos de mexicanos.

[Chicanos should not look to Wall Street or Washington to find their destiny. Our destiny is to the south with a people like us. . . . We are a family without borders, we are a family without orphans. I'll remind you in case you've forgotten that we are not the sons of the Immaculate Conception or of the Statue of Liberty. We are sons of Mexicans.][4]

A parallel insight began to emerge in the halls of the Mexican Office of the President. Members of the administration began to identify Chicanos as a potential source of political influence that could be brought to bear on U.S. policies toward Mexico. As one staffer recalls, her engagement with Chicano leaders enabled her to discern their strength as community leaders and the political opportunities that this strength could represent for the Mexican state: "I had the opportunity to meet with very important [Chicano] leaders . . . and I started to see the potential of collaborating with them" (Fundación Solidaridad Mexicano Americana interview, Mexico City, July 2003). The analogy that was raised was Israel, which had organized a powerful lobby with considerable sway on U.S. policies in the Middle East (A. Gutiérrez 1986; Shain 1999). Nevertheless, the commitment to Chicanos as a political arm of the Mexican state was still embryonic during Echeverría's sexenio and treated by most with a heavy dose of skepticism. The same staffer explained: "[Chicano leaders] represented a community that was beginning to stand out in the United States, with a unique proposal for their futures, looking for their own spaces, claiming their own territory politically, economically and socially. So I thought, well, this is fabulous. And the reference is always the obvious one: what Israel has accomplished, with all of the obvious and very marked differences, of course. Everyone thought I was crazy, and now I am a visionary. Going from crazy to visionary in one lifetime is a big accomplishment" (Fundación Solidaridad Mexicano Americana interview, Mexico City, July 2003).

Modest electoral gains by Mexican Americans in the 1970s and the extension of the protection of the 1965 Voting Rights Act to Latino voters in 1975 slowly lent credence to the view that Chicanos, and the Chicano movement in particular, displayed the potential to develop into a forceful organized constituency that would be responsive to Mexican interests, and that, more important, the U.S. government would no longer be able to ignore (A. Gutiérrez 1986: 48–49).

Difference and Discord: PRI Political Control and Mexican Emigration

While the engagement between Chicano groups and the Mexican government mapped out areas of common ground, the discussion also brought differences into perspective and ambition into stark relief. The first area of discord arose around the critical remarks that several Chicano leaders directed at the PRI, denouncing its authoritarian tactics and publicly questioning whether, by engaging with the Mexican state, Chicanos were not legitimizing these regressive policies—policies that, as they were careful to point out, had led to the hemisphere's most unequal distribution of wealth (de la Garza 1986: 41). Some were trenchant in their criticism of the interaction between Chicanos and the Mexican state. Rodolfo "Corky" Gonzalez, for example, excoriated the cofounder of La Raza Unida Party, José Angel Gutiérrez, for "support of a fascist Mexican government and a betrayal of the Mexican people" (Acuña, 1981, as quoted in de la Garza 1986: 40). The Echeverría administration, somewhat baffled at the Chicano groups' resistance to co-optation, bristled at such blunt critiques and progressively began to exclude Chicanos identified as critical of the government from participation in the dialogue (de la Garza 1986: 39).

The second area of contention was both more sensitive and more intrinsic to national interests on both sides. Discussions between the Echeverría administration and Chicano groups revealed that they were in fundamental disagreement over Mexican emigration policy. The administration began its sexenio by exploring the possibility, with the U.S. government, of resuscitating the bracero program. The moment for such negotiations seemed propitious: due to the sheer number of immigrants crossing the border without legal work permits, the phenomenon was emerging as a public policy concern for the United States. In 1972, U.S. border patrols made 430,000 apprehensions of undocumented immigrants, compared with the 55,000 apprehensions made in 1965.[5] Proposals to curtail illegal entry and apply sanctions on employers hiring immigrants who lacked work permits began circulating in the U.S. Congress (Corwin 1978: 197). As U.S. nativist sentiment seemed to be on an upsurge, Echeverría announced in 1973 that his administration would push hard for an agreement on labor emigration to afford Mexican workers protection from zealous border enforcement and egregious exploitation (Cornelius 1981; Corwin 1978: 78).

Mired in the Watergate scandal, the Nixon administration ignored Echeverría's proposals (Corwin 1978: 78), but Chicano groups noticed and expressed vociferous opposition. Unions involved in farm labor organizing drives, like the United Farm Workers, were joined by a host of Chicano groups registering their explicit disapproval with both the Mexican and U.S. governments. La Raza Unida held a formal meeting with the Echeverría administration to reiterate its rejection of a new bracero program and to lay out the minimal conditions under which it would refrain from launching a massive protest against the initiative. According to the organization's summary of the meeting, they sought guarantees to protect working conditions for those workers who were already across the border: "We had an interview with the Minister of Foreign Relations in Mexico and with Echeverría to voice our opposition to his policy with regard to the braceros. We are unconditionally opposed to a Bracero Program. We would only accept an agreement under the following conditions: 1) Mexican workers would have to have their own union or they would have to join our unions. . . . 2) Chicanos would have the right to veto such a program" (*Caracol*, November 1975, as quoted in Santamaría Gómez 1994: 58n25).

Ultimately, the negotiations between the Mexican and U.S. governments failed because the latter, destabilized by Watergate, was unable to withstand the pressure applied by organized labor. The quota of workers that the United States proposed was merely symbolic when compared to actual levels of undocumented Mexican immigration—a paltry 20,000 work contracts, when the number of Mexicans apprehended entering illegally had, by 1974, topped 700,000 (Corwin 1978: 198–201). The rhetoric that the Echeverría government adopted in the wake of the negotiations' collapse reflected its engagement with Chicano groups. In his State of the Union address to the Mexican Congress in 1974, following meetings with the Ford administration, Echeverría expounded the reasons Mexico did not sign a labor export agreement:

Concern for the dignity of man has impelled us to take a decided stand on the serious problem of migration of undocumented Mexican workers. . . . Today, in the highest tribunal of Mexico, we protest strongly the flagrant violation of human rights and the attempts against the life and dignity of our compatriots, who deserve the respect accorded to human beings by every civilized society, regardless of such formal considerations as those involved in their immigration status. . . .

We reject the idea of a new migrant worker agreement, for such agreements have never succeeded in preventing undocumented immigration in the past. The history of such agreements since the time of the Second World War shows us that quotas, far from solving the problem, have aggravated it. (Echeverría 1979: 125–26)

He added, "the solution to the migrant farm worker program is dependent on our own efforts . . . through the accelerated creation of jobs in agriculture and in industry" (1979: 125). During the remainder of his administration, Echeverría promulgated a series of measures designed to do precisely that, including an increase in spending on rural economic development and a population law devised to promote family planning (Corwin 1978: 189–99; Lustig 1998).

Throughout the negotiations over a new bracero arrangement, the Echeverría administration consulted neither with groups representing Mexican migrants nor with local governments representing migrants' communities of origin. In contrast to its engagement with Chicano groups, the state adopted a distinctly arm's-length approach to emigration. In 1972, the Mexican government created an interagency commission, Comisión Intersecretarial para Estudio del Problema de la Emigración Subrepticia de Trabajadores Mexicanos en los Estados Unidos, charged with researching the causes and consequences of undocumented migration. The commission's main findings, delivered in 1974, were twofold: first, that emigration had a significant impact on rural communities in central western Mexico, which had received the lion's share of the estimated $1 billion in annual migrant remittances sent home in the early 1970s; and second, that most emigration was temporary, with migrants returning to Mexico after a period, and that U.S. analysts had therefore overestimated the dimensions of the phenomenon (Corwin 1978: 198–99). In light of the commission's conclusions, and faced with political opposition from Chicano groups and their allies in Mexico, including the powerful Confederación de Trabajadores Mexicanos (CTM), binational consultations for a labor export agreement were shelved (Corwin 1978: 202; Shapira 1977).

The Echeverría administration's heavy public investment, combined with a resolute defense of the value of the peso in the context of the oil shocks of the mid-1970s and capital flight, produced a serious deficit in Mexico's balance of payments. By 1976, the government, having depleted its currency reserves, was forced to let the peso float. The currency quickly lost 40 percent of its value, and Mexico seemed destined for a serious recession (Lustig 1998; Santín Quiroz 2001). The discovery of oil, however, confirmed during the first year of López Portillo's sexenio (1976–82), meant that the government quickly shifted from the management of economic crisis to the "management of abundance" (*administración de la abundancia*), as the new president called it (Santín Quiroz 2001: 62), and ramped up its public expenditures dramatically (Lustig 1998; Santín Quiroz 2001). Managing the newfound abundance also involved managing Mexico's relationship with the main consumer of the oil and gas it produced: the United States (Meyer 1983). Throughout the López Portillo sexenio, the relationship between the neighbors was often strained. Sources of tension ranged from U.S. trade barriers to Mexico's foreign policy in Latin America, but central among them remained the question of undocumented Mexican migration (Vásquez and García y Griego 1983; Bustamante 1983). The progressive worsening of relations led the Mexican government to turn to its connections with Chicano groups as a source of political leverage. The López Portillo administration flirted with the notion of Chicanos acting as a lobby for Mexican interests and, to that end, created an official body to institutionalize Chicano interactions with the Mexican state. The government's attempts to control the engagement by formalizing it ultimately suffocated it, however, and marked the end of a rich period of interpretive interaction with Mexican Americans.

Bilateral Tensions and Chicano Offers of Help

In the summer of 1977, the U.S. government took unilateral steps to deal with the flow of Mexican migration. On August 4, President Carter sent a proposal to Congress, laying out plans for an amnesty program for migrants who had been in the United States since 1970, coupled with sanctions on employers who hired undocumented immigrants and an enhanced border patrol (Carter 1979). By August 7, a quarter of a million Mexicans from their country's interior had massed at Tijuana, determined to cross over to the United States before the amnesty plan went into effect.[6] Tijuana, a city of under a million inhabitants, was overwhelmed: "[migrants] beg on the streets . . . without lodging, food, or hope of public welfare [in this] congested, economically depressed city . . . [where] the unemployment rate exceeds forty percent," reported a dispatch for the *New York Times* (Holles 1977). Mindful of its "special relationship" with the United States, the López Portillo government limited itself to expressing "dismay" at the Carter proposals and the fact that they had been released without prior consultation with his administration (Riding 1977a).[7] (One Mexican analyst was blunter: "If we depend on American financing, if we depend on the United States buying our oil and our tomatoes, just how much choice do we have—just how much can we complain?" [as quoted in Riding 1977a].) In subsequent negotiations, the López Portillo administration pointed out repeatedly that so long as the United States refused to dismantle protectionist barriers against Mexican agricultural and manufactured products and insisted on purchasing gas from Mexico at below-market rates, Mexico would remain dependent on the "escape valve" that emigration represented to alleviate the pressure of high levels of unemployment (Riding 1977b, 1978).[8]

A delegation of Chicano leaders traveled to Mexico City in early 1978 to offer support to the government. The group, made up of familiar faces in the Chicano movement such as José Angel Gutiérrez from La Raza Unida and Eduardo Morga from LULAC, as well as new representatives from organizations solidly established in Washington political circles such as the National Council of La Raza, came to offer a united front against the Carter immigration control initiatives. "We are unanimously opposed to the Carter Plan," declared Gutiérrez. Eduardo Morga clarified that they had come to proffer support as an organized lobby. "We've never before told Mexico that we are all ready to help Mexico in the United States. We feel that in the future Mexico can use us as Israel uses American Jews, as Italy uses Italian-Americans, and so on. . . . [With 16 million Mexican Americans], we are just beginning to realize our potential strength." López Portillo responded with general encouragement of their efforts and a vague promise that should the U.S. and Mexican governments enter into formal deliberations over a labor export agreement, "Mexican-Americans would be represented on the Mexican negotiating team." He attached a caveat to his comments, however, emphasizing that he had "no intention of interfering in the internal affairs of the United States" (all quoted in *New York Times* 1978). López Portillo hedged his enthusiasm for the Chicano effort in part because his administration had contemplated using concessions around U.S. border control and immigration as a bargaining chip in its tortuous negotiations with its northern neighbor over a more favorable oil agreement (de la Garza 1980). As one Mexican analyst trenchantly observed in 1978, "the Mexican government may accept conditions which Chicanos wouldn't accept" (as quoted in de la Garza 1980: 573).

As deliberations over the sale of Mexican oil dragged on, Mexico's relationship with the United States continued to sour: a frustrated López Portillo declared that "Mexico is neither on the list of United States priorities nor on that of United States respect" (October 13, as quoted in Binder 1978). In the hope of improving the degenerating situation, he took the Chicano delegation up on its offer and drew on the connections that his predecessor had forged with Chicano leaders. In contrast to the engagement under the Echeverría administration, however, the López Portillo government sought to exercise control over the conversations. It strove to mold a haphazard series of interactions with a wide spectrum of Chicano groups into a disciplined lobby that could, in fact, influence the U.S. government (A. Gutiérrez 1986: 33n26). As one official in the López Portillo administration surmised, "President López Portillo [did] not want to develop relations with [Chicanos] until it [was] clear how each [could] help the other" (as quoted in de la Garza 1980: 578). To create that clarity and build a cogent political lobby, the administration narrowed the thematic scope of the conversations and carefully vetted the participants. Jorge Bustamante, chief architect of Echeverría's style of engagement with Chicanos, observed, "López Portillo preferred a new type of Chicano leader, one better suited to the political process of training public officials or representatives of legitimate organizations supported by foundations of national importance" (Bustamante 1986: 16), and the president's administration took pains to invite more moderate Chicano and Mexican American organizations to the table (Bustamante 1986; A. Gutiérrez 1986).

Disciplining Engagement: The Creation of the Hispanic Commission

To systematize the consultations between Chicanos and the Mexican state, the López Portillo government institutionalized their interactions. The administration took a request from Chicano groups for a formal legation in Mexico City and recast it as the Comisión Mixta de Enlace, or the Hispanic Commission, as it was called in English, in 1979. Although the word *Chicano* was glaringly absent from the commission's title, this group was designated to represent Chicanos in their discussions with the Mexican state (Santamaría Gómez 1994: 69, 80; A. Gutiérrez 1986: 54; G. Orozco 2001). Membership was confined to a permanent list of ten organizations, nine Chicano and one Puerto Rican. Only two of the Chicano organizations had strong grassroots traditions, with most of the remainder heavily dependent on foundation funding or the Catholic Church. Groups that had been very active in the relationship under Echeverría, like La Raza Unida Party, were excluded from the new body (J. Gutiérrez 1986: 29–32; A. Gutiérrez 1986: 55).[9] Moreover, the commission was relegated to the portfolio of the secretary of labor, Pedro Ojeda Paulada, moving engagement with the Chicano community out of the Office of the President, perhaps reflecting the president's lingering ambivalence. Furthermore, López Portillo transferred responsibility for managing the relationship from Bustamante, a dynamic proponent of engagement with a spectrum of Chicano organizations and intellectuals, to Guido Belasso, a career bureaucrat with a much more conservative view of the possibilities a Chicano lobby represented for Mexico (A. Gutiérrez 1986: 55). Chicano groups barred from the commission watched with dismay as López Portillo and his administration publicly dismissed their petitions for support in U.S. civil rights struggles (de la Garza 1980: 577).[10]

The relationship with Chicanos that the commission was designed to embody was reinforced through the extension of diplomatic gestures to Mexican Americans. López Portillo broadened his predecessor's scholarship program for Chicanos in Mexican universities and maintained the distribution of educational materials for American schools with large Mexican American student populations. Additionally, the secretary of education designed a summer course to train North American teachers in bilingual education (G. Orozco 2001).

These symbolic programs were not enough to keep the relationship from fraying.[11] Once the López Portillo administration institutionalized the conversations, the interactions lost the unscripted nature that made them so generative of insight. By reining in the content of the discussions and directing them to serve interests that were more narrowly those of the Mexican government, the administration sapped them of the vitality that had made them compelling to Chicano activists in the first place. Shortly after its creation, the commission morphed into a largely ceremonial expression of the relationship (A. Gutiérrez 1986: 55). The commission did not once meet with the Mexican president and was defunct by the end of López Portillo's sexenio (J. Gutiérrez 1986: 32).

Ultimately, López Portillo did not call on the commission to act as a lobby for Mexican interests in the United States or to influence North American policies toward Mexican emigrants. Instead, the government largely evaded the issue by retreating behind its principle of noninterference in the domestic affairs of other nations (Corwin 1978; Santamaría Gómez 1994). As the Carter and later the Reagan administrations floated a series of proposals to control Mexican immigration, all of which involved some combination of border militarization and the apportioning of a very limited number of work contracts, the López Portillo administration refrained from commenting publicly (Riding 1977a; Crewdson 1978; Pear 1981a, 1981c). (The only comment that López Portillo ever made regarding U.S. migration proposals was that he was "very intrigued" by a Reagan plan to legalize circular migration from Mexico, enabling migrants to work in the United States seasonally [Pear 1981b].) The López Portillo administration, however, also evoked judicial principle, refusing to continue transporting Mexican migrants, whom the U.S. border patrol had caught trying to cross illegally and had unceremoniously delivered back across the border, to the Mexican interior. The Mexican government thereby withdrew its material and moral support for U.S. border control (Santamaría Gómez 1994: 92–93). López Portillo declared that "Mexico is not a prison for its population" (as quoted in Corwin 1978: 210), and Jorge Castañeda, named secretary of foreign relations in 1979, asserted shortly after assuming his post that "Mexico can neither constitutionally, nor politically, nor judicially, nor morally, control the movement of Mexicans within and beyond its borders" (as quoted in Santamaría Gómez 1994: 92).

The López Portillo government, just like the Echeverría administration before it, engaged neither with the migrants who left for work in the United States nor with the communities they supported with their remittances. Instead, it adopted, once again, an arm's-length approach. In 1977, the government commissioned a follow-up study on undocumented migration to the United States. This study was much more extensive than the research ordered under Echeverría: approximately 150,000 surveys were conducted, at the border as well as in migrants' communities of origin (G. Orozco 2001; Riding 1980). But the findings, released in 1980, were consistent with the previous investigation: the magnitude of undocumented migration had been significantly overblown, as had the quantity of the remittances sent back to Mexico (Riding 1980).[12] The government's study lent credence to its reticent posture on migration questions and its continued underfunding and understaffing of its consular offices in the United States. In a further reflection of the state's reluctant attention to emigration, the detailed results of the study were never released, and when the administration of the office running the investigation—the National Commission on Population (CONAPO)—changed at the end of the López Portillo sexenio, the documentation of the survey was lost (Fundación Solidaridad Mexicano Americana interview, Mexico City, July 2003).

Transnational Labor Organizing: Emergent Conversations

The López Portillo administration's passive attitude toward emigration and, more specifically, toward the working conditions to which undocumented migrants were often subjected opened a vacuum that labor organizations on both sides of the border moved to fill. Ironically, the Carter and Reagan immigration proposals and Chicano mobilization against them brought increased public—and press—attention to the discrimination and exploitation experienced by Mexican workers and their families in the United States. Organizations ranging from the Mexican American Legal Defense Fund (MALDEF) to the more radical (and now defunct) Centro de Acción Social Autónoma (CASA) mobilized against insults such as indiscriminate and overly zealous U.S. Immigration and Naturalization Service (INS) roundups of Mexicans and Mexican Americans suspected of being in the United States illegally, and the lack of educational access for workers' children, regardless of their parents' legal status (Santamaría Gómez 1994: 86–97; Gómez-Quiñones 1990; Zazueta 1983). Chicano labor activists also began organizing undocumented Mexican workers in earnest; efforts by the UFW were joined by smaller drives by the International Ladies' Garment Workers' Union and the United Electrical Workers (Santamaría Gómez 1994: 86–97; Gómez-Quiñones 1990: 166–67). In response, some Mexican labor unions, including the Sindicato de Telefonistas (STRM) and the Central Independiente de Obreros Agrícolas y Campesinos (CIOAC), issued formal statements in defense of the rights of their co-nationals across the border. The STRM, for example, declared at its 1978 convention that "the human rights of migrant workers in the United States should stop being violated" and called for a national union drive in solidarity with migrants (as quoted in Santamaría Gómez 1994: 96). In 1980, ten U.S. and Mexican unions—including the United Auto Workers, the International Ladies' Garment Workers' Union, the STRM, and the CIOAC—congregated in Tlatelolco, Mexico City, for a binational convention on protecting the rights of Mexican migrant workers in the United States (Santamaría Gómez 1994: 97–98).

The unprecedented transnational mobilization launched by this event lost momentum fairly quickly, largely because of the decline of U.S. unions under Reagan, argues Santamaría Gómez (1994). The meeting between U.S. and Mexican unions in Mexico's capital, however, established leftist networks and set new conversations in motion that would come back to haunt the PRI in presidential elections less than a decade later, when the electoral dominance of the ruling party came under serious attack by a leftist coalition headed by a PRI defector, Cuauhtémoc Cárdenas.

The End of a Conversation: De la Madrid (1982–88)

By the end of his sexenio, it had become clear that López Portillo's gamble to stake Mexico's economic fortunes on newly discovered oil reserves had been a tragic miscalculation. As the price for crude began to drop in 1981, López Portillo's program of massive public spending, funded by oil revenues and significant international borrowing, began to fall apart. By 1982, Mexico was facing its worst economic crisis since the Great Depression.[13] Inflation surpassed 100 percent and was still rising; economic activity ground to a halt, with the economy registering a negative growth rate. Unemployment doubled, the peso lost most of its value in a matter of months, and the public deficit skyrocketed to almost 20 percent of GDP. The López Portillo administration suspended payment on the principal of its $80 billion foreign debt and nationalized the banking system. Miguel de la Madrid inherited an economy in shambles (Chand 2001: 25–31; Lustig 1998; Migdail 1987: 116–18).

The new president was compelled to embark immediately on a course of radical economic restructuring, including two brutal rounds of IMF-ordered structural adjustment programs. Under the mandate of fiscal austerity, public spending was slashed, with expenditures on health, education, and nutrition reduced by over one-third. Myriad government programs were discontinued or vigorously pruned (Lustig 1998; Santín Quiroz 2001; Migdail 1987: 116–18). The government's engagement with Chicanos was no exception. De la Madrid suspended the conversations with Mexican Americans that had, under his predecessor, grown stilted and routine, and he drastically reduced the Mexican state's cultural outreach to the Chicano community (G. Orozco 2001; Santamaría Gómez 1994: 111–28). Furthermore, government treatment of Mexican migrants remained skeletal; despite heroic efforts by certain individual consuls (most notably the consul in Los Angeles), consular protection of exploited migrants was stripped to the bare minimum. No new major studies of Mexican emigration were commissioned (G. Orozco 2001; Santamaría Gómez 1994: 111–28).

De la Madrid's sexenio, however, marked a crucial turning point for Mexican state policy toward emigrants, for three reasons. First, the state, through occasions as formal as presidential speeches, explicitly recognized the potential of Mexican Americans as a lobby; under de la Madrid, the Mexican state embraced the view extended by Chicano activists throughout the 1970s that they could serve as a lever with which Mexico could influence U.S. political outcomes (A. Gutiérrez 1986; Santamaría Gómez 1994). Second, during these years, the United States implemented a major amnesty program, known as the 1986 Immigration Reform and Control Act, which within the span of a few months changed the status of literally millions of Mexican migrants, giving them the legal right to live and work in the United States (Bean et al. 1998). Their new standing allowed them to emerge from the shadows, to organize, and eventually to petition—forcefully—both the U.S. government and, more significantly, the Mexican state for their political rights (Valdes 1995; Dresser 1993; Fitzgerald

2004). The Mexican government had no choice but to take notice. The reasons had to do with the third shift over which de la Madrid presided, no doubt unhappily, during his sexenio. The prolonged economic paroxysm that gripped Mexico for close to a decade also shook the PRI's monopolistic hold on power, galvanizing opposition and setting in motion a wave of politicization that would have ramifications well into the next millennium (Chand 2001; Shirk 2005).

Envisioning a Mexican Lobby in the United States

When de la Madrid was nominated as the PRI's candidate for the presidency, he was virtually unknown in Chicano political circles. Apart from a couple of brief visits to San Antonio and Los Angeles as the official representative of the López Portillo administration, he did not have much exposure to Mexican Americans or Mexican migrants. He reached out, however, to Bustamante, the erstwhile Mexican government liaison to Chicano groups, and asked him to lay out a plan for campaign outreach to Mexican Americans. Bustamante planned three meetings for him, with the participation of Chicano organizations and Chicano intellectuals. In keeping with the preferences made clear under López Portillo, no left-of-center groups were invited (A. Gutiérrez 1986: 56–58; Santamaría Gómez 1994: 111–14).

The first meeting was held in Mexico City on March 3, 1982, as the country was tumbling into economic crisis. The future president told "friends from the Mexican-American community and from Chicano organizations" that he would, in his administration, foster the development of a relationship "that is more systematic, closer, more profound than has emerged to date" (as quoted in Santamaría Gómez 1994: 111–12). Conceding that "we Mexicans have perhaps not had the energy, nor perhaps the possibility, nor have we paid the attention required to establish the mechanisms for communication, for dialogue, and for engagement with you" (as quoted in Santamaría Gómez 1994: 112), de la Madrid was emphatic in his insistence that "this meeting . . . should above all else be understood as a reaffirmation of the willingness of the Partido Revolucionario Institucional and its candidate to the Presidency of Mexico, to fortify, expand, and systematize these linkages, which, having as their base history and sentiment, can evolve into forms of cooperation even more dynamic and positive" (as quoted in A. Gutiérrez 1986: 56), intimating that these forms of cooperation would be part of a policy toward the United States that would be less defensive and "more dynamic, more responsible, and more active" (as quoted in Santamaría Gómez 1994: 112). At his subsequent meeting with Chicano intellectuals and organizations in April in Ciudad Juárez, de la Madrid noted that even cultural programs should be viewed as part of Mexico's strategy to defend the rights of Mexican Americans, because "to reaffirm their cultural identity and the solidarity produced within these communities . . . gives both of us more leverage in the process of social and political negotiation in the

United States" (as quoted in A. Gutiérrez 1986: 57). Thus he explicitly appropriated Chicano views of their organizations and communities as a potential lobby that could sway the United States' policy toward its southern neighbor.

Despite the candidate's enthusiastic pronouncements, however, the third planned meeting was never held. The final engagement, between de la Madrid and Chicano activists and journalists, was scheduled to take place in October immediately following the president-elect's audience with President Reagan. After the appointment with Reagan, the slated meeting with Chicanos was scuttled. In its stead, a gathering that included de la Madrid and a handful of Mexican American scholars was hastily convened. The improvised session would be the last time de la Madrid would meet with Mexican Americans during his administration (A. Gutiérrez 1986: 56–58; J. Gutiérrez 1986: 34). The formal explanation for suspending discussions was the resource constraints that the government confronted as the nation's economic difficulties escalated (J. Gutiérrez 1986: 34). Without a doubt, budgetary contraction made it financially difficult and politically untenable to dedicate funds to a dialogue with Chicanos and the cultural programs that supported it (G. Orozco 2001).

The economic crisis also generated political pressure from the U.S. government to snuff out Mexico's reemerging engagement with Mexican Americans (Santamaría Gómez 1994: 114; Castañeda, as cited in Santamaría Gómez 1994: 114n3). As early as 1978, ex-CIA director William Colby vocalized conservative opposition to the relationship when he warned that Mexican emigration was "a silent invasion" likely to represent a greater threat to the United States than the Soviet Union, because it could give rise to a separatist movement in the Southwest (Bustamante 1983: 318; Santamaría Gómez 1994: 123). In the months before de la Madrid took office, thirty-five U.S. congressional representatives sent a letter to President Reagan communicating their alarm at the state of affairs in Mexico: "The increasing instability in Mexico could potentially lead to a communist take-over unless the United States takes appropriate action to ensure that . . . president elect Miguel de la Madrid does not continue the socialist program initiated by the two previous administrations" (sent in September 1982, as quoted in Santamaría Gómez 1994: 129).

In response, the Reagan administration and its newly appointed ambassador to Mexico, John Gavin, offered friendly advice to the de la Madrid administration that the Mexican government should desist from political engagement with Chicano groups in the United States (Santamaría Gómez 1994: 114).

Changing Migration Patterns and the Immigration Reform and Control Act

The same economic vulnerability that made Mexico receptive to U.S. suggestions about how it should handle its relationship to Mexican Americans had a profound impact on emigration flows from Mexico. During the de la Madrid sexenio, real wages fell by approximately half, while the cost of the basic food basket almost doubled (Lustig 1998: 61–96). This confluence of forces had clear effects on the welfare of Mexicans, as captured most poignantly by the indicators of child malnutrition: according to Mexican government (ISSSTE) data, the percentage of Mexican children suffering ailments linked to insufficient nutrition as a proportion of all sick Mexican children rose by more than 3 percentage points in the same number of years, from 8.5 percent in 1981 to 11.7 percent in 1984 (Lustig 1998: 87–88). An even starker indicator of the effects of Mexico's economic turmoil was provided by a United Nations Children's Fund (UNICEF) study on world hunger, which reported that "in 1986, more children died of hunger in Mexico than in the Sudan" (Migdail 1987: 118). As Lustig observes, however, the welfare consequences for the poor and the middle class, as well as the resultant political protest, were less pronounced than the decline in real wages suggests (Lustig 1998: 61–96). Households adopted nonwage strategies to supplement income, chief among which, particularly for rural residents, was emigration (Lustig 1998: 74, 91). As indicated by case-based and survey studies in rural Mexico (Grindle 1989; P. Gregory 1986), out-migration increased substantially during the economic crisis of the 1980s, more than doubling in some of the surveyed communities, leading to labor shortages in agriculture in Mexico's center-west states. Furthermore, geographic origins became more diversified, with migrants emanating from states to the south and east of traditional sending states and possessing a wider range of educational levels, both lower and significantly higher as measured in years of schooling, than had been the norm (Bean et al. 1998; Massey et al. 1993; Bustamante et al. 1998; Jones 1995). Moreover, remittances, previously spent on investments in land, housing, or education, were increasingly devoted to subsistence expenditures (Grindle 1989; P. Gregory 1986). Data from the INS on the apprehension of illegal Mexican immigrants during this period seem to confirm the intensification of emigration during the economic crisis: the average number of apprehensions was 1,260,855 a year for 1981–86, peaking at 1,767,400 in 1986, a 50 percent increase from the average for 1971–80 (Vernez and Ronfeldt 1991).[14]

The increase in Mexican migration did not go unnoticed by restrictionist U.S. policymakers. After a decade of haggling over a possible immigration-control legislative package, anti-immigrant pressure groups, ascendant in the Reagan government, used the deterioration of the Mexican economy and the record number of INS apprehensions to push hard for an immigration law. Liberal opponents of the bill, also cognizant of the economic pressure that Mexico was under and its implication for migration flows, ceded, fearing that even more draconian legislation would be proposed in the future (Hayes 2001: 61; Alba 1998). Thus, the Immigration Reform and Control Act (IRCA) was passed in the 1986 legislative session. As part of the compromise that allowed for its passage, Congress also enacted the Special Agricultural Workers and the Replenishment Agricultural Workers programs to guarantee the agricultural lobby a steady supply of workers despite the new controls (Hayes 2001: 47–73; Chiswick 1988).

IRCA, popularly called the Simpson-Rodino Act, radically changed the character of Mexican migration to the United States. The act enabled more than 3 million undocumented Mexican migrants to change their legal status under its terms. Specifically, IRCA stipulated that migrants who had lived in the United States more or less continuously since 1982 were eligible for legal work and residence permits, and could, within six years, become naturalized citizens. 1.7 million Mexican immigrants changed their legal status under IRCA's terms. Additionally, those who had worked in agriculture for at least ninety days in 1986 could also qualify for legal status, and 1.3 million migrants took advantage of this option (Binational Study 1998). Once that status was obtained, migrants were free to follow the established procedures to bring family members to join them, and they did, in large numbers. In one fell swoop, the undocumented Mexican immigrants who had been so invisible that their numbers had been the subject of wild controversy, with estimates ranging from 400,000 to 6 million, emerged into the statutory light. With the passage of IRCA, over 3 million undocumented immigrants suddenly became visible to the Mexican state, their existence in the United States manifest and incontrovertible (Chiswick 1988; Hayes 2001; Bean et al. 1998; Bustamante et al. 1998).

IRCA also transformed the profile of this large segment of the Mexican immigrant population in certain key ways that would, over time, have important political ramifications for Mexico. As undocumented immigrants acquired legal status and settled indefinitely in the United States, rodinos—as newly legalized Mexican immigrants were often called—were able to cross the border more frequently, traveling back and forth between their new homes and their communities of origin (Cornelius 1989). Thus, they remained deeply rooted in Mexico and socially—not to mention materially—invested in its future (Kearney 2004; Fitzgerald 2006; R. Smith 1995). Yet living and working in the United States, they were not under the direct influence of the PRI and the political hegemony enforced through the party's corporatist networks, particularly in the Mexican countryside. In sum, IRCA created a significant, conspicuous population of Mexican migrants able to express critiques of the Mexican political system and mobilize against its excesses in a non-Mexican political space. The implications of the political latitude that migrants acquired as a result of the amnesty program would slowly become visible—and unsettling—to the PRI government as it faced the mounting political challenges generated by a sexenio of searing economic hardship.

The Gathering Political Crisis

The economic crisis that would come to define the de la Madrid presidency brought long-simmering social tensions to a head. Mexico's business interests and its middle class felt that the state, through its cavalier mismanagement of the economy, had squandered the wealth and social status they had worked so hard to achieve. The nationalization of the banking system and state control over their accounts, in particular, was felt to be clear evidence of their vulnerability to capricious state policy. Mexico's poor, its urban workers and rural campesinos, also felt alienated from a state and a party with which they had historically been identified. The precipitous fall of real wages, the successive dismantling of crucial nutritional and health subsidies, the utter abandonment of agriculture and the rise of rural misery in its wake, left them struggling with serious impoverishment. Moreover, the country's major unions, the Confederation of Mexican Workers (CTM) and the National Peasant Confederation (CNC), which had previously guaranteed some measure of economic redistribution, proved completely ineffective in defending the interests of their members and were ultimately discredited (Chand 2001; Shirk 2005).

The rise in social discontent gradually began to reinvigorate Mexico's electoral processes. Frustrated citizens began taking their grievances to the ballot box, progressively changing elections from a ritual of political pretense in which the winners were invariably the PRI's nominees to moments of real political contest in which politicians, and the parties they represented, were called to account. This trend was particularly pronounced in the north, where the National Action Party (PAN), a right-of-center party representing business and middle-class interests, was making sizable gains. In 1983, in the border state of Chihuahua, where the PAN achieved its most striking advances, it won the mayoral races for all of the main cities and carried important seats in the state legislature. "In one stroke," notes political analyst Vikram Chand, "over 70 percent of Chihuahua's population had fallen under PAN jurisdiction" (2001: 33). In response to the PAN's victories, the PRI fell back on tried and true strategies of election fraud. Irregularities became so widespread and blatant, however, that they produced a backlash. Chihuahua, where the electoral manipulation had been most egregious and in 1986 had robbed the PAN gubernatorial candidate of a widely expected victory, became the focal point for protests against PRI tactics and, more broadly, against the ruling party's obdurate hold on power (Chand 2001; Shirk 2005).

The fact that Chihuahua emerged as the site of a serious resistance movement against the PRI meant that the protests would spill across the border. Indeed, their organizers capitalized on the state's contiguity with el Norte to bring the electoral fraud Chihuahua had endured to international—and more pertinently, to U.S.—attention. In July, the PAN organized a six-day blockade of an important bridge over the Rio Grande, linking the cities of Ciudad Juárez and El Paso (Chand 2001). The blockade of this largest port of entry on the U.S.-Mexico border cost Mexico an estimated $15 million in export fees, but likely cost those U.S. enterprises that needed to transport products across the border from maquiladoras in Chihuahua far more (*New York Times* 1986). The protests, which lasted several months, raised concerns in Washington. By October, the CIA had warned that Mexico's political system "[would] 'rupture violently' unless Mexico's leaders make the country's 'rigid, authoritarian political structure' more democratic" (as quoted in Pear 1986). Encouraged by

PAN lobbyists, the U.S. Congress passed formal resolutions urging de la Madrid to "open up political channels for opposition parties" (Senator Dennis DeConcini, as quoted in Pear 1986; Santamaría Gómez 1994). The opposition in Chihuahua had successfully galvanized U.S. political pressure against the PRI. In doing so, they expanded the political arena of Mexican electoral contests into the United States. And in that arena, electoral integrity became *the* central issue.

By the middle of 1987, the PRI was showing the strain of governing amid the growing political discontent. Cuauhtémoc Cárdenas, governor of Michoacán and son of Lázaro Cárdenas, a PRI founder and one of the most revered populist politicians in Mexico's history, had split off from the party, taking with him a dissident faction christened the Democratic Current. He called for labor, peasants, and students to demand electoral transparency, declaring that Mexico's next president must emerge "not from the summit but from the grass roots" (as quoted in Rohter 1987). As the presidential elections of July 1988 approached, the charismatic politician left the PRI to run his own campaign for president under the banner of the National Democratic Front (FND), a hastily assembled coalition of leftist organizations and parties. The 1988 elections, which pitted the PRI's Carlos Salinas against both Cárdenas and the PAN's Manuel Clouthier, promised to be the most contested since the Mexican Revolution of 1929. In preparation, the FND and the PAN trained electoral monitors and schooled their supporters in techniques of civil disobedience, which they planned to use if the election proved fraudulent. Clouthier warned that the opposition would "paralyze all of Mexico" if fraud occurred (as quoted in Rohter 1988b).

The movement for electoral transparency quickly spread north of the border. The protests in Ciudad Juárez had demonstrated not only that the hegemony of the PRI was fragile, but that political mobilization in the United States could have significant impact in Mexico. The movement reenergized the networks of Chicano and leftist organizations forged during the sexenios of Echeverría and López Portillo. Groups and political relationships that had been worn down and worn thin by both the antileftist stance of the Reagan administration and de la Madrid's ostracism were revitalized by what they perceived as an unprecedented opportunity to push for democratic openness in Mexico (Martinez Saldaña 2002: 223–24; Santamaría Gómez 1994: 153–65). Veteran organizers of Chicano groups and the Mexican left who had been forced to migrate themselves due to the economic crisis of the 1980s were joined by scores of recent immigrants. Many were newly legalized under IRCA and thus able to take a public political stand without fear of deportation. Small but devoted groups of Mexican organizers were turning cities like Los Angeles, San Jose, San Antonio, and Chicago into sites where Mexico's electoral contest was also being staged (Calderón Chelius 2002; Martinez Saldaña 2002: 223–24; Santamaría Gómez 1994: 165–171; Dresser 1993: 98–99).

The Chicano groups and immigrants overwhelmingly rallied behind Cárdenas, whom they saw not just as the bearer of the populist legacy of the Mexican

Revolution and sympathetic to their concerns, but also as their best hope to challenge the PRI autocracy. Ben Garza, Chicano activist in the Los Angeles area and Cárdenas supporter, described the alliance: "For 4 or 5 years, we had been trying to organize people around the issue of democracy in Mexico. The 1988 election simply brought more people together. Many people of course supported Cárdenas, but others joined because of their desire to support democracy in Mexico. They were tired of the PRI and corruption" (as quoted in Dresser 1993: 99). Thus, the Cárdenas campaign became a vehicle through which Mexicans and Mexican Americans pushed for Mexican electoral reform.

As part of that reform, Mexican immigrants articulated their claim to the right to vote in Mexican elections even while residing in the United States and explicitly linked that demand to the exercise of transparent elections. They based their appeal for the vote on legal grounds, but also on their familial, cultural, and economic commitment to their country of origin (Calderón Chelius 2002; Ross Piñeda 2002). In a letter to President Miguel de la Madrid, a congress of twenty-two Mexican immigrant groups, Chicano organizations, and union locals, argued: "With the inalienable right with which our nationality endows us, our close family and cultural ties, our daily contribution to the wellbeing of our homeland, we demand that you guarantee effective suffrage and clear and impartial elections on the 6th of July. Furthermore, we will hold you responsible for the consequences that failure to comply may generate" (as quoted in Santamaría Gómez 1994: 158–59). Cárdenas, increasingly aware of the political leverage that migrants could represent, came out in support of voting rights for Mexicans living in the United States.

In response to this grassroots mobilization and the bold claims that it was provoking, the PRI speedily recovered its former interest in Mexican Americans and mounted a campaign to restore its connections with their leaders. As part of an initiative called Impact 1988, the Mexican government, in a familiar pattern, scheduled a series of meetings in early 1988 between Mexican American organizations and intellectuals and the PRI leadership, including Salinas. The meetings were to "explore in detail the opportunities and the challenges . . . of developing a strategy, made up of concrete actions, to improve the relations between Mexico and the United States" (as quoted in Santamaría Gómez 1994: 139), and the notion of Mexican Americans serving as an ethnic lobby for Mexico was once again invoked (Santamaría Gómez 1994: 137–42). The PRI's response to Mexican emigrants was just as familiar: it did not reach out to communities of emigrants in the United States (Santamaría Gómez 1994: 137–42).

The renewed engagement between the PRI and Chicanos was strained (Santamaría Gómez 1994: 137–42) and quickly began to disintegrate into bitter recriminations. In June 1988, a month before the Mexican elections, the California Democratic Party passed a resolution proposed by the Chicano caucus, "asking the U.S. government to pressure Mexico to respect human rights and to give Mexican citizens who reside outside the country the right to vote" (Acuña

1996: 233). It also asked "the North American government to intervene in the Mexican presidential elections of this year" (as quoted in Acuña 1996: 233). Through Bustamante, the Mexican government issued a virulent attack on the resolution, published in several major Mexican newspapers. "Just because Chicanos have Spanish surnames, that does not give them the credentials to understand what is happening in Mexico," railed Bustamante, adding that the resolution revealed that Chicanos "think like any other gringo." He cautioned Chicanos that if they wanted to be in solidarity with their Mexican brethren, they should refrain from criticizing "Mexican affairs" (Acuña 1996: 233).

On the eve of an election in which independent polls indicated that Salinas might not win a clear majority (Rohter 1988a), the PRI had alienated Mexican Americans and had confirmed its disinterest in Mexican emigrants. Salinas and his party would soon discover that this was a serious miscalculation.

Building a Lobby

Carlos Salinas de Gortari, PRI candidate for president, declared victory shortly after midnight on July 6, 1988. But official election results failed to come in to confirm his claim—a delay blamed on computer malfunction—and accusations of fraud began to mount. Opposition candidates charged that the PRI had stooped to ballot-box stuffing, the destruction of ballot boxes in pro-opposition municipalities, and the revival of hundreds of thousands of dead PRI supporters (Rohter 1988c). As official tallies continued to dribble in for days, Cuauhtémoc Cárdenas proclaimed that he had in fact won the election and that any PRI attempt to deny him the office of president would be "the technical equivalent of a coup" (as quoted in Branigin 1988). Public outcry began to mount, with small-scale protests flaring throughout the country. To draw international attention to the electoral crisis, opposition protestors in Chihuahua occupied the bridge linking Ciudad Juárez to El Paso, just as they had in 1986, bringing transnational commerce to a halt and costing the Mexican government and U.S. businesses millions of dollars (Treaster 1988). When the Federal Electoral Commission finally announced, more than a week after the election, that Salinas had indeed won, but only by just over 50 percent of the vote, a devastatingly—and suspiciously—slim margin for a party that had never garnered less than 70 percent in presidential elections, Cárdenas called for a protest rally in Mexico City. The demonstration drew over 200,000 people to the capital, which the PRI had lost in the elections. Cárdenas's supporters jeered at effigies of Salinas and chanted "Salinas lies, Cárdenas is President!" (Rohter 1988d). Shortly thereafter, Cárdenas embarked on a six-week postelection campaign throughout Mexico, which he christened his "journey for democracy and respect for popular sovereignty." At rallies where he was introduced as "the President-elect of the Mexican people," he called for protests and civil disobedience to challenge the election results (Rohter 1988c).

The events reverberated across the border. Coverage of electoral results hit the front pages of major U.S. newspapers, and analysts fretted over what the close contest would mean for Mexico's commitment to repaying its debt and sticking to its grueling austerity program (Rohter 1988e; Kissinger 1988). The embryonic network of Mexican and Mexican American supporters of Cárdenas went into high gear and organized protests in cities throughout California and the Southwest, with the most dramatic mobilizations occurring in Los Angeles (Dresser 1993; Martinez Saldaña 2002). Cárdenas took his postelection campaign across the border in 1989 as the head of the newly formed Democratic Revolutionary Party (Partido Revolucionario Democrático, or PRD), a consolidated version of the National Democratic Front (Reinhold 1989). Barnstorming in California and the Southwest, he energized the Mexican and Mexican American democracy movement that had rallied behind him, and helped to transform the spontaneous political mobilization into a formal branch of the PRD in the United States (Dresser 1993; Martinez Saldaña 2002; interviews, Chicago, August 2003). While in the United States, Cárdenas appealed forcefully to Mexican workers, decrying their neglect by the Mexican government and calling for a reform that would allow migrants to cast absentee ballots. Large numbers of migrants responded with enthusiastic support, while the PRI, from Mexico, derided the idea as a threat to national sovereignty, claiming that it would give the United States inappropriate and dangerous influence (Santamaría Gómez 1994).

Cárdenas also met with Chicano and non-Chicano leaders, including Senator Joseph Montoya, California state controller and future governor Gray Davis, former governor Jerry Brown, and civil rights leader Jesse Jackson (Santamaría Gómez 1994: 182–202). The Mexican opposition leader also traveled to Washington for meetings with various think tanks, toured prominent universities such as Harvard and MIT, where he was introduced as "the legitimate president of Mexico," and gave speeches about the ramifications of the Mexican elections for his nation's political future (Santamaría Gómez 1994: 182–202). Mexican political analyst Jorge Castañeda concluded in 1989 that "no other Mexican politician has moved masses in the United States like Cárdenas" (*Proceso*, November 1989, as quoted in Santamaría Gómez 1994: 202).

The political inroads he was making jolted Salinas and the PRI machine into action. Despite the PRI's dismissal of Cárdenas's supporters as "naïve" (López Pescador, consul of Los Angeles, November 1988, as quoted in Santamaría Gómez 1994: 183) and its accusations that his actions were "seditious" (*Uno mas uno*, December 1988, as quoted in Santamaría Gómez 1994: 286),[15] the mass anti-PRI rallies in cities throughout the United States, coupled with the warm reception that the opposition leader received at major American political and intellectual institutions, made it unequivocally clear that the Cárdenas campaign had transformed the United States into a staging area for Mexican politics (Dresser 1993; Martinez Saldaña 2002; Ramírez Paredes 1991). As López Pescador, consul in Los Angeles at the height of the anti-PRI demonstrations,

reflected, "[the protest activities] led to an awakening in Mexican political circles. The Mexican government realized that there [were] many anti-PRI Mexicans living in California who return[ed] periodically to their communities and
[had] influence in Mexico" (as quoted in Dresser 1993: 94). Furthermore, the
PRD was quickly gaining credence as an important political actor and ally for
Mexican American organizations: "We knew that the PRD, and PRD cells, had
gained a lot of ground in the Mexican American community," notes one program officer under Salinas (Fundación Solidaridad Mexicano Americana interview, Mexico City, May 2005). Salinas, with his party behind him, was determined not to cede the emerging political territory north of the border to his rival.
Months before assuming the office of president, he and his staff began a series
of high-level meetings with Mexican American leaders, which, in a break with
Mexican state tradition, also included a handful of Mexican emigrants, most of
them established entrepreneurs (Santamaría Gómez 1994: 182–202; Fundación
Solidaridad Mexicano Americana interview, Mexico City, May 2005; Reinhold
1989).

Initially, the goal of the PRI's renewed engagement with Mexican Americans
and its nascent interaction with U.S.-based Mexican nationals was to recoup
spheres of political influence lost to the PRD. Quickly, however, the engagement evolved into a set of policy principles and programs, the central tenet of
which was the distinction between Mexican Americans and Mexican emigrants. After a brief period of engaging with both groups and of conflating
them, often in gross oversimplifications, the Salinas administration began to
see them as fundamentally different, with different political values for Mexico
and for the PRI.

For the Mexican state, Mexican Americans were, without a doubt, the prize
to be captured: they were a segment of the U.S. population with increasing political and economic clout, they were represented by several large and established organizations, and they could serve as an "ideal vehicle"—in the words
of Salinas's foreign secretary Solana (as quoted in Reinhold 1989)—to press
Mexico's interests in the United States. Emigrants, on the other hand, had only
moderate political value to the Mexican government. Their grievances had
to be addressed, if only to dampen the opposition's ability to organize them.
Without voting rights in Mexico or the United States, however, they were primarily of consequence to their government as a vehicle through which the
Mexican state could strengthen its relationship with Mexican Americans. Emigrants, including upwards of three million newly legalized rodinos and agricultural workers, were essentially a means to an end.

The Salinas administration developed a bifurcated approach, echoing past
policy. With Mexican Americans, Salinas reopened the conversations that had
sputtered along under his predecessors and fortified them by carving out a
dedicated department in the Secretariat of Foreign Affairs charged with maintaining and augmenting them. Through engagement, Mexican American
groups and the Mexican state revived concepts articulated during interactions

of the 1970s and early 1980s, reinterpreted them, and created institutions to support and implement them. The most central of these was the definition of Mexican Americans as a lobby that could push for Mexican interests, especially the passage of NAFTA, in the United States. With emigrants, by contrast, the Salinas administrations and, subsequently, that of Zedillo limited their engagement to the provision of services. Mexican emigrants were mere recipients of state policy, rarely involved in the process of its development.

Reaching Out: Program for Mexican Communities Abroad

Within less than a year of taking office, Salinas de Gortari announced the creation of the Program for Mexican Communities Abroad (Programa para Comunidades Mexicanos en el Extranjero, or PCME), an umbrella program that would become the government's most important policy tool in its approach toward both Mexican Americans and emigrants living in the United States. A year of dedicated attempts to woo Mexican American leaders and organizations back into engagement with the government after several years of neglect culminated in two major meetings in the fall of 1989, one in Tijuana and one in Washington, D.C. At both gatherings, attended by prominent Mexican Americans as well as a few emigrants, the Mexican president emphasized the importance his administration attached to its relationship with Mexican Americans, stressing the value of a rapprochement for the construction of friendlier ties between the United States and its southern neighbor. At the Tijuana meeting, Salinas underscored the potential significance of a revived *acercamiento* or rapprochement with Mexican Americans for a redefinition of Mexico's relationship with the United States: "Without false antagonisms and for our mutual benefit, our two countries will find new areas of compromise and collaboration. [Our] rapprochement . . . occurs at a juncture in the relationship between Mexico and the United States that is especially interesting" (Tijuana, September 14, 1989, as quoted in Santamaría Gómez 1994: 209–10).

Mexican American leaders responded with some reticence, expressing their concern that the Salinas administration, just like its predecessors, was reaching out at a moment of political crisis and would callously sever its newly established ties the moment Mexican Americans raised issues that the regime found threatening (Fundación Solidaridad Mexicano Americana interviews, Mexico City, May 2005; Reinhold 1989; Santamaría Gómez 1994: 210–11; Dirección General para las Comunidades Mexicanas en el Extranjero [DGCME] 1990a). They insisted that the Salinas government institutionalize its engagement with the Mexican-origin population in the United States and create a formal program to host it: "One of the main conclusions [of these meetings]," reports the government account, "was that the relationship should be made more systematic, permanent, that things should not remain as they were, vulnerable to changes in administration and dependent on the goodwill of a few isolated groups in Mexico and the United States" (DGCME 1990a). The PCME was the Mexican government's response.

Formally launched on January 2, 1990, the PCME and the Dirección General para las Comunidades Mexicanas en el Extranjero (DGCME), the office that was to manage it, began with an extremely vague mandate. The Salinas administration did not have a clear idea of how to institutionalize its engagement with Mexican Americans, and the staff tasked with carrying out the assignment had had no contact with Mexican-origin communities abroad. As a former PCME staff member bluntly put it, "the people who were put in charge of the program had no exposure to the topic. They had never dealt with the issues. The reaction was 'how do I make heads or tails of this? [*con qué se come esto?*]' Who are these people? What do they want? What do they think?" (Fundación Solidaridad Mexicano Americana interview, Mexico City, May 2005). The official memo that created the PCME reflected this confusion: it stated generally that the mission of the program and of the DGCME was "to attend to Mexican communities abroad and to strengthen government links with them, given the singular resource they represent in this new stage of the bilateral relationship with the United States" (DGCME 1990d). The program goals were similarly amorphous, referring broadly to "the promotion of social relationships, the promotion of economic relationships, and planning and evaluation" (DGCME 1990d: 14–17). Throughout, the blurred PCME blueprint reiterates the need to open avenues for communication, as a means for program staff to familiarize themselves with Mexican-origin communities and to bring the implications of their mandate into sharper focus: in short, to figure out what to do (DGCME 1990d).

The program staff began scheduling a large number of meetings with Mexican American and Mexican emigrant groups in the United States, at which the DGCME consulted with them about the direction the PCME should take (SRE Archives 1990–91, DGCME program documents; Díaz de Cossio 1990a). As a former program officer in the DGCME remembered:

> The first thing that we did was to visit a large number of communities in the United States, in situ, and to ask, "if you were tasked with designing a program for Mexicans Abroad, what would you do? Because we don't want to sit at a desk and try to decide what it is that you want or you need." This was very healthy, because not only did it permit us to understand the needs with which we could begin to interact and address, and to look for mutual collaboration and benefits, but it also enabled a lot of people to learn about the program, and to get to know the director, and begin to trust him, as a person that came to them for the first time and asked, what shall we do and how shall we do it together. (Fundación Solidaridad Mexicano Americana interview, Mexico City, May 2005)

The interpretive conversations initiated in these meetings proved invaluable. They allowed DGCME staff to become acquainted with U.S.-based Mexican and Mexican American communities, equipping them with a more grounded sense of the constituency that their program had been created to address, but also allowing them to develop a rapport that would admit the generation of new insights about the relationship between the Mexican government and these communities. "The program wasn't something perfectly designed, planned by a group of experts, that decided that they were going to do this or that," explained a former PCME program officer: "No! It came out of the process, because the people involved were interested and open. . . . That was how it was. We didn't have a plan; we just took baby steps, and figured it out along the way. With obstacles along the way, of course, we stumbled a lot. But what I want to say is that the program was created because of the people involved and their commitment to the issue and to the journey, not because of an existing institutional framework" (Fundación Solidaridad Mexicano Americana interview, Mexico City, May 2005).

Articulating a Taxonomy: Mexican Americans and Mexican Migrants

The cardinal insight that the DGCME gleaned from its tour of Mexican communities in the United States—a tour that the director called "a voyage of wonder and discovery" (Díaz de Cossio 1990a)—was that Mexican Americans and Mexican migrants were fundamentally dissimilar, and that engaging with each of these constituencies would have radically different ramifications for Mexico and its relationship with the United States (Fundación Solidaridad Mexicano Americana interviews, Mexico City, May 2005). Early program documents display a persistent "slippage" between the two populations, generally describing the profile of long-standing Mexican American communities and tagging on migrants as an afterthought (DGCME 1990c, 1990d), but following the tour, the program officers began to distinguish between them (Fundación Solidaridad Mexicano Americana interview, Mexico City, May 2003). The DGCME ultimately determined that, in Mexico's quest to develop political and economic ties with the United States, migrants were essentially a liability, whereas Mexican Americans were an untapped resource. The needs that migrants enumerated in meetings with DGCME staff—assistance in regularizing their legal status, access to basic health and education services, defense of their rights as workers, and protection from excessive exploitation—put the government in a quandary: migrant grievances could not be fully addressed without raising the delicate question of migration, especially undocumented migration, and the treatment of migrant workers by U.S. authorities (Fundación Solidaridad Mexicano Americana interview, Mexico City, May 2005; González Gutiérrez 1993; Santamaría Gómez 1994: 182–214). Moreover, Mexican migrants could levy little political influence in the United States: they could not vote, had little positive standing in public opinion, and a weak level of political mobilization, especially after the electoral fervor died down and the anti-PRI mobilization behind Cárdenas had started to disintegrate (Martinez Saldaña 2002;

Dresser 1993; González Gutiérrez 1993). Migrants were, as the former administrator to the PCME bluntly assessed, "poor and disenfranchised" (González Gutiérrez 1993: 222).

Mexican Americans, on the other hand, were, as the same PCME officer put it, "aware of their political and economic power . . . and willing to exercise it" (González Gutiérrez 1993: 222). Not only could Mexican Americans vote, but they also had organized civil rights organizations that had successfully pushed for legislation to fight systemic discrimination. Their growing political clout was increasingly matched by rising purchasing power and economic status (González Gutiérrez 1993: 222–23; SRE Archives 1990–92, DGCME program documents). Moreover, as detailed in several DGCME papers (SRE Archives 1990–92, DGCME program documents), they were a population forecast to grow in number and influence. As a result, Mexican Americans were uniquely placed to rehabilitate Mexico's image in the United States, which had been badly battered by the accusations of wholesale electoral fraud (DGCME 1990c; Dresser 1993). Finally, Mexican American intellectuals and community leaders had, in the late 1970s, presciently begun to articulate proposals for reforms in the U.S.-Mexico relationship that, by the early 1990s, were poised to redefine this relationship radically and irrevocably (Zazueta 1983: 481n80). Most centrally, Chicano activists had raised the idea of a common market between the two countries, only to be brusquely rebuffed by the López Portillo administration (Zazueta 1983: 481n80; Santamaría Gómez 1994). At a time when Mexico was negotiating the reduction of trade barriers and seriously contemplating the creation of a North American free trade area, Mexican Americans' conceptual development of the idea, and their political support for it, became invaluable.

Serving Mexican Migrants

As the DGCME began to differentiate between Mexican migrants and Mexican Americans, the PCME program activities began to branch off in two different directions: one that addressed the needs of Mexican migrants and the other that cultivated a substantive engagement with Mexican Americans. In its approach to migrants, the DGCME focused on providing services, largely through local consulates, in areas that were politically innocuous, steering clear of their working and living conditions in the United States and of the economic constraints in Mexico that had compelled many to cross the border in the first place. The goals of these services were twofold: first, to minimize the negative impacts of labor emigration on communities of origin in Mexico, and second, and more important, to preserve migrants' cultural and political ties to Mexico as a way of accessing the political and economic clout of their Mexican American descendants (SRE interviews, Mexico City, May 2003; Fundación Solidaridad Mexicano Americana interviews, Mexico City, May 2003). As González Gutiérrez, program officer for the PCME in Los Angeles, stated, the program was part of "a long term strategy to use the generation of *rodinos* to build bridges to the Mexican diaspora's future generations" (1993: 233).[16]

Concretely, the PCME extended support to migrants in three main areas: health, education, and the promotion of sports and cultural activities. In the first, the PCME focused primarily on the diffusion of public health information on communicable diseases such as HIV/AIDS and tuberculosis, and on monitoring their epidemiological advance among migrants as well as in their communities of origin. Additionally, it lent some support to rural clinics that served migrant workers and their families. With regard to education, the PCME dedicated resources to promote bilingual education, targeting the children of migrants in particular, in an effort to preserve their linguistic affiliation with Mexico. The PCME organized training sessions and exchanges for U.S. teachers and distributed pedagogical material. Finally, to preserve migrants' cultural identification with their homeland, the PCME sponsored a series of cultural and sports events, including a binational soccer tournament in which Mexican teams on both sides of the border competed, and supported the traditional nationalist festivities organized by the consulate (González Gutiérrez and Schumacher 1998; DGCME 1990b, 1990c; *La Paloma*, nos. 7–22, January 1992–January 1995).

The process by which the DGCME designed these services was distinctly top-down. The program staff evaluated migrant needs on the basis of relatively limited interactions, as well as on information sporadically received from consular offices. Migrants were not involved in program formulation in any meaningful way: a clear distinction was maintained between the PCME program staff, which retained control over the design of services, and the migrants who were their beneficiaries. As a result, the programs reflected the Mexican government's perceptions of migrants' needs more closely than the actual constraints that migrants experienced. In the realm of education, for example, migrants expressed more interest in receiving assistance in English proficiency than in developing their Spanish skills, both for themselves, because of the edge it would give them in U.S. labor markets, and for their children, because of the boost it would give them as they tried to integrate themselves into U.S. schools. Nevertheless, the PCME focused almost exclusively on programs to promote Spanish competence (SRE and Fundación Solidaridad Mexicano Americana interviews, Mexico City, May 2003). Another striking instance of this disconnect was the Programa Paisano, an intervention deployed by a related office in the Mexican government, the National Migration Institute, drawn up in partnership with the DGCME, and based on the same information sources that the DGCME used in designing PCME services for migrants. The Paisano Program was crafted as a preventive program against abuses of migrants by Mexican customs authorities, an intervention prompted in part by Zacatecas governor Borrego's lobbying of the federal government (Borrego and SRE interviews, Mexico City, May 2003). In a blatant reflection of the government's patronizing definition of migrant needs, however, it focused

exclusively on returning migrants and did nothing to address the mistreatment of those who were exiting Mexico, leaving them vulnerable to racke-
teering by customs officials in cahoots with the migrant smugglers known as
coyotes. As the Mexican government's evaluation of human rights violations
against migrants conceded, "it would seem that the problem lies basically in
the fact that the design of the 'Paisano' Program involved the assumption . . .
that the migrants who enter and leave are different individuals" (Mexican
Human Rights Commission 1992: 46–47).

The state appraisal of the Paisano Program illustrates another feature of the
government's top-down approach. The PCME programs were subject to repeated evaluations, and with each round of assessment they were both narrowed and standardized. At the beginning of the PCME, consulates were afforded a fair amount of discretion in how they wanted to implement its services,
adapting the educational or cultural programs to the specific characteristics of
the community they were serving (well-established urban migrant communities in places like Los Angeles had very different needs from those based
around food processing plants in the rural Midwest, for example). By the final
years of the Zedillo administration, however, the interventions had been made
so uniform, with room for local improvisation and adaptation edited out, that
consular staff quietly abandoned or circumvented many programs (Fundación
Solidaridad Mexicano Americana and SRE interviews, Mexico City, May
2003).

In dramatic contrast to its approach to Mexican migrants, the DGCME took
pains to maintain and cultivate its interpretive engagement with Mexican
Americans. It continued to meet intensively with Mexican American organizations, calling for their reactions to its proposals, soliciting suggestions on how
to enhance their relationship with the Mexican government, and asking for
their perspectives on the meaning such a relationship could have for their communities as well as for Mexico as a nation. DGCME director Roger Díaz de
Cossio's entreaty to the National Council of La Raza, at a Washington, D.C.,
gathering, typified his overture to Mexican American groups. "Our futures are
inextricably linked," he asserted: "Without a doubt, it is to our mutual benefit
to work closely together. We still have many things to learn and relationships
to develop. We need your guidance and your suggestions on how to proceed.
We have so many things to do and, to repair years of neglect, we have to do
them very fast. We will be listening to your ideas and will be enriched by them"
(Díaz de Cossio 1990b).

The government reinforced its outreach with myriad goodwill gestures: it
bestowed the Aztec Eagle medal of honor on several Mexican American community leaders; it sponsored conferences on Mexican American issues in the
United States and in Mexico, including a Festival of La Raza in three border
cities; it underwrote several gallery exhibits and musical performances; and it
began publishing *La Paloma*, a bilingual newsletter recapping exchanges between Mexican Americans and the Mexican government whose circulation

would grow to three-quarters of a million (*La Paloma*, nos. 1–3, September 1990–February 1991). This engagement would generate new insights about the potential of a Mexican-origin lobby in the United States and how to mobilize that lobby for specific political goals.

Mapping Mejiamérica

While the notion of Mexican Americans acting as a lobby for Mexico had circulated since the late 1970s, the Mexican government had always been a recalcitrant participant in envisioning it. Under the Salinas administration, the DGCME reversed that historical reluctance and developed an accurate picture of the political possibilities such a lobby could represent. The Mexican government retrieved and reinterpreted a defining notion of the Chicano movement of the 1960s and 1970s: that the Chicano people constituted a nation, an imaginary homeland that they called Aztlán, which transcended political boundaries but where Chicanos were "free and sovereign," bound above all—and above all laws—by a duty to their people and their collective future (González Gutiérrez 1999; Gómez-Quiñones 1990; Santamaría Gómez 1994). The DGCME appropriated the concept of "a Mexican nation in the United States," a national entity distinct from both Mexico and the United States, but renamed the homeland "Mejiamérica" and stripped it of its message of political resistance, defining the nation instead as a "group of persons of the same ethnic origin, that generally speak the same language, and that have a common tradition" (DGCME 1990a; SRE Archives 1991). On the basis of this adaptation of a Chicano concept, the Mexican government reformulated its outreach to Mexican Americans as a foreign policy strategy rather than community outreach—a strategy that was "of the utmost national importance . . . for the preservation of [Mexican] national sovereignty and for our prosperity in the coming century." The DGCME informed Mexico's consuls that "Mejiamérica should be one of the most favored nations for our country in its relationships of cooperation," and that indeed, "[Mexico's] independent future [was] at stake" (DGCME 1990a).

Through its acercamiento with Mejiamérica and its Mexican American "inhabitants," the government was able to map out the imaginary homeland. PCME program documents began to reflect a new understanding of the crucial role that grassroots organizing, especially during the 1960s and 1970s, had played in the definition of Chicano identity and the development of the associated political base. The program memos showed an explicit understanding of the fact that Mexican American political leverage was not a natural or inevitable product of growing numbers. To its recognition of the legal and political victories of the Chicano movement, the government added a more sophisticated grasp of the historic processes of community mobilization through which Mexican Americans had wrested their power and the ways those processes, and the identities on which they were based, were still changing. "First as pachucos, then as Chicanos, then as La Raza Unida, and now as Hispanics, they struggle to obtain the place that they deserve in North American society, a place that is proportional to their growing numbers and economic power," summarized one memo (SRE Archives 1991). Additionally, the Mexican government began to describe with uncharacteristic acuity the specific leverage that Mexican Americans could apply to affect political outcomes. DGCME reports refer, for example, to the fact that they could provide swing votes in states like California or Texas with large electoral college delegations and thus determine the outcome of an American presidential election (SRE Archives 1991, DGCME program documents). Finally, PCME program documents began to reflect a recognition that Mexican Americans had developed a distinct set of cultural identities that were Mexican in affinity but hybrid at their core ("being Chicano is not being Mexicano"; de la Garza 1980: 575). The PCME papers also noted, however, that an essential part of that identity was an enduring need to search for one's Mexican cultural roots—"[Mexican Americans] have an enormous desire . . . to be recognized in the land of their ancestors which, for so many years, treated them with contempt and forgot them," stated one dispatch (DGCME 1990a)—and that an essential part of building a relationship with Mejiamérica was responding to that need.[17] Significantly, the documents added that the government could, and should, respond to those cultural needs by forging economic ties with Mexican Americans. Connecting Hispanic chambers of commerce and Mexican American entrepreneurs with Mexican business partners and banks quickly emerged as a major axis of PCME activities (*La Paloma*, nos. 1–7; SRE Archives 1990–92, DGCME program documents).

Mexican American organizations, in turn, gleaned new understandings of the potential that a collaboration with Mexico held for them. In the state's recognition of their history of community organizing, Mexican American groups saw the possibility of recruiting state help in new lobbying drives (SRE Archives 1990–92, DGCME program documents). Likewise, seeing the government's eager analysis of sources of their political influence, several Mexican American organizations and leaders became aware of their bargaining power and their ability to petition Mexico for support on a range of political issues (Acuña 1996: 231–54; Dresser 1993). Finally, in Mexico's recognition of their unique cultural identity and its overtures to business interests, Mexican American entrepreneurs as well as a quorum of Mexican American political organizations began to see the possibility of returning to their roots through investment. As relatively haphazard efforts to reduce trade barriers began to coalesce into a concrete proposal for a North American Free Trade Agreement (NAFTA), the insights that had emerged out of this interpretive engagement would prove critical in preparing a strategy to get the compact passed by the U.S. Congress.

Operationalizing the Lobby and Passing NAFTA

In June 1990, Presidents George Bush and Carlos Salinas publicly announced their intention to pursue a free trade agreement between their nations, and when Canada formally joined negotiations in early 1991, the debate over a North American Free Trade Agreement began in earnest (Kehoe 1994; Mayer 2001). The Salinas administration was soon flexing "the most visible [international] lobbying muscle in Washington" (Dresser 1993: 93). In a matter of months, Mexico tripled the lobbying contracts it registered with the Department of Justice and dispatched a small army of its own lobbyists and lawyers, who "regaled [U.S.] lawmakers with the country's efforts to modernize its economy, environment, and working conditions" (Dresser 1993: 93; Velasco 1997). To this blitz the Mexican government added efforts to enroll the support of Mexican American political and business groups. Before long this endeavor turned into a collaboration in which the Salinas administration and a quorum of Mexican American leaders and organizations worked together to persuade Mexican Americans that a free trade agreement was in their interest, and thus to bring Latino political influence to bear on NAFTA deliberations in the United States.

The DGCME orchestrated these consultations, with the PCME program staff traveling to meetings with business organizations and politicians. The Mexican office advanced the idea that Mexican Americans stood to gain the most from NAFTA, arguing that the agreement "basically involves small and medium-size companies pursuing growth opportunities" (*La Paloma*, no. 4, March–April 1991) and that "the Hispanic community will be a natural bridge between the U.S. and Mexico because of their natural advocacy, cultural roots and knowledge of the language" (Díaz de Cossio 1991e). Their Mexican American allies countered that although the symbolism of the bridge was seductive, the Mexican government needed to do the grassroots organizing and high-stakes lobbying work among Mexican Americans that was needed to construct it. Prominent Mexican American leaders—including José Niño, executive director of the U.S. Hispanic Chamber of Commerce, Congressman Bill Richardson, and Raul Yzaguirre, director of the National Council of La Raza—gave the Mexican government specific advice (SRE Archives 1991, DGCME program documents, January). For example, they suggested that Salinas meet personally with Mexican American business groups, that the government invite Mexican American organizations to Mexico for consultations with state offices that could address their specific concerns about the trade agreement, and that DGCME broaden its message to include Hispanics in general. An internal DGCME memo summed up the admonition as follows: "The message we received was that we should work this year more intensively with groups of political leaders and that at times the exclusively Mexican message that we project is at odds with the stage of political development of [Mexican American] groups in the United States, where they have been trying for several years to integrate themselves as Hispanics" (SRE Archives 1991, DGCME memorandum, Díaz de Cossio, January 16).

In response, Salinas, already planning U.S. travel in April for a summit meeting with Bush, added to his agenda several meetings with Mexican American organizations and a string of appearances at Mexican American community events. Additionally, shortly after the president's return, the Mexican government held a high-profile conference on NAFTA in Mexico City for Hispanic leaders, including representatives of Puerto Rican and Cuban organizations. The gathering was an opportunity for influential Latinos to consult with high-ranking members of the government, but it also enabled those in attendance to cross Democratic and Republican party lines and strategize about how to resolve differences over the trade agreement—particularly concerns over its impact on the environment and on workers—and mobilize the necessary support among Hispanics to steer the pact through the U.S. Congress. As one Hispanic politician observed, "True bipartisanship is occurring right here in Mexico City" (*La Paloma*, no. 4, April–May 1991). The conference was so successful that the Mexican government repeated it every year until NAFTA's ratification and backed up the gatherings with a packed schedule of individual appointments with Latino groups. The Mexican government was gradually constructing the political framework to hold up the bridge that it claimed Mexican Americans would be in the age of NAFTA. It also added economic cantilevers: Salinas pledged $20 million for joint business ventures between U.S. Latinos and Mexican nationals (Acuña 1996: 242; *La Paloma*, nos. 4–17, April 1991–January 1994; SRE Archives 1991–93, DGCME program documents).

Encouraged by the outcome of the meetings, the Mexican government developed a program to institutionalize the political lobby it had assembled. In late 1991, the DGCME launched a program to establish Mexican cultural institutes throughout the United States. The innocuous and somewhat misleading "cultural" designation notwithstanding, these were set up, according to PCME program documents, to be organizations that would make Mexico's "policy of *acercamiento* permanent" and would serve as "new instruments of political action" to "promote [Mexico's] national interests through political dialogue with Mexican-origin communities in the United States" (SRE Archives 1991, DGCME memorandum, Díaz de Cossio, July 25). The institutes were established as nonprofit organizations, jointly funded by private donations and the Mexican government, directed by a Mexican government appointee (often the local consul) but advised by a board of directors composed of prominent Mexican Americans. They were networked in a sort of decentralized political action group, and the leaders of the soon-to-be twenty centers were convened for biannual meetings with the Mexican government—both high-ranking officials and consuls—to bring their activities in line with Mexican state priorities. The government had grand ambitions for this web of lobbying instruments; as Díaz de Cossio, director of the DGCME, asserted, "the only limit is our imagination. In fact," he added "our national sovereignty depends on it" (Díaz de Cossio 1991a;

La Paloma, nos. 5–25, July 1991–August 1995; SRE interviews, Mexico City, May 2003; interviews, consulate, Chicago, August 2003).

How critical a role the Mexican government's lobbying played in NAFTA's passage through the U.S. Congress is difficult to establish (González Gutiérrez 1997; de la Garza 1997; Acuña 1996). What does seem clear is that the Mexican state's effort had some impact, although it may not have been decisive. The Salinas administration's effectiveness in organizing segments of Mexican Americans, and of Hispanics more broadly, into a pro-NAFTA lobby left an imprint on the compromises that Clinton eventually reached to override labor and environmental opposition to the pact. The most significant of these was the creation of the North American Development Bank (NADbank), designed to finance environmental infrastructure and economic development projects along the 2,000-mile border but also authorized to fund "economic adjustment" to NAFTA in communities in the United States, Canada, and Mexico. The NADbank was proposed by Mexican American lawmakers and activists as a means to level the income disparity between Mexican workers and those north of the border, but as Acuña observes, it was also viewed as a means to continue to "build a power base for Chicanos" (1996: 247).

The Zapatista Rebellion, Proposition 187, and the Collapse of a Lobby

Although NAFTA's ratification may have been evidence of the Mexican government's success in organizing a lobby in the United States, later events made clear that Mexico could not maintain this lobby without confronting the issues that had caused the government to break off its periodic *acercamiento* with Mexican-origin communities in the past. The government could not sustain its engagement with Mexican Americans unless it addressed their criticism of the PRI's seven-decade hold on power and dealt with all aspects of migration, from the treatment of migrant workers in the United States to the state policies that compounded the economic underdevelopment of migrant-sending communities.

On January 1, 1994, the day that NAFTA went into effect, the Zapatistas rose up in revolt against the Mexican government in the southern state of Chiapas. Their rebellion brought the limitations of Mexico's attempt to build a lobby to the surface. Named after Zapata, Mexico's populist revolutionary leader, the group occupied the state capital, San Cristóbal de las Casas, and a number of smaller towns. They called for a repeal of NAFTA and an end to the privatization of land. Salinas responded by sending the Mexican army to crush the rebellion (Davison 1994). Within days, outside Mexican consulates throughout the United States, Mexican and Mexican American activists began protesting the harsh military response, and by January 10 Mexican American activists had organized a delegation that traveled to Chiapas to document the government's human rights abuses (Santamaría Gómez 1994: 332–35). The Chiapas rebellion polarized the Mexican and Mexican American communities in the United States. Although support for NAFTA and the Salinas administration remained firm among a segment of Latino groups, the Zapatistas captivated Mexican and Mexican American leftists, confirming the opposition of many working-class Latinos to NAFTA and lending credence to the quietly harbored misgivings of those Latino organizations that had supported the agreement's passage. Moreover, just as it would in Mexico, support for the Zapatistas in the United States quickly morphed into a demand for electoral transparency in Mexico and for the end of the PRI's dictatorship.

Demonstrations in Mexico, with protestors carrying signs reading "Electoral Revolution of the Country Will Rise Up," were mirrored in cities north of the border (Santamaría Gómez 1994; Martinez Saldaña 2002; Houston Chronicle 1994). In a reprise of 1988, calls for electoral reform soon broadened to include demands that Mexican migrants in the United States be allowed to vote in the upcoming Mexican presidential election. To drive home their point, suffragists held parallel elections for the Mexican president in U.S. cities with large Mexican populations, most notably Los Angeles and Chicago, and thousands cast votes for their symbolic value. The government, through its engagement with Mexican communities in the United States, had once again made itself vulnerable to challenges and found itself facing accusations that it had duped Mexican Americans with eloquent proclamations about political reform going hand in hand with the economic reform that NAFTA would bring (Silen 1995; Santamaría Gómez 1994; 2001; Acuña 1996; Martinez Saldaña 2002; Calderón Chelius 2002).

The Mexican government's lack of response to Proposition 187, a virulently anti-immigrant legislative proposal on the 1994 ballot in California, revealed further problems with its lobby project. The proposition, titled "S.O.S.—Save our state" and championed by California governor Pete Wilson, would deprive undocumented immigrants of access to public services, including health and education, and require social service providers to report the illegal status of immigrant clients to U.S. authorities so that they could be deported. The campaign for the initiative had been the most jingoistic mobilization in California's recent history: with Wilson at the helm, the offensive called for "we Americans" to safeguard the state against "the invasion" of migrants, and ran television spots and newspaper advertisements depicting Mexicans rushing the border under the heading "Every day they just keep coming" (Acuña 1996: 156–62). Although the proposition targeted undocumented immigrants, the inflammatory rhetoric promoting it made little distinction between Mexican Americans, legal Mexican immigrants, and Mexicans who had entered illegally. Latinos throughout the state felt attacked. In response, a broad spectrum of Mexican American organizations joined forces with unions, social service providers, and Democratic politicians to challenge the proposition. Mass demonstrations, drawing tens of thousands of protestors, took place in cities throughout California in the months leading up to the referendum, and participants waved the Mexican flag as they chanted against the initiative. When Proposition 187 came to a vote in November 1994, almost 80 percent of Latinos voted against it. A by no means insignificant proportion of Mexican Americans supported some or all of the measures in the proposition—polls a month earlier suggested that a little less than half the Latinos in the state, the overwhelming majority of whom were Mexican Americans, would cast ballots in favor of 187 (Acuña 1996: 160)—but voted against it because of the racist discourse attached to it. Nevertheless, with Californians favoring it by a two-to-one margin, Proposition 187 passed easily (Acuña 1996; Santamaría Gómez 1994; Martinez Saldaña 2002; González Gutiérrez 1997; Olivares 1994).

Proposition 187 made clear that the position of Mexican Americans in society and the issue of Mexican migration were inextricably linked. This connection was one that the Mexican government did its best to ignore, having sidelined migrants in an effort to keep them invisible and based its strategy for a Mexican lobby in the United States on a firm distinction between migrants and Mexican Americans. The Mexican government's silence on Proposition 187, as on the anti-immigrant rhetoric that fueled its passage, was deafening. Apart from officially registering its opposition on two occasions—once when Governor Wilson attempted to attach anti-immigrant measures to NAFTA in 1993 and once during the heat of the campaign for the proposition—the Mexican government did nothing to slow the momentum of S.O.S. (Robles 1994; Acuña 1996). Its inaction was in sharp contrast to its intensive mobilization in favor of NAFTA. The distance it maintained from Mexican American organizations battling the initiative and the racist propaganda associated with it was chilling to many Mexican American groups and to Mexican immigrants. The coverage the proposed legislation received in *La Paloma*, the government newsletter, only underscored the difference: there had been pages upon pages devoted to pronouncements in favor of NAFTA, whereas Proposition 187 received not a single line in all of 1994 (*La Paloma*, nos. 1–21, September 1990–November 1994).

Instead of tackling the two issues that had repeatedly caused its engagement with Mexican communities abroad to fracture—censure of the PRI's political hegemony and migration—the government, now under the leadership of Ernesto Zedillo, opted for its traditional response and withdrew from any engagement with Mexican communities abroad that generated challenges to the regime. During the Zedillo sexenio, it abandoned efforts to create a powerful lobby in the United States and purposefully narrowed its engagement to certain segments of the Mexican American community, specifically business interests and staunch supporters of Mexico's neoliberal economic turn. NAFTA had bound the fortunes of Mexico and the United States together, and that fact alone made a large Mexican lobby in the United States redundant. When Mexico's decision to let the peso float in December 1994 precipitated a financial meltdown and Mexico's worst economic crisis since the Great Depression, the United States needed little encouragement to put together a $50 billion rescue package within a month (Lustig 1998). "Under Salinas, we built things up: there was a lot of activity, we created programs, new relationships, new institutions. Under Zedillo, we consolidated," tactfully concluded a program officer charged with emigrant affairs in the Secretariat of Foreign Relations (SRE interview, Mexico City, May 2003).

The Zedillo administration scaled back the outreach activities of the PCME and tightened the reins on institutions that embodied its engagement with Mexican Americans, especially the cultural institutes. Despite the enduring rhetoric of the institutes, in practice they reduced their already scant attention to working-class Mexican Americans, focusing on the elites who had been supportive of NAFTA. As a result, they atrophied into appendages of the consular system. Having turned away from one of the most important insights about Mejiamérica—that it was constructed through grassroots mobilization—the institutes never grew into the vital base of political support for the Mexican government or the dynamic networked lobby that the Salinas administration had envisioned. But they also never grew into a powerful political institution that could call the PRI to task, in any meaningful way, on its domination of the political system. Under Zedillo, the Mexican government replaced its programmatic engagement with Mexican Americans with a symbolic acercamiento.

In his National Development Plan for 1995–2000, Zedillo asserted that "the Mexican nation goes beyond the territory that is contained by the outlined borders" and referred to *México de afuera* in his speeches (presidencia de la republica, 1995, as quoted in González Gutiérrez 1997). After Proposition 187 sailed through, Zedillo pledged to "promote legal and constitutional reforms so that Mexicans can preserve their nationality, independent of the citizenship or residence they [have] adopted" and responded to a long-standing request by Mexican American organizers that Mexico allow dual nationality, thus enabling immigrants to become naturalized U.S. citizens without losing their status as Mexican nationals (presidencia de la republica, 1995, as quoted in González Gutiérrez 1997). In consultation with Mexican American organizations (and a handful of emigrant leaders), the PRI hammered out a legislative proposal for dual nationality—one that pointedly failed to grant suffrage along with nationality. The necessary constitutional change for dual nationality was passed in 1996 and went into effect two years later. In a compromise negotiated with the opposition parties that now represented a significant minority in the Mexican Congress, a law allowing Mexicans living abroad to vote was also passed that year. Yet as soon as the package became law, the PRI froze the migrant voting rights provision indefinitely by ordering the National Electoral Commission (IFE) to study its implementation (Calderón Chelius 2002; Ross Pineda 2002).

By passing legislation to allow for dual nationality, the administration transferred the responsibility of dealing with the consequences of Mexican immigration in the United States onto the immigrants themselves, and onto the Mexican American organizations that could enlist the newly naturalized voters in election drives. Zedillo's government had eschewed the responsibility of confronting U.S. political campaigns against Mexican migrants by vesting Mexican American groups with the constitutional tools to do so. (This point was not lost on the California Republican Party, which mounted a letter-writing campaign calling on the Clinton administration to oppose the Mexican constitutional reform on the grounds that it represented an attempt "to influence U.S. internal affairs" [as quoted in Leiken 2001: 38]). Moreover, the Zedillo administration remained conspicuously silent about accelerating emigration from Mexico in the wake of yet another financial crisis after the currency devaluation in 1994, one even more brutal than those before it, doubling unemployment and reducing real wages by 40 percent (Lustig 1998; Massey et al. 1993).

The administration had anticipated a huge reaction to the dual nationality amendment, but the level of response was low (Santamaría Gómez 2001; Fundación Solidaridad Mexicano Americana interviews, Mexico City, May 2003; SRE interviews, Mexico City, May and August 2003). The consulates received few petitions for reinstatement of Mexican nationality lost when Mexicans had adopted U.S. nationality, and naturalization rates—the lowest among any migrant group in the United States (Leiken 2001)—remained largely unchanged (Martinez Saldaña 2002). The magnitude of the disconnect between expectations and results reflected the Salinas and Zedillo administrations' disengagement with migrants. Uninterested in accessing the U.S. political system, Mexican emigrants had instead begun to build political power through grassroots organizing (González Gutiérrez 1995). In an irony that would cost the PRI state-level electoral contests, and ultimately the presidential contest in 2000, the Mexican government had overlooked the very dynamic it had identified as having created Mejiamérica: it had not paid attention to the community mobilization that was reshaping migrant political and economic influence in Mexico and in the United States.

8

From Interpretation
to Political Movement

State-Migrant Engagement in Zacatecas

From the sexenios of Echeverría through de la Madrid, from 1970 to 1988, the Mexican federal government had established a consistent pattern of engagement with Mexican Americans and Mexican migrants. Successive administrations courted Chicano groups and leaders with decided ambivalence, engaging them when closer ties seemed to be in Mexico's national interests and rebuffing them when that engagement produced challenges to PRI hegemony. Mexican migrants, meanwhile, were kept at a firm distance. Studied extensively, they were objectified and unceremoniously excluded from the political discussions over their status.

At the state level, though, a distinct pattern of engagement with migrants began to emerge during this same period. In a handful of states that had long and intense traditions of emigration, such as the central western states of Zacatecas, Michoacán, and Jalisco, the local government began reaching out to emigrants. In most cases, the initiatives were tentative and awkward. Sporadic visits to the United States by local officials, either from the governors' offices or from municipal centers, received a mixed reception, and attempts at collaboration to address the concerns of migrants and their communities of origin disintegrated just as quickly as they had begun (Oficina de Atención a Migrantes interviews, Michoacán, December 2002; interviews, Jalisco, December 2002 and May 2003; and Zacatecas and Jerez, January–May 2003; González Gutiérrez 1995).

In Zacatecas, however, state government efforts steadily gained momentum. Caught between a rural rebellion caused by the collapse of small-scale subsistence farming and a national economic crisis that slashed the state's budget, the government of Zacatecas turned to migrant remittances as a source of funds for rural development. After a few false starts, Zacatecan migrants and the state developed an informal matching-funds arrangement for the completion of basic infrastructure and other projects in migrants' communities of origin. Although the agreement channeled significant resources for public works, the core of the collaboration between migrants and the state was not the projects they were able to fund together. Rather, it was the quality of engagement that the state established. Through the conversations that were its medium, the engagement between migrants and the government of Zacatecas produced the conceptual basis to support new policies and creative approaches to economic development.

After several years, in the early 1990s, the state government of Zacatecas formalized the ad hoc partnership by officially adopting a model of local economic development that explicitly recognized migration and migrants. By turning the extemporaneous practice of matching migrants' funds donated for development projects into a formal program, the state of Zacatecas made its collaboration with migrants permanent but not static. The program provided an enduring structure for the relationship and, more important, for the interpretive conversations that were its sinews. Within that framework, the interpretive engagement grew, and migrants and the state articulated new relationships that captured the multiple causes and effects of labor migration in all their tangled complexity. The insights the interpretive conversation produced revealed new possibilities for action that neither side had imagined. Over time, the state and migrant groups together created new institutions to support the new concepts, even if conflict at times strained the collaboration to the breaking point. To do so, they drew on federal resources and structures, using them instrumentally when the federal government was unable to perceive the insights that drove their efforts. As this chapter shows, it was as if they had scavenged plywood and bricks from a federal construction site to build a home in another place so that they could hold their conversations in its living room. The institutions they built provided the migrants with new sources of power in dealings with the authorities. Ultimately, this power would enable them to redefine their partnership with the state, reversing it from one in which the state mediated migrants' relationship to Zacatecas's economic development to one in which migrants determined the ability of state government to shape Zacatecas's economic and political future.

Zacatecas's experience with a remittance-based matching-funds program illustrates more than the way that interpretive engagement can enlarge and transform a relationship. It also elucidates the dual properties of power and fragility that new meanings display. Through their interpretive conversations, the state of Zacatecas and Zacatecan migrants together blended meanings and understandings in otherwise inconceivable ways, and created completely new concepts. Without the collaborative process, the insights they had collectively would have been unavailable to migrants and the state separately. They would have remained out of their creative reach. But once those insights emerged, they transformed the language of development in the state of Zacatecas and cata-pulted emigration, politically invisible for so many decades, to the forefront of discussions about economic transformation.

Zacatecas's experience also, however, shows the fragility of new meanings, especially when they are still nascent. The meanings that emerged in these ex-changes suggested that migrants could play a vital role in shaping the economic and political transformation not only of their communities of origin, often small and isolated villages, but of the entire state. For meanings that were so politically controversial—so transgressive—to survive, they had to be embodied in a structure, made into formal institutions: a policy, an agreement, a state of-fice. Institutions gave the ideas, still emergent and inchoate in their tender new-ness, a protective shell. They endowed them with heft and authority, bestowing a kind of permanence and traction such that any maneuvers to destroy or disre-gard them could be executed only at significant political cost. Both migrants and government officials used the institutions to protect the interpretive process by which new, as yet unimagined meanings would surface. They viewed policy structures as containers for the collective process of interpretation—structures that they defended vigorously against attempts to dismantle them from within Zacatecas and without. Zacatecas's matching-funds arrangement was protected as an incubator for new ideas about how to involve migrants in development. And among the ideas that state bureaucrats and migrants created were strate-gies to acquire additional resources from an ambivalent federal government to strengthen and expand the policies that sheltered their interpretive engagement.

"We in Zacatecas have been visionaries"

In 1973, small farmers and landless peasants in Zacatecas began occupying vast tracts of privately owned land. They joined forces with student activists at the University of Zacatecas (UAZ) and agricultural unions to form the Zacate-can Popular Front (Frente Popular Zacatecano). Together they pitched tents and erected ramshackle huts in the middle of fields and pasture land. The shacks quickly grew into large protest camps where peasants and activists lived side by side and landless farmers used rocks and stakes to mark off small plots in which they cultivated staple crops for personal consumption (UAZ interviews, Zacatecas, March 2003). By 1976, the cresting movement had occupied fifty-seven private ranches and laid claim to some of the most fertile, best irrigated land in the state (Gómez Sánchez 1990: 191).

Behind the weatherworn roadside banners that sagged after the rains, the peasant-student settlement became entrenched. The squatters refused to leave until the government agreed to a large-scale land redistribution program. Peas-ants and students also made a series of ancillary demands, including improved irrigation, training in new agricultural techniques, and more flexible price ceilings set by the government for their crops (Gómez Sánchez 1990). Access to agricultural credit, most of which had previously been siphoned off by a small group of ranchers backed by a formidable private militia, and provision of basic infrastructure services featured most prominently (Gómez Sánchez 1990: 172; UAZ interviews, Zacatecas, 2003; Delgado Wise et al. 1991).

The poverty that had driven the peasants to act was crushing. The country's abandonment of its Green Revolution in the late 1960s in favor of industrially based growth had a serious impact on Zacatecan agricultural production, and the progressive reduction of state support for small-scale ejidal agriculture, in collectively owned plots, crippled the already underdeveloped economy (Gómez Sánchez 1990; Cross and Sandos 1981). By 1970, Zacatecas, a state which only a few decades before had had a lucrative mining industry and one of the nation's highest yields of beans and maize (Delgado Wise et al. 1991: 48), ranked as one of the poorest (Gómez Sánchez 1990: 175; Padilla 1998). According to a national study that compiled poverty indicators ranging from income to literacy to nutritional intake drawn from the 1970 census, Zacatecas ranked ninth out of 31 states in overall levels of poverty and marginalization (COPLAMAR, 1982, in Padilla 1998: 91).[1] It registered the second lowest income per capita in the country (after Oaxaca), a trend that continued into the 1980s, when the state came in last (Delgado Wise et al. 1991: 17–18). Similarly, it displayed some of the highest unemployment and underemployment rates in the republic for both decades (Padilla 1998: 91). In 1970, Zacatecas also suffered the lowest capacity to generate employment of all states (COPLAMAR, 1982, in Padilla 1998: 91). Not surprisingly, it also endured high rates of malnutrition: Zacatecas, one of Mexico's leading states in cattle farming in 1970, registered the lowest rate of meat consumption in the country that same year (Gómez Sánchez 1990; Padilla 1998: 91).

This generalized poverty was accentuated by the rural geographical isolation. The level of population dispersion was acute: even in 1980, 95 percent of the townships (a category that includes cities) in Zacatecas had less than 1,000 inhabitants, and 60 percent had less than 100. Moreover, the remote communities were equipped with minimal basic infrastructure: in 1970, almost 90 percent of rural households had no sewage lines, 80 percent had no source of electricity, and 60 percent had no ready access to potable water (Delgado Wise et al. 1991: 81–82; see table 8.1).

The call for land reform was as old as the Mexican Revolution at the turn of the twentieth century. Zapata's cry of "Land to the tiller!" was one of the most potent catalysts of a movement that brought an end to three decades of Porfiriato (the rule of Porfirio Diaz) and the crushing exploitation of the poor that characterized it. In the tumultuous years during and after the Revolution of 1910, modest amounts of land were redistributed, mainly as a stopgap measure to stem rebellion. Lázaro Cárdenas, president of Mexico from 1934 to 1940, incorporated this revolutionary call into the lexicon of Mexico's political establishment, making land reform central to the PRI's platform. His administration

TABLE 8.1
Living Conditions in Zacatecas, 1970–95

Measure (%)	1970	1990	1995
Population residing in towns of less than 5,000 residents	74.2	61.9	58
Households without sewage and toilets	79.4	53.1	39.9
Households without electricity	66.1	13.3	7.2
Households without potable water	56.6	27.1	17.6
Households with dirt floors	56	NA	NA

Source: Padilla 1998.

seized hundreds of thousands of hectares for redistribution, transforming Mexico's grand haciendas into *ejidos* that were communally owned,[2] and transforming restive peasants, many of whom fought determinedly in the Cristero Wars, into settled campesinos, a large constituency loyal to the PRI and its institutionalized revolution (Boyer 2003; Gilly 2006). The Frente Popular Zacatecano's demand for land was thus already vested with a political legitimacy derived from its association with the (now stale) revolutionary discourse of the ruling party. But as the campesinos would soon discover, land reform would provide no relief from the arduous conditions under which they lived.

A major staging area for the battles of the Mexican Revolution and the bitter Cristero Wars, Zacatecas had already undergone two major rounds of land reform, once immediately after the Mexican Revolution and once during the 1930s and 1940s under Cárdenas (Moctezuma Longoría 1989: 97–112). As a result, the allotment of agricultural properties was unusually equitable in terms of acreage, with the lion's share already parceled into small tracts or enclosed in *ejidos* (García Zamora 1997: 150–61). In fact, slightly more than half the agricultural land was owned communally, and with the exception of a small number of vast ranches, private tracts on the remaining land tended to be modest in size (García Zamora 1997: 156). The land allotted to petitioners during land redistribution was of poor quality, however: arid, rocky, and sandy. Far from the Rio Grande and other rivers that came close to the end of their journey in the state, agriculture on *ejidos* and other small parcels tended to rely on rainfall. Moreover, poor farmers were granted some of the craggiest land in a state where rugged terrain precluded the use of tractors in over 40 percent of its territory (Delgado Wise et al. 1991: 59; Gómez Sánchez 1990: 177–82; García Zamora 1997; López Moncada and Cerecedo Flores 2000).

If anything, the seemingly equitable land tenure patterns in Zacatecas interacted with national agricultural policy in a way that made poverty in the state more intractable (García Zamora 1997). The overwhelming majority of farmers used rudimentary agricultural techniques to cultivate small plots of maize and corn, the proceeds from which were regulated (and depressed) by price controls imposed by the federal government. The crop yields of small farmers were only about half per hectare of those of large farmers (Gómez Sánchez

1990: 177).[3] Even in banner years, peasants were unable to earn enough to cover subsistence needs, much less invest in technological improvements (Mines 1981; García Zamora 1997; Castro 1996; Delgado Wise et al. 1991).[4]

To supplement income, a significant proportion of Zacatecan peasants migrated to the United States. As Delgado Wise and Pozo (2002) argue, the structure of agricultural production in Zacatecas, aggravated by growing population pressures, reoriented the state from the production of crops to the production of labor for export. Land tenure patterns, combined with backward technologies, tethered Zacatecan agricultural production to labor markets north of the border because migrants had to travel to the United States for temporary periods to subsidize farming activities that were fundamentally unsustainable. Migration trends bear out this observation. Ever since the informal bracero program launched at the end of World War I, Zacatecans had been well represented among migrants to the United States, with emigration rates that were at least twice as high as those of states beyond the central western swath of the country (Cross and Sandos 1981: 9–14). Households in Zacatecas came to depend heavily on remittances for their economic welfare, and migration became an indispensable lifeline for rural communities up against the limits of an agricultural model characterized by small plots and scarce capital.[5] The state registered the highest rates of out-migration in the republic in 1970: an estimated 5 percent of the total population left for extended periods, whereas an unknown but significantly larger number—some estimates suggest that the ratio was as high as 5 to 1—migrated to the United States or Mexican cities for shorter seasonal stints in more promising labor markets in the 1970s (Delgado Wise et al. 1991: 19; Mestries Benquet 2002: 86–87). This trend would only accelerate in the 1980s and 1990s (Delgado Wise et al. 1991: 19–20; Padilla 1998: 133–46, 105).[6] Zacatecas's 1970 population of 1 million persons was almost a quarter lower than the population growth rate would have predicted:[7] Zacatecas had a population "gap" of 25,000 people (Padilla 1998: 16). Moreover, in 1975 it was receiving the highest remittance levels per capita in Mexico (Delgado Wise et al. 1991: 18). The influx of dollars, however, was not sufficient to blunt the poverty throughout the state, and economically and geographically marginalized campesinos felt they had no alternative but to continue seizing land.

As the squatter movement grew more entrenched and militant, the state government under Governor Pánames Escobedo, heavily influenced by Echeverría's use of land reform for political restitution after the traumatic massacre of Tlatelolco, initially negotiated with the squatters. A former general with strong ties to the central PRI political machinery, Pánames Escobedo had been dispatched to Zacatecas as the ruling party's candidate for governor to bring the increasingly powerful and independent cattle ranchers to heel and bring the state in line with national development policy. Mildly sympathetic to the campesinos' situation and directed by the Echeverría regime to resolve the crisis, he agreed to a modest round of land redistribution. From 1974 to 1976, about 100,000 hectares of privately owned land were reallocated to close to 4,000 protesting campesinos (del Alizal et al. 1995: 199). The gesture was even more limited than the area distributed suggests: virtually all the land reallocated was ill suited to agriculture, and the dry, uneven plots could barely support use as pasture land (Gómez Sánchez 1990; García Zamora 2000).[8] In a move to gild the meagerness of the measure, Pánames Escobedo also committed to creating a research center to investigate the causes of the state's agricultural collapse (Gómez Sánchez 1990; del Alizal et al. 1995). Despite these concessions, however, land seizures escalated, and rural unrest grew more volatile and destabilizing. Ranchers, merchants, and other well-to-do residents took to the streets of the state capital in a massive protest in February 1976, and public protest was shadowed by increasingly brutal attacks by ranchers' private militias on squatting campesinos (Gómez Sánchez 1990: 191–92).

By 1976, the state government, with no land left that it could reallocate without causing a political crisis and with the federal government under the newly instated López Portillo having lost its appetite for land distribution, changed tack and used force to expel the squatters from private plots. Pánames Escobedo called in the army, enrolled the ranchers' private militias, and applied harsh measures against the Popular Front, including detentions, beatings, and kidnappings. Undaunted, campesinos and their student allies continued the land seizure movements into the late 1980s. On several occasions, unrest flared into violent confrontation, with protests staged increasingly in urban centers. The movement posed a constant and at times significant challenge to state authority (del Alizal et al. 1995; Delgado Wise et al. 1991: 101–24).

The state government tried to buy social peace. Resorting to traditional PRI-ista corporatist tactics, it handed out subsidies and cash gifts to peasant participants in the movement, which, according to the memoirs of the assistant attorney general serving at the time (1974–80), "helped a great deal in calming the aggressiveness of people" (Murillo Belmonte, as quoted in Delgado Wise et al. 1991: 110). The state also began to address the other demands of the peasant movement. Pánames Escobedo launched several initiatives to increase technical assistance to small farmers, provide them with improved seeds, and connect small plots to irrigation systems (Gómez Sánchez 1990).

With only so much that government could do to turn the arid gravelly plots it had distributed to protestors into fertile parcels, the state and municipal governments began to tackle the insufficiency of basic infrastructure. Pánames Escobedo turned his attention to providing isolated villages with amenities such as potable water, electricity, and roads, and the initiatives he began, his successor, José Cervantes Corona, embraced with even greater zeal (del Alizal et al. 1995: 201). Over time, the provision of infrastructure in rural areas would act as a measure of government responsiveness. As one municipal president in Zacatecas explained, "Infrastructure is how people hold us accountable now. The more concrete we pour, the more votes we get" (interview, Zacatecas, March 2003).

Remittances and Infrastructure Provision

Despite its plans to soothe rural discontent with infrastructure provision, the state government of Zacatecas was cash-strapped; after the national liquidity crisis of 1982, and cut loose from federal purse strings, it had to find new sources of funding within its borders. Faced with the prospect that rural unrest would flare again, it began to explore the possibility of drawing on private monies for basic infrastructure projects (del Alizal et al. 1995). (The state government also pursued its crackdown on land occupations and prolonged protests: eyewitness accounts describe police or army forces beating campesinos, bulldozing their homes, and slaughtering their livestock [Gómez Sánchez 1990: 193].) Tapping the resources of wealthier residents of the state's dispersed villages—resources that consisted of the monies they earned al Norte, in U.S. fields and factories—quickly emerged as an attractive source of funding to supplement the costs of laying down pipes, putting up electricity networks, and rolling out concrete.

Zacatecan migrants, on their own initiative, had long financed the construction of infrastructure in their communities, and rural hamlets throughout the state boasted projects from the drilling of new wells to the renovation of the local church funded through migrant donations (Moctezuma Longoría 2003; Goldring 2002; interviews, Zacatecas, March–April 2003). But their methods were intimately related to the way they migrated and the implications their stays across the border had for their status in their communities. Zacatecan migrants were overwhelmingly—by a ratio of three to one in 1970 (E. Rivas, 1989, as cited in Delgado Wise et al. 1991: 71)—what Mines (1981) calls "shuttle migrants": they left Mexico to work for delimited periods, but did so repeatedly, "shuttling" to the United States to subsidize their agricultural activities in Zacatecas, to which they returned every year. The contrast between the level of infrastructure provision in the United States and that in their home villages "arouse[d]," as Mines understatedly puts it, "interest in a higher standard of living" (1981: 157). Faced with government inadequacy in this area, migrants, the new rural elites of their villages, undertook the public works themselves (interviews, Zacatecas, December 2002, March–April 2003; Mines and Massey 1985). For the many instances in which these endeavors required the consent of state authorities, the Zacatecans enlisted the help of the Catholic Church to negotiate the terms of their contributions to public works. Village churches often acted as behind-the-scenes intermediaries with the municipal and state governments, haggling with bureaucrats who sometimes resented what they viewed as the new village elites' overly assertive efforts to obtain permits (Delgado Wise et al. 1991: 94).

Whereas the vast majority of Zacatecan migrants spent multiple short periods working in the United States, a fraction had settled there permanently, and the way they gifted funds for community projects reflected their migration histories (Moctezuma Longoría 2003; Goldring 2002). Because of the way that employment and social networks were intertwined, with migrants accessing jobs through friends and relatives in their home community, those from a given village tended to settle in the same area in the United States, creating what migration scholars have termed "daughter communities" (Delgado Wise and Rodríguez Ramírez 2001; R. Smith 1995; Levitt 2001). Mines, in his study of the Zacatecan village of Las Animas and its daughter communities in Tijuana, Los Angeles, and San Francisco (1981), demonstrates, for example, that networks that Las Animas forged in California industry during and after the first informal bracero program following World War I enabled villagers who migrated north under the second program to escape exploitative conditions in agriculture for jobs in San Francisco and Los Angeles. Small clusters of Animeños quickly established themselves in those cities; villagers who settled there brought family members and abandoned the shuttle pattern of migration, as well as many, but not all, of the agricultural activities that temporary migration supported (Mines 1981).

Zacatecan migrants in those daughter communities would often organize hometown associations for the express purpose of funding community projects. These clubs, created on the fly, were frequently no more than informal collection drives, dissolving once a project was complete. One migrant who organized a club in Los Angeles in the mid-1970s remembered how spontaneous it was: "When I made good, I told my mother, 'I have a few dollars now, what can I get you to make you happy?' And she said, 'Son, what I want is for you to help me build a chapel in the village where we were born.' Nothing more, nothing less. So I started organizing migrants from our village, collecting money for the chapel, writing down names and donations on a piece of paper: Juan—fifty cents, Pedro—a dollar fifty . . . and that's how we became a club, as simple as that" (interview, Zacatecas, March 2003).

A handful of groups, however, took on a more enduring character, serving as social clubs and mutual aid societies that institutionalized relationships of reciprocity in the daughter communities (Moctezuma Longoría 2003). Some were patterned on the *mutualistas* founded by the Mexican consulate during the heyday of consular support in the 1920s and 1930s, and sought a relationship with the current local Mexican consulate (González Gutiérrez 1999), but in the 1970s and early 1980s, when the Mexican government was striving to pretend that emigration did not exist, they were rebuffed. Without institutional support, even the most solid of these organizations was fragile and tended to disintegrate over time (interviews, Zacatecas, March 2003; Mexico City, February 2003; and Chicago, April 2003).

Failed Partnerships: Formal and Informal Initiatives to Channel Remittances

In 1982, the state government of Zacatecas launched a program for infrastructure development that required a contribution from the beneficiaries; its defining assumption was that community contributions would consist primarily of

remittances that migrants sent or brought home. It was, according to histori-
ans del Alizal et al., "the first institutional attempt to channel a portion of the
resources sent home by migrant workers to the construction of public works"
(1995: 202). The policy was embedded in Zacatecas's 1982 Unifying Agreement for Development (Convenio Único de Desarrollo) with the federal government, a compact that the de la Madrid administration, in its bid to decen-
tralize the execution of government programs, signed with each state to
formalize the transfer of federal resources (Rodríguez 1997: 136–37).

    After only a couple of years, however, the initiative to use private financing,
derived from remittances, for infrastructure construction was discontinued.
The main reason the program faltered was that it was based on the perception
that migrants were not meaningfully distinct from other small-scale farmers in
Zacatecas. In a reflection of the larger national political practice, migration
was unacknowledged, and migrants were counted in local populations (UAZ
interviews, Zacatecas, March 2003). As Genaro Borrego, who would become
governor of Zacatecas in 1986, observed: "The topic of migrants in the 1980s
was a taboo subject. No one wanted to touch it; it wasn't in the political discourse of the party. . . . Especially in Zacatecas . . . policymakers avoided it.
There was no desire to recognize or deal with it as a reality, which, like all realities, has aspects that are both positive and negative" (interview, Mexico City,
May 2003).

    The perception that migrants were full members of their communities was
not without basis: most migrants returned to Zacatecas for extended periods
during the year. They purchased land or livestock, built houses, and invested in
agriculture. However, because their wealth primarily derived from wage labor
in the United States rather than from crops produced locally, their emigration
bifurcated villages economically and socially into two distinct classes: households
that sent one or more men abroad on a regular basis, and households that did
not. How migrants participated in agriculture depended on their access to employment north of the border. Their success—their survival—as small-scale
farmers was informed by the ability to move easily in U.S. labor markets and
earn enough to subsidize, and even invest in, agriculture on poor soil. With
their welfare more contingent on short stints in the United States than on local
relationships or government assistance programs, migrant households had economic, social, and even political needs distinct from those of nonmigrants. Although the government of Zacatecas was keen on funneling migrants' money
toward state projects, it showed little interest in addressing their special concerns (Delgado et al. 1991; Mines 1981; Mines and Massey 1985).

    The slippage between the state view of migrants as ordinary members of their
community and the economic and social realities produced by migration proved
to be the Achilles' heel of the formal state initiative. This flaw compounded the
second factor that caused the program's failure: mutual misunderstanding and
mistrust. Migrants wanted a greater say in how money collected from them was
spent. Although they were often the elites of their little ranchos, they were no

match for the wealthy cattle ranchers who dominated the state's agricultural economy and political scene. Although in theory the increase in infrastructure investment was supposed to placate striking campesinos' demands for land reform, the plans as to where roads would be rolled out and pipes laid down, as migrants complained, tended to favor large agriculturalists. In addition, the infrastructure planned through the Unified Agreement for Development reflected federal priorities for basic service provision. Indeed, the agreements were designed to promote a mild version of decentralization: one that allowed state autonomy but only within the firm parameters laid out by the central government. Both state and municipal governments perceived migrants' desire to exercise some measure of control over how the funds they donated were allocated as an affront to their authority. Evaluations of the use of migrant resources for programs through the Unified Agreement allude to these tensions: in a manner that was highly unusual for official documents drafted during this period, they hint at accusations levied at the state government regarding the mismanagement of private funds under the program and of the politically motivated disbursal of monies (del Alizal et al. 1995; interviews, Zacatecas, March–April 2003).

Evidence suggests that in addition to using remittances through this short-lived formal government program, municipal presidents explored avenues to use the funds for community projects during the late 1970s and early 1980s. Those municipalities that experimented with this possibility tried to fund infrastructure construction jointly with migrant clubs. Oral histories of these informal partnerships indicate that the earliest attempts at such collaborations date to 1974, when the Tepetongo club of Los Angeles offered the municipal government of Tepetongo, Zacatecas, a small grant to construct a sports field (interviews, Zacatecas, April 2003).

Such informal partnerships faltered because municipal governments conflated migrants with other residents in the communities that they governed. Clubs, however, were generally made up of migrants who had settled abroad and did not return regularly or for extended periods, so the failure to recognize migrants as a separate group, with distinct needs and concerns, created serious problems. Chief among unrecognized needs was a mechanism that allowed migrants to hold the state accountable and ensure that the municipal government would spend migrant funds as promised (interviews, Zacatecas, March–April 2003).

Migrants who had settled in the United States were wary of graft at home and concerned that the needs they saw in their home communities would be sacrificed to the wants of local elites. Among these elites were shuttle migrants, who, with the resources they earned abroad, were able to pressure local authorities into redirecting settler migrant funds from projects that held important symbolic and cultural value to that group, such as the construction of churches, toward those of greater benefit to themselves, such as irrigation systems or roadways.

The recollections of the man who was mayor of Tepetongo during the early 1980s capture the suspicion with which migrants and the state viewed each other and illustrate how their interactions escalated miscommunication. The Los Angeles Tepetongo club wanted to build a sports field to honor one of its members, a Tepetongo native who played minor league baseball in a California, but also to demonstrate their collective success to the village. Through construction of a baseball diamond, the village's absent sons would remain forever present. As the mayor recounted, however, the project had been stalled for several years under his predecessor, due to "a lot of funny business, a lot of theft" (interview, Zacatecas, April 2003). To resolve the dispute, the mayor traveled to Los Angeles to meet with the club in 1980.

> I said to myself, I'm going to see what all of this is about. And it was during that trip that I uncovered a whole lot of stuff. . . . The migrants took me to the Casa del Mexicano. We had a meeting there. There were like ten people. We practically came to blows [*puro madrazos*]. It was like being on trial. They wanted me to sign stuff. They asked me things . . . trick questions, and I answered them with whatever came to mind, nothing real, just to get out of answering. And then they asked me to sign something, and I signed like this [draws a scribble on a piece of paper] and they got mad. And I said, "well that's my signature." I mean, how was I going to sign a paper with off-handed answers [*pendejadas*] I gave them to the trick questions that they asked me. I mean, the whole thing was a trap. . . . Anyway, I decided that I didn't want to work with them because I didn't want to be accused of stealing their money. (Interview, Zacatecas, April 2003)

After much negotiation, the project went forward, but only after the municipality agreed that migrants would maintain full control over their contributions by sending money to a representative in the community rather than to the municipal offices. The completion of the sports field set a precedent, and other collaborative projects followed. The experience, however, was short-lived: the municipal government never institutionalized the relationship or created an institutional container for the trust that the migrant club had placed in the municipal president. Once that president left office, the partnerships petered out and the Tepetongo club tore itself apart through infighting (interviews, Zacatecas, April 2003).

Nevertheless, the formal and informal attempts to draw on migrant remittances for infrastructure provision suggested the potential of such a partnership. The floundering attempts at collaboration transformed an initiative the state had explored out of political necessity into an idea that seemed commonplace and plausible. Partnerships between migrants and the state government, framed in a formal policy, were possible, if complicated, but a policy that did not open clear channels of communication between the two sides would fail. By the time Genaro Borrego became governor in 1986, not only had the political rationale for an engagement with migrants been well established, but the elements that could be combined into effective institutional structures to support a partnership had also been identified. The insights and institutional models produced by the failed collaboration provided the new administration with space and resources to explore a qualitatively different engagement, one allowing for interpretive conversations and a genuine exploration of migrants' roles in the state's economic development.

Principles of a Partnership

Chroniclers of the development of the various federations of Zacatecan Clubs throughout the United States, which would later become some of the largest and most influential organizations of Mexican migrants, cite 1986, when Borrego began his term as governor, as the year the federations' engagement with the state and efforts at community organizing began (Goldring 2003; Moctezuma Longoría 2003). The conversations that migrants began with him would grow into a nationwide matching-funds program for community projects and radically revise views about the role that migrants could play in local economies and political contexts. So modest and haphazard was their beginning that it would have been impossible to imagine the national program, renowned worldwide, they would establish.

Borrego's first real contact with migrants was during his campaign for governor. His friend and campaign volunteer Juan Guillermo Zazati encouraged him to meet with Zacatecans who had migrated and settled in the United States. For Zazati, settler migrants were peripheral to Zacatecas's political and economic life until he had had occasion to meet many of them in southern California, where he had gone to seek care for his wife, who was ill with cancer. "I got to know about their lives, how they lived there. It was a hard time in my life and the company I found meant a lot to me" (interview, Zacatecas, March 2003). Zazati, a successful contractor in Zacatecas, concluded agreements with some of these migrants to build their houses in their communities of origin. "But I was having trouble finishing them on time because the places where they wanted me to build weren't urbanized yet [they lacked basic infrastructure]. It was a problem I wanted to resolve; it was a problem they wanted to resolve. It was clear that there was an opportunity to do something there" (interview, Zacatecas, March 2003).

During one of his final campaign tours through rural Zacatecas, the future governor met with a group of migrants who worked in Los Angeles but had returned to Zacatecas for short stays (interview, Zacatecas, March 2003). "They told me about how they were doing," recalls Borrego. "About how they organized themselves, how they wanted to organize themselves, what ideas they had, what grievances they had, what discomfort they felt, what struggles they faced every day over there in the United States, and what were their proposals, their concerns" (interview, Mexico City, May 2003). The candidate invited them to meet with him once he took office to explore the possibility of capitalizing on remittances for rural development (Borrego interview, Mexico City, May 2003; del Alizal et al. 1995; UAZ interviews, Zacatecas, March 2003). The migrants took the governor up on his offer, and one of them, Julian Estrada, traveled to the capital for an audience. The conversation quickly progressed beyond negotiations over the ways remittances could be channeled and toward specific infrastructure projects. As the governor recalls:

> Julian came to tell me, "We exist. We exist, we are Zacatecanos, we love our land, we hurt for her, we want her to develop, and we want to contribute to that. But at the same time, we have problems in the United States, no one listens to us, no one pays attention to us, we are strangers there, we suffer discrimination. In the consulates, they focus [especially at that time] on bureaucratic matters, but there is no political dialogue, no humanistic dialogue to deal with social problems that come up for us." So I got really interested, so I asked Julian to put me in touch with others there [in Los Angeles]. (Interview, Mexico City, May 2003)

These conversations gave rise to a plan for the governor to visit Los Angeles to meet with Zacatecan migrants. Borrego would not be the first Zacatecan governor to go there; several of his predecessors, including governors José Rodríguez Elías in 1962 and Fernando Pánames Escobedo in 1978, had made official visits to the city (González Gutiérrez 1995: 77–78n24). Borrego's exploratory approach, however, transformed the trip into the inauguration of a sustained engagement with migrants; as he explained: "I decided to make a formal visit [to Los Angeles] in my capacity as governor to meet with them *without a pre-defined agenda.* Simply and sincerely to let them know that I recognized them as Zacatecanos, just as if they were living here [in the state], and that I was the governor of the Zacatecanos over here, but I was also the governor of the Zacatecanos over there. To make a long story short, a date was picked, and I invited several Zacatecanos who were interested to join me" (interview, Mexico City, May 2003, emphasis mine). The visit was set for mid-November 1986, arranged to coincide with a dance that a group of Zacatecan clubs had planned for compatriots in the Los Angeles area (interviews, Zacatecas, March–April 2003; Borrego interview, Mexico City, May 2003; UAZ interviews, Zacatecas, March–April 2003; González Gutiérrez 1995).

The heart of the encounter was a meeting between Borrego, the retinue he brought from Zacatecas (which included the bishop of Zacatecas and a handful of municipal presidents), and about fifteen Zacatecan migrants who lived in Los Angeles. They gathered in a hotel meeting room and had an extensive discussion about the challenges that migrants faced in the United States, the needs that they and their communities of origin had, and the possibilities for collaboration with the state government. The conversation had no other goals than to allow Zacatecan migrants and the governor to get acquainted and to "try and put some of our ideas in some sort of order," as Borrego described it.

The discussions, which lasted all day, were for the most part freewheeling and gregarious, although tense at times. In the end, participants left the meeting having articulated a series of conceptual insights about migrants, their economic and political lives in the United States, and their ties to their communities of origin. Of these, three would define the relationship between migrants and the state of Zacatecas for years to come.

The first of these insights was that migrants—and, in particular, permanent settler migrants who had made their home in cities like Los Angeles—were a distinct group, with needs and identities that differed from those prevalent in their communities of origin. They were not campesinos who migrated north a few months out of the year, or a few years out of their lives, to subsidize their failing ranches. Rather, they settled north of the border and farmed the plots that they still had in Zacatecas, primarily as an act of nostalgia. When they had saved enough, they would uproot their neat rows of bean stalks and peach trees to make room for California-style homes (Moctezuma Longoría 1999; Mines 1981).

Second, unlike the impact of temporary migrants, who lived "on-site" in the village and held sway over their poorer neighbors, the impact of settler migrants on their communities of origin was tightly correlated to their level of community organization. By organizing, migrants could combine efforts to better their villages by pooling monies, energy, and most of all, vision, to carry out projects they believed in. Organizing also gave them an advantage in navigating labor markets in the United States and enabled them to perform better economically. Migrants who had created clubs—later called hometown associations in the migration literature (M. Orozco 2002; Garza and Orozco 2002)—could use their social contacts to hear about jobs, to compare notes about working conditions, and even to strategize about challenging what they considered exploitative behavior by their employers (interviews, Zacatecas, February 2003; Cornelius 1998). A cross between an informal union and an ad hoc hiring hall, the clubs helped migrants do better economically, as they themselves would later insist, and as a result they were able to remit more money.

The third and final insight was that the state could magnify the impact that organized settler migrants had on their communities by contributing resources and embedding the projects migrants wanted to carry out in larger state development plans. But the state would be able to play this role only if it earned the migrants' trust, and the trust required was deeper than mere confidence that the state government would act as a good-faith partner. Migrants not only had to trust that the state would not swindle them out of the resources they donated for community projects, but they had to trust that the state, in its function as an intermediary between migrants and their communities of origin, would faithfully reflect and carry out migrants' intentions to their villages. These three insights, jotted down on a lined piece of notebook paper, would serve as a charter that guided the creation of new organizations and policies to support an on-going engagement.

In the course of their discussion, fueled by watery coffee and cigarettes, the migrants and Borrego articulated five clear objectives. The first was to promote the grassroots organizing of migrants and their consolidation into a formal organization, "a network of solidarity" (Borrego interview, Mexico City, May 2003) that was transnational in character and encompassed migrants and the communities from which they came on an equal basis. The second objective was to defend the rights of migrant workers. These rights included labor rights and human rights, as well as cultural and civic rights, and the participants committed "to us[ing] any means necessary . . . formal and informal, diplomatic and political, whatever was required" (Borrego interview, Mexico City, May 2003), to protect those rights and guard migrants from exploitation. The third goal was to ensure that migrants received fair treatment in transit from Zacatecas to the United States and back, with a special focus on eradicating abuses by Mexican customs officials (Borrego interview, Mexico City, May 2003). The fourth was to create channels for migrants to foster the development of their villages of origin, so that "the fruit of their labor, their sacrifice, their efforts should have a beneficial impact on their communities" (Borrego interview, Mexico City, May 2003). The fifth and final aim was the creation of employment in Zacatecas. At the end of the meeting, the participants added these objectives to the sheet of paper and committed to meet regularly to evaluate progress toward them (UAZ, Federación de Clubes Zacatecas del Sur de California [FCZSC], and Zacatecas Planning Department interviews, Zacatecas, March–April 2003; interviews, Zacatecas, April 2003; Borrego interview, Mexico City, May 2003).

Over and above the insights the charter encapsulated, the fact that such a document was drafted at all was itself a recognition that migrants were a group distinct from their communities of origin. It was an acknowledgment that the migrants had unique goals and needs. Moreover, if the state government wanted to partner with them and access their resources, it had to form a relationship with them that was separate from any relationship it had or would maintain with the residents of their ranchos of origin in Zacatecas, including the shuttle migrants who lived there.

The following evening, at the annual gala the Zacatecans held in the Los Angeles area to crown a local Zacatecan beauty queen—a huge affair, according to the governor, who was moved at the sight of a ballroom filled to capacity with his compatriots—Borrego publicly announced the state's recognition that migrants were a distinct constituency to which, he emphasized, it had an undeniable responsibility. The declaration represented a radical reversal of decades of governmental silence, especially at the state level, on the question of migration: "I am the governor of the Zacatecanos over here [in the United States] just as much as I am the governor of Zacatecanos over there [in Zacatecas]" (Borrego interview, May 2005). He baptized the day of the event—November 11—as the Day of the Migrant (Día del Migrante) in Zacatecas and promised to return yearly to celebrate the occasion with them. He then presented the charter to the crowd, outlining its elements, and thus declared in a public forum the state's commitment to building a lasting partnership (interviews, Zacatecas, March–April 2003; FDZSC interviews, April and July 2003; UAZ interviews, Zacatecas, 2003).

Zacatecans who attended the dance remember the governor's explicit recognition of settler migrants and their needs as a watershed moment. They became visible to the government as a constituency, but even more important they became visible to themselves as a group that could have a hand in creating new futures for themselves and their families on both sides of the border. A migrant who would become a major organizing force among his compatriots some years later remembered the effect of the governor's acknowledgment: "He made our excitement and our commitment grow . . . ah, the governor is here! It was because he was Borrego but mostly because he was governor. Because in Mexico, like in California, it's almost impossible to see the governor, but that night at the ball, then through the clubs, the events we organized . . . well, the governor comes and greets you, he sits down at your table . . . maybe because he was in another country [laughs] but it was important to us. It really helped us move forward. We saw ourselves as people who could change things" (interview, Zacatecas, March 2003).

Organizing Migrants

At the same meeting held in the Los Angeles hotel conference room, the migrants and the governor agreed on an institution to serve as a vehicle for migrants' community organizing efforts. They chose the newly reinaugurated Federation of Zacatecan Clubs, which had organizational roots stretching to 1972. That year, eight Zacatecas clubs decided to form a loose association to help each other with fund-raising and expand their social networks in Los Angeles beyond people from their particular hamlet.[9] The federation they created met at the Casa Mexicana, headquarters of Comité de Beneficencia Mexicana, a large and well-established mutual aid society that had been under the tutelage of the Los Angeles consulate since its founding in 1931. The Casa Mexicana was the gathering place for Mexicans from various states, and soon clubs from Durango, Michoacán, and Jalisco asked to join the federation. In 1980, the alliance of Zacatecanos was renamed the Federation of Mexican Clubs to reflect its more inclusive structure, although it remained dominated by Zacatecan clubs (five as opposed to only three from the rest of Mexico). In anticipation of Borrego's visit, the Zacatecan clubs broke with the larger Federation of Mexican Clubs and reestablished their own state-based association. Until the governor's arrival, however, the organization existed only on paper (http://www.federacionzacatecana.org; Moctezuma Longoría 2003: 5–6; González Gutiérrez 1995; Borrego interview, Mexico City, May 2003; UAZ interviews, Zacatecas, March–April 2003; Goldring 2003).

At the first conclave between migrants and the state, it was decided that the Federation of Zacatecan Clubs would serve as the organization representing Zacatecan migrants in Los Angeles, and Borrego designated it as the government's interlocutor in its relationship with the *paisanos* of southern California (Borrego interview, Mexico City, May 2003; interviews, Zacatecas, April 2003). In a recursive cycle, the state brought an organization into being by acknowledging it, which gave the fledgling group the political legitimacy to engage with the state on behalf of Zacatecans in Los Angeles, which in turn justified the state's ongoing interactions with the federation. In this sense, the state was a key participant in the grassroots organizing that created the federation; the association of Zacatecan clubs became a robust organization because of the exchanges between migrants and the state, rather than because of the efforts of either party on its own. In the process, the state and migrants redefined each other. Migrants became a visible constituency represented by an organized group vested with political recognition and, by extension, clout, and the Zacatecan state government became a partner and a vehicle through which migrants could assert their belonging to their state and, less directly, to their villages of origin.

The governor was careful to publicly vest the Federation of Zacatecan Clubs with official sanction and raise the profile of the organization to other Zacatecans in Los Angeles, as well as to the Angelino authorities. He announced the creation of the federation in front of hundreds of Zacatecan migrants during the short speech he gave at the ball, and explained he would stay in contact with Zacatecans "*de aca*—over here" through ongoing conversations with their federation. At a rodeo the following day, in an arena packed with migrants, the governor descended onto the dusty showground and solemnly delivered a Mexican flag to a representative from each of the Zacatecan hometown associations that belonged to the federation. Los Angeles mayor Tom Bradley, who attended the event to meet the Mexican governor, watched the whole performance: "I wanted the mayor to see that the Federation was going to be an important representative of Mexican interests, a representative in Zacatecas, deserving of respect," recalled Borrego (Borrego interview, Mexico City, May 2003; interviews, Zacatecas, March–April 2003; UAZ interviews, Zacatecas, March–April 2003).

Building Trust

"Oiga, Señor, why don't you help us with getting potable water for our community, with getting a road, with this, with that . . . people came up to the governor the whole time he was in Los Angeles and kept asking him for help," recalled a government employee who accompanied him (interview, Zacatecas, March 2003). Indeed, during the daylong meeting at the hotel, they also drafted a matching-funds arrangement to finance development projects in migrants' communities of origin. This agreement was high on the migrants' list of priorities—without it, the handwritten compact and the governor's recognition of the Federation of Zacatecan Clubs would have remained empty gestures.

The arrangement recycled insights and institutional structures from Zacatecas's previous attempts to capture remittances for public works. It built on the idea that a stable partnership between migrants and the state would enable migrants to contribute to public works in a manner benefiting local development. "There was no correspondence between their desire [to donate funds for amenities] and the structures to make it happen. So we had to organize, create a methodology, put the structures in place," recalled the governor (interview, Mexico City, May 2003). The agreement incorporated the insight that migrant clubs could be important vehicles for identifying community projects.

The arrangement also reflected an awareness of why previous attempts at collaboration had failed—flaws the migrants in the room recalled for Borrego and his retinue. Thus, building infrastructure faded as the main goal, replaced with the aim of fostering trust between migrants and the state government, without which all essays at collaboration would collapse. As Borrego clarified:

> The objective was twofold: to create an incentive to increase their contributions to community projects, and even more, to build trust [para dar confianza]; if they contributed a dollar, and contributing that dollar involved some risk, well, it just seemed fundamental to me in terms of equity that I contribute a dollar and run the same risk. I wanted them to know that we were in it together. (Interview, Mexico City, May 2003)

The methodology used to select community projects reflected the governor's aspiration to build migrants' confidence in the state as an intermediary that could help carry out the vision *they* had for their villages of origin. In that initial phase, when the relationship was still tentative and fragile, migrants were given absolute discretion over the projects they wanted to fund, and the governor agreed to match their contributions on the spot. Moreover, he embraced the ad hoc organizing style that migrants had used both to collect monies for community projects and to set up migrant clubs. At the same meeting, a list of projects was drawn up. As Borrego recounts:

> We said, "Who here wants to do a project in their community?" And because they had already been organizing themselves, they responded, "Well, some of us have a fund that we've been collecting for months—sometimes years!—because we want to contribute to the lighting of public space in such and such a village." "Okay, let's write that down. How much do you have?" "This amount." "Okay, we'll put together a budget, and once we have that, I'll tell you how much more you have to collect, and I'll find the amount to match it. Okay, who else has a project? And who else?" And we took notes right then and there. So then, I returned back to Zacatecas with something like 20 projects that the migrants

wanted to carry out. And we completed them all—within the year. (Interview, Mexico City, May 2003)

Finally, the migrants and the governor agreed to create citizens' committees in communities of origin to oversee the completion of the projects and ensure that the resources that the migrants had contributed were accounted for (FDZSC interviews, Zacatecas, April 2003; UAZ interviews, Zacatecas, March–April 2003; Borrego interview, May 2003).

The drive to support migrant community organizing and the careful labor of building a relationship of trust were mutually reinforcing. As migrants saw their projects completed, more clubs were organized, more projects proposed to the governor's office, and the conversations between the state government and migrants grew more substantive. They began to tackle increasingly contentious questions, such as the responsibility of the Mexican state to protect the labor rights of migrant workers, or the measures the Zacatecan government could take to rescue villages from a downward economic spiral, including the provision of agricultural extension services and the revision of price controls on staple crops. In another synergistic loop, the breadth of those conversations and the quality of engagement with the state that they reflected endowed the federation with community legitimacy in Los Angeles as well as in Zacatecas, which in turn encouraged migrants' involvement in larger municipal projects (FDZSC interviews, Zacatecas, April 2003; UAZ interviews, Zacatecas, March–April 2003; Borrego interview, May 2003).

Although the matching-funds arrangement remained informal for the duration of Borrego's six-year term, leaving no dedicated records to document the public works supported through migrant donations, the data available suggest that the projects were modest in size but significant in the precedent they set: twenty clubs, most with membership of only several dozen Zacatecanos, collected a total of about $200,000 for projects ranging from the paving of roads, to the installation of potable water systems, to the renovation of local plazas and churches. Additionally, a small group of entrepreneurial Zacatecan migrants, having succeeded handsomely through agribusinesses they set up in the United States, and heartened by their new relationship with the state, invested privately in tourism projects that the government promoted, with their contributions topping $2 million (*La Paloma*, no. 7, January–March 1992).

Borrego broadened the trust on which the state government's *acercamiento* with Zacatecanos in Los Angeles depended beyond the matching-funds program by fulfilling his commitment to work to resolve the problems that migrants faced *because of their status as migrants*. On repeated occasions, he advocated for his paisanos with the federal government. After corroborating migrants' complaints that the consulate in Los Angeles was negligent in addressing their needs and treated them with disdain, he traveled to Mexico City to convey their grievances to President de la Madrid and the secretary of foreign relations. The consultations set in motion a redefinition of the role of consular offices in migrant communities in the United States. "It marked the beginning of a conceptual transformation about what a consulate should do into one that was built on the understanding that the consulate should be a center where integrated services are provided to migrants, a place where they are heard, and a place where they can seek protection," recalls Borrego (interview, Mexico City, May 2003). The presiding consul in Los Angeles, whom migrants characterized as elitist and unavailable, was replaced with a diplomat who was "more disposed to interact and engage with the community" (interview, Mexico City, May 2003). In meetings with federal authorities, Borrego also decried the flagrant extortion that migrants reported they experienced at the hands of Mexican customs officers every time they crossed the border. The concerns that the governor relayed directly to President Salinas, according to his recollection, provided the impetus for a federal program—the Paisano Program—to clamp down on abuses against migrants (Borrego interview, Mexico City, May 2003; UAZ interviews, Zacatecas, March 2003; SRE interview, Mexico City, May 2003).

"What Borrego did that was groundbreaking was that he earned the trust—*la confianza*—of the Zacatecanos in the United States," concluded the director of the matching-funds program under Borrego's successor (interview, Zacatecas, April 2003). After the passage of the U.S. Immigration Reform and Control Act (IRCA) in 1986, the number of Zacatecan settler migrants in the United States shot up dramatically; to the amnesty and family reunification that the law allowed, Zacatecas added a 40 percent increase in the number of migrants who crossed the border each year (Mestries Benquet 2002: 105). A decade after IRCA became law, one in four Zacatecan households had a family member living, more or less permanently, in the country to the north (Mestries Benquet 2002: 105). The *confianza* between migrants and the state government and the interpretive engagement that it supported would soon begin to transform the role of migrants in Mexico and in the United States. Through their partnership with the state, migrants would become agents who shaped the economic and political trajectories of villages, of municipalities, of their state, and eventually of their country as a whole.

With the Mexican federal government's *acercamiento* in ruins at the end of the de la Madrid administration, the state government of Zacatecas was the only branch of the Mexican government that had any meaningful engagement with Mexicans abroad. Over the next decade, Zacatecanos would create formal institutions that would provide the building blocks for a radically revised federal policy toward migrants.

Institutionalizing Insight

When Arturo Romo assumed the office of governor of Zacatecas in September 1992, he was determined to continue the engagement with emigrants that his predecessor had begun. The ad hoc matching-funds arrangement for community projects under Borrego convinced Romo of the potential that the partnership held for village development, and the new governor had plans to expand. He sent a director from the state planning office to Los Angeles to lay the groundwork for his victory tour there and to schedule meetings.

What the director found when he arrived was profoundly disquieting. Migrants in the Federation of Zacatecan Clubs were up in arms: they had painstakingly raised thousands of dollars for community projects by organizing raffles, holding dances, and passing the hat among friends and neighbors, and they had handed those funds to the state government for public works in their communities of origin, but the projects had never been completed. "The pipes we bought for the water network have been lying in the mud in the village for months, and the state still hasn't put in its share. Our money is turning into rust," exclaimed one migrant club leader (interview, Zacatecas, April 2003). Many projects had not even been started. The migrants had no written documentation of their agreement with the state; their contracts were verbal, guaranteed by the *confianza* they had placed in the person of Genaro Borrego. The abandoned projects revealed that toward the end of Borrego's sexenio, some rot had set in. For the bureaucrats who had to carry out the projects, excitement about the matching-funds arrangement had fizzled after the first few years. Staff at the state planning office and in municipal governments had begun to chafe at Borrego's commitment that the California residents should have complete authority to determine which projects to initiate and support. With migrants showing a preference for remodeling village chapels and carving out sewage gullies and electricity networks that didn't always connect well with state systems, government employees had become downright lethargic in implementing the matching-funds initiative. The migrants felt deeply betrayed and were ready to cut off all engagement with state authorities (UAZ interviews, Zacatecas, March 2003; Secretaria de Planeación y Desarrollo Regional [SEPLADER] interviews, Zacatecas, April 2003; FCZSC interviews, Zacatecas, April and July 2003; interviews, Zacatecas, April 2003; Goldring 2002).

When their outrage was conveyed to the new governor Romo, he decided to formalize the matching-funds arrangement in an official government program. Under Borrego, the state government had matched migrant contributions by quietly funneling federal monies to migrant-sponsored projects, without ever officially declaring their unorthodox use. To turn the ad hoc arrangement into a state program, the government of Zacatecas had to make its draw on federal funds explicit. In addition to restoring the damaged relationship with migrants, the creation of a formal matching-funds program would enable the state to capture a larger portion of the monies the federal government was allocating to the nation's poorer municipalities. Under Salinas, the federal government was channeling money directly to municipalities classed as marginalized (Rodríguez 1997). Not only was Zacatecas receiving less than the share it would have expected given its crushing poverty, but the funds were bypassing the state government completely, flowing directly into municipal coffers, thus escaping the Romo administration's control (interviews, Zacatecas, March 2003).

Immediately upon his staff member's return from California, Romo approached the federal authorities about the possibility of laying out a formal procedure for the use of federal monies for migrant community projects. Several rounds of discreet negotiations with Luis Donaldo Colossio, then director of the Secretariat for Social Development (SEDESOL), followed, with discussions occurring under the cover of other events, including a seminar on Mexico at UCLA, which was attended, somewhat unexpectedly, by a cohort of Zacatecan migrant leaders. The result of the talks was a tripartite matching-funds program, popularly called Dos por Uno or Two for One, in which the state and federal governments each apportioned a dollar for every dollar contributed by migrants. In the fall of 1992, the governor of Zacatecas and the president of the Federation of Zacatecan Clubs of Southern California, Manuel de la Cruz, traveled to Mexico City to sign a binding convention with the federal government formalizing the groundbreaking arrangement in time for Romo to unveil the new program at his meeting with migrants in Los Angeles on November 13 (interviews, Zacatecas, March 2003; and Mexico City, May 2003).

Despite the excitement among many migrants and state officials about formalization of the matching-funds arrangement, the Two for One program had gotten off to a slow start: "it took six months to . . . begin the first project. The migrants didn't trust us with their money anymore. When we'd ask them to deposit their money in the state treasury, they'd say 'we're not letting go of our money—you give us the money and we'll build the project,'" remembers a government employee (interview, Zacatecas, March 2003). However, after "a lot of personal negotiation, a lot of personal convincing, a lot of visits and a lot of phone calls," the program flourished, and over three hundred projects were completed during Romo's term in office (Goldring 2002; interview, Zacatecas, March 2003). To rebuild the trust between migrants and the state that had collapsed during the interstices of the Romo and Borrego sexenios and to expand the engagement beyond the tight-knit outpost of Zacatecan migrants in Los Angeles, the Zacatecan government drew heavily on federal resources. Armed with the conceptual understandings that emerged under the Borrego administration, the Romo government was able to exploit federal programs—especially the Program for Mexican Communities Abroad (Programa para Comunidades Mexicanos en el Extranjero, or PCME; see chap. 7)—to foster grassroots organizing in the United States and deepen migrant ties with local communities in Zacatecas. The resulting community mobilization among Zacatecan *paisanos alla*—"over there"—was a joint effort between the state authorities and migrants, nourished by countless rounds of interpretive conversation. The institutions transformed the power they had acquired to shape meaning into solid organizational structures that could not be swept away when the political winds changed. Whether the Zacatecan state authorities—and the Zacatecan branch of the PRI—liked it or not, they were soon locked into an engagement that migrants had amassed the institutional authority to enforce.

Interpretation versus Translation: Solidaridad Internacional

From the start, the federal government's participation in the Two for One program was built on a misunderstanding. For the Federation of Zacatecan Clubs and the state government, the program was the formalization of an existing relationship. It was also a contractual commitment from the state to continue to engage with migrants, for the development of their communities of origin and support for their organizing drives in the United States. It was, as a government summary of the program explains, "a response to the concerns of the Federation of Zacatecan Clubs" and an institutional structure designed "so that the good intentions we [the state and the migrants] have articulated in our encounters [will] be transformed into deeds . . . for the development of Zacatecas and Mexico" (Zacatecas n.d. [c. 1996]: 4–6). For the Mexican federal government, however, the Two for One agreement was an extension of its National Solidarity Program, a view captured most blatantly in the fact that it named the compact Solidarity International, a name pointedly not used in Zacatecan state documents.

The National Solidarity Program—or Solidaridad—was Carlos Salinas's brainchild, and would become the signature project of his administration (Cornelius et al. 1994: 12). ("The whole country was plastered with billboards for Solidaridad," griped a formal government official in Zacatecas [interview, Zacatecas, 2003].) Designed as an antipoverty initiative to replace the social safety net hopelessly tattered after a decade of belt-tightening, it was founded, in Salinas's words, on the notion of citizen "participation and co-responsibility" (as quoted in Díaz-Cayeros and Magaloni 2003: 3) and required communities to contribute to financing and implementation. Moreover, it called for beneficiaries to create Solidarity committees to mobilize local resources for projects. In principle, the more than 150,000 Solidarity committees set up throughout Mexico were supposed to define the priorities for spending the estimated $12 billion allocated to the program, but in practice localities had little say. Decisions were instead made by the SEDESOL bureaucrats in Mexico City to meet what many analysts have argued were thinly disguised political goals (essentially to recoup ground lost to Cárdenas in the 1988 election) (Cornelius et al. 1994; Dresser 1994; Díaz-Cayeros and Magaloni 2003; Kaufman and Trejo 1997). When viewed through the lens of Solidaridad, migrant clubs were no different from citizens' committees contributing to the completion of public works in their communities—public works that the federal government would have selected. So well did this arrangement seem to fit the program lines of Solidaridad that the SEDESOL extended it to half a dozen other states (Goldring 2002).

Almost immediately after the convention for the Two for One program—Solidarity International to the federal government—was signed, friction arose between the state and federal government over its implementation. Tensions flared because the state of Zacatecas's goal was to intensify a partnership that rested on the three key insights that had emerged from the engagement between migrants and the state under Borrego, whereas federal authorities, blind to those insights, were interested primarily in furthering a program that bordered on a national obsession (García Zamora 1994: 204–47). The first of the three foundational understandings strengthened under the Two for One program was that migrants were a group distinct but not separate from their communities of origin and that they funded community projects for complex reasons. Migrants donated funds for projects not solely to foster development but also to maintain ties to the villages they left behind and to assert their identities as members of their specific rancho in the larger Zacatecan, Mexican, and multicultural context of Los Angeles and, more broadly, the United States. By supporting these public works, they expressed their identities as Jerezanos, as Valparaisanos, as Jomulquillenses who happened to have settled in southern California. Through the lens of Solidaridad Internacional, the migrants were reduced to community members like any other, and their resources were considered no different than those contributed on site, vested with no symbolism beyond a generic desire for development.

The second insight concerned the role of migrant clubs and their adherence to a larger federation. The Zacatecan state's sensitive engagement with the clubs reflected an understanding that they served a function much broader than the completion of a community project. They were organizations that enabled migrants to represent and defend their interests in their villages of origin, as well as in U.S. labor markets. Moreover, they were the interlocutor through which the state could access an otherwise dispersed and invisible constituency, and converse with it about both the role that migrants could play in the development of Zacatecas and the ways the state could advocate for migrants in the United States and with the Mexican government. For SEDESOL bureaucrats, the clubs were indistinguishable from ordinary solidarity committees, most of which had a short life span, disbanding after their project was complete. The bureaucrats' approach to the clubs was brazenly instrumental: the clubs were merely the vehicle by which funds for public works were collected.

The final insight about the importance of building trust with migrants was also lost on SEDESOL. The state government of Zacatecas, in a deliberate fashion, used the Two for One program to strengthen the bonds of *confianza* between with migrants and the state. State planning officials took pains to engage migrants in extensive consultations about the types of projects completed under the formal partnership, and about the vision for Zacatecas's development that the projects implied. They did this both through formal channels, such as a joint migrant-state working commission to evaluate proposed projects incorporated in the Two for One program design, and through informal venues, such as phone conversations, visits to the United States, and meetings with migrants in Zacatecas. ("It seemed like I was in the United States every weekend," remembered the director of the program under Romo.) The state government also demonstrated a recognition that migrant participation in the program was voluntary, and that earning migrants' trust meant demonstrating that the state also trusted *them* as a partner. Within the framework of Solidarity International, trust was irrelevant. Participation in the program was conditional on the contribution of funds, and both community deposits and federal disbursement of monies had to follow program norms that the federal government laid down. Moreover, to receive federal resources, the projects had to adhere strictly to the priorities defined by the federal government (Díaz-Cayeros and Magaloni 2003; Kaufman and Trejo 1997). The state government of Zacatecas was more flexible. Although no longer granting migrants exclusive say over what projects would be constructed and how, especially when projects affected state-level infrastructure planning, bureaucrats remained amenable to migrants' preferences. Not only were they willing to support cultural projects that fell outside the range of poverty alleviation initiatives sanctioned by the Salinas administration, but their engagement with migrants opened a window onto why the churches, rodeos, and plaza renovations were so important. As one former state employee working on the Two for One program recalled:

> The federal government wanted basic infrastructure projects, poverty alleviation projects, but the paisanos over there, what they wanted were churches and rodeo rings. Things they considered an expression of their tradition. Why? Because these are parts of themselves they couldn't express over there. They came here, came home, to be who they were, to be proud. . . . So we supported them in that and once they had their little church, once that hunger was satisfied, then they also wanted to build projects to help their communities and we were there to support them with that. We had projects to offer them. (Interview, Zacatecas, March 2003)

Along with the bureaucrats' increasing empathy for the migrants' priorities was a growing conviction that migrants would pull out of the program if their needs were not respected, so the state government battled federal authorities to defend projects that even it viewed as superfluous in the marginalized villages from which many migrants hailed (interviews, Zacatecas, March 2003; and Mexico City, May 2003).

Because of these frictions, "it took forever to implement the first small project," remembers a director of planning charged with Two for One implementation. The federal government displayed little willingness to modify Solidaridad norms. It was even less disposed to engage or negotiate with migrants in any meaningful way, which would have meant recognizing them as political and social actors, not just as the recipients of services. Disputes with the federal authorities immediately erupted over project selection, project design, and the procedure for migrants' contribution of resources. A former state planning official captured these tensions in his characterization of interactions concerning an electrification project:

> The federal official was like, I am going to the site and I am going to lay out the project. But we were like, wait, this is a migrant project, we've already worked out a layout, we have it right here, why would you define the site plan? [He answered], that's the procedure. Just get the money, deposit it, and deal with the migrants however you like. The federal money is available, and you need my signature if you want it. . . . There was a lack of trust: of the migrants toward the government and of the government toward the migrants; I mean, [the federal bureaucrats] were like, who are these people anyway? (Interview, Zacatecas, March 2003)

To resolve such impasses, Zacatecan state officials leveraged the rapport that the Borrego and, increasingly, the Romo administrations had cultivated with the migrants to comply with federal norms. The former Two for One director explained:

> We talked to the brother of one, who talked to the cousin of the other, who was the president of the club [funding the electrification project], and we talked to the president of the federation whose relatives also lived in the village. . . . In the end, we worked out that one of the elders [*ancianos*] in the rancho that everyone trusted would hold the money until the very last minute, and the day everything was ready to go, with all the government monies already there, he would deposit it in the account. (Interview, Zacatecas, April 2003)

The state also repackaged projects that were important to migrants but that the federal government did not consider conducive to development, to match federal priorities more closely. Churches were recast as "community centers" and rodeo rings were filed as "sports centers"—"because that is in fact what they are," argued one bureaucrat. "They are places where people get together for a collective purpose—to pray or to enjoy themselves together—*para convivir*" (interview, Zacatecas, April 2003). The state's robust partnership with migrants, invested with meaning and *confianza*, was translated into flat programmatic terms that the federal government could understand (interviews, Zacatecas, March–April 2003).

Because the federal government was reluctant to engage with migrants in an interpretive process and thus unable to absorb the insights that had made the collaboration between Zacatecan migrants and their state government so effective, federal attempts to extend Solidaridad Internacional to six other states failed miserably. From the start, the percentage of funds allocated to Zacatecas through the program was disproportionately large—almost 30

TABLE 8.2
Zacatecas and Total Expenditures for Solidaridad Internacional, 1993–97

Expenditure	1993	1994	1995	1996	1997
Zacatecas's Two for One (in thousands of pesos)	1,877	3,769	3,905	7,066	16,826
Solidaridad Internacional (in thousands of pesos)	6,497	10,544	9,798		
Zacatecas's share of total (%)	29	36	40		

Source: Secretaria de Planeación y Finanzas, 1998, in Goldring 2002: 75.

percent. In a reflection of the SEDESOL difficulties with the program in other states, that proportion grew to 40 percent two years later (see table 8.2; Goldring 2002). When the National Solidarity Program, tainted with accusations that it had been deployed for political ends, was scrapped in 1995 after Zedillo took office, Solidaridad Internacional was swept away with it (Goldring 2002; Kaufman and Trejo 1997). Federal contributions to matching-funds programs were discontinued in all states but Zacatecas, where the partnership depended not on the federal program but on a relationship developed locally. In the other states where Solidaridad Internacional was tried, matching-funds arrangements with migrants became dormant, revived only when Zacatecas's program was made national some years later (interviews, Michoacán, December 2002; Guanajuato, December 2002; Jalisco, December 2002 and May 2003).

Organizing Interpretation: Expanding the Two for One

While the federal government's inability to grasp the conceptual basis of the Two for One program and its unwillingness to engage with migrants undermined its ability to replicate the model in other states, the Zacatecan state government and Zacatecan migrants employed federal structures and resources to intensify their partnership. They used state programs as tools to build the new institutions that supported their partnerships, tinkering with the architecture of those institutions as they went along. Specifically, the Federation of Zacatecan Clubs and the Zacatecas state government exploited federal programs to organize three additional federations, one in the north of Texas, one in Chicago, and one in Denver, and they stimulated the creation of unaffiliated Zacatecan clubs in Oklahoma, Nevada, and Florida. The state government consolidated new grassroots community groups by immediately getting them to coalesce around the completion of a community project through the Two for One program.

The proliferation of clubs and migrant projects in municipalities throughout the state soon raised the question of what role municipal government should play in determining which projects were carried out and in contributing resources. "Project after project was getting done in villages, and the municipal presidents just stood by and watched. It was becoming very complicated for them politically, and they wanted to get involved," remembered one staff member from Romo's Office of Planning (interview, Zacatecas, April 2003). The state government began to devise means to draw municipal governments into the engagement, involving them in community mobilization among migrants in the United States, in the design of public works projects under the Two for One, and in the informal contribution of resources—generally in-kind, like cement, the municipal truck, a few masons—for the construction of the projects. In that endeavor as well, the state government relied on the scaffolding provided by federal programs to make the ties between migrants and the municipal governments in villages of origin thicker and more resilient (interviews, Zacatecas, April 2003; UAZ interviews, Zacatecas, March–April 2003).

The main federal programs used by the state government to amplify its relationship with Zacatecan paisanos in the United States were those designed to provide services to Mexican emigrants. In particular, the Zacatecan authorities relied on the program structures erected under the PCME to extend health, education, and sports and cultural services to migrants. The DGCME increasingly began to delegate provision of these services to state authorities; in its view, programs that targeted Mexican migrants were tangential to its main mission (González Gutiérrez and Schumacher 1998; González Gutiérrez 1995; Fundación Solidaridad Mexicano Americana interviews, Mexico City, May 2003). Before long, the state government of Zacatecas was an active participant in many PCME programs, most notably in educational services, with the state training teachers and supplying educational materials. The state authorities also organized sports tournaments and obliged consulates and Mexican cultural institutes by supplying musical troupes and art shows for cultural expositions in the United States (Zacatecas n.d. [c. 1997]; interviews, Zacatecas, March–April 2003).

Involvement in the PCME proved a boon to the state government's efforts to strengthen its partnership with migrants in three main ways. First, it furnished the state with information on Zacatecan migrants in the United States. The PCME programs, along with applications for the consular identification card—*la matricula consular*[10]—supplied the Zacatecan state government with names and addresses of Zacatecan migrants in various U.S. cities, information the state combined with its own informal registries collected by municipal presidents, who interviewed relatives and neighbors of emigrants to discover where they had settled. Second, it offered the state government access to Zacatecan migrants who availed themselves of PCME services. Zacatecan state authorities were able to connect with paisanos who joined the baseball tournament or sent their children to summer lessons organized by the state government under the PCME umbrella. Third, the PCME provided the Zacatecan state government with the funds to cover the travel costs of its bureaucrats and, as the state role in PCME service provision increased, of its municipal presidents. State employees took advantage of travel for PCME purposes to organize Zacatecan migrants and strengthen their partnership with the state as well. Even as the federal government proffered these resources to Zacatecan state authorities, they were unable to see the value of the community organizing drive taking place right under their noses.

The story of how the Federation of Zacatecan Clubs in Denver was formed exemplifies the way the state of Zacatecas and migration federations used federal government structures to further their engagement. In 1995, the DGCME held a meeting on the PCME binational education initiative to which it invited those state governments implementing aspects of the program, as well as consular staff and representatives from the Mexican cultural institutes. The following year, the director of the Mexican Cultural Institute of Denver approached Zacatecas state officials he had met at that meeting about the possibility of putting together an exhibition about the art, culture, and tourism of the colonial state for a convention that the institute was hosting for the National Council of La Raza, a Mexican American organization. The state government agreed and immediately contacted the president of the Federation of Zacatecan Clubs in Los Angeles to prepare for an organizing drive in Denver. Municipal presidents were tasked with finding out whether they had a large population of migrants living in Denver and, if so, to discover their addresses. The municipal authorities also prepared plans and budgets for modest but necessary projects that they felt were good candidates for the Two for One program. The Zacatecan delegation, which included the executive director of the Two for One program, the president of the Federation of the Zacatecan Clubs in Los Angeles, and the municipal presidents of Luis Moya and Ojocaliente, two municipalities well represented among Zacatecan migrants in Denver, traveled to Colorado at the federal government's expense (interviews, Zacatecas, March 2003; Zacatecas n.d. [c. 1997]: 17).

The group perfunctorily delivered their presentation on Zacatecas to the Mexican American organization during the day, and in the evenings it got to work mobilizing Zacatecan migrants in the area. Using home and work addresses they managed to collect from municipal governments, along with those gleaned from consulate lists, the group went knocking on doors; they got airtime on the local Spanish-language radio station to advertise that they were in Denver; and they invited all the Zacatecanos in town to a dinner meeting at a Mexican restaurant. In a repeat of Borrego's trip to Los Angeles a decade earlier, the meeting began with open-ended discussions about who the migrants were and what relationship they wanted to have with the state. "We talked about Zacatecas, about all of us as Zacatecanos, about the times they came home for feasts and holidays, about how they lived in Denver, about their work—everybody there seemed to work for the same landscape company," remembered the Two for One director (interview, Zacatecas, April 2003). The migrants were encouraged to form clubs, and the municipal presidents presented their proposals for public works projects that the migrants could support, complete with budgets, drawings, and emotional appeals as to what the project would mean for the people of the municipality and how the bridge, the electricity network, and so on would serve as a memorial to the villages' *hijos ausentes*—absent sons—who had sacrificed for the good of their communities. The president of the California Zacatecan Federation explained the importance of creating an umbrella organization and provided a point-by-point "how to" model for establishing a Federation of Clubs.

Over the next several months, the Zacatecans of Denver modified the proposals they had received, choosing to consolidate them into a couple of larger highway and potable water projects and establishing themselves with that move as a significant factor in the development of their municipalities. They also continued to work closely with the Federation of Zacatecan Clubs from California to build the fledgling Denver federation into a resilient network that could marshal political influence tailored to the contexts of Luis Moya and Ojocaliente, of Zacatecas, and of Colorado. Variations on the Denver experience were repeated in cities throughout the United States (interviews, Zacatecas, March–April; FCZSC interviews, Zacatecas, July 2003; Zacatecas, Secretaría de Planeación y Finanzas 1996–98).

These collaborative efforts and the repeated interpretive cycles on which they were based transformed the partnership institutionalized in the Two for One program. By the end of Romo's administration in 1998, Borrego's improvised matching-funds agreement had expanded into a major vector for public works financing. Migrant clubs and their federations in the United States had funded 137 community and infrastructure projects in villages throughout the state, in the amount of approximately $20 million dollars (Zacatecas, Secretaría de Planeación y Finanzas 1993–98). "The Two for One program has gained such momentum," observed Rodríguez Márquez, director of planning and development under Romo, "that in practice it has come to be considered as an alternative source of funding for municipal development programs" (as quoted in Moctezuma Longoría 2003: 24; see table 8.3).

Migrants, moreover, emerged as important constituents who increasingly defined development strategies in Zacatecan municipalities as a result of the convergence of two key trends. First, under the New Federalism that Zedillo championed after he took office, federal funds for local development were increasingly channeled through municipalities. The new strategy was designed to promote decentralized decision making, but also to draw a thick line between poverty reduction and political manipulation, in the hopes of shedding the stigma that had tainted the Solidaridad program as a scheme to buy votes in the guise of providing services. Federal funds for the Two for One program in Zacatecas were no exception and were funneled directly to municipal governments (Goldring 2002). Second, as growing numbers of municipal presidents participated in organizing drives among paisanos in the United States— under Romo's tenure, presidents from at least a third of Zacatecas's fifty-two

TABLE 8.3
Two-for-One and Three-for-One Program Budget and Projects, 1993–2002

Year	Investment (thousands of pesos)	Investment in 2002 currency (thousands of pesos)	No. of projects	No. of counties benefited	Average cost of project (thousands of pesos)
1993	1,877	7,026	7	No data	268
1994	3,769	13,176	30	No data	125
1995	3,905	8,983	34	No data	114
1996	6,946	12,512	61	17	113
1997	16,825	26,192	77	No data	218
1998	772	1,013	8	7	96
1999	48,179	56,296	93	27	518
2000	60,000	64,344	108	28	555
2001	72,000	73,956	130	30	553
2002	140,000	140,000	240	35	583

Sources: Zacatecas, Secretaría de Planeación 1993–98; Moctezuma Longaría 2003.
Note: In 2002, 10 pesos equaled approximately US$1.

municipalities made trips to the United States to meet with migrants—direct, vital relationships were forged between migrants and municipal authorities. Interpretive conversations between the migrants and the Zacatecan state government expanded to include municipal authorities.

As Goldring (2002) reports, those conversations were contested, often difficult, and mired in misunderstanding and ambiguity. Migrants and municipal governments engaged in heated discussions about which projects would be funded, what their implications were for local development, and what ramifications they would have for local political contests in an era of fierce election battles. One state official working on the matching-funds program offered this description of the negotiations:

For example, a group of migrants wants to put a system of potable water in their rancho. . . . But that would only benefit twenty inhabitants of the locality. We tell them, "okay, we also want your locality to have water, but we can do this in such a way that we can provide water for the municipal capitol and other localities. Instead of using the water source in your locality which will get used up very quickly because the well has very little water, why don't we put the water system near the municipal capital where the underground water table is documented, plentiful, clean, and not contaminated, so that we can contribute water to all the surrounding communities?" Negotiations and conversations and conversations, until we all come out in agreement, having reached consensus on the project. Sometimes they know things about their rancho that we don't. And they demand a lot of accountability. *Cuentas claras, amistades largas*—good bookkeeping, good friendships. Sometimes the plan is better at the end, but the meetings and all the discussions, and the municipal government can also be very stubborn about its priorities, especially near elections . . . well, it can be very, very difficult. (Interview, Zacatecas, March 2003)

Those conversations, however, produced new understandings of how municipal economies were tethered to U.S. labor markets and how community life was shaped by migrant social and cultural practices across the border—that the rodeo ring favored by migrants, for example, was as important to the municipality's development as a new sewage system.

Satisfied with the matching-funds setup, municipalities expanded their partnership with migrants beyond the confines of the Two for One program and initiated ad hoc matching-funds arrangements through other funding streams from the federal government. They negotiated a sliding scale of migrant contributions depending on the project: from 50 percent for a project such as remodeling a church to 20 percent for "poverty alleviation" projects such as electrification (municipal government employee interviews, Zacatecas, March–April 2003; survey of municipal presidents, April 2003[11]; FCZSC interviews, Zacatecas, July 2003; other interviews, Zacatecas, April 2003; Goldring 2002).

The events in Zacatecas were emulated to varying degrees by other state governments in areas with high emigration rates. Borrego's and Romo's journeys to meet with migrants were followed by a cascade of visits from other governors. By 1995, Los Angeles alone had received the governors of Jalisco, Sinaloa, Nayarit, Michoacán, Aguascalientes, San Luis Potosi, Tlaxcala, and Guanajuato (González Gutiérrez 1995). Their visits prompted the creation of umbrella organizations, and by 1996 the Mexican consulate reported that the California city was host to six functioning federations or associations of migrant hometown clubs (Goldring 2002). The trend was most pronounced in southern California, but it quickly took root in areas with large concentrations of migrants such as Chicago, Dallas, and Seattle. The Federation of Zacatecan Clubs from Southern California worked with the nascent federations to help them get organizing drives off the ground, instruct them on how to register as nonprofit organizations, and advise them on how to establish engagements built on dialogue and exchange with their respective Mexican state governments. In Los Angeles alone, the number of clubs jumped from a little over 100 in 1995 to nearly 250 five years later (Leiken 2001). Although no state other than Zacatecas had been able to develop a substantial matching-funds arrangement by 1998, migrant federations from other states donated monies for community projects and emergency assistance to municipal and state authorities in a small-scale and ad hoc manner (Mexican consulate interviews, Chicago, August 2003; interviews, Jalisco, May 2003, and Michoacán, December 2002; González Gutiérrez 1995; Leiken 2001; Goldring 2002; Zabin and Escala Rabadan 1998).

The Mexican federal government's attempts to delegate service provision for migrants to state governments only accelerated this process. DGCME officials organized a number of conferences for municipal and state authorities on

PCME program provision and encouraged the creation of state Oficina de Atención a Migrantes y Sus Familias (OFAM)—service centers for migrants and their families—which they then networked into an overarching commission (CONOFAM) (SRE interviews, Mexico City, May and July 2003; Fundación Solidaridad Mexicano Americana interviews, Mexico City, May 2003; González Gutiérrez and Schumacher 1998). States varied in their institutional commitment to the OFAMs: those with large emigrant populations set up separate, although generally understaffed and poorly resourced, offices, whereas those with new or paltry emigration streams made only symbolic attempts to comply. "In some states, they just added an inbox labeled OFAM on some desk in the corner, and that was their OFAM" (Fundación Solidaridad Mexicano Americana interviews, Mexico City, May 2003). The network the federal government established in the CONOFAM, however, and the regular conferences of OFAMs it sponsored allowed the states to exchange information about how to deal with their emigrant populations, such as how to support bilingual education and the logistics of transporting the bodies of deceased migrants back to their home villages for burial. They also shared knowledge about migrant clubs and their organization into federations, about the possibilities of partnering with them for public works projects, and, tentatively, about the political sway that migrants—as an organized constituency with local credibility— could wield in municipal and state electoral contests (SRE interviews, Mexico City, May 2003; interviews, Michoacán and Jalisco, December 2002; and Zacatecas, April 2003). Ironically, federal attempts to farm out what was considered a less desirable portfolio ultimately diffused information about how to engage with migrants among migrant-sending states, and helped bring the potential of migrants as a political force to the attention of state governments. The Zacatecan gubernatorial elections at the end of Romo's term would soon make the full weight of the political influence they had garnered over the previous decade abundantly clear.

Ricardo Monreal, the PRD, and the Frente Cívico Zacatecano

Zacatecas, an agricultural state with a dense corporatist root bed, had long had the dubious distinction of being the most PRI-ista state in the Mexican federation (Delgado Wise 2002; Delgado Wise and Pozo 2002; Moctezuma Longoría 2003). Ricardo Monreal's winning campaign for governor as the Democratic Revolutionary Party (PRD) candidate shattered that image: not only did the renegade candidate defeat the PRI, but Zacatecas became the first state in the nation to have a governor from a leftist opposition party. Migrant support of his candidacy was decisive; Zacatecan groups in the United States backed the candidate with funds and aggressive lobbying tactics on both sides of the border. "It's thanks to them that I became state governor," Monreal would later freely acknowledge (as quoted in Lizarzaburu 2004). With their candidate's victory, the migrants demonstrated the political influence they had acquired. The

Two for One program, with all of its attendant organizing, had institutionalized that power.

In the early phase of the governor's race, the PRI initially chose Ricardo Monreal Ávila as its candidate, and the Federation of Zacatecan Clubs in Los Angeles, now officially called the Federación de Zacatecanos Unidos del Sur de California and the largest and most powerful of all Zacatecan federations (it claimed to represent 45,000 Zacatecan families [Goldring 2002]), officially announced its support for him. The PRI, however, changed candidates midstream, designating José Antonio Olvera Acevedo as its nominee just a few months before the election. Just like Cuauhtémoc Cárdenas before him, Monreal remained in the race, running first as an independent backed by a patchwork of smaller parties and eventually becoming part of the PRD. In true Mexican corporatist fashion, the president of the Federation of Zacatecan Clubs of Southern California retracted his support for Monreal and pledged allegiance to the PRI's new candidate. This switch opened an enormous rift in the federation, between a minority who remained loyal to the PRI and a large majority who complained that Romo was increasingly trying to bring the Federation of Southern California, as well as other federations throughout the United States, under government control. The federation hemorrhaged members, and the dissidents founded the Frente Cívico Zacatecano—the Zacatecan Civic Front—as a political action group to back Monreal.[12]

Reflecting its members' organizing experience in the federation, the Frente Cívico was dynamic and immediately effective. Its members donated generously and campaigned vigorously for the renegade politician, both in Los Angeles and in their communities of origin, advertising on village radio shows, calling home, traveling back to their villages to encourage people to vote for change. Monreal's campaign manager recalled how migrants mobilized: "The network [of migrants supporting Monreal] grew and grew and grew, and in the end they financed a lot of Monreal's campaign. They organized visits for Monreal in all of their communities, paying for all of the governor's expenses out-of-pocket. Those who could not attend just sent their funds to relatives for the governor's campaign. They would call into radio shows here in Zacatecas and they would say, 'This is so-and-so, and I just want to tell all of my relatives in the town of such-and-such that all of you have to vote for Monreal because of this and this and this, and he came to see us in the United States, he spent time with us. Don't lose this important opportunity. Don't be afraid of the PRI. Vote for Monreal'" (interview, Zacatecas, April 2003). The exhortation not to be afraid was especially poignant: many migrants, including several not directly involved with the Frente Cívico, remember being threatened by the national PRI machinery and its representatives in state government and in consulates in the United States at that time (interviews, Zacatecas, March 2003). In fact, the federal government, which had been so reticent in its support for the matching-funds arrangement, showed no compunction in using it to imply that Monreal supporters would "lose their opportunities for collaboration with the government" (interviews, Zacatecas, April 2003).

Although both candidates were well aware that winning the governorship required them to win over Zacatecanos in the United States, and both traveled north to push their tickets, the Monreal camp displayed a more prescient understanding of the political leverage that migrants could represent and made strengthening migrants' participation in Zacatecas a central component of Monreal's platform. More to the point, the candidate promised to institutionalize their involvement in their communities of origin by creating a series of additional formal structures.

Cognizant that Monreal, a long-shot candidate who could not even get PRI party bosses to take him seriously, sailed into the governor's office on a wave of organized and well-funded migrant support, the new PRD administration fulfilled its campaign promises to Zacatecan paisanos north of the border. As soon as Monreal was inaugurated, the state government more than doubled the budget for the Two for One program and ratcheted up the matching-funds program into a "Three for One" arrangement, adding a dollar from municipal governments to the two state and federal dollars already apportioned to match migrant donations. This revision institutionalized municipal participation in the program and provided an additional incentive for municipal presidents to foster the organization of clubs. To restore the bonds of *confianza* after a traumatic race, the new administration expanded the consultation procedures for project selection, giving migrants more say over various aspects of the projects (including quality control and bidding procedures), and negotiated with the federal government to enable migrant clubs to deposit their contributions in accounts they controlled rather than in the state treasury. Finally, Monreal named a cabinet-level liaison with migrants in the United States and opened a Zacatecan state office in Los Angeles. A consummate politician, Monreal also brokered a truce between the Federation of Zacatecan Clubs and the Frente Cívico, such that the federation would concentrate on Three for One projects and the Frente Cívico would take on issues identified as explicitly political.[13] And take on political issues it did.

The Frente Cívico quickly established itself as a major political advocate for Mexican migrants in California and the United States as a whole. The organization joined a number of campaigns to back pro-immigrant legislation or policies, ranging from a proposed amnesty program to defending undocumented immigrants' access to drivers' licenses. It also forged close ties with the AFL-CIO, supporting its organizing drives among Mexican immigrants and endorsing its resolution for the legalization of immigrants and the repeal of sanctions against those who hired undocumented workers. Additionally, the Zacatecan PAC backed the campaigns of numerous Latino and Mexican American candidates for a range of public offices, from Lou Correa (of Zacatecan ancestry) for the Orange County Board of Supervisors to Cruz Bustamante in his bids for lieutenant governor and governor. As a further indicator of its lobbying skill, the Frente Cívico, representing predominantly lower-middle-class immigrants, many of whom were undocumented, established high-level contacts in the U.S. government by securing regular access to then governor Gray Davis and obtaining several meetings with the presidential candidates Al Gore and George Bush.[14]

The Frente Cívico, in partnership with the federation, held enormous sway in Zacatecas, shaping numerous pieces of state legislation that affected migrants or their communities of origin. The frente and federation, often conflated in Zacatecan communities, had tremendous popular appeal: Moctezuma Longoría recounts that when Guadalupe Gómez, president of the Frente Cívico and after 2000 president of the federation, visited his native municipality of Jalpa to promote various Three for One projects, "he received a massive reception in numerous communities, as if it were the Zacatecan governor himself who was visiting" (Moctezuma Longoría 2003: 31; Goldring 2002; FCZSC interviews, Zacatecas, April and July 2003).

The frente and the Monreal administration established an alliance to advance the *political* rights of emigrants in Mexico and in the United States. That coalition quickly became an important vehicle by which emigrant suffragists from throughout Mexico pushed for their cause. A few months after assuming office, in November 1998, the Monreal administration, together with the Autonomous University of Zacatecas and the Frente Cívico, held a major voting rights conference attended by representatives of migrant groups, scholars, and politicians. The meetings were one of an avalanche of conferences on the topic as Mexico was approaching the national elections of 2000, but the quality of engagement between the Zacatecan state government and Zacatecan migrant organizations—an engagement that increasingly involved the historically leftist and activist Autonomous University of Zacatecas—attracted activists in particular as a channel that would transmit their demands with fidelity. A conference on voting rights was again held in Zacatecas in 2001, and at that meeting the suffragists penned the manifesto they titled "The Declaration on the Political Rights of Mexicans Abroad," but which was more commonly known as "The Declaration of Zacatecas." In an echo of the insights articulated during the initial encounters between Governor Borrego and Zacatecan migrants in 1986, the Declaration states that Mexican migrants' lack of political voice is "the major obstacle that we face to obtain the recognition of our dignity and to exercise our influence on the development of the country where we live and of our country of origin" (in Ross 2002: 176; Santamaría Gómez 2001: 172–75; UAZ interviews, Zacatecas, March–April 2003).

Through engagement, the migrants of Zacatecas and their state government together managed to accomplish what the Mexican federal government had struggled unsuccessfully to do for decades. The government and migrants of one of Mexico's poorest and most agricultural states, with a population of little more than 1 million in a country of 100 million, had created a powerful lobby that was determining political outcomes in the United States and in Mexico. Yet, even as the political movement of Mexican migrants was gathering momentum, the federal government—and more specifically, the PRI—chose to ignore it, pretending that the political storm gathering on its horizon did not exist.

9

The Relationship between "Seeing" and "Interpreting"

The Mexican Government's Interpretive Engagement with Mexican Migrants

Shortly after 11:00 p.m. on July 2, 2000, Mexican president Ernesto Zedillo announced: "The next president of Mexico will be Vicente Fox Quesada" (as quoted in Preston 2000). With this terse statement, Zedillo conceded that his party, the PRI, had lost the presidency for the first time since its creation in 1929. The PRI's seventy-one-year vise on power had finally been loosed. Fox supporters streamed into the streets of Mexico City, chanting "Vicente Presidente!" and serenading the president-elect with boisterous renditions of "Las Mañanitas," a traditional Mexican song in praise of birthdays and new beginnings (Collier 2000). Over the coming days, cities throughout Mexico saw celebrations of the election results: news bulletins reported tens of thousands of people dancing in the streets, mariachi bands playing, flags waving, and roaring cheers of "Yes we could!—Si se pudo!" in state capitals throughout the republic (Amador 2000a; Collier 2000; Preston 2000). The celebrations in Mexico were matched by festivities in numerous cities in the United States. In Chicago's Mexican neighborhood, Fox supporters poured into the streets and "cheered, hugged, sang Mexico's national anthem, and even cried" (Jackson 2000); in Cleveland, Mexicans rejoiced openly in community centers and social clubs, making statements to eager visiting reporters about the hope they felt for Mexico's future: "Now Mexican people have a choice" (Kaggwa 2000); in California's Bay Area, Mexican migrants who had been glued to their television sets celebrated in the streets and taquerias of San Francisco's mission district, and in heavily Mexican towns in northern California, residents hung homemade posters from lampposts that read "Yes we could! Si se pudo!" echoing the victory cry that rose up south of the border (Fernandez and Pence 2000).

For migrants, Fox's electoral upset represented more than the end of the PRI's seventy-one-year rule. It marked the end of the political invisibility with which they had struggled for over three decades. With Fox's victory, they strode onto Mexico's political stage. During his campaign the National Action Party (PAN) candidate had avidly courted migrant support, and after his win he continued to solicit their political backing by making numerous trips to the United States and promising to institute policies to involve migrants in the political and economic development of their country of origin. Throughout his campaign and in the months after his victory, Fox had significant credibility because of his attention to migrants during his tenure as governor of Guanajuato. Even before Fox took office in the state, the government of Guanajuato had begun to elaborate policies directed at Guanajuatenses in the United States. As governor, he continued and amplified them. On the presidential campaign trail, which he pushed north of the border, Fox called migrants "Mexico's heroes and heroines" and invoked Guanajuato's policies to demonstrate that he was prepared to walk his laudatory talk. He pledged that building a relationship with migrants would be one of his administration's top priorities.

In the PAN candidate, migrants saw a bridge over which they could bring their local initiatives and local mobilization to the federal level, a means to make the interpretive engagement that was emerging between them and a small handful of state governments national. Ultimately, the instinct of the migrant leaders who backed Fox proved correct, and migrants were able finally, after decades of federal neglect, to establish an interpretive engagement with the Mexican government. However, they only succeeded because Fox failed.

The Fox administration's approach to migrants both in Guanajuato and at the federal level was solidly analytical. His PAN government strove to track, tabulate, and measure migration and migrant remittances in order to channel them to meet state priorities for economic growth and political development. The state defined the potential that migration and migrants represented for Guanajuato, and then for Mexico as a whole, and designed policies to manipulate that potential to achieve what the state determined to be the maximum gain. Migrant leaders were right in deducing that Fox and his state and then federal administrations "saw" migrants and were willing to stand by their political visibility. Yet because of its approach to policy making, the state under Fox saw only what it wanted to see, which quickly became obvious. Migrants were reduced to an economic and political resource—to objects of policy—and were excluded from the process of policy design and the generation of the concepts on which the policy was built.

Judith Jordan, in her work on relationship and disconnection (2004), argues that engagement based on fixed understandings of the participants inevitably leads to the collapse of that engagement, regardless of context. When participants adhere to preconceived meanings and, over time, marshal increasing resources to defend those meanings, their perceptions of one another become further and further removed from the realities. This route, suggests Jordan, eventually leads to an impasse, at which point either the relationship is abandoned or one party consolidates its power over the other in an effort to keep increasingly scripted and unreal meanings from shifting. The Fox administration precipitated a collapse like the one Jordan presages. It stubbornly clung to its definitions of who migrants were, the resources they represented, and the role they could play in Mexico. As a result, the relationship that the Fox administration tried to establish with migrants reached a breaking point within months of his taking office. Instead of a bridge that would allow migrants to engage with the Mexican government in an interpretive fashion, the Fox administration was revealing itself to be much more of a barrier. The tentative relationship migrants had established with Fox began to disintegrate rapidly as migrants began eschewing dealings with the Mexican state.

The collapse of the relationship discredited many of the meanings and definitions that the Fox administration had superimposed onto migrants and their experiences. The failure was not one that the administration could sweep under the rug: its aggressive courting of migrant political support made adopting the federal government's tried and true strategy of pretending—with a wink and a nod—that emigrants did not exist impossible. The state could not deny having seen a constituency it had taken pains to make visible without incurring significant political cost. The relationship's collapse, however, cleared away the state-fabricated meanings about migrants that were limiting, inconsonant, or simply incorrect. Freed from the shackles of those meanings, migrants and the government were able to engage interpretively, to collaborate in the construction of new meanings. In yet another reinterpretation of interpretive engagement, federal bureaucrats reinvented the institutions and methods that had been used to foster conversations with Mexican Americans, but this time, they applied them to Mexican migrants as well as Mexican American interlocutors. The conversations broke old paradigms about migration in Mexico and led to the articulation of new connections. Those insights, and the policies they have inspired, have recast the relationship among migration, development, and political power in ways likely to have significant ramifications for Mexico's political and economic future.

The implosion of Fox's somewhat condescending and narrow rapport with migrants and the emergence of a vital interpretive engagement with migrants out of its ruins illustrate the often overlooked relationship between two approaches to governing so different that they are virtual opposites. The first focuses on analyzing social dynamics by dissecting them and probing them for possible targets of intervention, and it lead to policy intervention *on* society. The second draws the participants in the social dynamics into a process of interpreting their significance and potential, and produces policy *with* society. In Mexico's experience with migration and development policy, one approach gave rise to the other: analysis made migrants visible, and interpretation with the migrants the state chose to finally see transformed state practices of seeing.

Analyzing Migrants

On April 1, 1993, 140 mushroom pickers in Kennett Square, Pennsylvania, walked off their jobs, demanding wage increases and the recognition of their organization as a union (Slobodzian and Rhor 1993). The strikers, like the rest of the mushroom pickers in the tiny capital of the U.S. mushroom industry, were almost exclusively from Guanajuato, and most of them from a handful of small ranchos in the municipalities of Morelia, Uriangato, and Yuriria (V. Garcia 1997). Although small, the strike was the first organized expression of simmering labor unrest in the agricultural enclave. Ever since an estimated 4,000 undocumented Mexican laborers in the area had regularized their status under the Immigration Reform and Control Act of 1986 and the Special Agricultural Workers program in 1987 (Bustos 1989), those who did not simply leave their jobs in search of better employment began resisting the worst of the illegal practices common in the mushroom hothouses. No longer afraid of deportation, Mexican workers began to protest low wages, unpaid overtime, abysmal working conditions, and the frequency of on-the-job injury and to demand the improvement of seriously substandard employer-provided housing, especially the lack of running water, electricity, and toilet facilities in the trailers (Bustos 1991; Barrientos 1993; Henson 1993).

The strike, mobilized with the help of a New Jersey farm workers' group (Comité de Apoyo a los Trabajadores Agrícolas, or CATA), was endorsed by the AFL-CIO and the Teamsters, as well as the American Friends Service Committee, and received extensive local and national coverage (Slobodzian and Rhor 1993; interviews, Philadelphia, August 2003). Within a few weeks of the walkout announcement, Cuauhtémoc Cárdenas, having received a call from a Mexican labor organizer while gearing up for his 1994 presidential bid, visited the strikers. With Spanish-language press in tow,[1] he offered them his public support and held them up as heroes for resisting the endemically poor conditions under which Mexican migrants labored (Slobodzian and Rhor 1993; interviews, Philadelphia, August 2003). True to form, the PRI, unnerved by all the attention the migrant workers were receiving, sent representatives to meet with prominent Mexican American and Mexican businessmen in the area to devise a solution to the conflict and make the whole mess—and especially the migrants—disappear. "It was all very secretive. We met in the [Philadelphia] consulate on a day it was closed," remembered one businessman. "They made sure to keep the curtains pulled shut the whole time" (interview, Philadelphia, August 2003).

The governor of Guanajuato, Carlos Medina Placensia, also traveled to Pennsylvania "to let the paisanos know that their state government was supporting them and backing them," as he put it (interview, Mexico City, July 2003). Medina was from the PAN party, and Guanajuato was still only the third state with an opposition governor. Notoriously inept at courting migrant support and weak in rural areas, the PAN sought to emulate Cárdenas's strategy and build a loyal base among Mexican workers in the United States. The headline-grabbing mushroom pickers' strike provided an ideal opportunity (interviews, Philadelphia, August–September 2003; and Guanajuato, July 2003).

The Beginnings of Guanajuatan Policy

Medina, named governor in 1992 instead of the party's candidate, Vicente Fox, after a negotiation between the PRI and the PAN over contested election results, was already developing an interest in migration. Appointed to the post unexpectedly, the former mayor of Leon embarked on a tour of his state, visiting municipalities with intensive emigration patterns. "For me, in that moment, it was a surprise," recounted Medina, and he approached the issue with analytic zeal: "I told my staff that I wanted to know exactly how many migrants there were in the United States, and exactly where they had settled. Numbers and locations, that's what I wanted" (interview, Mexico City, July 2003). On the basis of those data, the governor's office laid out a plan to set up Guanajuatan centers in the United States, after the federal model of Mexican cultural institutes. Just like the institutes, they would serve as the hubs of a lobbying network that, as Medina specified, would be "in keeping with the philosophy and doctrines of [the] National Action [Party]" (interview, Mexico City, July 2003). Moreover, the centers, to be called Casas Guanajuato, would explicitly foster a state-based, and not a municipal, identity. As the former governor specified, this was part of a statewide strategy to build cultural cohesion in Guanajuato to promote economic integration, but more important, to create a political base for the right-of-center opposition party:

> In the northern part of the state, we ha[d] municipalities that ha[d] a very low level of economic development, and some . . . had closer economic ties and activities with bordering states than with the rest of Guanajuato itself. So . . . we needed to reinforce the Guanajuatan identity of Guanajuatenses. We wanted people to look toward Guanajuato and its government for their future. And that's why we decided that the Casa Guanajuato should have a larger state identity, rather than be identified with a given municipality. And anyway, how much can a municipality really do for migrants? (Interview, Mexico City, July 2003)

Once in Kennett Square, the governor met with the striking workers but squandered the opportunity to initiate an interpretive conversation with Guanajuatan migrants. In contrast to the open-ended engagement of the Zacatecan government, Medina's interaction skimmed the surface: he made several speeches in support of the strikers, which were perceived as genuine by the mushroom pickers, but he displayed little interest in the details of their lives and in building a relationship with them. Instead, his approach was to solve the problem at hand. He consulted with growers about addressing, as he saw it, "flaws in their human resource management system" (Medina interview, May 2003). He also talked with county government officials about Guanajuatan workers in Kennett Square. On the basis of information he received from the Chester County public health service about the prevalence of HIV among the workers, which was matched by an anomalous cluster of cases in isolated ranchos in the municipality of Moreleon, the governor drafted a system with U.S. authorities to map out migrant networks and to track the movement of disease among them. The program, appropriately named the Binational Health Information System for Epidemiological Surveillance of Mexican Migrant Workers, was launched as a pilot project for the exchange of health information between Mexican and U.S. authorities. The Guanajuato government, satisfied with the results, later replicated it for Guanajuatan migrant populations in Texas, Colorado, and Illinois (Velasco-Mondragón et al. 2000; Consejo Estatal de Población [COESPO] interviews, Guanajuato, July 2003).

Medina also established a Casa Guanajuato for the migrants—the first to be built from the blueprints drawn up in Guanajuato state offices. Although the Casa was set up to give migrants a venue to "gather and meet" (Medina interview, May 2003), the governor specified that concern about the spread of HIV to Guanajuatan ranchos and the resulting desire to canvass migrant populations were the main impetus behind the program: "It was the catalyst that really got the Casas Guanajuato program going. It's why we decided to finally allocate funds to the project after so many months of tinkering with the design" (interview, Mexico City, July 2003). This thrust was maintained as a central mission of the program; as the director of the program under Medina's successor, Vicente Fox, emphasized: "Casas Guanajuato is where we have been monitoring and assessing the location and networks of the migrants" (Ramon Flores, as quoted in M. P. Smith 2003).

On his return to Guanajuato, the governor formally established a separate agency, the Dirección General de Atención a Comunidades Guanajuatenses en el Extranjero (DACGE), to implement the Casas program and design other interventions for migrants. The formal mission of the DACGE was broad—to offer migrants "connection, communication, support, and services" (*Pa'l Norte* 1994: vol. 1, no. 1)—but the purpose it served in practice was twofold: first, to trace emigration from Guanajuato, assess and map its impacts on local communities, and mitigate the negative effects where possible; and second, to capture the political capital that migrants represented. The DACGE's newsletter, *Pa'l Norte*, continues to make these two goals explicit through regular publication of articles on migration flows from Guanajuato, bulletins with preventive health tips, and invariably a message from the governor wooing Guanajuatenses abroad with generic expressions of admiration and support, tinged with condescension (*Pa'l Norte* 1994–2001; DACGE interviews, Guanajuato, July 2003; M. P. Smith 2003).

The Casa Guanajuato in Kennett Square did not even survive long enough to make it into the government's official records on the Casas program; it disintegrated soon after the governor left Pennsylvania. The migrant mushroom pickers did not see themselves primarily as Guanajuatenses but identified instead with their communities of origin or, at most, with the municipalities in which those were located. The Casas, which explicitly promoted a state-level Guanajuatan identity, and implicitly advanced a PANista political agenda, did not resonate with them. Turning a blind eye to their obvious lack of interest, the DACGE doggedly continued to set up Casas Guanajuato. The state office poured substantial resources into the initiative: the DACGE staff traveled to cities throughout the United States to establish the Casas; they handed the Guanajuatenses they managed to gather a standardized mimeographed charter with only the names of the Casa president and treasurer left blank; they granted the groups seed money; they shipped them regular supplies of materials designed to foster a Guanajuatan identity, ranging from history books to artisans who conducted craft workshops; and eventually they founded a branch of the DACGE in Illinois to provide the Casas with more "hands-on" support (DACGE interviews, Guanajuato, July 2003, and Chicago, August 2003; DACGE Casas Archives 1998–2002; *Pa'l Norte* 1996–2001). Despite this prodigious expenditure of effort and resources, the program, at its peak in 2000, could boast only 18 Casas in the United States, although Fox claimed 33 during his campaign (G. Orozco et al. 2000; Hegstrom 2000; DAGCE interviews, Guanajuato, July 2003; Leiken 2001).

The Casas had extremely short life spans. The DACGE heroically tried to prop them up with more funds and patch them together in the face of reams of letters that they received from Casa members accusing each other of graft and power-mongering, but the agency met with little success. "So many of them were just empty shells, with one or two people claiming to represent dozens and collecting state money," commented one DACGE staff member in Illinois (DACGE interview, Chicago, August 2003). Further, they were shadowed by a network of Guanajuatan migrant organizations independent of the state government. These were patterned after the municipality-based hometown clubs championed initially by the Zacatecans and copied by migrants from states throughout Mexico (COESPO interviews, Guanajuato, July 2003; interviews, consulate, Chicago, August 2003). By 2000, Mexican consulates reported that there were at least 24 known clubs compared to 18 government-sponsored Casas (G. Orozco et al. 2000). The DACGE dragged its feet on recognizing these clubs, and progressively morphed into a state-level expression of the federal government's Programa para Comunidades Mexicanas en el Extranjero (PCME), with its social service approach toward migrants, whom it treated like clients rather than an organized political group. This development was one the federal government was only too happy to support as it meant that it could continue to delegate service provision for migrants to state governments (DACGE interviews, July 2003).

Channeling Remittances: The Comunidades Program

The Guanajuato state government's attempts at building collaborative programs with migrants fared even worse than the Casas. Championed by Fox, who became governor in 1995, these programs' main priority was capitalizing on the remittances migrants sent to the state, estimated at $1.36 million a day (Instituto Nacional de Estatistica y Geografía, in Delgado Wise 2004). These efforts, however, invariably collapsed because the state defined where and how those remittances would be used, rather than engaging with migrants to develop ideas about how it could help them fund projects that they and their communities wanted, or how migrant-driven projects might support statewide economic development.

The government's most famous effort at building a partnership with migrants to foster development was its Mi Comunidad program (sometimes called the Comunidades program) launched by the Fox administration in 1996 and heavily promoted by the presidential hopeful. The scheme seemed a brilliantly straightforward way to redirect migrant remittances toward productive investment: through a series of incentives and an aggressive public relations campaign, the state would raise remittance funds from migrants and use them for start-up capital for maquiladoras located in migrants' communities of origin (Torres 2001). The state pledged comprehensive technical assistance, and in some cases, the requisite machinery to help get maquilas up and running. The initiative was heralded by policymakers, scholars, and international development banks alike as a new model for development, a "for-profit" market-driven version of remittance matching-funds arrangements, and its drafters had visions of turning isolated and impoverished hamlets into vibrant, if diminutive, de facto export-processing zones (Martinez Saldaña 2002; Moctezuma Longoría and Rodríguez Ramírez 2000). In fact, inspired by the clusters of garment factories in the north of Italy, which had become centers for the production of clothing for high-end niche markets, government planners viewed Mi Comunidad as an initiative that, at the height of Guanajuato's garment assembly boom during the honeymoon period after NAFTA's passage, simply could not fail (interviews, Guanajuato, July 2003; M. P. Smith 2003).

Thanks to its public relations blitz among Guanajuatan migrants, the state raised the money for thirteen maquilas, each requiring a minimal investment of $60,000, and matched the funds with generous technical assistance, wage subsidies, and discounted loans. The maquilas were all very small, the largest among them employing no more than a dozen people. Then-governor Fox visited several of them with much fanfare and confidently proclaimed that the workshops would quickly distinguish themselves as catalysts of economic growth for their municipalities (interviews, Guanajuato, July 2003).

Within five years, it became clear that Mi Comunidad was a dramatic failure. Despite intensive hands-on assistance from government staff and larger than anticipated state subsidies, only four maquilas out of the thirteen established remained. Moreover, these barely hobbled along: they were either producing for low-end local markets or found themselves assembling at the tail end of global commodity chains, having been subcontracted to sew simple low-quality garments for relatively low returns. The remaining maquilas also faced chronic labor shortages as their workers, once trained, left for better prospects in garment firms in Guanajuato's larger cities or U.S. garment centers like Los Angeles, or simply dropped out of the workforce for extended periods when they received remittances from relatives abroad. Migrant investors who had returned to their communities of origin to rescue their failing maquilas found themselves planning to migrate once again to raise the capital needed to keep the firms afloat (Martinez Saldaña 2002; Moctezuma Longoría and Rodríguez Ramírez 2000; interviews with maquila owners and state officials, July 2003).

In retrospect, the failure of Mi Comunidad was predictable. From the start, the program faced a host of obstacles—some structural, some social. The workshops it set up were cut off from major production and distribution centers by substandard infrastructure ranging from barely passable roads to unreliable phone lines. They were tenuously connected, if at all, to the commodity production chains for garment production, and as a result, had little access to mechanisms to help them improve quality. The shortage of workers in the villages stemmed from the same patterns that had inspired the state to launch the program: well-established migration networks made job possibilities north of the border almost as accessible as local employment. Finally, and perhaps most important, migrant firm owners found themselves torn between complying with a business model and fulfilling social obligations, feeling compelled to give relatives and neighbors jobs or pay advances to compensate for the remittances they had sunk into the maquilas. All the factors that condemned the Mi Comunidad maquiladoras to failure would have been obvious to bureaucrats had they taken the trouble to engage with migrants as they were developing the program. State employees made a Sisyphean effort to overcome the obstacles that the program ran up against:

> We tried to organize working groups among the firms that were in the same geographic area so that they could learn from each other; we linked them to maquilas in the hopes that the larger firm would subcontract to them; we had weekly management meetings with them, and we went over their operating budget with them item by item . . . but the work was too irregular. . . . In the end, the program went from being a business development program to a social service program. . . . It became about building the self-esteem of women—because it was mostly women—who were employed in the workshop. (Interview, Guanajuato, July 2003)

The program also opened up bitter fissures within Guanajuatan emigrant groups, many of which had made a Herculean effort—among migrants earning relatively low wages—to pool the $60,000 minimum required to participate.[2] In addition to wiping out the life savings of dozens, the program also erased any *confianza* that migrants had placed in the state government as a result of its provision of services to migrants and its enthusiastic promotion of the Comunidades program (interviews, Guanajuato, July 2003; Iskander 2005).

Frustrated with this scheme, the same Guanajuatan migrant clubs that the state was reluctant to recognize pressured the government into emulating the Three for One matching-funds program in Zacatecas. By early 1999, the program had already spread to Jalisco and Guerrero, a couple of states in the migrant-sending area of central western Mexico (SEDESOL interviews, Mexico City, December 2002 and May 2003; and Jalisco office, May 2003). It seemed to offer a well-established framework that guaranteed migrants a voice, protecting their role in identifying what kind of projects—basic infrastructure, cultural spaces, health services—they wanted to support (interviews, Guanajuato, July 2003, Chicago, August 2003). In 2000, with Fox still governor but with his presidential campaign well under way, the state government acquiesced and created its own version of the matching-funds initiative, a more modest Two for One program.

In the Guanajuatan adaptation, however, every dollar contributed by migrants would be matched by two from the state government, rather than the state and federal governments each supplying a dollar. The PAN, which governed Guanajuato, was by then in a presidential dead heat with the PRI and had no interest in begging resources from the PRI-dominated federal government. Furthermore, Guanajuato applied a distinct style of program implementation, using rigid criteria for the projects to be funded. It explicitly prioritized those it viewed as catalyzing development and discouraged, if not completely excluded, those it saw as an extension of the dead-end consumption patterns it attributed to migrants. "We fund about one in four of the projects the migrants ask us to fund," explained a manager of the program. "We fund the projects the municipal governments prioritize, and we look for the projects that are likely to have the largest economic impact" (interview, Guanajuato, July 2003). Officials set up so many bureaucratic hurdles to filter out "unproductive" projects, such as plazas and churches, that it took migrant communities almost the entire fiscal year to get a project authorized. Getting approval required navigating fifty-six bureaucratic steps, including the massive hurdle of drawing up a community development plan in a format defined by the state government. The labyrinthine process left only a few weeks at the end of the year for the actual construction of a project before the municipal authorities had to return any unused funds. So frustrating was the process that participation in the Two for One—and later Guanajuato's version of the federal Three for One, when the fifty-six bureaucratic steps were reduced to thirty-two—remained sluggish and at times actually dipped. The effect of this bureaucratic filter was that Guanajuato's matching-funds projects had a larger overall budget than did those in other states, and they were skewed toward larger infrastructure instead of the churches, rodeos, and community spaces that migrants clubs preferred. In 2001, for example, 50 percent of the program's budget went to the paving of rural roads (Guanajuato 2003; interviews, Guanajuato, July 2003).

The Guanajuato government's response to these policy disappointments was to be stubbornly analytic, ordering a new batch of studies after each blunder. In 2002, it partnered with the Colegio de la Frontera Norte to conduct two detailed household surveys on migration and its social and economic impacts—two of the largest surveys of their kind ever conducted in Mexico. "Our programs weren't working and we were at a loss. So we decided we needed to know more, about migrants and their families, and that's why we embarked on this study," explained the director of the surveys at Guanajuato's State Council on Population (Consejo Estatal de Población, or COESPO; interview, Guanajuato, July 2003). The state government also subjected each of its policy failures to several, arguably redundant, rounds of evaluation. The Comunidades program, for example, underwent at least four, one internal, two commissioned by local and international research centers, and one comprehensive independent study (Brynes 2003). Finally, the state government restructured the organization that carried out its migrant programs. In 2001, it split the DACGE portfolio in two, leaving the agency with the services for migrants, but apportioning services for migrants' families in communities of origin to a new division called the State Commission for the Support of Migrants and Their Families (Comisión Estatal de Apoyo Integral a los Migrantes y Sus Familias). The reorganization reflected an obvious misunderstanding of the relationship between migrants and their communities in Guanajuato: the state government saw a divide between migrants in the United States and their families in Guanajuato. The strong ties that bound them were invisible to a state government resolved to act on migrants instead of engaging with them. As the director of migrant services at the commission put it, "migrants leave behind families, dependents with lots of problems. And we are left shouldering responsibility for solving them" (Comisión Estatal de Apoyo Integral a los Migrantes y Sus Familias interview, Guanajuato, July 2003).

A Brief Engagement: Migrants and Mexico's Democratic Revolution

Even as his programs for migrants were ailing, presidential candidate Vicente Fox paraded them during his campaigning north of the border as proof of his engagement. In his large, energetic rallies in cities throughout California and his swaggering march through Calle 26, the Mexican heart of Chicago, he invoked his programs repeatedly to show that he understood migrants and their relationships with their communities of origin (Oppenheimer 2000; SRE interviews, Mexico City, May 2003). Both opposition parties had begun courting migrant support early on: in 1999, the PRD and the PAN proposed joint legislation calling for the federal government to implement measures to allow migrants to vote in the 2000 election. The bill was defeated by PRI, but both opposition candidates took up the cause in their presidential campaigns (Quiñones 1999). Cárdenas and Fox both made campaign promises about using government resources to protect migrants from a variety of abuses and to negotiate changes in U.S. policy toward them. By May 2000, however, as the campaign was drawing to a close and Cárdenas and Fox were barnstorming through the United States so intensively that their schedules practically overlapped (Robles 2000), a distinction between the two candidates seemed to be emerging. (Labastida, the PRI candidate, in a rebuff to Mexican migrants that only underscored the ruling party's deep reluctance to engage with them, vowed not to leave Mexico until the elections were over [Leiken 2001; Belluck 2000].)[3]

To migrants, Fox seemed to emerge as the candidate who grasped that migration was a local phenomenon: that it had local causes and very specific local effects. The Casas and Comunidades programs, their shortcomings still unclear to observers beyond Guanajuato and even to many observers in the state, were viewed as evidence that his pledge to be the president of "118 million Mexicans"—100 million in Mexico and 18 million beyond its borders—was more than rhetorical, and that the presidential hopeful's direct experience with programs for migrants and their communities meant that he had a pragmatic vision of what that commitment would look like in practice. Moreover, Fox's campaign promise to take the hugely popular Two for One program national, and to raise the government contribution to three dollars for every dollar migrants gave, was seen as an indication that he saw a role for government in supporting migrants' ties to their communities of origin (SRE interviews, May and July 2003; FCZSC interviews, Zacatecas, July 2003; UAZ interviews, Zacatecas, 2003; Hegstrom 2000). The existence of programs for migrants in Guanajuato and the promised expansion of the matching-funds program were cited in informal surveys of migrants as reasons for backing the PAN candidate. In Fox, an overwhelming majority of migrants saw their best hope to unseat the PRI after seventy-one years of uncontested rule. Indeed, as Levitt and de la Dehasa state, "in simulated elections organized among emigrants, Fox got 10,985 votes; Cárdenas got 2,673; and PRI candidate Labastida got 1,789" (2004).

Many migrants also saw in Fox a bridge to take local initiatives—and the partnerships that migrants had established with local governments in particular—to the federal level (SRE interviews, May and July 2003; FCZSC interviews, Zacatecas, July 2003; UAZ interviews, Zacatecas, 2003). So, while the Fox campaign mobilized to use migrants as a source of political influence in Mexico, migrants were also using Fox to achieve policy objectives that were important to them. The migrant groups that rallied around him were mainly concerned with new economic and political *relationships* that they wanted to forge with government and communities of origin. Little did they know that those relationships had gone unaddressed in Guanajuato, when they had not actually been severed by government policy. The approach that Fox and the government of Guanajuato had used to make policy for migrants, objectifying with its meticulous studies and vaguely patronizing in its rhetoric, distracted them from the potential that a rich engagement between migrants and the government could offer for the state's economic transformation.

Although thousands of valiant migrants streamed back into Mexico to vote, their direct effect on the election was infinitesimal. (Out of 37.6 million ballots cast nationwide, migrants were thought to represent fewer than 50,000 [Fitzgerald 2004].) Their indirect effect may have been more significant, however. Fox told the *Washington Post* that "[migrants] are the people who are sustaining the economy [in their hometowns] and they have the moral authority to influence votes" (as quoted in Leiken 2001), and he urged migrants at every opportunity to tell their relatives and friends to vote the PRI out of power. His campaign in the United States, spearheaded by Mimexca (Migrantes Mexicanos por el Cambio), a counterpart to Amigos de Fox in Mexico, distributed millions of postcards and phone cards so that migrants could exhort family members to "vote for change" (Leiken 2001; Levitt and de la Dehasa 2004). According to a statistical analysis run by Joseph Klesner (2005) in which he controlled for the demographic, socioeconomic, and religious factors that favored the PAN, Fox did unexpectedly well in the central western region of Mexico, the region with the highest emigration rates both historically and at the time of the election. However, irrespective of the actual magnitude of migrant influence on the electoral outcome, Fox and his team viewed migrants as an important political group that had not only helped bring them to power but that would continue to shape political events.

VIPs—Very Important Paisanos

Before even formally assuming the office of president, Fox announced that he was establishing an Office for Mexican Migrants Abroad, to be headed by a director who would have a cabinet-level position. At a meeting with seventy leaders of migrant organizations in Los Angeles in November 2000, itself a politically unprecedented event, the president-elect told them that the office, patterned on the DACGE in Guanajuato, would "address your demands and your proposals on a daily basis, so that you can remind us every day of our obligations [to you]" (as quoted in Amador 2000a). Adding that the office would be directed by "migrants themselves, I don't want intermediaries to represent them" (as quoted in Amador 2000a), he named Juan Hernandez, a Mexican American wheeler-dealer who had campaigned for him in the United States, as head of the office. Fox also renewed his pledge to fight to get migrants living abroad the right to vote in Mexican elections. Soon afterward, two hundred presidents of migrant organizations received invitations to his inaugural festivities. Meetings to discuss future steps with Fox and Hernandez were to follow the ceremonies. (Not coincidentally, perhaps, fifteen Mexican migrant leaders from Los Angeles were also invited to the inauguration of George Bush.) "Never have we initiated a relationship this close and this good with a [Mexican] president," beamed Rafael Barajas, president of the Federation of Zacatecan Clubs of Southern California (Amador 2000a).

Despite their optimism, however, migrant leaders left the meetings in Mexico City feeling apprehensive. Many publicly expressed concern that Hernandez had an incomplete understanding of the realities that migrants and their communities faced and also intimated that Fox's grasp of the programs he had promoted on the campaign trail was less than perfect. In interviews with *La Opinión*, a Los Angeles Spanish-language daily newspaper, they concurred that Hernandez "isn't familiar with the whole situation [of migrants and their communities]," and one flatly added, "he is unaware of the real problems of Mexicans, simply because he is a Chicano and doesn't represent Mexicans" (as quoted in Amador 2000a). Even more disappointing was that Fox displayed a murky understanding of how the Two for One program worked and seemed to be advocating a revision of its fundamental purpose. His comments seemed to herald a downgrade from an arrangement that offered two or three dollars in matching funds, to one that offered only a single dollar for each migrant dollar. Furthermore, they seemed to presage a redirection of funds toward projects that the government viewed as productive and away from the cultural and social public works migrants favored. "For every dollar that you want to invest in your communities, building maquilas, creating jobs, creating these types of opportunities for your children, your families in these communities, the government will match your dollar," Fox told the migrant leaders (as quoted in Robles 2000).

Their fears were soon confirmed. The Fox administration, with Hernandez as its spokesman, seemed to view migrants primarily as a source of capital. Remittances were reduced to money, stripped of their significance as the language in which migrants reasserted their ties to their families and communities, and migrants were becoming invisible behind the dollar signs. Hernandez announced that migrants were "VIPs—Very Important Paisanos" and would be treated as such "because they are creating wealth" for Mexico, not because the Mexican state had any inherent responsibility toward them (Amador 2001). In addition to repeating ad nauseam the amount migrants sent to Mexico every year— between $7 billion and $9 billion according to the Office for Mexican Migrants Abroad in 2001—the proposals all focused on channeling those funds toward the creation of firms. Hernandez shamelessly touted the three remaining Comunidades maquiladoras in Guanajuato, all on the verge of foreclosure, as the embodiment of a best practice the administration wanted to extend to the rest of Mexico. "We did it in Guanajuato and we are going to reproduce it in all 32 states. Within 100 days, we are going to be opening the maquilas" (as quoted in Amador 2001). In conjunction with the Inter-American Development Bank and the Nacional Financiera, a Mexican development bank, the Fox administration set up a program for small-firm creation using remittances, which

sputtered along and never showed more than mediocre results (http://www.
iadb.org). An additional way devised to capitalize on remittances was the
Padrino—Godfather—program. Also called the Adopt-a-Community program,
it was designed to convince wealthy Mexican American businessmen to invest
in job-creating partnerships in impoverished microregions. It was soon abandoned as the business ventures in the isolated communities failed (*Migration
News* 2001).

The emphasis on remittances, although alienating to many migrants, combined with U.S. security concerns after the September 11, 2001, attacks to give
new impetus to the Mexican government's long-standing program of granting
consular identification documents. The cards, generally called by their Spanish
name, *matrícula consular*, identified the bearer as a Mexican national living
abroad. The Fox administration pushed hard to get the document accepted as
an official form of identification by U.S. police and government officials, but
more importantly, by U.S. banks and money transfer outfits. The Mexican government's intensive lobbying encouraged a number of financial establishments,
led by Wells Fargo in late 2001, to recognize the card as sufficient identification to open a bank account and to wire remittances to Mexico (*La Opinión*
2001).

From the Three for One Program to the Citizens' Initiative

In 2002, the Fox administration finally made the matching-funds program into
a national one under SEDESOL. In scale it was patterned after the Zacatecan
version, the Three for One, which matched each migrant dollar with a dollar
from the federal, state, and municipal governments. In a major change, however, the federal government opened the program to all Mexicans, migrant or
not, and renamed it Iniciativa Ciudadana—Citizens' Initiative. In essence, the
government had transformed a program that had served as the vector for migrant community mobilization into just another poverty alleviation program.
Iniciativa Ciudadana became just a recycled version of Salinas's Solidaridad
program, complete with the same embedded misunderstandings of migrants
and their relationships to their communities of origin. Migrants were again
subsumed into their communities, treated merely as the elites of local hamlets,
and given no special access to the matching-funds arrangement. There was no
recognition of the function that the program served over and above the simple
construction of public works, no appreciation that it had provided an institutional structure to generate new understandings about the relationship between migration and development, between citizens and the state, and between
economic and political locations in the United States and in Mexico. As if that
were not problematic enough, the federal government, just as in the original
Solidaridad program and in Guanajuato's Two for One, applied its own criteria in selecting which programs would receive funding, dismissing as "unproductive" and unnecessary "consumption" projects like churches and plazas. In

doing so, it paternalistically dismissed migrants' vision for the development of their communities, effectively excluding them from conversations about their own future (SEDESOL interviews, Mexico City, December 2002 and May 2003; Zacatecas, April 2003).

Not only did the federal demotion of the program show a lack of engagement with migrants, but the policy shift began to undermine the very dynamics that had made the matching-funds program valuable to migrants and local government in the first place. It neutered the program's ability to act as a catalyst for organizing among migrants in the United States. The motivation to form a club in order to carry out a project in their community of origin that would, as one migrant leader put it, "make us proud, make our sacrifice clear," disappeared, and with it, so did potential interlocutors with the government. When the program was recast as Iniciativa Ciudadana and opened to all citizens, migrants were again submerged in the general population, and their concerns were lost among the many pressing petitions made to the government (interviews, Zacatecas, March 2003; Mexico City, July 2003; and Chicago, August 2003).

Nowhere was this shift more poignant than in Zacatecas. Leaders from various federations of Zacatecan clubs, who, under the new federal guidelines, were no longer formally included in project selection, traveled to the state capital on their own initiative to remind Zacatecan authorities of the reasons that the program had been a catalyst for change in migrants lives, as they lived them out on both sides of the border, as well as in the lives of the communities they came from. "Keep the projects for the migrants. This is our program. We started it. We negotiated it. Everyone in the room here today knows that," asserted one federation representative at a meeting with the state planning officials and the fifty municipal presidents in attendance. "You need to help us out. We need this program to help us organize, and fight for our rights as workers [in the United States]" (plenary Three for One planning meeting, Zacatecas, March 2003). The president of the Federation of Zacatecan Clubs in Southern California, José Guadalupe Gómez, cautioned that clubs were disbanding because they no longer felt motivated to participate in a program that ensnared projects the state defined as unproductive in miles of red tape, stalling them for months on end; at least 20 Zacatecan clubs in California, out of an estimated 130 nationwide, dissolved in 2003 out of frustration (Amador 2003b; M. Orozco 2003). "We need to be more demanding with the Mexican government so that projects that the community considers priorities are supported, and not only those that the authorities determine are worthwhile," asserted the president of the largest and most powerful Mexican federation of clubs in the United States (as quoted in Arredondo 2003). The program no longer embodied a relationship that constituted a partnership; it embodied a clientelistic power dynamic in which migrants had to appeal to an authoritative state.

The Collapse of a Relationship

Within two years of Fox's taking office, the migrants who had been so enthusiastic about their relationship with an administration that finally saw them after so many decades of neglect—"*que nos toma[ba] en cuenta*" (as quoted in Amador 2000b)—were thoroughly disillusioned. "We thought that . . . the relationship and the dialogue [with the Mexican government] would grow, but it didn't happen. There is a real disenchantment," commented one Mexican leader at a conference of Mexican and Mexican American intellectuals (Serenses, as quoted in Arredondo 2002). The Presidential Office for Mexicans Abroad seemed to be a vehicle for much talk but little substantive engagement. Moreover, apart from the modest pressure it had applied to private remittance transfer companies to get them to lower their fees, the administration made no progress on its other campaign promises to migrants: the PAN had yet to submit legislation to enable them to vote in Mexican elections and, despite a few symbolic gestures, had made no headway in negotiating new migration agreements or an amnesty with the U.S. government. Migrant groups began to threaten "remittance boycotts" to protest the Mexican government's lack of responsiveness (Kammer 2002).

Additionally, a low-grade war of attrition between Juan Hernandez and Jorge Castañeda, the secretary of foreign relations who was responsible for Mexico's network of consulates, was further undermining services to migrants. Perhaps in an attempt to give Hernandez the rope with which to hang himself, the Secretariat of Foreign Relations (SRE) staff significantly reduced outreach activities and concentrated instead on providing existing services to Mexican migrants through the still-operating Programa para Mexicanos en el Extranjero (PCME) (SRE interviews, Mexico City, May 2003). The Presidential Office for Mexicans Abroad did not have the staff or the budget resources to make up the difference, and Hernandez's ambitious plans were shown up as just talk. In the summer of 2002, the office was eliminated and Hernandez was dismissed. Castañeda did not survive the skirmish and was replaced soon afterward.

The Presidential Office's closure was an implicit admission of the failure of its outreach to migrants—an effort that had always been more of a public relations campaign than it was a substantive engagement. It also was an acknowledgment of the limits of the administration's approach in dealing with migrants. The Fox government, in a break from past Mexican administrations, was not only willing to "see" Mexican migrants but also perceived the political usefulness of a relationship with them. It was also determined to strictly define the terms of engagement. The relationship it sought was one-way. With the implosion of this top-down approach, however, the administration was forced to respond to migrant demands for a substantive engagement, similar to the one that had blossomed in Zacatecas. These demands were backed with clout provided both by increasingly mobilized grassroots organizations and also, ironically, by a more precise awareness of migrant economic contribution, thanks to the administration's tabulation and advertisement of remittance levels.

Within days, Fox announced that an Institute for Mexicans Abroad—Instituto de los Mexicanos en el Extranjero (IME)—would be created. It was the product of an agreement negotiated within the government at the end of the turf war between the SRE and the Presidential Office for Mexicans Abroad. The administration spun the new agency as evidence of the president's renewed commitment to migrants, but most commentators both in and out of government acknowledged that it was a last-ditch effort to salvage whatever was left of the Fox administration's—of the PAN's—credibility with the ever more influential emigrant population. "It's our last chance. There won't be another one. We have to get this one right or we will have lost the migrants forever," conceded a program officer at the new institute (SRE interviews, Mexico City, 2003).

Institute for Mexicans Abroad: Bringing Together "Seeing" and "Engaging"

The Mexican government envisioned the IME as an "institutional strategy more modern and effective in generating policies" for Mexicans abroad (SRE 2002a). Created at a crisis in the relationship between migrants and the state, the new institute represented both an abandonment of well-worn government strategies to assert political control over the engagement with migrants and the surrender of willful blindness toward them. The IME, which would be housed in the Secretariat of Foreign Relations, would instead blend the strengths of the new PAN-ista Fox administration and the capacities developed by the PRI administrations before it. It would merge the Fox administration's willingness to acknowledge migrants—to both "see" them and discern them in all of their specificity—with the decades of SRE experience in fostering and reinventing interpretive engagement generative of new insights and sources of power, even though that engagement had heretofore been only with Mexican Americans, to the exclusion of Mexican migrants.

The executive order that authorized the IME's establishment made this amalgam explicit. The new strategy would combine the Presidential Office for Mexicans Abroad's ability to "connect the president of Mexico with Mexican communities abroad and to detect their most pressing concerns, demonstrating the importance of a government body dedicated to connecting with those communities," with the SRE's "significant experience developed since 1990 through the Program for Mexican Communities Abroad . . . [elaborating] strategies of *acercamiento*" with Mexican-origin groups in the United States (SRE 2002a). Moreover, the official mandate recognized that this combination of capacities was critical to respond to "new demands" that migrants would have in a host of areas, from "political representation" to "health and education"—demands that could not be anticipated because they had yet to be articulated (SRE 2002a and 2002b). With the IME, the federal government, for the first time, opened a space to hold interpretive conversations with migrants.

To erect an organizational structure that could accomplish these things, the government, and the SRE in particular, revived knowledge of how to host an interpretive conversation. Just as it had done every time it reinitiated engagement with Mexican Americans after having closed it down, the federal government recovered knowledge necessary to support interpretive exchange, knowledge encapsulated in the insights those exchanges had produced. Just as before, it was forced to reinterpret knowledge held in practices that had been abandoned and that existed only in institutional memory. And just as it was each time the Mexican state tried to restart conversations with Mexican Americans, that act of reinterpretation was situated in specific historical and political contexts. With the creation of the IME, the context required the Mexican state to recognize and embrace relationships it had studiously tried to ignore and even negate.

Chief among these was the connection between Mexican Americans and Mexican migrants. For decades, the Mexican government had maintained that the two were either completely separate groups, and thus required radically different strategies, or that they could be subsumed into a single group, with Mexican Americans representing migrant interests, thus requiring the government to engage only with Mexican Americans. The IME's structure had to reflect an acknowledgment that the two groups were not wholly distinct but were also not the same, that they were bound together by multiple complex relationships sometimes not of their own creation, and that alliances and frictions arose among and between them in unexpected ways around the dynamic of Mexican labor emigration.

The second relationship that the IME had to build into its structure was that between migrants and their communities of origin. The federal government had historically discounted—had chosen not to "see"—the myriad and densely woven ties between migrants and the communities from which they hailed. It either suspended migrants "above" their communities, treating them as generic Mexican identities, a habit the state of Guanajuato also adopted, or it subsumed them into their villages of origin, addressing them as elites participating in the local economy (and in the social relationships that were its infrastructure) in a straightforward way. To break with this view, the IME's structure had to reflect a recognition that migrants were integral members of their communities of origin, but also divided from them by space, social environment, and economic context, and thus also had separate existences, experiences, and interests. Similarly, the organizational format had to recognize that migrants' needs and aspirations were defined as much by the local, even parochial, contexts of their villages as by national and international politics, most notably by the asymmetrical relationship between Mexico and its overbearing northern neighbor.

Finally, the IME could not be set up in a way that included migrants in interpretive exchange without an explicit avowal of the relationship between participation in interpretive engagement with the state and the development of political power. As the federal government had discovered through its engagement with Mexican Americans, once engagement enabled new connections and insights to be articulated, those insights could not be "unsaid." The only way to neutralize them (and their ramifications for state action) was to pull out of the engagement, a tactic to which the government had resorted over and over again. Although disengagement was possible with Mexican Americans, who after all were U.S. citizens, it was not an option in the same way for any strategy aiming to marginalize migrants to whom the Mexican state had a juridical responsibility. Once relationships were articulated and embodied in the IME, particularly relationships that underscored the connection between emigration and economic and political development, migrants' role in shaping the future of their communities of origin, and by extension, of the nation, became visible. The government could only disregard those connections at significant political cost. To address this dynamic, the IME provided clear institutional channels for migrants to hold the state accountable and exercise the political power they would accrue through engagement, and it protected conduits to contain migrant grievances and keep them from spilling over into voting behavior in communities of origin.

Structuring Engagement: Organizational Profile of the IME

The SRE instantiated these relationships in an institutional structure that stood out as one of the most innovative in the entire Mexican government. The IME consisted of an executive body flanked by two advisory councils: one representing the federal government, the National Council (Consejo Nacional), and the other Mexican-origin communities in the United States, the Consultative Council (Consejo Consultivo). The role of the executive body, made up of about two dozen bureaucrats, was to facilitate interpretive conversations between the councils and among their members. As the legislative decree that mandated the IME stated, the institute's function was "the creation of meeting spaces and opportunities and to foster the communication with and between Mexican communities that live abroad" (SRE 2003).

The National Council for Mexican Communities Abroad was composed of representatives from twelve major secretariats in the Mexican government, with responsibilities as different as those of the Secretariat of Health and the Treasury Department, but all with portfolios that touched either directly or indirectly on the issue of migration or the interests of migrants.[4] These were the implementing agencies for any policy recommendations that emerged from the conversations supported by the IME. Their participation in the institute represented the recognition that migrant needs and contributions were multifaceted, local and national, and affecting everything from local agricultural development to international relations.

The Consultative Council for Mexicans Abroad was essentially an advisory board made up of three constituencies: approximately 100 Mexican migrant and Mexican American community leaders; representatives from 10 prominent Mexican American and Hispanic organizations in the United States;[5] and representatives from 32 state governments. The breakdown of the membership encapsulated the Mexican state's acknowledgment of the relationship between Mexican Americans and Mexicans by bringing members of both groups into the conversation: out of an initial 100 community leaders, 72 were Mexican migrants, and 29 of those were leaders of federations of Mexican clubs or club presidents. Furthermore, 12 were identified as activists who engaged in political activity on both sides of the border (C. Morales, pers. comm., 2003). Community leaders were voted in through elections held at the Mexican consulates throughout the United States, in which people of Mexican origin who had registered could participate—both migrants and Mexican Americans (although participants were overwhelmingly migrants) (SRE interviews, Mexico City, May 2003). The representatives were apportioned according to the number of Mexican-origin people living in a given area of the United States; so, for example, the consulates of Chicago and Los Angeles held elections for 13 and 17 community leaders, respectively, whereas the Boston consulate held an election for 2 and the Philadelphia consulate an election for 1 (http://www.sre.gob.mx/ IME). The elections not only gave the council significant legitimacy in Mexican communities in the United States but were viewed by many as a break with the Mexican federal government's habitual clientelistic condescension toward migrants. "This is an historic event," exclaimed the secretary general of the Federation of Clubs of Michoacán in California. "For the first time, we were able to vote and select the people that are going to bring the agenda of Mexicans abroad back to Mexico" (as quoted in Amador 2002a). It was also significant because it belied the government's persistent assertions that organizing migrant participants in an electoral contest was logistically unfeasible for the Mexican government.

Mexican American organizations represented on the council were, on the other hand, selected by the SRE. The criteria were twofold: first, that the organization have a history of engagement with the Mexican government and, as a result, an institutional knowledge of how to participate in interpretive conversations with the state. Groups like the National Council of La Raza and the League of United Latin American Citizens had engaged with the Mexican government since the late 1970s and would thus be able to help resuscitate interpretive dialogue by drawing on their own institutional memories. The second criterion was that the organizations should be "the most representative in the United States" and explicitly address needs of both Mexican Americans and Mexican migrants (SRE interviews, Mexico City, May 2003 and May 2005; http://www.sre.gob.mx/IME, May–October 2005).

The SRE also selected the state governments represented on the council, choosing states with some of the highest emigration rates and longest emigration traditions in the nation, stretching back in some cases before 1900. Their selection manifested the SRE's admission of the importance of involving state governments in the process of developing conceptual insights, rather than simply delegating to them the implementation of prefabricated services for migrants. Initially, the SRE allotted seats on the board to representatives from ten states: President Fox's home state of Guanajuato, Michoacán, Jalisco, Chihuahua, Durango, Mexico State, Guerrero, Oaxaca, Puebla, and, of course, the trendsetting state of Zacatecas (C. Morales, pers. comm., 2003). The IME quickly grew into such an influential institution in shaping policies that affected migrants, and through them, the regions from which they hailed, that state governments began to petition for council seats. By 2005, the council had expanded to include representatives from all Mexican states (http://www.sre.gob.mx/IME, May–October 2005; SRE interviews, May 2005).

The director nominated for the IME also embodied the Mexican government's explicit recognition of the relationships it had tried to ignore. In an unprecedented move, Fox appointed a Mexican migrant. Candido Morales, a native of Oaxaca and president of the Mixteca Club of Sonoma, California, was chosen after an exhaustive search during which the government considered *only* migrant candidates (Robles 2002; SRE interviews, Mexico City, May 2003).

Morales stressed that the IME's mission was to "advise the government of Mexico in the design and formulation of policies for Mexican communities in the United States" (as quoted in Robles 2002). It was pointedly not to build a lobby that the Mexican government could direct to further political goals. Moreover, the former migrant club leader, who had opened interpretive spaces in his community and his village of origin, made explicit the value of an inclusive interpretive engagement that involved migrants, Mexican Americans, and government authorities. In doing so, he signaled to the Mexican communities abroad that the federal government was finally willing to engage with migrants in a mutually constitutive relationship, one in which participants shaped each other's future. "We have sought to open the process of the exchange of ideas and different opinions as wide as possible," explained Morales to *La Opinión*, Los Angeles' Spanish-language daily newspaper. In an interview with me, he identified the multiplicity of experiences and views as the source of the Consultative Council's generative capacity: "This consultative council has a lot of diversity, it has teachers, it has businessmen, it has community leaders. This group has fresh ideas, especially for us as the consumers of those ideas, so that the programs that emerge become more and more attuned to the needs of the communities they are created for, and that we don't produce formulaic policy that the bureaucracy here thinks is good for people. That's the main difference that differentiates this approach from previous ones" (Mexico City, May 2003).

He was also cognizant that historically the Mexican government had given migrants short shrift, providing only skeletal services and edging them out of the process of program design. "In Mexico, for decades, we were not heard by the government and our human rights, our social rights and our political rights were not a priority for the national authorities," Morales reminded the participants in the Consultative Council (C. Morales, interview, 2003). For that reason, he emphasized that bringing the Consultative Council and the National Council together was essential for operationalizing the insights and turning them into actionable policy. The secretariats represented on the National Council, he explained, "can bring the budget necessary to implement [the ideas], to make these proposals concrete, so that they don't stay in the realm of the rhetorical, so that the programs become solid and real, so that we move from words to action" (interview, Mexico City, May 2003).

Morales boldly broadened the scope of the discussions that migrants could hope to have with the Mexican state. Shortly after accepting the position of director, he announced that he anticipated that one of the "principal themes" that the IME would address was that of "the situation of undocumented migrants" and the measures the state could take to ameliorate it. He added that he foresaw the conversations addressing not only the actions that Mexican Americans and migrants could take in the United States to tackle challenge, but the ways the Mexican state could support their efforts (Amador 2002b).

Practices of Engagement: Operating Procedures of the IME

The SRE also set up procedures to foster the conversations that were interpretive engagement's medium. The IME was to use as models practices that the SRE had previously employed to engage with Mexican Americans, but it would reinvent them to fit the new broader constituency and the new mandate.

In March 2003, the IME held its inaugural plenary meeting in Mexico City. The conference brought together both advisory councils in their entirety, and President Fox formally recognized and welcomed their members. In its grandeur and in the interactions orchestrated between high-level government authorities and representatives of Mexican communities abroad, the meeting echoed conferences sponsored by the Salinas administration a decade earlier during its frenzied efforts to drum up a lobby to push NAFTA through the U.S. Congress. The profile and tone of the IME conference was different, however. Instead of a meeting with a select group of Mexican American representatives who were seduced with promises of cultural belonging to their ancestral homeland through economic investment, migrant leaders were there in full force, and the tenor of government pronouncements was much more humble, laden with references to collaborative work and exchange. "I want to express my gratitude for your presence in Mexico," announced Fox: "I want to express my gratitude for your having accepted the great challenge of joining with us in doing the work of being close, of bringing together the Mexicans that are here, on this side of the border, and the Mexicans that are over there, on the other side of the border. . . . From now on, I give you my full commitment to work alongside you, shoulder to shoulder, to be close and to support you the way that you deserve" (Fox 2003a).

The meetings did in fact involve a lot of work. The Consultative Council was divided into six groups, each addressing a different facet of migrant and Mexican American concerns. The groups, called "commissions" in an evocation of the commission that the federal government had set up to engage with Mexican Americans under López Portillo, tackled issues on a wide range of topics that included the economy and business, education, law, politics, community building, and health, culture, and the border. During that first plenary, the commissions met intensively and drew up lists of recommendations for the various secretariats in the National Council. The government bodies on the National Council committed themselves to responding to—although not to acting on—each recommendation. The IME coordinated the exchange, posting both recommendations and responses on its website in a sort of virtual conversation, and sent out almost daily bulletins reporting on the exchange to anyone who subscribed to its list.

The IME plenary conferences were repeated twice a year. Just as at the first, migrant and Mexican American representatives met with high-level government officials, and the National Council and Consultative Council were brought together for substantive discussion. The six commissions submitted new recommendations as well as iterations of previous suggestions, in light of the government's responses. Between plenary sessions, the commissions met regularly to hone proposals in their focus areas, and IME staff, often accompanied by bureaucrats from the relevant government offices, traveled to participate in the discussions.

Reinterpretation in Action: From Iniciativa Ciudadana to Four for One

By 2006, after only two years, the IME had facilitated the transformation of policies in myriad areas that affected migrants and Mexican Americans. The interpretive conversations it fostered led to the reconceptualization and reformulation of state practices as they related to issues ranging from the health of Mexican communities in the United States, to customs duties, to the political rights of migrants in Mexico. Nowhere was their impact more dramatic than in the case of the matching-funds program that had been so important to migrants both as a means of participating in their communities of origin and as a vehicle to organize and develop their political power, which had compelled the Mexican government to enter into a conversation with them in the first place. Not only did the conversations hosted by the IME reverse the federal government's transformation of the Three for One matching-funds program into a run-of-the-mill (and neoliberal) poverty alleviation scheme; it reinvented it as a transnational forum for participatory community development planning.

At the time the IME was set up, Mexican migrant clubs and the federal government were at an impasse over the Three for One matching-funds program, which the federal authorities had renamed the Iniciativa Ciudadana—Citizens' Initiative. "The program has been spoilt," said the president of the Federation of Zacatecan Clubs of Southern California. "Iniciativa Ciudadana has significantly reduced the importance of migrant participation." The SEDE-SOL countered with frustrated assertions that the government could not legally and ethically extend a program to certain segments of the population and not to others (SEDESOL interviews, Mexico City, December 2002 and May 2003). And although the migrant clubs continued to submit proposals for church construction and plaza renovations along with projects for basic infrastructure, SEDESOL viewed its role as educating migrants about the type of project that it considered conducive to economic development: "mak[ing] them more civilized about the type of projects that they want to execute," as the secretarial staff put it (SEDESOL interview, Mexico City, May 2003).

At the first IME plenary meeting in March 2003, the economic issues commission submitted a series of recommendations regarding the matching-funds program. These were essentially twofold: first, the commission requested that the SEDESOL revise the operating rules for the program, giving preference to projects proposed by migrant clubs over those submitted by citizens' committees formed solely for the purpose of building infrastructure. Moreover, the commission asked that the SEDESOL clarify its criteria for funding projects and specifically asked it to explain why it did not consider the construction of churches, plazas, and rodeo rings—spaces migrants viewed as critical for community building and community dialogue on both symbolic and practical levels—useful for economic and social development. Second, the commission entreated the SEDESOL to run training seminars for migrants in the United States on the matching-funds program, asking the secretariat in effect to support grassroots mobilization through the program much as the state government of Zacatecas had done since it initiated the arrangement in 1986 (http://www.sre.gob.mx/IME, May 2004 and May–October 2005).

These requests started an intensive conversation between the Consultative Council's economic commission and the SEDESOL, one often but not always mediated by the IME. Through this exchange, the federal government began to understand that the Three for One had a much broader function than infrastructure development: SEDESOL officials began to perceive that the program organized migrant interlocutors into federations of clubs and enabled the state to mediate migrants' relationships with their communities of origin. They also began to grasp the political power and economic clout that migrant federations were starting to represent, and the kind of impact that they could have on political and economic outcomes in Mexico. Federations of migrant clubs, in turn, assimilated the government's view of their potential, broadened their vision beyond their villages and states of origin, and began to contemplate the role they could play in the development of the nation of Mexico as a whole (UAZ interviews, Mexico City, November 2004).

Within months of receiving the suggestions, SEDESOL responded: it extended an informal pledge to prioritize projects submitted by migrant clubs, and it created an institutional mechanism to give migrants greater say over the projects funded. Specifically, SEDESOL mandated the establishment of project selection committees with equal representation from the three levels of government that were contributing funds and migrants for each state participating in the program. In an explicit recognition of the economic and organizational capacity that migrant club federations had achieved, it also raised the ceiling for federal contributions per project substantially, from 250,000 pesos ($25,000) to 500,000 pesos ($50,000), and in doing so, it doubled the possible size of projects from $100,000 to $200,000. The SEDESOL also partnered with migrant clubs and consular authorities to hold workshops for migrants in cities throughout the United States about the matching-funds program. By the end of 2004, the agency had completely rewritten the program guidelines and scrapped the title Iniciativa Ciudadana, renaming it the Three for One Program for Migrants. As the slightly modified but rehabilitated name indicated, the SEDESOL formally limited participation to migrants organized in clubs, and it privileged as one of the program's three goals "the development of ties of identity between [Mexican] nationals residing abroad with their communities of origin" (SEDESOL 2005: sec. 2). It also increased once again the maximum federal contribution for projects from $50,000 to $80,000, and upped the total budget for the program from the $10 million allocated in 2003 to $16 million for 2005 (http://www.sedesol.gob.mx/IME, May–October 2005; SEDESOL interviews, May 2005).

The conversation about the program did not end there. Instead, it expanded to include other conversations about the program's potential for economic development that had been occurring about the same time. These had been taking place primarily—not surprisingly—in Zacatecas and its communities in the United States. Throughout 2004, the Federation of Zacatecan Clubs of Southern California, in collaboration with the University of Zacatecas (UAZ), the University of Southern California, and the Rockefeller Foundation, held a series of workshops that brought migrants, state and municipal government officials, entrepreneurs (from Zacatecas and from the United States), and academics together to discuss the possibility of linking migration with the creation of investment opportunities (García Zamora 2005). These produced several interesting pilot projects. Among them were a proposal to modify the Three for One guidelines in Zacatecas to fund business investments and twenty-six business plans for small firms that could then be supported under the matching-funds program, and a proposal for the creation of an Advisory Center for Community and Business Development that would be housed at the University of Zacatecas and steered by a board that included migrants, community leaders, government officials, and representatives of industries with bases in the state (García Zamora 2005).

As the conversations between government and migrants expanded, they incorporated many of the innovations produced through the discussions in Zacatecas. Not only did the Zacatecan pioneers inform the federal government of these proposals, but many of the participants in the two conversations—the one in Zacatecas and the one at the federal level—were the same. They brought to their interpretive engagement with the federal government the insights that drove the proposals and an intimate familiarity with the process of conceptual development that produced them—a process that contained insights not yet fully articulated (http://www.sre.gob.mx/IME, Jan.–Sept. 2004; interviews, Zacatecas, August 2004).

As a result of the new directions that the conversation about the matching-funds program was beginning to explore, SEDESOL and the economic issues commission set up a special working group at the end of 2004 to formulate ways that the Three for One could be expanded to include business ventures. Specifically, the working group was charged with investigating the feasibility of expanding to a Four for One program, with investors adding their dollar to the pot. More significantly, however, the group explored the relationships on which such a collaboration would need to rest. It gauged the interests and concerns of possible investors and identified the social connections that needed to be forged between migrants, communities, investors, and government as well as the physical connections in terms of communications and transportation infrastructure needed for the projects to work (http://www.sre.gob.mx/IME, Dec. 2004–Sept. 2005). In a sense, what the working group attempted to do was to reinvent Guanajuato's Comunidades program. It appropriated the idea of using migration as a catalyst for economic investment. Instead of a program that, like Comunidades, was defined and directed by a government that paid scant attention to the social context of its scheme, the working group endeavored to create an initiative that relied on the weave of mutually constituting relationships, where the participants together chose the projects and envisioned their function in a broader context of community development. The conversations initiated in the working group eventually grew into a partnership, launched in 2006, between migrants, the Mexican government, and Western Union to promote investment in projects that advanced both community development and job creation. The dual-use projects included agricultural infrastructure, natural resource conservation efforts, community-based economic development projects such as structural improvements or technical upgrades to existing small businesses, and educational facilities (*Business Wire* 2006).

Interpretation for Political Change: Getting the Vote

The IME supported a similar interpretive conversation around migrant suffrage. Procedurally, it resembled the exchange around the matching-funds program, but the conversation about franchise rights highlighted the connection between interpretive engagement and political power. Migrants used their engagement with the federal government to question rationales it offered for not extending suffrage to them. Through repeated cycles of interpretive exploration, they discredited the government's prevarication and uncovered the deep political insecurity about how migrants would affect electoral outcomes that underlay presidential proclamations that "we have been working, dialoguing, insisting . . . on the importance of taking this grand step forward" (Fox 2004).

The reforms required to enable migrants to vote were primarily logistical. The constitutional amendment of 1996 (see chap. 7) had granted migrants the right to vote in Mexican elections, but the government had yet to solve the logistical and budgetary hurdles (some of them added after the amendment passed) that prevented migrants from exercising this right.

At the second plenary meeting of the IME in August 2003, the Consultative Council, through the political issues commission, submitted a request for a binational forum on the migration vote. The PAN dragged its feet, despite the president's claim that the party was working on the issue with "determination and diligence" (Fox 2003b). Seeing a strategic opportunity, the PRD moved to the forefront in advocating suffrage for migrants, and in early 2004 it began organizing PRD committees in the United States in anticipation of the 2006 presidential contest (PRD interviews, Chicago, August and October 2003). The political momentum created by the PRD-sponsored conferences, as well as raucous meetings organized independently, made it impossible for the IME to delay responding without undermining its own credibility.

In April 2004, the IME hosted a blitz of conferences on the topic in cities throughout the United States—most notably in Los Angeles, Chicago, and Houston—and brought together legislators from the Mexican Congress and migrants. The discussions gave migrants an opportunity to take government officials to task for waffling and, more important, to suggest solutions to the obstacles that legislators argued stood in the way of allowing Mexicans to vote from the United States. Migrant members of the Consultative Council offered, for example, to subsidize the logistical costs of such balloting with a portion of their remittances. The IME meetings thus enabled migrants to discredit the government's—more precisely, the PAN's—excuses for not providing them with a means to vote. In December 2004, at the fourth IME plenary session, the Fox administration's time to act was clearly running out: the Consultative Council drowned out the president's welcome with chants of "Voto! Voto!" Mexican American leaders joined migrants in their demand: "Mexicans are not Mexicans without the right to vote," announced Hector Flores, the president of the League of United Latin American Citizens, during a visit to Mexico City in early 2005. The Fox administration's failure to act on the vote was seriously damaging its renewed relationship with migrants and threatening the survival of the IME, the institution it had described as its "last chance" to engage them (IME 2005).

Soon thereafter, the Chamber of Deputies in the Mexican Congress overwhelmingly approved a series of reforms to the laws that dictated the logistics of electoral procedures, making it clear that it was politically possible to move the necessary bills through Mexico's legislative bodies. Without Senate approval and the president's ratification, passage of the amendments remained symbolic. As the elections of 2006 neared, however—and with them the deadline for changes in electoral procedure—the political costs of not acting appeared increasingly steep. In an attempt at political damage control, PAN-headed state governments, like those of Jalisco and Puebla, began the process of moving bills allowing Mexican migrants to vote in state elections through their own legislative bodies. (IME 2005)

In late June 2005, the political momentum had become impossible to withstand, and, in an extraordinary session, the Mexican Senate and Chamber of Deputies approved a negotiated revision of the earlier amendments. Passed with 455 votes in favor, 6 against, and 6 abstentions, the new law allowed Mexican migrants to vote by absentee ballot in future presidential elections, including the election of 2006. The amendments also stipulated, however, that campaigning beyond the nation's borders would henceforth be illegal, a condition designed to dampen the exponential growth of migrant political influence. Nevertheless, the delegation of fifty migrant leaders who had traveled to Mexico City to witness the vote in the Chamber of Deputies greeted the passage as a historic victory for migrants who had been politically invisible for decades. As the results came in, chants of "Yes we could! Yes we could! Yes we could!" rose up from the public boxes in the Congress. The Los Angeles paper *La Opinión* reported that when passage was formally announced, "the migrants embraced each other, left the legislative auditorium mad with happiness . . . and began to shout in unison: México! México! México! México! México!" (Robles Nava 2005).

Voting to Cement the IME: Political Power and Protecting Interpretation

During the legislative debates over the bills that would enable Mexican migrants to vote from the United States, the Fox administration invoked a 2003 study completed by Marcelli and Cornelius which estimated that only a small fraction of migrants who lived north of the border would actually participate in an election. According to the survey's analysis, only 125,000 to 1.1 million expatriate Mexicans—or between 1.5 and 12 percent—would vote in the 2006 presidential election. (A finding less publicized by the PAN was that fewer than a quarter of these would vote for the party [Marcelli and Cornelius 2003].) The validity of these findings was hotly disputed, but their accuracy is peripheral to the debate about migrant suffrage. With the vote, migrants came out of the political shadows and have become undeniably visible political actors in Mexico as well as in the United States.

In describing the objectives of the IME, its director stated that the institute had been set up as an enduring governmental structure that would "lend more permanence to the effort [of engaging with migrants] so that whatever we create now does not end at the end of this presidential term" (interview, Mexico City, May 2003). It was not the first time that a Mexican government official charged with nurturing the state's relationship with migrants had uttered such a pledge. Mexico's history of engagement with migrants was strewn with the wreckage of institutions established with the same promise of permanence, only to be abandoned when they ceased to be advantageous to the federal government. For the first time, however, the right and the ability to vote had given migrants the political clout to hold IME director Morales to his word. The vote made retreating from an engagement with migrants politically costly for any party at the helm of the federal government, although this was due more to voting's symbolic weight than to the actual number of votes migrants would cast in national elections. In fact, in the coming years migrant participation in the Mexican elections would be sparse, with the exception of migrant Zacatecans, who would participate heartily as voters and candidates for office. Out of the 11 million Mexican nationals in the United States old enough to vote, fewer than 60,000 registered, and the Mexican Election Commission (Instituto Federal Electoral) received only 32,621 votes from outside Mexico, with a little less than 29,000 coming from the United States—much fewer than the 400,000 predicted by scholars and pollsters (Suro 2005; Instituto Federal Electoral, 2006, as cited in R. Smith 2008: 726). The poor showing was a direct result of the logistical hurdles that the Mexican government placed in migrant voters' path, including everything from restrictions on campaigning and fund-raising outside of Mexico, to a requirement that migrants possess a voter ID card that could be issued only in Mexico, to onerous procedures for submitting the ballot (R. Smith 2008; Kapralos 2006). As one migrant leader concluded, Mexican political parties passed the initiative to give migrants the vote because "[they] didn't want to take the blame that they didn't pass anything, so they passed something symbolic" that curtailed migrants' actual ability to vote (as quoted in R. Smith 2008: 727).

That "something symbolic," however, cemented the status of migrants as actors in local and national Mexican politics. Their right to vote was hemmed in by legislative barriers to be sure, but migrants had become powerful as community organizers with transnational appeal, skilled negotiators with local and national governments, and valuable contributors to the economic development of the villages, towns, and states from which they hailed. Migrants from states throughout the republic had mobilized themselves, often with the support of state government, into clubs and organizations the federal government could not only see but with which it felt compelled to engage. Through a series of interpretive conversations with government, first at the state and then at the federal level, migrants had developed the political power to compel the Mexican state to continue the conversation indefinitely. Not only did they draw the federal government into an interpretive exchange, but they also transformed state practices through which the Mexican government "saw" them. They staked a permanent claim to a seat at the table where Mexico's future was discussed, imagined, and built.

10

Conclusion

Creating the Creative State

At the heart of Moroccan and Mexican migration and development policies is a paradox. The governments that created these effective policies linking emigration to grassroots development had never intended to do so, and in the end these policies were so effective that they came to be regarded as "best practices" and were emulated around the world. Neither the Moroccan nor the Mexican government had any intention of using migration to advance a strategy of economic change that would include migrants and their communities in such a meaningful way. On the contrary, both governments had neglected the villages and urban neighborhoods from which the migrants had come, and showed little interest in migrants' welfare. When the governments had engaged with migrants, it was either in an attempt to bring them to heel or to seize their resources. Sometimes, it was a combination of both. How, then, did the governments of these two nations create such innovative and useful policies for building a bridge between emigration and local economic development?

The search for the answer to this paradox uncovered the tangled root bed of creative practices that underlay these policies, a root bed some forty years deep and so wide that it connected the halls of government, the factories and fields in the United States and Europe where migrants worked, and the communities in Morocco and Mexico that migrants still called home. The sap that ran through those roots was an ongoing engagement between the state and migrants of both countries. Here, I have called that engagement interpretive, because policymakers and migrants from both countries interacted in an attempt to make sense of—to interpret—the massive social and economic changes that large-scale emigration was causing in Morocco and Mexico. The motives that drove government and migrants to engage with one another could not have been more different. Government bureaucrats from Morocco and Mexico joined in conversations with emigrants in order to develop an understanding of migration that was robust enough to enable them to capture the wages emigrants had earned abroad, the skills they had acquired, or the political clout they had amassed. Migrants engaged with their governments in an attempt to make sense of the implications that migration had for their lives and for the welfare of their communities. In some cases, they used their interaction with the state as a form of reconnaissance that would allow them to identify and better resist the strategies of control that both governments deployed across their borders. But it was precisely because their agendas were in opposition and their perspectives divergent that the engagement between migrants and their states was so rich and generative.

With much at stake, migrants and their governments found themselves compelled to explore their differences, however incomplete and outdated, about the significance of migration. Although the exchanges were often tense, even adversarial, participants were able to draw out new understandings, not always shared but always mutually intelligible, about the possibilities and constraints that migration could represent. By exploring the slippage between the different meanings articulated in the conversation, they discovered the places where new possibilities could be imagined. They combined the insights, still embryonic, that the exchanges produced with well-worn views and created concepts that were hybrids but that were also wholly new.

In addition to providing the basis for innovative migration and development policies, the engagement between migrants and their states also swept away any meanings that would have blocked the implementation of those new policy approaches. It called into question assumptions or assertions so ingrained that they had seemed natural, like the separation of le Maroc utile—the useful Morocco—from the rest of the kingdom, which had defined development planning in Morocco, and the hard-and-fast distinction between Mexican migrants and Mexican Americans that had been maintained by the Mexican government for so long. It unearthed forms of power so entrenched that they appeared to be part of the social bedrock, and showed them to be no more than contingent practices used to achieve specific goals. The interpretive engagement between migrants and the state in Morocco undermined the representation of migrants as homogenous purveyors of remittances without ties to local villages and challenged state neglect of migrants' communities of origin. In Mexico, the interpretive engagement between state-level government authorities and migrants took on the federal government's habit of pretending, with a wink and a nod, that emigrants did not exist.

Interpretive engagement allowed migrants and their states to explore new ways of relating that would have been inconceivable to them before they interacted in an ongoing way. Migrants were recast as protagonists who could mediate between the state and their communities and, because of their special position as integral members of societies on both sides of a national border, could bring together political, economic, and geographic spaces typically conceived of as separate. The state and its function were redefined, and its purview and responsibilities extended into new social, geographic, and national arenas. In Morocco, the Ministry of the Interior engaged with migrants who had organized to build electricity networks in their villages of origin, and as a result of that interaction, the ministry, also responsible for the heavy-handed repression of any form of social mobilization, soon began promoting autonomous community mobilization as key to the success of national infrastructure programs. Government authorities from the Mexican state of Zacatecas met with Zacatecan migrants in a Los Angeles hotel room and, through their interpretive exchanges, hashed out the beginnings of a model for labor organizing in the United States that was based primarily on migrants' identification with their communities of origin in Zacatecas rather than on their employment in cities like Fresno, Houston, or Tulsa.

Interpretation can allow the unimaginable to be imagined. As these Moroccan and Mexican experiences demonstrate, it was imagination itself, as much as the policies to which it gave rise, that wove an enduring connection between migration and development. The new political possibilities that interpretation opened were weapons of political transformation as powerful as any of the rallies, street demonstrations, or strikes that migrants staged.

That imagination, however, was potent only because it was anchored in the specific contexts, the specific experiences, and the specific meanings that migrants and state bureaucrats interpreted in their exchanges. It was because migrants and bureaucrats tried to make sense of the unique grind that migrants endured at work, to tend to the special kind of economic stagnation of each village suffered, to respond the opportunistic political ambitions that emerged at a given historical juncture, and to examine the demarcations of the development plan that government adopted that their imagination remained grounded and useful. As a result, the strategies they developed to engage with the resources that migration generated were realistic and cogent even while being innovative. Migrants and their states were able to envision new and more hopeful futures because their imagination remained anchored in the specificity of the present. And because they were able to do so in an ongoing way, Moroccan and Mexican migration and development policies remained vital, adapting to changing contexts and taking advantage of emerging opportunities. Through their interpretive engagement, migrants and policymakers would continue to develop new visions for the future, even after the future they had imagined had become a reality.

Processing Development

In addition to producing creative policy, the interpretive exchanges between migrants and the state allowed new understandings of economic development to emerge. Over time, they gave rise to a view of development as processes of learning and innovation rather than a product of the division of labor for economic production, and privileged the generation of knowledge over the extraction of wealth. This take on economic development as an ongoing and indeterminate process is at variance with the way the term has commonly been understood. The technical definitions of economic development are myriad: an increase in national revenue, a rise in per capita income, an improvement in the standard of living and reduction of poverty produced by economic growth, or a broadening of opportunities and capacities for all members of a society. Implicit in all of those designations, however, is the belief that development is a dogged march toward an end-stage. Economic development is a goal to move toward; it is the means to an end in a scenario where the end is the only thing that matters. This perspective was one that both the Moroccan and Mexican governments shared, but as Morocco's authoritarian monarchy and Mexico's one-party system engaged in joint interpretation with their migrant constituencies, their approach shifted over time from driving toward a clearly defined vision of economic development, described in detail in so many Moroccan five-year plans and Mexico's regular succession of party platforms, to supporting the practices of development. As they provisionally stepped away from the notion of development as outcome, they began to tend to the processes of development even though they had no definitive sense of where those processes would lead.

The reconceptualization of economic development as process rather than a predetermined result has important implications for how we consider the migration and development policies elaborated in Morocco and Mexico. If the policies presented in this book were evaluated in terms of the progress they made toward some preconceived idea of what a developed economy should look like, they might be considered disappointing interventions. In Morocco, the engagement between the state's Banque Centrale Populaire and emigrant workers did create banking services for migrants and did enable the state to invest the wages they earned in Europe in national development projects. The state development bank, however, rarely channeled any of those captured resources into the rural communities migrants were from, favoring instead already industrialized coastal cities over the country's underserved heartland. Even as Rabat, Tangiers, Casablanca, and Agadir benefited from new gleaming infrastructure and generous business support, rural areas languished, isolated and often without even basic electricity or water services. Similarly, Mexico's Three for One matching-funds program encouraged local government to partner with migrants to pave roads, lay down sewer lines, build schools and community centers, and renovate churches and plazas. However, many of the villages that received infrastructure services and were beautified through the program were being emptied out by a steady and often growing exodus of residents to the United States. In many ranchos, only a handful of elderly residents were left to enjoy the improvements.

When those same policies are considered an expression of a process of development, they are revealed as powerful vehicles for economic and social transformation. They emerge as catalysts that spark future development processes, each more innovative and more vital than the last. The hundreds of thousands of bank accounts that the Banque Centrale Populaire opened for a previously overlooked migrant population quickly turned emigrants into financial actors with enormous clout in the Moroccan economy, with influence so significant they were able to redirect the state's attention to their rural communities of origin. As interpretive attention focused squarely on how to provide rural areas with basic infrastructure, not only did standards of living in previously forgotten hamlets rise dramatically, but rural Morocco became the setting for boutique agro-processing ventures that, for the first time, exported goods instead of labor to Europe. Likewise, Mexico's matching-funds program helped migrants organize into clubs, and within the space of a short decade they were galvanized into a movement which gained enough momentum to affect Mexican presidential elections. After decades of disregarding them, the Mexican federal government created formal institutional structures to collect their counsel and to collaborate with them in defining services to improve migrant conditions on both sides of the border, some as straightforward as a consular identification card (*matrícula consular*) and others as nuanced as transnational HIV-education campaigns and drug rehabilitation centers in communities of origin.

When the notion of development as a clearly defined outcome is called into question by policies like those elaborated in Morocco and Mexico, so too is the controversy regarding whether migration produces development. The effect of migration on development can be definitively assessed only if development is viewed as an end-point: its impact can then be measured by judging whether it brought an economy closer to a fully developed state, and if so, by how much. When development is viewed a process and the outcome is not overdetermined, then attention shifts to the ways that migration shapes patterns of social and economic interactions. Evaluations of migration and related policies are no longer based on how close they bring an economy to a fixed idea of development, but consider instead whether the interactions they foster create opportunities for economic growth, support learning, and improve the welfare of individuals and communities. And if development is process and not product, then the effectiveness of policy in building a relationship between migration and development is found in the ways it enables migrants to construct, manage, and imagine their relationship to their countries of origin, and in the ways it empowers them to participate in the charting of their own futures.

From "Best Practice" to Practicing Policy

Moroccan and Mexican migration and development policies continued to evolve as the engagement that nurtured them grew. In the first few years of the twenty-first century, when the importance of migration to development became obvious, governments of migrant-sending countries and numerous organizations, ranging from multilateral development banks to private firms, approached the governments of Morocco and Mexico as sources of expertise in this field. They consulted with policymakers from both countries in an attempt to understand in great detail the policies that they wanted to reproduce in other contexts. In the process, they were drawn into the interpretive conversations that fed Morocco's and Mexico's migration and development policies. Soon, those conversations swelled beyond an engagement between migrants and the state and expanded to include these governments, organizations, and enterprises that sought out advice. The conversations stretched in new directions, tackled new problems, and made new connections. The policies, which depended as much on the interpretation that renewed them as on their design, began to reflect the new mix of interlocutors and the new insights they produced. By the end of 2005, the policies already reflected those new directions: they had sprouted offshoots, encompassed new partnerships, and embodied new versions of tested practices.

In Morocco, where the emphasis of the interpretive engagement between migrants and the state has always been on the financial resources that migrants bring back to the kingdom, the conversation has widened to include private banks and international remittance companies. A number of privately held Moroccan banks now provide financial services tailored to Moroccans living abroad that echo the BCP's targeted approach to emigrants. The BCP, as well as its new competitors, has forged partnerships with money transfer firms, like MoneyGram and Western Union, so that emigrants can now send their money to Morocco using those companies but doing it through the banking service window. Additionally, conversations between the Moroccan government and governments of other sending countries that have migration and development policies in place have led to the creation of new institutions to support the engagement between migrants and the state. The centerpiece of these new institutions is the Council for the Moroccan Community Abroad (Conseil de la Communauté Marocaine à l'Étranger, or CCME), founded on December 21, 2007. Reminiscent of the emigrant board attached to Mexico's Instituto de los Mexicanos en el Extranjero, the CCME is made up of emigrant members and serves in an advisory capacity to the Ministry for Moroccans Living Abroad. It has five working groups that focus on broad topics the government has prioritized, including religious education and practices, economic development, and citizenship rights. In a particularly Moroccan interpretation of that institution, however, the council members are not elected (however imperfect those elections have tended to be in the Mexican case); rather they are appointed by the king, until such time as the government determines that elections can yield members it deems to be truly representative of the Moroccan community abroad.

In Mexico, the expansion of interpretive conversations to include multilateral and bilateral donor organizations, independent foundations, and private companies has shifted the emphasis of those discussions somewhat. The interest in using migrants, and migrant clubs in particular, as vectors for economic development has displaced the government's concern about Mexican migrants organizing political lobbies that can affect political outcomes on both sides of the border. To be sure, some donor organizations like USAID and the Ford Foundation have collaborated with Mexican migrant hometown associations to strengthen their capacity for community organizing. The main thrust of interpretive conversations about migration and development, however, has veered toward an exploration of how to support emigrant entrepreneurship in communities of origin. This shift began with the Inter-American Development Bank's backing of the Invierte en México—Invest in Mexico—program through the Mexican development bank Nacional Financiera, in 2004. It has continued as Western Union has joined with the Mexican government and migrant clubs to launch a pilot program in the state of Zacatecas that ratchets up Mexico's matching-funds program to a Four for One program. Western Union has stretched the boundaries of the matching-funds program, pledging to add a fourth dollar to the three dollars that federal, state, and municipal governments offer migrants for every dollar they contribute to community projects, only provided the Mexican government accede to Zacatecan migrant demands and support their entrepreneurial initiatives ranging from mescal distilleries to cheese factories, which had, until recently, been excluded from the program.

The evolution of Morocco's and Mexico's policies resulting in the expansion of the interpretive conversations on which they are based underscores the lesson their experience offers to other nations seeking to link emigration to economic development. Both countries' experience demonstrates that the solution is not to copy existing policies and apply the unaltered facsimiles in other contexts—not to "cut and paste" policies that have been identified as "best practice." Neither is it to identify key institutional ingredients—like the size, organization, and sophistication of emigrant communities, the capacity and credibility of the state, and the support of powerful political parties (Levitt and Dehasa 2004; Portes et al. 2007)—which can be combined to produce migration and development policy.

Instead, a more useful approach is to nurture locally the processes that gave rise to those policies that have been singled out as models of excellence. Morocco's and Mexico's trajectories in this realm demonstrate the value of initiating conversations in which policymakers, migrants, and others can interpret various aspects of migration and development, and in so doing, can cultivate their own creativity in designing policy. Rather than imitating Moroccan and Mexican migration and development policies, it may be more constructive to bring both countries' policies and the practices they engender into conversations in which they can be reinterpreted. What, for example, can the Moroccan experience offer Indian policymakers interested in the formalization of the arrangements many migrants use to send money to their families in order to channel remittances into the financial system to fund industrial activity? What insights can Mexico's experience with matching-funds programs and migrant investment in community development offer Brazil as it considers the growing ranks of its citizens in the United States and Japan? When used more like Rorschach ink blots than architectural blueprints, Mexican and Moroccan migration and development policies can serve as inspiration for creative interpretation.

Moroccan and Mexican experiences in this field also show, however, that interpretive conversations must be accompanied by a willingness to allow the thick lines that demarcate the state's boundaries to fade. The potential for interpretive exchanges to produce truly innovative ideas depends on whether they include nonstate actors, especially those that bring perspectives critical of established policies and the understandings that legitimate them. Tapping the creative potential of interpretation requires disaggregating the task of designing policy into a set of practices and inviting those outside the state to participate in these practices, even to redefine them. The Moroccan government could not have developed its cutting-edge financial services for Moroccans living abroad had it not included migrants in the ongoing process of designing and refining them, or allowed migrants to appropriate the services as signifiers of their own identities as transnational citizens whose lives spanned the Mediterranean. Nor could the Mexican government have expanded a few local experiments in fostering migrant community development projects into a federal program had it not involved migrants in the movement that pushed the policy onto the national stage, or heeded migrants' demands to establish the Institute for Mexicans Abroad (IME), an institutional vehicle that allowed them to continue to shape the policies that affected their lives. The interpretive engagement that was the fount of Moroccan and Mexican state creativity demands a particular readiness to view the state as a set of ongoing, ever-changing practices rather than a cluster of solid institutions.

Practicing Accountability

Letting the state dissolve into a set of practices and opening those practices to actors outside the walls of government carries with it its own risks. How can the state be held accountable if no arm or agency of government is responsible for sole authorship of the policies that it rolls out? Whom do you sanction when the policy fails? How can you monitor whether or not government has completed the tasks with which it was charged if what those tasks involve is constantly being redefined? How can you ensure transparency if policies, as well as the practices by which they are carried out, are mired in ambiguity, and if the understandings on which they are based have not yet been articulated clearly enough to be identified, much less evaluated? Here, too, the experiences of Morocco and Mexico with migration and development policy offer valuable lessons.

Throughout the process of policy development, Moroccan and Mexican migrants held the states with which they engaged to a kind of procedural accountability. They required that the practices of interpretation adhere to certain norms; otherwise, they would simply withdraw from the engagement. These norms were essentially twofold: first, a heightened attentiveness to nascent meanings and a respect for their fragility in their embryonic stage; and second, a recognition of participants' mutual interdependence in the process of interpretation, since none of them could have created whatever new meanings emerged on their own. These principles served as the basis of the contingent trust that kept migrants in conversation with their states. Participants in the interpretive engagement that produced Moroccan and Mexican migration and development policies report that this trust—*confiance, confianza*—was indispensable to the success of the process, but that it was conditional on emergent understandings being valued as expressions of creativity rather than being targeted as political threats that needed to be suppressed. It only lasted when the meanings that arose were used to include migrants and their communities rather than being deployed as a weapon of political repression that exiled them, or any of their concerns, from the conversation. This provisional trust, extended over and over again in repeated interpretive exchanges, gave the relationships between migrants and their states the tensile strength to withstand the anxiety that both policymakers and migrants felt, at times acutely, about the process of interpretation lacking a clear goal and offering few guarantees about the political consequences of the meanings that might arise. When states violated this trust, as the governments of both Morocco and Mexico did on several occasions, restarting an interpretive engagement with migrants required a significant investment of resources and political capital. For example, in a bid to reopen interpretive conversations with migrants, both governments established new institutions, like the Hassan II Foundation in Morocco and the IME in Mexico, or made major amendments to policies that affected migrants, like the allocation of parliamentary seats to emigrants in Morocco and the extension of the right to vote to emigrants in Mexico.

Moroccan and Mexican migrant strategies for exercising accountability offer guidelines for holding governments responsible even when the state is viewed as a flow of practices. They intimate the importance of expecting the practices of government to abide by certain principles of conduct, regardless of whether those practices are carried out by government bureaucrats or involved citizens. In the examples featured in this book, those principles were a heightened attentiveness and respect for emergent meanings and a commitment to inclusiveness, but they could have been others. What is important is that those principles be agreed on by all who participate in the practices or are touched by them in some way. Requiring government to adhere to these shared norms rather than to rigid regulations affords it the autonomy to engage in practices, like interpretive conversations, that may not be fully intelligible to outside observers, and it creates space for new meanings to emerge and for existing practices to evolve in unexpected ways. Holding the state accountable for how it practices government, rather than for whether it met a predefined list of performance targets, allows us to view state practices as provisional responses to social problems and to evaluate their usefulness. How helpful are state practices in creating new opportunities for development? How effective are they at protecting the welfare of the communities they affect? Whom do they exclude? Whom do they favor? What assumptions do they reflect? This style of procedural accountability with its potential for inquisitive, exploratory, multifaceted review of government practice is in itself a form of interpretation, and thus it can also generate new ideas and new approaches. By holding the state accountable in this manner, we also feed state creativity.

Interpreting Time

Viewing state practices as provisional responses to social problems also reserves room for them to evolve, which is important in that the benefits of participating in interpretive conversations may only become clear over time. In both Morocco and Mexico, the full significance of the insights and relationships developed through interpretive conversation took years to become clear. Before they coalesced into the policies now celebrated as "best practices," the conversations considered in this book meandered for quite a while. They intensified and weakened before gathering renewed momentum; they traveled across space and then became anchored in a particular place before they crossed national borders again. Moreover, at various times, the conversations seemed to produce only failure. In Morocco, for example, the conversations that would one day reform national infrastructure provision began in the south of France during a labor mobilization against layoffs in French heavy industry, a battle that was ultimately lost. If the immediate effects of the conversation that workers initiated at the time in an attempt to keep their jobs had been evaluated alone, the interpretive exchange would seem like a bust. When followed over a longer span of time, however, the conversation emerges as part of an interpretive thread woven into the contexts of migrants' villages of origin, and eventually into state bureaucracies, changing those bulky administrations in fundamental and politically radical ways. Similarly, the Zacatecan matching-funds arrangement that would grow into a nationwide program and mobilize Mexican migrants throughout the United States began as an informal agreement, hastily scribbled down on a sheet of notebook paper. If it had been evaluated when still nascent, the arrangement might have appeared at best an instrumental use of migrant funds to build just enough infrastructure to ensure social peace, or at worst, an instance of government corruption, with the governor diverting funds from other programs to capture a new constituency. When considered over time, however, the arrangement's institutional function as shelter for interpretive engagement becomes apparent, and its role as a catalyst for formidable migrant organizing becomes clear.

Respecting the time it took for policies to reach their "best practice" form is important because eliding time would also erase the lessons that the development of those policies can offer. It would obscure the extent to which innovation is a relational process, one that depends on the lengthy engagement of multiple voices and multiple perspectives. This quality is true of innovation in all areas, but in terms of policy, the inclusion of various social actors—especially those who are politically marginalized—in the process of interpretation is indispensable for creating policies that will enable communities to work with the state as they author their own futures, define development, and determine the significance that globalization will have for their lives. To paraphrase a Moroccan emigrant activist, taking the state "by the hand" often first requires a lengthy dance of seduction, but one that is ultimately worthwhile because sharing in interpretive exchanges allows the state to be a vehicle through which communities can shape their own destinies.

The elision of time and the emphasis on the instantaneous erase the gradual, and undervalue the potential that an insight, a new relationship, or a nascent, still informal policy can represent if allowed the time to mature. Collapsing time forecloses the opportunity for the as-yet-unimagined, for the innovations of which we have not yet begun to dream. It ruthlessly truncates the processes that produce innovation, processes that occur laboriously over time. It obscures the multiple, unfinished, and blurry iterations that successful policies go through before they attain a form that is singled out as a "best practice." It privileges the actual over the possible, enforces the dominance of the factual over the intuited, and curtails the envisaging of what a policy might become and the effects it might have. For innovation to emerge, the space for ambiguity that time allows is required. Innovation needs to be indeterminate for a while before it can be novel.

Creative State

Promoting state creativity is not a "paint-by-numbers" exercise. There are no clearly defined, sequential steps to follow; there is no blueprint to which to adhere. However, as the Moroccan and Mexican experiences with migration and development policy demonstrate, we can identify practices that nurture innovation and turn the state, even in its most sclerotic, repressive, and bureaucratic incarnations, into a site of creativity. Fostering government innovation requires that actors on both sides of the boundary that separates the state from society together delve into the confusion that surrounds social challenges, and then together interpret the specific meanings and the particular phenomena that they find there. It also demands that together they construct the policies, institutions, and informal accords to shelter the contingent exchanges on which interpretation depends as well as the emergent, ephemeral insights it produces. It entails adopting new principles for accountability and developing a resilient patience when separating successes from failures. It involves taking a long-term view and entertaining the possibility that failures are important precursors to success.

The receptiveness to engage without a strict agenda, the willingness to reexamine meanings so ingrained that they have become invisible and to consider meanings so foreign that they are incomprehensible, and the courage to tolerate the anxiety that inevitably results is the essence of the creative state. As we confront new problems, many of which will not only reconfigure our lives as radically as migration has reshaped the lives of the people and nations but will also disarm us just as completely, it is a state we need to enter. It is not just that the state can be creative; it is that we cannot afford for it to be otherwise. As one Moroccan activist who engaged with the state said of interpretive conversations, "they are our treasure" (as quoted in Daoud 2005: 193). And as our treasure, as the foundation of the creative state, practices of interpretation must be nurtured and defended.

Appendix

Methodology

The research on which *Creative State* is based spanned the years 2001 through 2006. At its heart was fieldwork in both Morocco and Mexico; I lived about a year in each location. In both countries, I spent time in the places where the policies were formed and in the places where they were implemented. In Morocco, I conducted research in Rabat and Casablanca, but I also conducted focused localized research in the province of Taroudant, in Tangiers, and in Fez. In Mexico, I conducted research in Mexico City, but I also conducted research in the states of Jalisco, Michoacán, and more intensive research in the states of Guanajuato and Zacatecas. During my fieldwork, I also conducted research in receiving sites for emigrants of both countries. I spent several weeks doing interviews for this project in Paris and Brussels, two cities where large Moroccan populations were instrumental in shaping Moroccan government policy. I also conducted research in Chicago, a city with an important, deeply rooted, and politically active Mexican emigrant population, as well as the Philadelphia area, the site of emigrant activism that led to policy change in Mexico. In keeping with a case-study approach, I selected the receiving-country sites based on emerging findings from research in Morocco and Mexico.

At all of these research sites, I used mixed methodology, ranging from statistical analyses of remittance transfers, to surveys, to open-ended interviews, oral histories, and participant observation (see table A.1 for a summary of methods). The methodologies I used for given settings and given moments were tailored to the context and processes that I was observing and grew out of the conceptual understandings I developed as the research progressed. Although I used a wide variety of methods, I favored qualitative approaches because they are uniquely suited to the study of ambiguity and shifts in meaning (Piore 1979).

In terms of qualitative research, I interviewed current and former government officials, focusing first on government agencies charged with implementing policies for emigrants, at both national and local levels, and then extending outward from there to government offices that may not have directed policy toward migrants but that were affected by the interpretive engagement between migrants and the state. I interviewed migrant activists, participants in emigrant organizations, and members of migrants' communities in both sending and receiving areas. I also spoke with researchers, consultants, representatives of multilateral organizations such as the World Bank and the United Nations Development Program, staff from nongovernmental organizations, and members of the press who had either participated in the interpretive processes I was studying or who had followed the conversations or their outcomes. In total, I conducted 148 structured and semistructured interviews for the Morocco portion of the study, and 132 for the Mexico portion. I also conducted innumerable open-ended, informal interviews. Most of the oral life histories that people shared with me happened in this way. Apart from a handful of interviews in the Amazigh (Berber) language, for which I relied on the generous help of a translator, I conducted the interviews directly, in Spanish, French, or Arabic, depending on the context.

In addition to interviews, I engaged in ethnographic participant observation. I visited dozens of emigrant-driven development projects in communities throughout Morocco and Mexico. I observed strategy meetings called by emigrant activists, in both migrant-sending and migrant-receiving areas. I attended plenary sessions and town-hall meetings organized by government officials and observed a number of internal government meetings. I also went to consular offices and observed interactions between migrants and consular staff, and I traveled to major border transit sites—at Tijuana and Tangiers—crossed the border, and interviewed government officials, independent observers, and migrants on both sides. I also observed service provision to migrants at local and national government offices (including banks) that had programs directed to them. Additionally, I attended fairs and conferences that were either expressly organized for emigrants or addressed issues relating to emigration and to the relationship between migration and development in particular. Finally, and most importantly, I spent a lot of time "hanging out" in emigrant communities—again, in sending and receiving areas—participating in the everyday practices of daily life, as well as attending community festivities, such as holiday celebrations and weddings.

I also conducted extensive documentary research. Most of the government agencies and nongovernmental organizations involved in the process of policy development that I examined graciously opened their archives to me, as did the World Bank. I took full advantage of their generosity and used their archives extensively. I also conducted thorough reviews of government publications and video produced for emigrants, and completed searches in the local and national print media on emigrant issues. Finally, I drew on data in electronic media, including websites produced by government offices and migrant groups, electronic newsletters sent by government and emigrant organizations, and postings to blogs and chat rooms.

In October 2003, about halfway through my fieldwork, I also organized a conference in conjunction with the Massachusetts Institute of Technology's globalization project on migration and development policy. Morocco, Mexico, the Philippines, Haiti, and Spain were represented. From each country, we invited the highest ranking government official charged with overseeing emigration and its impact on economic development, a representative from a prominent nongovernmental migration organization, and a leading academic studying the phenomenon. The conference was closed to the public so that government officials, activists, and academics could have an honest and unguarded conversation about the challenges and opportunities that migration presented for development, as well as the ways that policy intervention could address both. Thus, my organization of and involvement in the meeting served as a form of participant action research in which I was able to observe a process of interpretive engagement, between actors from the same country and among actors from other countries, unfold over two days. Indeed, the interpretive conversations in those meetings may very well have refined the Moroccan government's design of the Council for the Moroccan Community Abroad (Conseil de la Communauté Marocaine à l'Etranger), patterned so closely on Mexico's Institute for Mexicans Abroad (Instituto de los Mexicanos al Extranjero), which the participants discussed at length.

TABLE A.1
Summary of Methods

Methods	Morocco (12 months)	Mexico (11 months)
Principal government authorities (federal/central)	Ministry of Foreign Affairs; Fondation Hassan II; Banque Centrale Populaire; Bank al-Amal; Office National de l'Electricité	Ministry of Foreign Affairs; SEDESOL
Localized case sites	Taroudant; Tangier/Algecsiras; Casablanca	Zacatecas; Guanajuato; Jalisco; Michoacán
Receiving-country sites (2 months total)	Paris; Brussels	Chicago; Philadelphia
Semistructured and structured interviews	148	132
Open-ended interviews	Many	Many
Participant observation	Project sites (M/D); migrant group meetings; transit reception sites; consular offices; BCP branches	Project sites (Three for One; Mi Comunidad); government meetings, plenary sessions, migrant group meetings; consular offices
Press review	Local and national press (EU and Morocco); emigrant publications in EU; government newsletters/glossies for migrant population; development organization publications	Local and national press (U.S. and Mexico); emigrant publications in U.S.; radio interviews; government newsletters/glossies for migrant population
Archives	National archives; bank archives; migrant organization archives; Fondation Hassan II archives and databases	SRE archives; Guanajuato, Zacatecas, Jalisco municipal and state archives; local church archives
Conferences/fairs	MIT Migration and Development Conference; EMIM conference (Brussels); FH2 Fair for Moroccans living abroad (Casablanca); and other	MIT Migration and Development Conference; migration and development conferences (Zacatecas and Mexico City); *movilidades* conferences (Satillo); and others.
Other data sources	Migrant group websites; government websites; blogs; state and INSEA surveys; state television features	Hometown Association Federation websites; government websites; blogs; SRE electronic newsletter; e-mail lists; state- and university-produced surveys, processed and unprocessed; author survey (Zacatecas)

Notes

2. Discretionary State Seeing

1. French land policy in Morocco would undergo a meaningful shift during the forty-four years of Morocco's status as a French protectorate (1912–56). Under Maréchal Lyautey, the first resident general dispatched to Morocco (1912–26), colonial land policy was more tempered: Lyautey established an unbreakable rule that no land should be confiscated from Moroccans and that land to be cultivated had to be legally purchased. This stipulation, while principled, was more flexible in actual practice: at the time of the French incursion, only a small fraction of Moroccan lands were registered with legal title. The rest were invested with communal or individual property rights that were recognized informally, without the backing of legal documentation. While these rights were binding in the Moroccan context, the French colonial administration generally did not recognize these traditional property rights, and French colonists could appropriate the lands with relative ease. Lyautey was eventually removed from his post because he was viewed as too lenient in his administration of the Moroccan protectorate and was replaced with a series of hardliners under whose governance the outright appropriation of Moroccan lands became more commonplace (Bidwell 1973).

2. Albert Sarraut, minister of the colonies after World War I, was the architect of the Plan Sarraut that called for the division of agricultural labor among the colonies. Swearingen summarizes the plan as follows: "Each colony should specialize in the production of certain primary materials for the metropole. Thus, for example, Madagascar would produce meat and minerals; the Antilles, sugar and coffee; Indochina, cotton, rubber and silk; and Equatorial Africa, oil, crops, and wood" (1985: 351). In the context of this grand colonial plan, Morocco would produce grain and fruit (Swearingen 1985; Hoisington 1985).

3. Jacques Berque, historian and sociologist of Morocco under the French protectorate, also reported that even land-grabbing practices illegal under French colonial law became commonplace, especially in the 1930s and 1940s when the movement to colonize Morocco picked up momentum; he called it "the golden age for the advocate and the lawyer," when large numbers of Moroccans were swindled out of their land in case after case of "scandalous behavior" by the French colons (Bidwell 1973: 213).

4. Pasha el-Glaoui of the Souss region of Morocco was among the most powerful and, as a result, wealthiest of the caïds of the protectorate. The protectorate authorities gave him wide latitude to multiply his landholding and to exercise nearly absolute administrative control over Moroccan commerce and agriculture in southwest Morocco (American University 1965). One historical account describes this caïd's exploitation of the area: "Every inhabitant of the Moroccan South

has to supplement his regulation taxes by providing presents for Glaoui's journeys, whether he goes to Mecca or takes the waters in Vichy. He has to furnish presents each time one of his numerous progeny celebrates a marriage; each time the Resident General pays a visit; not to speak of all the payments required when an official document is needed, or a judgment; when one wishes to leave prison or to avoid entering it. Glaoui has the monopoly of the trade in almonds, saffron and olives. He is the only buyer of these products, paying, at the most, half of their open market value. . . . He requisitions labourers to cultivate his lands and does not pay them; he has also, by various means, appropriated an appreciable part of the good land throughout Southern Morocco. It is literally true that he is the largest exploiter in North Africa" (Bourdet and Barrat, as quoted in Hoffman 1967: 164). In my interviews in the Souss (December 2003–January 2004), several of the people I spoke with referenced their tribe's oppression and exploitation under el-Glaoui and noted that the historical memory of that period was one of the reasons they felt compelled to organize against any sort of arbitrary administrative control by the state.

5. These requirements included the submission of a finalized work contract for employment in France, an identification document, a summary of the candidate's anthropometrics, a certificate of good health, and a certificate testifying to the candidate's proficiency and aptitude for the work described in the contract. For the vast majority of Moroccans, any one of these requirements would have been practically impossible to meet (Belguendouz 1987: 39).

6. The forced labor practices employed by agriculturalists were extremely varied, ranging from financial practices such as high-interest loans, that resulted in bonded labor, to violent intimidation— all with the tacit approval of colonial authorities and the Moroccan caïds, many of whom also engaged in the same practices. Additionally, commercial agriculturalists, desperate for labor, began using Moroccan women and children as farm laborers (Belguendouz 1987: 40).

7. The World Bank indicates that the estimates cited in its report are likely to be conservative because of sampling differences between the Household Consumption Survey conducted in 1959–60 and the Household Consumption Survey conducted in 1970–71 (World Bank 1981: 218–27).

8. During this period, Morocco displayed a healthy growth rate: an average annual GDP growth rate of 4 percent from 1960 to 1964, and of 2.4 percent from 1965 to 1967. The rate, however, was not sufficient to generate the urban employment growth required to cope with the large-scale migration to the cities that the country was experiencing at the time. Moreover, an important share of this growth rate was due to agricultural production, which represented a third of the GDP during the 1960s (World Bank 1981).

9. Hassan II refused to visit the Rif at any point during his almost forty-year reign (1961–99) (White 2001). The region also suffered persistent government underinvestment in infrastructure and industrial development (Bossard 1979).

10. The documentary was a CBS film titled *Harvest of Shame* and released on Thanksgiving Day in 1960. The documentary sought to depict the deplorable living and working conditions of immigrant and U.S. born migrant workers who had harvested the food on the traditional Thanksgiving table. According to observers of the documentary's impact, the film "touched off a reaction of astonishing proportions" (Healey 1966, as quoted in Calavita 1992: 143), and would help put farm worker conditions on the political agenda. The flood of mail sent to the network and Congress by a "conscience-stricken" public led, in part, to the passage of the Migrant Health Act in 1962, which called for the establishment of clinics for farm workers and their families, among other measures (Discovery Times Channel 2005; Calavita 1992: 143)

11. See Lipshultz (1962) for the variety of expressions of this opposition. Lipshultz notes that U.S. growers drew on racial discourse to counter moves to deport Mexican agricultural laborers, arguing that because they were of "inferior racial stock," Mexican immigrants posed no threat to domestic workers. Ralph Taylor, executive secretary of the Agricultural Legislative Committee of California, for example, told the House Committee on Immigration and Naturalization in 1930 that "the Mexican does not have this ambition, to get ahead and consequently, is a . . . desirable person to have around, for he will work for other people. He is not ambitious, either to own land, to control local, state, or national policies, or to displace Americans in those spheres of life where they want to work" (as quoted in Lipshultz 1962: 11).

12. This perspective was shared at least in principle by the U.S. government, if not in practice. President Truman's Commission on Migratory Labor specified that "the negotiation of the Mexican International Agreement is a collective bargaining situation in which the Mexican Government is the representative of the workers and the Department of State is the representative of our farm employers" (President's Commission on Migratory Labor, 1951, as quoted in Calavita 1992: 18).

13. These demands were made under a short-lived bracero program (1943–45) for railroad track construction and maintenance; see Driscoll (1999).

14. In a summary of a 1980 briefing session sponsored by the Rockefeller Foundation on the topic of Mexican emigration, and attended by U.S. and Mexican government officials, representatives of lobby groups, including Chicano organizations, and academics, Ann Craig reports that "for the Mexican policymakers and politicians, the more general problem of rural-to-urban migration within Mexico has been a higher-priority concern than emigration to the U.S., because the results of the internal migratory flow are both more visible and more politically and economically costly to Mexico" (1981: 19).

3. Reaching Out

1. Daoud reports that companies charged emigrant workers a premium for the services they did provide: for example, workers were charged 10 percent of their monthly salary for the electricity that supplied one naked light bulb. They were charged similarly exorbitant fees for water use and laundry services (2004: 17).

2. The same pattern of engagement between Moroccan students and Moroccan workers also emerged in Belgium, West Germany, and the Netherlands—countries that also recruited Moroccan labor (Ouali 2004; Van der Valk 2004; Daoud 2004). In Belgium, the second most important recruiter of Moroccan workers after France, Moroccan students began to mobilize in 1966 in response to the needs they noticed among Moroccan workers. Although Belgium was a heavy importer of Moroccan labor through formal channels, the majority of Moroccans traveled to Belgium on their own initiative, entering as "tourists" who secured a work permit after arriving in the country (Ouali 2004). Mohamed el-Baroudi, a Moroccan student in exile at the time, recalls how student activists initiated their relationship with these Moroccan "tourists": "Myself and a group of friends who were also in exile, we quickly noticed that Moroccan workers who arrived in Belgium to work found no structures to receive them. . . . Except for workers who were contracted by the mines [and transported directly to their place of work] the workers who arrived did not have a single point of reference—other than La Gare du Midi [the main train station in Brussels]. Starting from [the station], they would start venturing out into the neighboring streets. . . . Nothing existed to help orient Moroccan workers either administratively or socially, Belgium had not put in place a system to receive the workers. . . . Faced with this observation, we [found] a space to set up a reception area [for Moroccan workers] where we offered various services" (As quoted in Berwart 2004: 13). Student activists provided services that included everything from literacy classes and letter writing to the collection of funds for the repatriation of bodies when workers died in the Belgian coal mines, a tragedy that Baroudi noted "happened all too often" (Belwart 2004). The nascent organization, which would eventually evolve into the largest Moroccan opposition organization in Belgium, the Moroccan Democratic Association (Regroupement Marocain Démocratique, or RDM), reinforced the casual connection that the students had established with the Belgian union movement and, in the process, made Moroccan workers visible to the labor organizations that had ignored them. The group of student leftists also enlisted the help of Belgian doctors to care for injured workers, and Belgian lawyers to advocate for them, linking migrants to Belgian social service networks in this way (Belwart 2004; Ouali 2004).

3. Michel Foucault was also active in pro-immigrant and pro-Arab mobilizations during this period. Throughout the 1970s, he set up and participated in a number of commissions investigating the working and living conditions of Arab workers (Zancarini-Fournel 2002).

4. This data is also available at the Moroccan Ministry of Labor. It is not a formal data series but is available for the asking.

4. Relational Awareness and Controlling Relationships

1. Some observers of Morocco's political economy have revised upward the World Bank estimate for government expenditures on the Western Sahara military engagement, arguing that the cost represented close to 45 percent of the government's annual budget (Layachi 1998).

2. Article 11 in the Franco-Moroccan convention on migrant labor is typical of the provisions for family reunification in the other conventions that Morocco negotiated with Germany, Belgium and the Netherlands. While it allows for family reunification, it also opens a loophole for the French government to insert legal caveats at will. It reads: "The families of Moroccan workers can join them and the French government will afford them all the facilities necessary for them to do so, provided that it occurs within the legislation and regulations that are in force at the time" (Convention 1963—mimeo).

3. So scandalized was the French labor movement by the incident that a short documentary on the subject was produced (Daoud 2004; Vidal 2005).

4. The quotation in the heading is from an interview, Paris, 2004.

5. The full passage of this excerpt from the speech that Hassan II delivered on November 29, 1985, to representatives of the Moroccan community in Paris, in the presence of François Mitterrand (president at the time), was full of allusions that would have been interpreted clearly and powerfully by the Moroccan community abroad. It reads as follows: "I do not want to end this speech without exhorting you to remain authentically yourselves, even while opening yourself to your current situations and the future of your world; you live alongside a certain number of foreign communities, and you have surely noticed that you are at once light and anchored because you have an authenticity that is real, that you radiate and that you communicate and that demands that you be respected. Well, remain Moroccan, remain Moroccan because always, be it in peace or in strife, myself or those that will succeed me may one day need to take up another Green March. Well, I want for you, in the name of all Moroccans living abroad, not just in France or in Paris, to take a vow that all the young Moroccans that are born in foreign lands will be dedicated, even in their cribs, to the marches that history will ask of them" (as quoted in Belguendouz 1999: 151).

6. The organizations were, in Belgium, Regroupement Démocratique Marocain en Belgique; in Holland, Association des Travailleurs Marocains en Hollande; and in West Germany, Union des Travailleurs Marocains en Allemagne.

7. The king's sentiments on integration come across even more clearly in the remainder of the excerpt. About integration, Hassan II said: "I am against it . . . for the simple reason that for me, there is no distinction between a Moroccan born in Morocco and raised in Morocco and a Moroccan born in France and raised in France. They are both Moroccan. When I told the Moroccans, march! and they marched and . . . when I told them stop and they stopped. . . ." *Interviewer:* "You are referring to the Green March." *Hassan II:* "Yes, and I want, in the centuries to come, that we be able to recover this same national fiber, and it gets diluted outside the Motherland. I am against integration, in any sense of the term. . . . I am against it. I said it in front of the president of the republic himself, M. Mitterrand, and in front of the Moroccan community here." *Interviewer:* "Now, it's in front of all of the French." *Hassan II:* "I told them [Moroccan emigrants]: you shouldn't fill your head and your spirit, at night before going to bed, with electoral problems that do not concern you, that are not yours. Because you are definitely not French. They'll always court your voices but then they'll always forget you afterwards. You won't even dare to . . . I know the Moroccans, they are very humble and modest [*pudique*]. They won't even go ask for the few crumbs that are due them the next day. So it's not worth it, it won't work and it's not worth it. It will just lead to underhandedness, and I don't want that. The relationship between the French and the Moroccans has always been what it has been. We confronted one another, we embraced one another, but it never became underhanded. And I want it to stay that way" (Morocco, Ministère de l'Information 1990, Heure de Verité, antenne 2, December 17, 1989).

5. Practice and Power

1. A bureaucrat at the ONE explained the urban policy bias regarding electricity provision to a journalist investigating rural electrification in the mid-1990s as follows: "Isn't it heretical to want to connect isolated *douars* to electricity, when we don't even know for sure that they will still be inhabited in 2000? Is it necessary to prioritize dispersed settlements? Cities are growing, urbanization is a dynamic process. Any policy intervention ultimately modifies the human landscape" (Daoud 1997: 41).

2. During the 1990s, M/D received numerous requests for help from villages that had independently set up their own electricity networks, only to have them fall into disrepair and become nonfunctioning.

3. Although women were always formally welcome to participate in the village association, gender norms made it difficult for them to attend meetings. This situation has recently started to change in several village associations.

4. In villages that had no significant emigration, M/D contributed additional funds for construction to compensate for the absence of remittances (Daoud 1997: 42; interviews, Taroudant, December 2003).

5. Exact numbers for PNER 2 are difficult to obtain because the program would be folded into the Global Program for Rural Electrification (Programme d'Électrification Rurale Globale, or PERG) in 1995–96. Villages provided with electricity from 1995 onward would be double-counted: they would be tallied in the evaluations of PNER 2 (see World Bank 1998), but they would also be counted—more accurately—as villages electrified under the PERG (see ONE 1999).

6. The ONE managed power production, while distribution and the construction of electricity networks were handled either by the ONE or by the *regie*, an administrative unit larger than a

municipality but smaller than a province. A lack of logistical and financial coordination between the ONE and the *regies* involved in electricity distribution, most explicitly manifested in the huge debts many *regies* had accumulated to the ONE, undermined the financial solvency of the state power producer.

7. The ONE combined reduced tariffs at off-peak hours for industry with a public relations campaign. The ONE also engaged in heated negotiations with industrialists from 1992 through 1995 to schedule power outages. It sent its "vigilance committees" to enforce the electricity usage schedule it had established in Morocco's industrial centers, especially in the Casablanca-Rabat-Kenitra corridor (e.g., Ain Sebaa and Mohammedia). Larger producers complained that the government policies were forcing them to cut production by 30 percent at a time when they were trying to penetrate foreign markets. In a trend that worried the ONE, an important proportion of companies in Morocco's major industrial centers (e.g., Ain Sebaa) built independent generators.

8. Privatization resulted in a rise of production capacity from 2,400 megawatts in 1993 to 3,400 megawatts in 1996 (Belyazid 1996).

6. Process as Resource

1. Until 1987, Moroccan emigrants received a 2.5 percent bonus on all deposits they made in Moroccan banks, primarily the Banque Centrale Populaire. The National Treasury paid 1.25 percent and the banks receiving the deposits—again, primarily the BCP—paid the remaining 1.25 percent. When the bonuses were discontinued in 1987, the government required banks holding emigrant deposits to continue paying an equivalent amount into a government fund. In 1990, the bonuses were directed to institutions the government established to strengthen the ties between emigrants and Morocco, especially the Hassan II Foundation and Bank al-Amal (Belguendouz 2006: 8; Fondation Hassan II interviews, 2004).

2. The fungibility of the funds allocated to the two institutions would lead to accusations of corruption and the misallocation of funds. The accusations were backed by the Ministry of Foreign Affairs, whose bureaucrats felt threatened by the new ministry. The ministry and the foundation were audited, and the foundation was reorganized in the mid-1990s as a consequence of the investigation (Brand 2002; Hassan II Foundation interviews, Rabat, December–March 2004).

3. Moreover, the BCP was not unaware that a number of private banks—which had entered the emigrant market in earnest after Morocco reformed its financial sector in 1993—were capturing a greater share of the market and that the BCP would have to excel in emigrant service provision to maintain its lead. In 2004, the BCP market share had shrunk to about 60 percent of the emigrant market, with the BCME and Wafabank representing approximately 15 and 20 percent of the market, respectively. The BCME and Wafabank merged in 2004 and mounted an offensive to capture a greater portion of the emigrant market (BCP and BCME [during the merger with Wafabank] interviews, Casablanca, March 2004).

7. The Reluctant Conversationalist

1. Diplomat Jorge Castañeda is one of the government officials who watched the massacre from the Ministry of Foreign Affairs building facing the plaza, where most of the students had gathered. He issued one of the first public accounts of the event, in a letter sent to the *New York Times* on October 11 and published ten days later. In his description of the incident, most of the students had already cleared the square by the time the soldiers appeared, an account that contradicts the version offered by several other eyewitnesses, who remember the crowd of unarmed students caught helplessly between two lines of advancing soldiers, some of whom shot at each other in the chaos. Not only were the events of the Tlatelolco massacre highly disputed, but the actual number of dead and injured has also been the subject of considerable controversy, with estimates as high as 800 shot dead. The dispute over the death toll was in part a result of government efforts to censor information about the massacre immediately after it occurred (Braun 1997: 532–33nn89–91).

2. See Poniatowska (1971) and Ramírez (1969) for information not published in contemporary press accounts of the events.

3. César Chávez consistently declined invitations from Chicano leaders and the Mexican government to participate in discussions with the Echeverría administration. Instead, Chavez and the UFW forged a working relationship with CTM (Confederación de Trabajadores Mexicanos), a major Mexican union that was at loggerheads with Echeverría throughout his *sexenio*. The goal of the UFW was to try and organize Mexican workers in Mexico prior to their arrival in California.

Eventually, Chavez did meet with Echeverría's successor on a handful of occasions (J. Gutiérrez 1986: 30, 34).

4. *Caracol*, November 1975, as quoted in Santamaría Gómez (1994: 60). I have provided the original followed by a translation in which I have attempted to maintain the integrity of the message about linguistic identity embedded in the original statement. The mixed use of Spanish and English reflected an important statement about cultural *mestizaje*—mixing—that Chicano writers embraced as part of their vindication of their mixed-heritage identities. For more on this topic, see Anzaldua (1999).

5. The number of apprehensions is not the same as the number of migrants who tried to cross over into the United States: individual migrants were often counted more than once because they were apprehended and released several times.

6. Smugglers were charging $250 to help migrants cross into the United States and offered to "obtain bogus, back-dated documents, such as rent receipts, utility bills, Social Security cards, and American work permits" for an additional $300 to $400 (Holles 1977).

7. One Mexican government official admitted, "We have to be very careful what we say because we don't want to affect the magnificent relations we've had with the United States since President López Portillo took office" (as quoted in Riding 1977a).

8. Mexico wanted to sell its natural gas to the United States at $2.60 per thousand cubic feet—a price worked out by Mexico and six American companies. Washington, however, was determined to pay no more than $2.16, the price it had negotiated with Canada. After Mexico suspended negotiations, the U.S. secretary of energy cavalierly commented that "sooner or later" Mexico would lower its price, to which the Mexican administration replied that "sooner or later" the United States would have to raise its offer (Riding 1978). In the end (1980), Mexico sold only one-seventh of the gas initially negotiated to the United States. The remainder was consumed internally or burnt off (Meyer 1983: 186–88).

9. The ten members of the Hispanic Commission were the Puerto Rican group ASPIRA, Project SER, LULAC, American G.I. Forum, MALDEF, National Association of Farmworker Organizations (NAFO), Mexican American Women National Association (MANA), IMAGE, National Hispanic Forum, and the National Council of La Raza. Chicano community groups had several complaints about the list of participants: for example, NAFO did not include the United Farm Workers of America (founded by César Chávez); the National Hispanic Forum was composed of organizations based in Washington, D.C., and was heavily dependent on the support of the Catholic Church; National Council of La Raza had an agenda that was staff-directed rather than member-directed and relied on Ford Foundation funding; and some of the organizations' leaders had dual roles as representatives to the commission and members of the U.S. Department of State Hispanic Advisory Committee (A. Gutiérrez 1986: 29–32).

10. The Mexican government's treatment of Chicano land grant petitions illustrates this shift in attitude well: the López Portillo administration moved from a considered response to Chicano requests to simply deriding them. See de la Garza (1980) for more on this change in attitude.

11. De la Garza recounts one particularly low point of the relationship between Chicanos and the Mexican government. The López Portillo administration adamantly objected to the appointment of Julian Nava, a Chicano lawyer, as U.S. ambassador to Mexico, feeling that it represented a diplomatic slight to Mexico. A senior member of the Secretariat of Foreign Relations charged with U.S. affairs is said to have remarked, "Just because he looks like us, they think he will be more acceptable to us." De la Garza wryly adds, "As the [speaking] official is of European rather than *mestizo* origin, his remarks are said to have elicited the following response, 'Isn't that why they appointed you to deal with U.S. affairs?' " (de la Garza 1986: 42).

12. The study concluded that the number of undocumented migrants from Mexico was somewhere between 480,000 and 1.22 million depending on the season, far lower than the U.S. administration's estimate of anywhere between 3 and 6 million. Furthermore, the study placed the level of remittances at $310 million, as opposed to the $3 billion suggested by U.S. estimates (Riding 1980).

13. Although much of the literature on the 1982 economic crisis attributed Mexico's economic nosedive to the mismanagement of public funds and a foolhardy prognosis of oil prices continuing on their upward trend, Lustig (1998) rightly points out that Mexico's public spending choices as well as its view of the oil market were roughly in keeping with the directives of organizations like the World Bank and the International Monetary Fund.

14. Data on apprehensions represent a rough measure of migration flows. They are as reflective of border control practices as actual migration movements. For the time periods covered by the data presented here, however, there was no significant increase in border control activities, as evidenced by the level of federal funds allocated to them, roughly constant in real terms through-

out the period considered here. With the passage of IRCA, the federal government significantly increased border control activities (Hayes 2001). For more on other methods used to measure levels of undocumented migration, please see Bean et al. (2001).

15. In addition to calling him seditious, the PRI senators who leveled this charge also accused the opposition leader of "a lack of professional and political ethics, and compared him to those who had gone to Maximilian of Hamburg [and asked him] to come and govern [Mexico]" (*Uno mas uno*, December 1988, as quoted in Santamaría Gómez 1994: 186).

16. The DGCME proposal "Academic Interchange" refers to this function of *rodinos* more explicitly. The document reads as follows: "Mexican-origin communities in the United States have acquired a great importance in the last few years. A few numbers suffice to illustrate this. 3.4 million Mexicans applied for amnesty under the Simpson-Rodino law; 1.6 million have applied under SAW.... Since many of them are heads of households, and had already or have recently brought their families to join them in the United States, we can estimate conservatively that there are about 10 million Mexicans living in the United States.... What influence will they have on us in twenty years? If we count their descendants as well as new emigrants, they can grow to 30 or 40 million people" (SRE Archives 1990, DGCME memorandum, April 28). Observations such as these about *rodinos* abound in early DGCME documents (SRE Archives 1990–92).

17. The DGCME was emphatic about the strategic importance of Mexican American cultural longing to the Mexican government. In a dispatch to consuls, the DGCME cautioned: "If we do not engage with them now, if we do not carry out projects that are of mutual interest, we will lose Mexican Americans for good because they will end up incorporating themselves into the Anglo-Saxon society that discriminated against them but that gives them opportunities to work and to climb the socioeconomic ladder. And they will incorporate themselves with resentment. Resentment, not against their poor relatives in Mexico, but toward the government and the Mexican institutions that never acknowledged them. This will be true, regardless of whether these institutions are the consulates, the service providers in the tourism sector, the police that dock them, the businessmen that won't receive them. They will feel resentment toward us because we smirk with contempt at the Spanish that they speak and don't realize that they were mistreated at school every time that they spoke it" (DGCME 1990a).

8. From Interpretation to Political Movement

1. The national study, conducted by the Coordinación General del Plan Nacional de Zonas Deprimidas y Grupos Marginados (COPLAMAR), used the following indicators to construct its metric of marginalization: wage levels, unemployment and underemployment, agricultural employment, lack of rural transportation and communication infrastructure, illiteracy and educational levels, child mortality, mortality, doctors per capita, households without piped water, households without electricity, households without sewage, household crowding, households without access to radio or television, nutritional levels, and use of shoes.

2. *Ejido* is a colonial term that originally simply denoted public land. After the revolution, much of the land reform in Mexico consisted of giving peasants usufruct rights to private land that could not be taken from its owner. Cárdenas's policy represented a radical shift because it gave ownership property rights to *ejidatarios*: instead of being mere users of the land, peasants, many of whom were formerly landless, would own *ejidos*, albeit communally (http://www.les1.man.ac.uk/multimedia/mexican_land_reform.htm).

3. For example, between 1979 and 1984, large farms on well-irrigated land in the districts of the Rio Grande and Tlaltenango harvested an average of .596 tons of pinto beans per hectare, whereas the state average, which included small farms in more arid regions, was only .394 tons per hectare (Gómez Sánchez 1990: 177).

4. According to Mines's (1981) in-depth study of agricultural production in the Zacatecan village of Las Animas during the banner years of 1977 and 1978, each *yunta*—about 3.5 hectares of tillable land—earned between $260 and $355 per year. Less than a third of all farmers had enough land to meet the basic subsistence needs of their families, at a poverty line which he estimated at $1,464 per year for a family of seven.

5. Agriculture in Zacatecas continued to follow the same pattern of underinvestment in the following decades. In 1990s, for example, genetically improved seeds were only used on 6 percent of cultivated land as opposed to 35 percent in Mexico as a whole. Additionally, fertilizer was only used on 50 percent of the cultivated area in Zacatecas as compared to 65 percent in the country as whole. Finally, although the use of agricultural machinery was slightly higher in Zacatecas than it was in the rest of the country, a large proportion of the machinery was obsolete (García Zamora 2000: 15). These data are consistent with a pattern of emigration to earn capital for

agricultural investment, but in the end not enough capital to make significant, transformative improvements to agricultural methods.

6. Lindstrom and Lauster, in their 2001 study of the causes of out-migration from Zacatecas, present a picture consistent with this argument. On the basis of a Mexican Migration Project sample from 1986–90, they observe that rates of emigration were related to the kinds of economic opportunities available in the municipality of origin. In municipalities with abundant employment opportunities, the probability of emigration was relatively lower. In municipalities where opportunities for investment—including agricultural investment—were higher, the probability of emigration was also higher (Lindstrom and Lauster 2001).

7. The population growth rate factors were fertility, morbidity, and documented emigration (Padilla 1998).

8. A total of 11 percent of the land in *ejidos* in Zacatecas in 1980 was land that could be irrigated. The remaining 89 percent was fed only by Zacatecas's irregular rainfall (Moctezuma Longoría 1999).

9. The clubs that belonged to this initial version of the Federation of Zacatecan Clubs included the Zacatecas Social Club, the Jalpa Club, the Fresnillo Club, the Guadalupe Victoria Club, the Jerez Club, the Calera Club, and two others which are unknown (Moctezuma Longoría 2003).

10. The Mexican government began issuing consular identification cards in 1871. The official purpose of the card is to provide documentary evidence that the bearer is a Mexican citizen who lives outside of Mexico.

11. In April 2003, I conducted a survey of sitting municipal presidents in the state of Zacatecas. The survey asked whether matching-funds projects were put forth by the municipality, migrant clubs, or both, and asked what types of projects had been carried under the matching-funds program in the municipality to date. The response rate was around 78 percent: out of a total of 27 municipal presidents who had active projects in the program, 21 responded to the survey. The survey was administered at a plenary session of municipal presidents in Zacatecas. The research project was explained in the meeting, and the survey was distributed during a coffee break. Almost all of the presidents in attendance responded to the survey.

12. The Frente Cívico Zacatecano was formally registered in the United States as a PAC in 2000 (Goldring 2002).

13. Within a couple of years, the federation and the Frente Cívico had reconciled so well that leadership actually moved from one organization to the other and back again. The most explicit example is that of Guadalupe Gómez, who was president of the Frente Cívico until 2000, when he left to take office as president of the federation.

14. The Frente Cívico and the Federation of Zacatecan Clubs from southern California also established strong ties with important think tanks, such as the InterAmerican Dialogue, and development banks in Washington, such as the Inter-American Development Bank, largely based on its development of the Three for One program. As Manuel Orozco of the InterAmerican Dialogue has observed, attention to remittances and the effects that they can have for development through matching-funds programs like the one elaborated in Zacatecas can have a legitimizing effect on migration (interviews and meetings, Washington, D.C., February 2003).

9. The Relationship between "Seeing" and "Interpreting"

1. Univision, for example, produced an in-depth television report on the strike in 1993 (interviews, Philadelphia, August 2003).

2. Interestingly enough, despite its dramatic failure, the Mi Comunidad program was enthusiastically cited by multilateral development agencies as a policy example to be followed. See, for example, the Inter-American Development Bank's description of its $2.5 million Capitalization of Remittances for Local Economic Development initiative for Mexico—otherwise known as Invierte en Mexico—launched in 2004 (2006).

3. Fox used Labastida's refusal to travel north of the border to his advantage in a characteristically provocative–and effective–public relations move. He told the Mexico City daily *La Reforma* that he was going to "visit Mexicans expelled by Labastida's PRI, that had to leave because the regime is murdering them in their own land with starvation" (as quoted in Leiken 2001: 20).

4. The government departments represented on the National Council for Mexican Communities Abroad included Secretariat of the Interior (Gobernación); Foreign Relations; Treasury and Public Credit; Social Development; Economy; Agriculture, Livestock, Rural Development, Fisheries and Nutrition; Environment and Natural Resources; Health; and Tourism, Work, and Social Security (http://www.sre.gob.mx/IME).

5. These organizations included the Association of Farmworker Opportunity Programs, the Hispanic National Bar Association, the Hispanic Scholarship Fund, the League of United Latin American Citizens, the Mexican American Legal Defense and Educational Fund, the National Association for Bilingual Education, the New American Alliance, the U.S. Hispanic Chamber of Commerce, and the United Farm Workers (http://www.sre.gob.mx/IME, May–October 2005).

References

Ababou, A. 2002. Les MRE ne savent investir que dans l'immobilier! Bladi.net. August 12. www.bladi.net.

Ackerman, J. 2004. Co-Governance for Accountability: Beyond "Exit" and "Voice." *World Development* 32(3): 447–63.

Acuña, R. 1996. *Anything but Mexican: Chicanos in Contemporary Los Angeles*. New York: Verso.

A.D.N. 1993. Résultats bancaires pour 1992: BCP: Les RME constituent 65% des dépôts. *L'Économiste*, May 6.

Agence Française pour la Maîtrise de l'Énergie (AFME), Ambassade de France/Service de la Coopération Technique, and Royaume du Maroc, Direction de l'Énergie et Direction des Collectivités Locales. 1988. *Programme pilote de pré-electrification rurale: Dossier de projet préliminaire*. Rabat.

Alanís Enciso, F. S. 1999. *El primer programa bracero y el gobierno de México, 1917–1918*. San Luis Potosí: El Colegio de San Luis.

——. 2004. Nos vamos al norte: La emigración de San Luis Potosí a Estados Unidos entre 1920–1940. *Migraciones Internacionales* 2(4): 66–94.

Alba, F. 1998. Mexico's 1982 Economic Crisis. In *Binational Study/Estudio Binacional: Migration between Mexico and the United States*. Washington, DC: Mexican Ministry of Foreign Affairs and U.S. Commission on Immigration Reform.

Alizal, L. del, V. M. Munoz Patraca, and A. Rodríguez Kuri. 1995. Un retrato actual: 1940–1991. In *La fragua de una leyenda: Historia mínima de Zacatecas*, ed. J. Flores Olague. Mexico City: Editorial Limusa.

Aly, N. al-. 1999. Morocco: Emigrants Press for True Citizenship Back Home. *Africa News*, August 20.

Amabile, T. 1996. *Creativity in Context: Update to The Social Psychology of Creativity*. Boulder: Westview Press.

Amador, L. 2000a. Guanajuato se vistió de azul: Las celebraciones duraron casi toda la noche en las primeras ciudades del estado. *La Opinión*, July 4.

——. 2000b. Mexicanos de LA irán a la toma de poder. *La Opinión*, December 2.

——. 2001. Prioridades: Las remesas y evitar abusos de paisanos; Nueva oficina protegera intereses de los mexicanos en el exterior. *La Opinión*, January 19.

——. 2002a. Eligen a los miembros del Consejo Consultivo del IME. *La Opinión*, November 22.

——. 2002b. Los indocumentados serán el tema central. *La Opinión*, September 20.

——. 2003a. Consejo Consultivo se reunirá con Fox. *La Opinión,* January 9.

——. 2003b. Programa 3×1 regresaría a manos de migrantes; Comunidades en el exterior recuperan el poder de decidir sobre las inversiones. *La Opinión*, November 19.

Amalki, S. el-. 2004. L'émigrant n'est pas une machine à devises. *Al Bayane*, August 11.

American University. 1965. *Area Handbook for Morocco.* Washington, DC.

Amsden, A. 2001. *The Rise of "The Rest": Challenges to the West from Late-Industrializing Economies.* New York: Oxford University Press.

Anderson, B. 2002. *Imagined Communities: Reflections on the Origin and Spread of Nationalism.* London: Verso.

Anzaldua, Gloria. 1999. *Borderlands = La Frontera.* San Francisco: Aunt Lute Books.

Argun, B. E. 2003. *Turkey in Germany: The Transnational Sphere of Deutschkei.* New York: Routledge.

Arizpe, L. 1981. The Rural Exodus in Mexico and Mexican Migration to the United States. *International Migration Review* 15(4).

Arredondo, M. L. 2002. Tibios nexus a ambos lados de la frontera: Mexicanos y mexico-americanos empiezan a acercarse, más allá de canales oficiales. *La Opinión*, February 25.

——. 2003. Consejo Consultivo busca aporte de mexicanos. *La Opinión*, February 9.

Ashford, D. 1969. The Politics of Rural Mobilization in North Africa. *Journal of Modern African Studies* 7 (2): 187–202.

Association des Travailleurs Marocains en France (ATMF). 1984. *Ils ont écrit . . . dignité.* Gennevilliers.

——. 1987. *La société française et l'immigration maghrébine: Questions et perspectives culturelles.* Paris.

——. 1989. La communauté marocaine en France: Quelles évolutions? Quelles perspectives? Rencontre Nationale ATMF, January 28–29.

Association des Travailleurs Marocains en France (ATMF) Archives. 1978–88. Organization documents, internal documents, promotional materials, press releases, newspaper clippings, formal letters of complaint to French and Moroccan government agencies, lists of missing persons, lists of persons deprived of consular documents, documentation of working conditions and violations of employment contracts. Paris.

Association Marocaine d'Études et de Recherches sur les Migrations (AMERM). 2000. *La migration clandestine: Enjeux et perspectives.* Rabat: Fondation Hassan II.

——. 2002. *La migration sud-nord: La problématique de l'exode des compétences.* Rabat: Fondation Hassan II.

Association pour la Valorisation des Echanges par la Coopération (AVEC). 1992. *Project Maroc: Chantier d'électrification, région de Taliouine, village de Tinfate.* Nice.

Atouf, E. 2004. Les migrations marocaines vers la France durant l'entre-deux-guerres: Vers un lieu de mémoire de l'immigration. *Hommes et Migrations (January–February), no.* 1247, 12.

——. N.d. *Les marocains en France de 1910 à 1965: L'histoire d'une immigration programmée.* Paris.

Banco de Mexico. 1995–2009 (series). Ingresos por remesas. www.banxico.org.mx.

Banque Centrale Populaire. 1996–2000. Internal documents on Operation Transit.

Banque Centrale Populaire du Maroc (BCP). 1986. *25 ans d'expansion: 1961–1986.* Casablanca.

——. 1991. *30 ans: 1961–1991 (30th Anniversary of the Crédit Populaire du Maroc, 1961–1991).* Casablanca.

——. 2003. *Crépo flash: Bulletin de communication interne du Groupe Banques Populaires.* Accueil MRE.

Banque Centrale Populaire du Maroc (BCP) *Rapports annuels.* 1978–2005 (series). Casablanca.

Baroudi, M. 2005. Marocain du mois. *Wafin.be: Au service des belgo-marocains* (http://wafin.be).

Barrientos, T. 1993. Pickers' Work Is Fast, Filthy and Grueling. *Philadelphia Inquirer*, April 18.

Basch, L., N. Glick Schiller, and C. Szanton Blanc. 1994. *Nations Unbound: Transnational Projects, Postcolonial Predicaments, and Deterritorialized Nation-States*. Amsterdam: Gordon and Breach.

Basfao, K., and H. Taarji, eds. 1994. *L'annuaire de l'émigration*. Rabat: Fondation Hassan II.

Al-Bayane. 1998. Operation transit: L'effort est poursuivi pour un meilleur accueil. August 4.

BBC. 2002. Monitoring Middle East—Political. Morocco: King Mohammed VI Tells Parliament "Democracy Not an End in Itself." October 11.

Bean, F., R. Corona, R. Tuirán, and K. Woodrow-Lafield. 1998. The Quantification of Migration between Mexico and the United States. In *Binational Study/Estudio Binacional: Migration between Mexico and the United States*. Washington, DC: Mexican Ministry of Foreign Affairs and U.S. Commission on Immigration Reform.

Bean, F. D., J. V. Hook, K. Woodrow-Lafield, and Pew Hispanic Center. 2001. *Estimates of Numbers of Unauthorized Migrants Residing in the United States: The Total, Mexican, and Non-Mexican Central American Unauthorized Populations in Mid-2001*. Washington, DC: Pew Hispanic Center.

Bechky, B. 2003. Sharing Meaning across Occupational Communities: The Transformation of Understanding on a Production Floor. *Organization Science* 14(3): 312–30.

Belbahri, A. 1994. Commerçants: Un rôle à la fois économique, culturel et social. In *L'annuaire de l'émigration*, ed. K. Basfao and H. Taarji. Rabat: Fondation Hassan II.

Belguendouz, A. 1987. L'émigration des travailleurs marocains. In *La grande encyclopédie du Maroc*, 37–64. Rabat.

———. 1999. *Les marocains à l'etranger: Citoyens et partenaires*. Kénitra: Boukili Impression.

———. 2003. *Marocains des ailleurs et marocains de l'intérieur*. Rabat: Imprimerie Beni snassen Impression.

———. 2006. *Le traitement institutionnel de la relation entre les marocains résidant à l'étranger et le Maroc*. San Domenico di Fiesole: CARIM Research Reports.

Belluck, P. 2000. Mexican Presidential Candidates Campaign in U.S. *New York Times*, July 1.

Belyazid, K. 1996. Énergies: Le grand tournant libéral. *L'Économiste*, March 7.

Benguigui, Y., director. 1997. *Mémoires d'immigrés: L'héritage maghrébin*. Documentary film. Canal + éditions, Paris.

Bennani, D. 2004. Rétrospective: Il était une fois la presse. *Telquel* 130.

Bennoune, M. 1975. Maghribin Workers in France. *MERIP Reports*, no. 34.

Bentaleb, N. 2004. Électrification rurale décentralisée dans le sud. *Vertigo—La revue en sciences de l'environnement* 5(1).

Berdai, M., and V. Butin. 1993. Mettre en oeuvre l'électrification décentralisée dans une démarche participative: Un nouveau service et une stratégie d'équipement rural: Le cas de Programme Pilote d'Electrification Rurale Décentralisée (PPER) au Maroc. Rabat.

———. 1994. Dynamique institutionnelle et mobilisation des populations: Le PPER au Maroc. *Liaison Énergie-Francophonie*, no. 23.

Berhoumi, J. and A. Krouss. 1993. En exclusivité: Le ministre marocain de l'immigration. *Horizons Magazine* (February).

Bernstein, R. 1984. Renault's Turnaround Hopes. *New York Times*, October 8.

Berriane, M. 1995. Fonctionnement du système migratoire et naissance d'un petit centre urbain (Taouima) dans la banlieue de Nador (Maroc). In *Les nouvelles formes de la mobilité spatiale dans le monde arabe*, ed. R. a. P. S. Escalier, 151–66. Tours: URBAMA.

———. 1998. La ville, le développement sectoriel et la relance des provinces du Nord. In *Le développement du Maroc septirégional: Points de vues de géographes*, ed. M. Berriane and A. Laouina. Neustadt an der Aisch: Justus Perthes Verlag Gotha.

———. 2003. Les marocains résidant en Allemagne. In *Marocains de l'extérieur*. Rabat: Fondation Hassan II.

Berriane, M., and H. Hopfinger, eds. 1999. *Nador (Maroc): Petite ville parmi les grandes*. Tours: URBAMA.

Berrissoule, B. 1998. La Fondation Hassan II s'organise autour de six structures. *L'Économiste*. January 15.

Berwart, F. 2004. 40 ans d'engagement: interview de M. el Baroudi. *Agenda Interculturelle* 220 (February 2004): 11–13.

Berwart, R. 1994. Le bassin minier de Charleroi et de la Basse-Sambre: L'héritage des gueules noires de l'histoire au patrimoine industriel. In Charleroi: Archives de Wallonie, file 276. Wallonie-Limbourg-Nord/Pas de Calais-Aix-la-Chapelle. Also available at http://www.terrils.be/fr/Terrils/Histoire/charleroi/charleroi.pdf.

Bidwell, R. 1973. *Morocco under Colonial Rule: French Administration of Tribal Areas, 1912–1956.* London: Frank Cass.

Binder, D. 1978. U.S., Alarmed at Decline in Ties with Mexico, Drafts New Policy. *New York Times*, November 20.

Blanchard, P., E. Deroo, D. el-Yazami, P. Fournié, and G. Manceron. 2003. *Le Paris arabe*. Paris: La Découverte.

Borrego Estrada, G. 2002. *Desde el escaño*. Monterrey: Cámara de Senadores.

Bossard, R. 1979. Un espace de migration: Les travailleurs du Rif oriental (province de Nador) et l'Europe. In *Rural Geography*. Montpellier: Université Paul Valery.

Boudoudou, M. 1988. Esquisse d'une histoire économique et politique de l'émigration en France. In *Le Maroc et la Hollande: Études sur l'histoire, la migration, la linguistique et la sémiologie de la culture*, ed. A. Kaddouri, J. Saib, and Z. Abdelmajid. Rabat: Université Mohammed V.

Boukhima, A. 2000. La Fondation Hassan II trace ses priorités. *L'Économiste*. April 4.

Bousetta, H., Sonia Gsir, and Dirk Jacobs. 2005. *Active Civic Participation of Immigrants in Belgium: Country Report Prepared for the European Research Project POLITIS.* Oldenburg: European Research Project POLITIS.

Bouzerda, A. 1990. At Least 33 Die during Rioting in Morocco. *Independent*. October 8.

Boyer, C. 2003. *Becoming Campesinos: Politics, Identity, and Agrarian Struggle in Postrevolutionary Michoacán, 1920–1935.* Stanford: Stanford University Press.

Brand, L. 2002. States and Their Expatriates: Explaining the Development of Tunisian and Moroccan Emigration-Related Institutions. Working paper no. 52. La Jolla: University of California, San Diego.

Branigin, W. 1988. Mexican Opposition Presses Vote Claims. *Washington Post*, July 11.

Braun, H. 1997. Protests of Engagement: Dignity, False Love, and Self-Love in Mexico during 1968. *Comparative Studies in Society and History* 39(3): 511–49.

Brikerhoff, J. 2009. *Digital Diasporas: Identity and Transnational Engagement.* Cambridge: Cambridge University Press.

Broder, J. M., and Douglas Jehl. 1999. In Scenes of Tumult, Moroccans Bury King. *New York Times*, July 26.

Brouksy, L. 2002. *Makhzénité et modernité: Révolution tranquille d'un roi.* Rabat: Diwan.

Brynes, D. 2003. *Driving the State: Families and Public Policy in Central Mexico.* Ithaca: Cornell University Press.

Buncombe, A. 1999. Morocco in Final Homage to Hassan. *Independent*, July 26.

Burawoy, M. 1998. The Extended Case Method. *Sociological Theory* 16(1).

Business Wire. 2006. Western Union Expands Initiative to Promote Community, Economic Development in Mexico; Mexican State of Michoacán the Second State to Benefit from 4x1 Program. June 23.

Bustamante, J. 1983. Unequal Exchange in the Binational Relationship: The Case of Immigrant Labor. In *Mexican-U.S. Relations: Conflict and Convergence*, ed. C. Vásquez and M. García y Griego. Los Angeles: Chicano Studies Research Center, University of California.

——. 1986. Chicano-Mexicano Relations: From Practice to Theory. In *Chicano-Mexicano Relations*, ed. T. J. Mindiola and M. Martinez. Calhoun: University of Houston.

Bustamante, J., G. Jasso, J. E. Taylor, and P. Trigueros Legarreta. 1998. Characteristics of Migrants: Mexicans in the United States. In *Binational Study/Estudio Binacional: Migration between Mexico and the United States.* Washington, DC: Mexican Ministry of Foreign Affairs and the U.S. Commission on Immigration Reform.

Bustos, S. 1989. Amnesty: "Adios" to Mushrooms. *Philadelphia Inquirer*, May 7.
——. 1991. Mushroom Workers Protest, Walk Off Jobs over Work Rule. *Philadelphia Inquirer*. June 4.
——. 1994. For Farmworkers, a Year in Limbo. *Philadelphia Inquirer*, May 18.
Butin, V., and Migrations et Développement. 1993. *Electrification rurale décentralisée: Électrification par Groupe Electrogène et Mini-Réseau Local*. Rabat: Migrations et Développement.
Byrnes, D. 2003. *Driving the State: Families and Public Policy in Central Mexico*. Ithaca: Cornell University Press.
Calandra, R., and J. Lahoussain. 1992. *Projet Maroc: Chantier d'electrification, region de Taliouine, village de Tinfate*. Nice: Assocation pour la Valorisation des Echanges pour la Coopération.
Calavita, K. 1992. *Inside the State: The Bracero Program, Immigration, and the I.N.S.* New York: Routledge.
Calderón Chelius, L. 2002. "Para no volverse ausencia": La construcción de la identidad política en le proceso migratorio, el caso Mexicano. In *La dimensión política de la migración mexicana*, ed. L. Calderón Chelius and J. Martinez Saldaña. Mexico City: Instituto de Investigación Mora.
Canales, A., and I. Montiel Armas. 2004. Remesas e inversión productiva en comunidades de alta migración a Estados Unidos: El caso de Teocaltiche, Jalisco. *Migraciones Internacionales* 2(3).
Cans, C. 2005. Comment l'Anti-Atlas reprend vie. *Jeune Afrique*. April 12.
Cárdenas, E. 1996. *La política económica en México, 1950–1994*. Mexico City: El Colegio de México.
Cardoso, L. 1980. *Mexican Emigration to the United States*. Tucson: University of Arizona Press.
Carter, J. 1979. Proposals concerning Illegal Mexican Labor. In *Mexican Workers in the United States: Historical and Political Perspectives*, ed. G. Kiser and M. Kiser. Albuquerque: University of New Mexico Press.
Castañeda, J. 2007. *Ex-Mex: From Migrants to Immigrants*. New York: New Press.
Castro Castro, I. 1996. Depresión económica y transmutaciones sociales en el agro zacatecano. In *Facultad de Derecho*. Zacatecas: Universidad Autónoma de Zacatecas.
Central Bank of Mexico (Banco de Mexico). 2002. Remesas Familiares. Data series. www.banxico.org.mx.
Centre d'Études et de Recherches Démographiques (CERED). 1991. *Population l'an 2062*. Rabat: Ministère de la Prévision Économique et du Plan, Royaume de Maroc.
——. 1999. *Dynamiques urbaines et développement rural au Maroc*. Rabat: Ministère de la Prévision Économique et du Plan.
Centre Régional d'Investissement (CRI). 2004. *Investir à Casablanca: Le guide*. Casablanca.
Chami, R., C. Fullenkamp, and S. Jahjah. 2005. *Are Immigrant Remittance Flows a Source of Capital for Development?* Washington, DC: International Monetary Fund.
Chand, V. 2001. *Mexico's Political Awakening*. Notre Dame: University of Notre Dame Press.
Chaoui, M. 1994. Sur les chemins du retour. *Rivages* 11: 34–38.
Charef, M. 1981. Les transfers d'épargne des émigrés marocains en France: Évaluation de leur importance et de leurs effets. In *Maghrébins en France: Émigrés ou immigrés?* ed. L. Talha, 217–28. Aix-en-Provence: Edisud.
——. 1995. Migrations internationales et mutations socio-économiques dans le Souss-Massa (Maroc). In *Les nouvelles formes de la mobilité spatiale dans le monde arabe*, ed. R. a. P. S. Escalier, 167–76. Tours: URBAMA.
——. 2003. Des hommes passerelles entre l'Europe et le Maghreb: Marocains de France et d'Europe. *Hommes et Migrations* 124: 6–17.
Chattou, Z. 1998. *Migration marocaines en Europe: Le paradoxe des itinéraires*. Paris: L'Harmattan.
Chattou, Z., and M. Belbah. 2002. *La double nationalité en question: Enjeux et motivations de la double appartenance*. Paris: Éditions Karthala.

Chaudhry, K. A. 1989. The Price of Wealth: Business and State in Labor Remittance and Oil Economies. *International Organization* 43(1): 101–45.

Chekrouni, N. 2004. La place et le rôle des émigrés—Immigrés dans le développement local. July 26. http//:www.marocainsdumonde.gov.ma.

Chiswick, B. R. 1988. Illegal Immigration and Immigration Control. *Journal of Economic Perspectives* 2(3): 101–15.

Chumer, M., R. Hull, and R. Prichard. 2000. Situating Discussions about "Knowledge." In *Managing Knowledge: Critical Investigations of Work and Learning*, ed. R. Prichard, R. Hull, M. Chumer, and H. Willmott. New York: St. Martin's Press.

Claisse, A. 1987. Makhzen Traditions. In *The Political Economy of Morocco*, ed. I. W. Zartman. New York: Praeger.

Clément, J. F., and J. Paul. 1984. Trade Unions and Moroccan Politics. *MERIP Reports*, no. 127.

——. 1986. Morocco's Bourgeoisie: Monarchy, State and Owning Class. *MERIP Reports*, no. 142, 13–17.

Cohen, J. 1997. Deliberation and Democratic Legitimacy. In *Deliberative Democracy: Essays on Reason and Politics*, ed. J. Bohman and W. Rehg. Cambridge: MIT Press.

Cohen, M., J. March, and J. Olson. 1972. A Garbage Can Model of Organizational Choice. *Administrative Science Quarterly* 17:1–25.

Collier, R. 2000. Vicente Fox Wins Landmark Ballot, Ending 71 Years of Single Party Rule. *San Francisco Chronicle*, July 3.

Contu, A., and H. Willmott. 2003. Re-Embedding Situatedness: The Importance of Power Relations in Learning Theory. *Organization Science* 14(3).

Cook, S., and J. S. Brown. 1999. Bridging Epistemologies: The Generative Dance between Organizational Knowledge and Organizational Knowing. *Organization Science* 10: 381–400.

Cornelissen, J. 2006. Making Sense of Theory Construction: Metaphor and Disciplined Imagination. *Organization Studies* 27(11): 1579–97.

Cornelius, W. 1981. *Mexican Migration to the United States: The Limits of Government Intervention*. La Jolla: Program in U.S.-Mexican Studies, University of California, San Diego.

——1989. Impacts of the 1986 U.S. Immigration Law on Emigration from Rural Mexican Sending Communities. *Population and Development Review* 14(4): 689–705.

——. 1998. The Structural Embeddedness of Demand for Mexican Immigrant Labor: New Evidence from California. In *Crossings: Mexican Immigration in Interdisciplinary Perspectives*, ed. M. Suarez-Orozco. Cambridge: Harvard University Press.

Cornelius, W., A. Craig, and J. Fox. 1994. Mexico's National Solidarity Program: An Overview. In *Transforming State-Society Relations in Mexico: The National Solidarity Strategy*, ed. W. Cornelius, A. Craig, and J. Fox. La Jolla: University of California, San Diego.

Cornelius, W., and E. Marcelli. 2001. The Changing Profile of Mexican Migrants to the United States: New Evidence from California and Mexico. *Latin American Research Review* 36(3).

Corrado, F. 2003. Territorial Resources as Levers of Local Development in a Globalized Context. Paper delivered at the thirty-ninth IsoCaRP Conference, Cairo, September 30.

Corwin, A. F. 1978. Mexican Policy and Ambivalence toward Labor Emigration to the United States. In *Immigrants—and Immigrants*, ed. A. Corwin. Westport, CT: Greenwood Press.

Courbage, Y. 1996. La population maghrébine a l'étranger: Dynamique démographique, caractéristiques socio-économiques. In *Migration internationale*, ed. CERED. Rabat: Premier Ministre and Ministère Chargé de la Population.

Craig, A. 1981. *Mexican Immigration: Changing Terms of the Debates in the United States and Mexico*. La Jolla: Program in U.S.-Mexican Studies, University of California, San Diego.

Craig, R. 1971. *The Bracero Program: Interest Groups and Foreign Policy*. Austin: University of Texas Press.

Creagan, J. 1965. Public Law 78: A Tangle of Domestic and International Relations. *Journal of Inter-American Studies* 7(4): 541–56.

Crewdson, J. 1978. Plans for "Berlin Wall" at El Paso Assailed. *New York Times*, November 7.

Cross, H., and J. Sandos. 1981. *Across the Border: Rural Development in Mexico and Recent Migration to the United States.* Berkeley: University of California Press.

Cubertafond, B. 2001. *La vie politique au Maroc.* Paris: L'Harmattan.

Cunty, G. 1990. *Programme pilote de pré-electrification rurale: Phase 1, Programme d'Accompagnement.* Aix-en-Provence: Royaume de Maroc, Ministry of the Interior, Direction of Local Collectivities.

Dades, A. 1998. SMAP '98: Trois jours du Maroc à Paris pour se ressourcer, édifier, s'enrichir. *La Vie Économique*, May 8.

Dalle, I. 2001. *Maroc 1961–1999: L'espérance brisée.* Paris: Maisonneuve et Larose.

Dalpé, R., C. DeBresson, and H. Xiaoping. 1992. The Public Sector as First User of Innovations. *Research Policy* 21(1992): 251–62.

Danish Enterprise and Construction Authority. 2007. Program for user-driven innovation. June 17. http://www.deaca.dk/userdriveninnovation.

Daoud, Z. 1981. Agrarian Capitalism and the Moroccan Crisis. *MERIP Reports*, no. 99, 27–33.

——. 1990. Le devenir de la société rurale marocaine. *Lamalif*, 28–32.

——. 1997. *Marocains des deux rives.* Paris: Éditions Ouvrières.

——. 2003. En 1977, comment voyait-on le Maroc de l'an 2000. *L'Économiste.*

——. 2004. *Travailleurs marocains en France: Mémoire restituée.* Casablanca: Tarik Éditions.

——. 2005. *Marocains de l'autre rive.* Casablanca: Éditions Maghrébines.

Davison, P. 1994. Zapatistas Head for State Capital. *Independent*, January 7.

Dean, M. 1999. *Governmentality: Power and Rule in Modern Society.* London: Sage.

Delal Baer, M., and S. Weintraub. 1994. The Pressures for Political Reform in Mexico. In *The NAFTA Debate: Grappling with Unconventional Trade Issues*, ed. M. Delal Baer and S. Weintraub. Boulder: Lynne Rienner.

Delgado Wise, R. 2002. *México en el primer año de gobierno de Vicente Fox.* Zacatecas: Universidad Autónoma de Zacatecas.

——. 2004. The Hidden Agenda of Mexico's Fox Administration. *Latin American Perspectives* 31: 146.

Delgado Wise, R., V. Figueroa Sepúlveda, and M. Hoffner Long. 1991. *Zacatecas: Sociedad, economía, política, cultura.* Mexico City: Universidad Nacional Autónoma de México.

Delgado Wise, R., M. Moctezuma Longoría, and H. Rodríguez Ramírez. 2000. Evaluation de programas y projectos comunitarios y productivos con participacion de los migrantes: El caso de Zacatecas. Unpublished manuscript, Zacatecas.

Delgado Wise, R., and R. Pozo. 2002. *Minería, estado y gran capital en México.* Mexico City: Universidad Nacional Autónoma de México.

Delgado Wise, R., and H. Rodríguez Ramírez. 2001. Los dilemas de la migración y el desarrollo en Zacatecas: El caso de la región de alta migración internacional. *Red Internacional de Migración y Desarrollo 2.*

Demir, M. 1990. Human Rights Briefing. *MERIP Reports*, no. 163.

Derderian, R. L. 2004. *North Africans in Contemporary France: Becoming Visible.* New York: Palgrave Macmillan.

Desrues, T., and E. Moyano. 2001. Social Change and Political Transition in Morocco. *Mediterranean Politics* 6(1): 21–47.

Dewar, R. D., and J. E. Dutton. 1986. The Adoption of Radical and Incremental Innovations: An Empirical Analysis. *Management Science* 32(11): 1422–33.

Díaz de Cossio, R. 1990a. Speech delivered to the Mexican American Opportunity Foundation. October 19. Ed. Dirección General para las Comunidades Mexicanas en el Extranjero (DGCME). SRE Archives, Mexico City.

——. 1990b. Speech delivered to the National Council of la Raza. July 16. DGCME. SRE Archives, Mexico City.

——. 1991a. Building Bridges for the Free Trade Agreement. DGCME memorandum. SRE Archives, Mexico City.

——. 1991b. Derivaciones politicas. DGCME. SRE Archives, Mexico City.

——. 1991c. Institutos mexicanos en los estadoes unidos. DGCME. SRE Archives, Mexico City.

——. 1991d. Un cambio de vision, un cambio de actitud: Una oportunidad historia. Reunion de consules, Chicago. November 9, 1991. DGCME. SRE Archives, Mexico City.

——. 1991e. Memorandum. SRE Archives, Mexico City. June 4.

Díaz-Cayeros, A., and B. Magaloni. 2003. *The Politics of Public Spending: The Programa Nacional de Solidaridad (PRONASOL) in Mexico*. Washington, DC: World Bank.

Diouri, M. 1992. *A qui appartient le Maroc*. Paris: L'Harmattan.

Dirección General de Atención a Comunidades Guanajuatenses in el Extranjero (DACGE) Casas Archives. 1998–2002 (series). DACGE Casas program documents. Guanajuato, Mexico, DACGE office.

Dirección General para las Comunidades Mexicanas en el Extranjero (DGCME). 1990a. Actividade sugeridas a los consultados para el cumplimiento de los proyectos. Internal memo. September 11. SRE Archives, Mexico City.

——. 1990b. La atencion a las Comunidades mexicanas en el extranjero. SRE Archives, Mexico City.

——. 1990c. Los mexicanos en los Estados Unidos. Speech to be given June 4, 1991. SRE Archives, Mexico City.

——. 1990d. *Racionalidad, organizacion, funciones, presupuesto, y programas para 1990*. SRE Archives, Mexico City.

Discovery Times Channel. 2005. *Harvest of Shame*. Classic 1960 CBS documentary, created by Edward R. Murrow. Aired on Discovery Times Channel, April 25.

Dresser, D. 1993. Exporting Conflict: Transboundary Consequences of Mexican Politics. In *The California-Mexico Connection*, ed. A. Lowenthal and K. Burgess. Stanford: Stanford University Press.

——. 1994. Bringing the Poor Back In: National Solidarity as a Strategy of Regime Legitimization. In *Transforming State-Society Relations in Mexico: The National Solidarity Strategy*, ed. W. Cornelius, A. Craig, and J. Fox. La Jolla: University of California, San Diego.

Driscoll, B. 1999. *The Tracks North: The Railroad Program of World War II*. Austin: University of Texas.

Drissi Semlali, F., and L. Lakhdar. 1991. Contribution des travailleurs marocains à l'étranger (T.M.E) au développement de l'économie marocaine. In *University Mohamed V*. Rabat.

Drummond, J. 2002. Royal progress stirs Morocco reform: Incentives for investors highlight the constraints placed upon the democratically elected government. *Financial Times*, February 12.

Dubet, F., and D. Lapeyronnie. 1992. *Les quartiers d'exil*. Paris: Éditions du Seuil.

Dumont, A. 2008. Le mouvement associatif des immigrés marocains en France. Poitiers: Université de Poitiers.

Durand, J., and D. Massey. 1996. Migradollars and Development: A Reconsideration of the Mexican Case. *International Migration Review* 30(2): 423–44.

Echeverría, L. 1979. Mexico's Recent Position on Workers for the United States. In *Mexican Workers in the United States: Historical and Political Perspectives*, ed. G. Kiser and M. Kiser. Albuquerque: University of New Mexico Press.

Économie et Entreprises. 2003. La diaspora rencontre le Maroc (special issue).

The Economist. 1990. The Fury in Fez. December 22.

——. 1999. King Hassan of Morocco. July 31.

L'Économiste. 1992. Alimentation électrique: Les entreprises bousculées par les coupures et délestages.

——. 1993a. Concertation ONE-industriels pour programmer les coupures. January 21.

——. 1993b. ONE: Campagne pour les économies. April 22.

——. 1993c. Pour veiller à l'application du plan de charge: Déficit électrique: Des comités de vigilance effectueront des contrôles dans les entreprises. September 16.

——. 1994. L'ONE ne peut plus payer son pétrole. November 10.

——. 1996. Secteur énergétique: 1996, l'année des réformes. October 10.

——. 2003. Les forums de l'Économiste: La parole of MRE. August 12.

Elster, J. 1998. Introduction to *Deliberative Democracy*, ed. J. Elster. Cambridge: Cambridge University Press.

Ennaji, M. 2005. *Multilingualism, Cultural Identity, and Education in Morocco.* New York: Springer.

Entelis, J. 1980. *Comparative Politics of North Africa: Algeria, Morocco, and Tunisia.* Syracuse: Syracuse University Press.

Fantasia, R., and K. Voss. 2004. *Hard Work: Remaking the American Labor Movement.* Berkeley, University of California Press.

Farnsworth, C. 1974. France's Economy Is in Growing Difficulty. *New York Times,* December 1.

Farsoun, K., and J. Paul. 1976. War in the Sahara: 1963. *MERIP Reports,* no. 45, 13–16.

Fathallah, H. 2002. Le dilemme des MRE. *Économie et Entreprises* (August, special issue).

Fawcett, E. 1974. Europe's Imported Work Force. *New York Times,* June 23.

Feldman, M. 1989. *Order without Design: Information Production and Policy Making.* Stanford: Stanford University Press.

Fellat, F. M. 1996. Transferts et politiques d'incitation aux investissements des émigrés (Maroc). In *Migration internationale.* Rabat: Centre d'Études et de Recherches Démographiques.

Fernandez, M., and A. Pence. 2000. Epochal Vote Celebrated in Bay Area. *San Francisco Chronicle,* July 4.

Fitzgerald, D. 2004. "For 118 Million Mexicans": Emigrants and Chicanos in Mexican Politics. In *Dilemmas of Political Change in Mexico,* ed. K. Middlebrook. La Jolla: Center for U.S.-Mexican Studies, University of California, San Diego.

——. 2006. Inside the Sending State: The Politics of Mexican Emigration Control. *International Migration Review* 40(2): 34.

Flowers, S. 2008. Harnessing the Hackers: The Emergence and Exploitation of Outlaw Innovation. *Research Policy* 27: 177–93.

Fondation Hassan II. 1996–2000 (series). Internal documents on Operations Transit.

——. *Annual Reports.* 1997–2001 (series). Rabat.

——, ed. 2003. *Marocains de l'extérieur.* Rabat.

Fonseca, Jose. 2002. *Complexity and Innovation in Organizations.* New York: Routledge.

Foucault, M. 1991. Governmentality. In *The Foucault Effect: Studies in Governmentality,* ed. C. Gordon, G. Burchell, and P. Miller. Chicago: University of Chicago Press.

——. 1994. *The Essential Foucault: Selections from Essential Works of Foucault, 1954–1984.* New York: New Press.

Foulani, H. 1999. Plus on est jeune moins on envoie d'argent au pays. *L'Économiste,* August 15.

Fox, V. 1998. *Dreams, Challenges and Threats.* Dallas: University of Texas.

——. 2003a. Palabras del Presidente Vicente Fox, durante la ceremonia de instalación del consejo consultivo del instituto de los Mexicanos en el Exterior. Mexico: Secretaría de Relaciones Exteriores (SRE). March 20.

——. 2003b. Versión de las palabras del Presidente Vicente Fox Quesada durante la ceremonia inaugural de la Segunda Reunión del Consejo Consultivo del Instituto de los Mexicanos en el Exterior, que este mediodía encabezó en La Hondonada de la residencia oficial de Los Pinos. Mexico: Secretaría de Relaciones Exteriores (SRE). Nov 7.

Freeman, G. 1979. *Immigrant Labor and Racial Conflict in Industrial Societies: The French and British Experience, 1945–1975.* Princeton: Princeton University Press.

Frennet–De Keyser, A. 2004. La convention belgo-marocaine de main d'oeuvre: Un non-événement? In *Trajectoires et dynamiques migratoires de l'immigration marocaine de Belgique,* ed. N. Ouali. Louvain–La Neuve: Bruylant-Academia.

Fung, A., and E. O. Wright, eds. 2003. *Deepening Democracy: Institutional Innovations in Empowered Participatory Governance.* London: Verso.

Galarza, E. 1964. *Merchants of Labor: The Mexican Bracero Story*. Santa Barbara: McNally and Loftin.

Gamboa, E. 1990. *Mexican Labor and World War II: Braceros in the Pacific Northwest, 1942–1947*. Austin: University of Texas Press.

Ganz, M. 2009. *Why David Sometimes Wins: Leadership, Organization and Strategy in the California Farm Worker Movement*. New York: Oxford University Press.

Garcia, J. A. 1987. The Political Integration of Mexican Immigrants: Examining Some Political Orientations. *International Migration Review* 21(2): 17.

Garcia, J. R. 1980. *Operation Wetback: The Mass Deportation of Mexican Undocumented Workers in 1954*. Westport, CT: Greenwood Press.

Garcia, M. 1989. *Mexican Americans: Leadership, Ideology, and Identity, 1930–1960*. New Haven: Yale University Press.

Garcia, V. 1997. *Mexican Enclaves in the U.S. Northeast: Immigrant and Migrant Mushroom Workers in Southern Chester County, Pennsylvania*. Lansing: Julian Samora Research Institute, Michigan State University.

García-Acevedo, M. R. 1996. Return to Aztlán: Mexico's Policies toward Chicanas/os. In *Chicanas/Chicanos at the Crossroads*, ed. D. Maciel and I. Ortiz. Tuscon: University of Arizona Press.

García Zamora, R. 1994. *Crisis y modernización del agro en México*. Mexico City: Universidad Autónoma Chapingo.

——. 1997. *La agricultura en el laberinto de la modernidad*. Zacatecas: Universidad Autónoma de Zacatecas.

——. 2000. *Agricultura, migración y desarrollo regional*. Zacatecas: Universidad Autónoma de Zacatecas.

——. 2002. Los proyectos productivos con los migrantes en México Hoy. Segundo Coloquio Sobre Migración Internacional: Mexico-California. University of California, Berkeley, March 28.

——. 2005. Migración internacional y remesas colectivas en Zacatecas. *Foreign Affairs en Español* 5(3): 11.

Garson, J.-P. 1986. L'exemple français: Continuités historiques, mutations productives et rôle structurel des migrations clandestins en France. In *Économie politique des migrations clandestins de main-d'oeuvre*, ed. Y. Moulier-Boutang, J.-P. Garson, and R. Silberman. Paris: Publisud.

Garson, J.-P., and M. Bennabou. 1981. Les marocains. In *L'argent des immigrés: Revenues, épargne et transferts de huit nationalités immigrées en France*, ed. J.-P. Garson and G. Tapinos. Paris: Presses Universitaires de France.

Garson, J.-P., and G. Tapinos, eds. 1981. *L'argent des immigrés: Revenues, épargne et transferts de huit nationalités immigrées en France*. Paris: Presses Universitaires de France.

Garza, R. de la. 1980. Chicanos and U.S. Foreign Policy: The Future of Chicano-Mexican Relations. *Western Political Quarterly* 33(4): 571–82.

——. 1986. Chicanos as an Ethnic Lobby: Limits and Possibilities. In *Chicano-Mexico Relations*, ed. T. J. Mindiola and M. Martinez. Calhoun: University of Houston.

——. 1997. Foreign Policy Comes Home: The Domestic Consequences of the Program for Mexican Communities Living in Foreign Countries. In *Bridging the Border: Transforming Mexico-U.S. Relations*, ed. R. de la Garza and J. Velazco. Lanham, MD: Rowman and Littlefield.

Garza, R. de la, and B. L. Lowell, eds. 2002. *Sending Money Home: Hispanic Remittances and Community Development*. Lanham, MD: Rowman and Littlefield.

Garza, R. de la, and M. Orozco. 2002. Binational Impact of Latino Remittances. In *Sending Money Home: Hispanic Remittances and Community Development*, ed. R. de la Garza and B. L. Lowell. Lanham, MD: Rowman and Littlefield.

Gastaut, Y. 1994. Le rôle des immigrés pendant les journées de mai-juin 1968. *Migrations/Société* 6(32): 9–29.

Gellner, E. 1983. *Muslim Society*. Cambridge: Cambridge University Press.

Gharbaoui, A. 1971. Les travailleurs maghrébins immigrés dans la banlieue nord-ouest de Paris. *Revue de Géographie du Maroc* 19:3–55.

Giddens, A. 1984. *The Constitution of Society: Outline of a Theory of Structuration.* Berkeley: University of California Press.

Gilly, A. 2006. *The Mexican Revolution: A People's History.* New York: New Press.

Giniger, H. 1972. Never Sure He'll Be King at Nightfall. *New York Times*, August 20.

———. 1973. Hassan Is Keeping Opposition at Bay. *New York Times*, September 17.

Glick Schiller, N. a. G. F. 2001. *Georges Woke up Laughing: Long Distance Nationalism and the Search for Home.* Durham, NC: Duke University Press.

Glytsos, N. 2002. The Role of Migrant Remittances in Development: Evidence from Mediterranean Countries. *International Migration* 40(1): 5–26.

Goldring, L. 1999. The Power of Status in Transnational Social Fields. In *Transnationalism from Below*, ed. L. E. Guarnizo and M. P. Smith. New Brunswick, NJ: Transaction Publishers.

———. 2002. The Mexican State and Transmigrant Organizations: Negotiating the Boundaries of Membership and Participation. *Latin American Research Review* 37(3): 55–99.

———. 2003. *Re-thinking Remittances: Social and Political Dimensions of Individual and Collective Remittances.* Toronto: Center for Research on Latin America and the Caribbean, York University.

Gómez-Quiñones, J. 1990. *Chicano Politics: Reality and Promise, 1940–1990.* Albuquerque: University of New Mexico Press.

Gómez Sánchez, P. 1990. La cuestión agraria en Zacatecas, periodo 1970–1985. In *Historia de la cuentión agraria mexicana: Estado de Zacatecas*, ed. P. Gómez Sánchez, 171–215. Zacatecas: Universidad Autónoma de Zacatecas.

González, G. G. 1990. *Mexican Consuls and Labor Organizing: Imperial Politics in the American Southwest.* Austin: University of Texas Press.

———. 1994. *Labor and Community: Mexican Citrus Worker Villages in a Southern California County, 1900–1950.* Urbana: University of Illinois Press.

González, G. G., and R. Fernandez. 2003. *A Century of Chicano History.* New York: Routledge.

González Gutiérrez, C. 1993. The Mexican Diaspora in California. In *The California-Mexico Connection*, ed. A. Lowenthal and K. Burgess. Stanford: Stanford University Press.

———. 1995. La organización de los inmigrantes mexicanos en Los Ángeles: La lealtad de los oriundos. *Revista Mexicana de Politica Exterior* 46 (Spring).

———. 1997. Decentralized Diplomacy: The Role of Consular Offices in Mexico's Relations with Its Diaspora. In *Bridging the Border: Transforming Mexico-U.S. Relations*, ed. R. de la Garza and J. Velazco. Lanham, MD: Rowman and Littlefield.

———. 1999. Fostering Identities: Mexico's Relations with Its Diaspora. *Journal of American History* 86(2).

González Gutiérrez, C., and M. E. Schumacher. 1998. El acercamiento de México a las comunidades mexicanas en Estados Unidos: El caso del PCME. In *México y Estados Unidos: Las rutas de la cooperación*, ed. O. Pellicer and R. Fernández de Castro. Mexico City: Instituto Matías Romero de Estudios Diplomáticos–Instituto Tecnológico Autónomo de México.

Granotier, B. 1970. *Les travailleurs immigrés en France.* Paris: François Maspero.

Grason, D., and B. Massera. 2004. *Chausson: Une dignité ouvrière.* Paris: Syllepse.

Gregory, J. 1999. Hassan II of Morocco Dies at 70; A Monarch Oriented toward the West. *New York Times*, July 24.

Gregory, P. 1986. *The Myth of Market Failure: Employment and the Labor Market in Mexico.* Baltimore: Johns Hopkins University Press.

Grindle, M. S. 1989. The Response to Austerity: Political and Economic Strategies of Mexico's Rural Poor. In *Lost Promises: Debt, Austerity, and Development in Latin America*, ed. W. Canak. Boulder: Westview Press.

Grosclaude, M. 1990. *Maroc: Mission de suivi des projets "Pré-électrification rurale" et télé-detection; Compte-rendu de mission au Maroc*. Paris: Ambassade de France à Rabat—AFME.

Groupe d'Études et de Recherches Appliquées (GERA). 1992. *Étude des mouvements migratoires du Maroc vers la communauté européenne*. Rabat: Université Mohammed V.

Guanajuato. Comisión Estatal de Apoyo Integral a los Migrantes y Sus Familias. 2001–2005 (series). Programa Social Migrantes 2x1. Guanajuato.

Guarnizo, L. E. 1998. The Rise of Transnational Social Formations: Mexican and Dominican State Responses to Transnational Migration. *Political Power and Social Theory* 12:45–94.

———. 2003. The Economics of Transnational Living. *International Migration Review* 37(3): 666–99.

Guarnizo, L. E., and M. P. Smith. 1999. The Locations of Transnationalism. In *Transnationalism from Below*, ed. L. E. Guarnizo and M. P. Smith. New Brunswick, NJ: Transaction Publishers.

Gulyani, S. 1999. Innovating with Infrastructure: How India's Largest Carmaker Copes with Poor Electricity Supply. *World Development* 27(10).

Gupta, A. 1998. *Postcolonial Developments: Agriculture in the Making of Modern India*. Durham, NC: Duke University Press.

Gutiérrez, A. 1986. The Chicano Elite in Chicano-Mexicano Relations. In *Chicano-Mexicano Relations*, ed. T. J. Mindiola and M. Martinez. Calhoun: University of Houston.

Gutiérrez, J. A. 1986. The Chicano in Mexicano-Norte Americano Foreign Relations. In *Chicano-Mexicano Relations*, ed. T. J. Mindiola and M. Martinez. Calhoun: University of Houston.

Gutmann, A., and D. Thompson. 2004. *Why Deliberative Democracy*. Princeton: Princeton University Press.

Haas, H. de. 2003. *Migration and Development in Southern Morocco: The Disparate Socio-Economic Impacts of Out-Migration on the Todgha Oasis Valley*. Amsterdam: CERES.

Hall, R. 1993. A Framework Linking Intangible Resources and Capabilities to Sustainable Competitive Advantage. *Strategic Management Journal* 14(8).

Halliday, F. 1984. Labor Migration in the Arab World. *MERIP Reports*, no. 123.

Hamdouch, B., T. Baddou, A. Berrada, and L. Lassounde. 1981. *Migration internationale au Maroc*. Montreal: Université du Québec.

Hamdouch, B., A. Berrada, W. Heinmeyer, P. de Mas, and H. van der Wusten. 1979. *Migration de développement, migration de sous-développement? Une étude sur l'impact de la migration dans le milieu rural du Maroc*. Rabat: INSEA.

Hamdouch, B., A. Berrera, M. Lahlou, M. el-Manar Laalami, and M. Mahmoudi. 2000. *Les marocains résidants à l'etranger: Une enquête socio-économique*. Rabat: Institut National de Statistique et d'Économie Appliquée.

Hansen, T. B., and F. Stepputat. 2001. Introduction: States of Imagination. In *States of Imagination: Ethnographic Explorations of the Postcolonial State*, ed. T. B. Hansen and F. Stepputat, 1–40. Durham, NC: Duke University Press.

Haour-Knipe, M., and R. Rector. 1996. *Crossing Borders: Migration, Ethnicity and AIDS*. London: Taylor and Francis.

Hart, G. 2002. *Disabling Globalization: Places of Power in Post-Apartheid South Africa*. Berkeley: University of California Press.

Hayes, H. 2001. *U.S. Immigration Policy and the Undocumented: Ambivalent Laws, Furtive Lives*. Westport, CT: Praeger.

Hegstrom, E. 2000. Lifting Barriers at Border Urged. *Houston Chronicle*, June 16.

Heller, P. 2001. Moving the State: The Politics of Democratic Decentralization in Kerela, South Africa, and Porto Alegre. *Politics and Society* 29(1): 131–63.

Henson, R. 1993. Mushroom Workers Sue over Pay in the Federal Action, the Strikers Say Kaolin Broke the Law by Not Paying Some Workers Overtime. *Philadelphia Inquirer*, April 20.

Herradi, J. E. 2003. Casablanca: Un industriel initie les bidonvillois à la gestion locale. *L'Économiste*, September 10.

Hoffman, B. G. 1967. *Structure of Traditional Moroccan Rural Society*. The Hague: Mouton De Gruyter.

Hoisington, W. 1985. The Selling of Agadir: French Business Promotion in Morocco in the 1930s. *International journal of African Historical Studies* 18(2): 315–24.

Holles, E. 1977. 200,000 at Tijuana Wait to Be Smuggled into U.S. by Deadline. *New York Times*, August 8.

Houdaigui, R. el-. 2003. *La politique étrangère sous le règne de Hassan II*. Paris: L'Harmattan.

Houston Chronicle. 1994. Marchers Seek Fair Elections, Mexican Peasants Leaving Jungle to Attend Peace Talks. February 14.

Hughes, S. 1968. Thirsty Moroccans Turn to Irrigation. *New York Times*, January 26.

Ikram, R., and M. E. Jouhari. 1997. Essoufflement des transfers financiers. *L'Économiste*, October 23.

Institut National de Statistique et d'Économie Apliquée (INSEA). 2000. *Les marocains résidant à l'étranger: Une enquête socio-économique*. Rabat.

Instituto de los Mexicanos en el Extranjero (IME). 2005. Cronos: Voto de los mexicanos en el exteriors: Sintesis cronológica. Mexico City.

Inter-American Development Bank, Multilateral Investment Fund. 2006. Remittances: Promoting Financial Democracy. Washington, DC.

International Monetary Fund (IMF). 2005. *Morocco: Statistical Appendix Country Report No. 05/420*. Washington, DC.

International Monetary Fund (IMF) *Balance of Payments Statistics Yearbooks*. 1977–2005 (series). Washington, DC.

Iskander, N. 2005. Social Learning as a Productive Project: The Tres por Uno (Three for One) Experience at Zacatecas, Mexico. In *The Development Dimension: Migration, Remittances and Development*. Paris: Organisation for Economic Co-operation and Development (OECD).

Jackson, B. 2000. Chicago Supporters Celebrate Victory. *Chicago Sun-Times*, July 3.

Jacobs, J. 2004. *Dark Age Ahead*. New York: Random House.

Jafry, A. 2005. Chaouia-Ouardigha: Le CRI veut apporter des solutions au foncier. *L'Économiste*, April 1.

Jansen, D. 1991. Policy Networks and Change: The Case of High-T Superconductors. In *Policy Networks: Empirical Evidence and Theoretical Considerations*, ed. B. Marin and R. Mayntz, 137–74. Boulder: Westview Press.

Jehl, D. 1999. In Morocco, Too, a Young King for a New Generation. *New York Times*, July 27.

Jenkins, J. C. 1978. The Demand for Immigrant Workers: Labor Scarcity or Social Control. *International Migration Review* 12(4): 514–35.

Jeppesen, L. B., and L. Frederiksen. 2006. Why Do Users Contribute to Firm-Hosted User Communities? The Case of Computer-Controlled Music Instruments. *Organization Science* 17(1): 45–63.

Jeppesen, L. B., and M. J. Molin. 2003. Consumers as Co-developers: Learning and Innovation Outside the Firm. *Technology Analysis and Strategic Management* 15(3): 363–83.

Jibril, M. 1994. Les émigrés dans la fièvre de l'immobilier. *Rivages* 12 (Winter): 24–28.

Joffe, E. G. H. 1985. The Moroccan Nationalist Movement: Istiqlal, the Sultan, and the Country. *Journal of African History* 26(4): 289–307.

Johnson, H., and G. Wison. 2000. Biting the Bullet: Civil Society, Social Learning and the Transformation of Local Governance. *World Development* 28(11): 1891–1906.

Jones, R. 1995. Immigration Reform and Migrant Flows: Compositional and Spatial Changes in Mexican Migration after the Immigration Reform Act of 1986. *Annals of the Association of American Geographers* 85(4).

Jordan, J. 2004. Relational Awareness: Transforming Disconnection. In *The Complexity of Connection*, ed. J. Jordan, M. Walker, and L. Hartling. New York: Guilford Press.

Kaggwa, L. 2000. Fox's Win Viewed Favorably in Region; Hispanics Expecting Democracy in Mexico. *Plain Dealer*, July 8.

Kaioua, A. 1999. Place des émigrés marocains en Europe dans l'investissement industriel à Casablanca. In *Migrations internationales entre le Maghreb et l'Europe: Les effets sur les pays de destination et les pays d'origine*, ed. M. Berriane and H. Popp. Casablanca: University Mohammed V.

Kammer, J. 2002. Mexican Immigrants Invited to Meet with Fox. *Copley News Service*, August 1.

Kapralos, K. 2006. Expatriates' Votes Trickle into Mexico. *Everett (WA) Herald*, July 2.

Kastoryano, R. 2002. *Negotiating Identities: States and Immigrants in France and Germany*. Princeton: Princeton University Press.

Katloft, R., H. Boer, R. Chapman, F. Gertsen, and J. Nielsen. 2006. Collaborative Improvement—Interplay but Not a Game. *Creativity and Innovation Management* 15(4): 348–58.

Kaufman, R., and G. Trejo. 1997. Regionalism, Regime Transformation, and PRONASOL: The Politics of the National Solidarity Programme in Four Mexican States. *Latin American Studies* 29:717–45.

Kearney, M. 1991. Borders and the Boundaries of the State and Self at the End of Empire. *Journal of Historical Sociology* 4(1): 52–74.

———. 2004. *Changing Fields of Anthropology: From Local to Global*. Lanham, MD: Rowman and Littlefield.

Kehoe, T. J. 1994. Toward a Dynamic General Equilibrium Model of North American Free Trade. In *Modeling Trade Policy: Applied General Equilibrium Assessments of North American Free Trade*, ed. C. R. S. Joseph F. Francois. Cambridge: Cambridge University Press.

Khachani, M. 2004. *Les marocains d'ailleurs: La question migratoire à l'épreuve du partenariat euro-marocain*. Rabat: AMERM.

Khaldi, M. 2003. Les marocains résidant en Espagne. In *Marocains de l'extérieur*. Rabat: Fondation Hassan II.

Kingdon, J. 1995. *Agendas, Alternatives, and Public Policies*. New York: Harper Collins.

Kissinger, H. 1988. The Rise of Mexico. *Washington Post*, August 17.

Klesner, J. 2005. Electoral Competition and the New Party System in Mexico. *Latin American Politics and Society* 47(2): 103–42.

Kogut, B., and U. Zander. 1992. Knowledge of the firm, combinative capabilities and the replication of technology. *Organization Science* 3:383–97.

Ksikes, D. 2004. Mémoire: Le rif, notre mauvaise conscience. *Telquel* 118.

Kutschera, C. 1984. Immigrés, les "orphelins" de la politique française. *24 Heures*, September 12–13.

Laftasse, B., A. Haoudi, and M. Fhal. 1992. Les transferts d'Epargne des R.M.E. PhD diss. Université Mohammed V, Rabat.

Lahoussain, J., and R. Calandra. 1992. *Projet Maroc: Chantier d'electrification, region Taliouine, village de Tinfate*. Nice: Association pour la Valorisation des Exchanges par la Coopération.

Lakhani, K. 2005. Distributed Coordination Practices in Free and Open Source Communities. PhD diss., Sloan School of Management, MIT.

Lakoff, G. 1987. *Women, Fire, and Dangerous Things: What Categories Reveal about the Mind*. Chicago: Chicago University Press.

Lalutte, P. 1976. Sahara: Notes toward an Analysis. *MERIP Reports*, no. 45, 7–12.

Lamlili, N. 2004. Centres régionaux d'investissement: Les premiers fruits de la réforme. *L'Économiste*, March 1.

Latour, B. 1987. *Science in Action*. Cambridge: Harvard University Press.

Lave, J., P. Duguid, N. Fernandez, and E. Axel. 1992. Coming of Age in Birmingham: Cultural Studies and Conceptions of Subjectivity. *Annual Review of Anthropology* 21:257–82.

Lave, J., and E. Wenger. 1991. *Situated Learning: Legitimate Peripheral Participation.* Cambridge: Cambridge University Press.

Layachi, A. 1998. *State, Society and Democracy in Morocco: The Limits of Associative Life.* Washington, DC: Center for Contemporary Arab Studies, Georgetown University.

——. 1999. Economic Reform and Elusive Political Change in Morocco. In *North Africa in Transition: State, Society, and Economic Transformation in the 1990s,* ed. Y. Zoubir. Gainesville: University Press of Florida.

Lazaar, M. 1995. Migration internationale et croissance des villes du Nord-Ouest marocain: Les cas de Tétouan et de Tanger (Maroc). In *Les nouvelles formes de la mobilité spatiale dans le monde arabe,* ed. R. a. P. S. Escalier, 145–50. Tours: URBAMA.

Leiken, R. 2001. *The Melting Border.* Washington, DC: Center for Equal Opportunity.

Lester, R., and M. Piore. 2004. *Innovation: The Missing Dimension.* Cambridge: Harvard University Press.

Leveau, R. 1976. *Le fellah marocain: Défenseur du trône.* Paris: Fondation Nationale des Sciences Politiques.

——. 2000. The Moroccan Monarchy: A Political System in Quest of a New Equilibrium. In *Middle East Monarchies: The Challenge of Modernity,* ed. J. Kostiner. Boulder: Lynne Rienner.

Levitt, P. 2001. *The Transnational Villagers.* Berkeley: University of California Press.

Levitt, P., and R. de la Dehasa. 2004. Transnational Migration and the Redefinition of the State: Variations and Explanations. *Ethnic and Racial Studies* 26(4): 587–611.

Levy, D., and G. Székely. 1983. *Mexico: Paradoxes of Stability and Change.* Boulder: Westview Press.

Levy, H. 2004. *Rural Roads and Poverty Alleviation in Morocco.* Washington, DC: World Bank.

Lewis, F. 1974. Giscard Asserts World Is in Grip of Fiscal Crisis. *New York Times,* October 25.

Lewis, P. 1986. France's Iacocca. *New York Times,* December 7.

Lindstrom, D., and N. Lauster. 2001. Local Economic Opportunity and the Competing Risks of Internal and U.S. Migration in Zacatecas, Mexico. *International Migration Review* 35(4): 1232–56.

Lipshultz, R. 1962. American Attitudes toward Mexican Immigration, 1924–1952. Master's thesis, University of Chicago.

Lizarzaburu, J. 2004. Mexican migrants' growing influence. *BBC News,* May 18.

Lloyd, C. 2000. Trade Unions and Immigrants in France: From Assimilation to Antiracist Networking. In *Trade Unions, Immigration, and Immigrants in Europe, 1960–1993,* ed. R. Pennix and J. Roosblad. New York: Berghahn Books.

Locke, R., and K. Thelem. 1995. Apples and Oranges Revisited: Contextualized Comparisons and the Study of Comparative Labor Politics. *Politics and Society* 23(3).

López Flores, S., and J. Palma Vargas. 1991. Movimiento mexicano-chicano en el estado de California. In *El sistema politico Mexico visto por los mexicanos de afuera,* ed. G. Ramírez Paredes. Mexico City: UNAM.

López Moncada, J., and A. Cerecedo Flores. 2000. Jornaleros agricolas en el ejido de chaparrosa, Villa de Cos, Zacatecas. Master's thesis, Universidad Autónoma de Zacatecas.

Lugan, B. 1992. *Histoire du Maroc: Des origines à nos jours.* Paris: Criterion.

Lustig, N. 1998. *Mexico: The Remaking of an Economy.* Washington, DC: Brookings Institution Press.

MacPherson, R. 1999. World Leaders, Subjects Bid Farewell to Morocco's King Hassan. *Agence France Press,* July 25.

Mahfoud, Y. 2001. BCP: Il faudra un très très grand Omary. *L'Économiste,* February 12.

Majid, M. 1987. *Les luttes de classes au Maroc depuis l'Indépendance.* Rotterdam: Éditions Hiwar.

Malet, E., and P. Simon, eds. 1996. *Les banlieues: Europe, quartiers et migrants.* Paris: Passages.

Mana, A. 1993. Les porteurs du savoir. *Rivages* 6: 22–24.

Mansour, A. 2004. Il était une fois Laraki. *Casablanca Maroc-Hebdo Press*, March 11.

Mansouri, E. H. el-. 1996. La communauté marocaine à l'étranger: Evolution et caratéristiques socio-économiques. In *Migration internationale*, ed. CERED. Rabat: Premier Ministre and Ministère Chargé de la Population.

Marcelli, E., and W. Cornelius. 2003. Immigrant Voting in Home-Country Elections: Potential Consequences of Extending the Franchise to Expatriate Mexicans. *Mexican Studies/ Estudios Mexicanos* 21(2): 429–60.

March, J. 1994. *A Primer on Decision Making*. New York: Free Press.

———. 1997. Understanding How Decisions Happen in Organizations. In *Organizational Decision Making*, ed. Z. Shapira. Cambridge: Cambridge University Press.

Marie, C.-V. 1996. En première ligne dans l'élasticité de l'emploi. *Plein Droit* 31 (April).

Markham, J. 1980. King Hassan's Quagmire. *New York Times*, April 27.

Marsh, D., and M. Smith. 2000. Understanding Policy Networks: towards a Dialectical Approach. *Political Studies* 48(1): 4–21.

Martin, P. 2001. *There Is Nothing More Permanent Than Temporary Foreign Workers*. La Jolla: Center for Immigration Studies, University of California, San Diego.

Martinez Saldaña, J. 2002. Participación política migrante: Praxis cotidiana de ciudadanos excluidos. In *La dimensión política de la migración mexicana*, ed. L. Calderón Chelius and J. Martinez Saldaña. Mexico: Instituto de Investigadora Mora.

Massey, D., J. Arango, G. Hugo, A. Kouaouci, A. Pellegrino, and J. Taylor. 1993. Theories of International Migration: A Review and Appraisal. *Population and Development Review* 19(3): 34.

Le Matin. 2004a. Un atelier à Paris sur le développement local dans le Royaume. November 22.

———. 2004b. Les MRE et la mère-patrie: Une logique de lucidité et de responsabilité. July 11.

———. 2004c. Opération transit 2004: Important dispositif sanitaire. June 18.

———. 2004d. Rendez vous des MRE: L'immobilier marocain à l'honneur à Paris. February 30.

Matthiessen, P. 1969. *Sal Si Puedes: Cesar Chavez and the New American Revolution*. New York: Random House.

Mayer, F. 2001. Negotiating NAFTA: Political Lessons for the FTAA. Working paper SAN01-17. Terry Sanford Institute, Duke University.

M'barki, S. 2003. Les Marocains residant en Italie: caractéristiques démographiques et sociales. *Marocains de l'exterieur*. Rabat: Fondation Hassan II.

MERIP Reports. 1977. Wave of Repression Sweeps Morocco. No. 57, 18–19.

Mernissi, F. 1998. *ONG rurales de Haut-Atlas: Les ait débrouille*. Marrakesh: Éditions Le Fennec.

Mestries Benquet, F. 2002. El rancho se nos llenó de viejos: Crisis del agro y migración internacional en Zacatecas. *Estudios Agrarios* 19:81–136.

Mexican Human Rights Commission. 1992. *Report on Human Rights Violations of Mexican Migratory Workers: On Route to the Northern Border, Crossing the Border, and upon Entering the Southern United States Border Strip*. Mexico City: Comisión Nacional de Derechos Humanos.

Meyer, L. 1983. Oil Booms and the Mexican Historical Experience: Past Problems—Future Prospects. In *Mexican-U.S. Relations: Conflict and Convergence*, ed. C. Vásquez and M. García y Griego. Los Angeles: Chicano Studies Research Center, University of California.

M'hammed, M. 2004. *La rencontre: Essai sur la communication et l'éducation en milieu intercultural*. Paris: Presses Université Laval.

Michener, V. 1998. The Participatory Approach: Contradiction and Co-option in Burkina Faso. *World Development* 26(12): 2105–18.

Middlebrook, K. 1995. *The Paradox of Revolution: Labor, the State and Authoritarianism in Mexico*. Baltimore: Johns Hopkins University Press.

Migdail, C. 1987. Mexico's Failing Political System. *Journal of Interamerican Studies and World Affairs* 29(3).

Migration News. 2001. INS: Border Deaths, Trafficking. Vol. 7, no. 3. University of California, Davis. Migrations et Développement (M/D). 2002a. *Evaluation capitalisation des initiatives locales, 2000*. Taroudant.

Migrations et Développement (M/D). 2002a. *Evaluation capitalisation des initiatives locales, 2000*. Taroudant.

———. 2002b. *Rapport ECIL: Evaluation capitalisation des initiatives locales*. Taroudant Migrations et Développement (M/D) *Note de présentation*. 1990–2001 (series). Marseille.

Migrations et Développement (M/D), and Migrations et Développement Local. 1996. *Programme d'electrification décentralisée sur initiative locale*. Marseille and Rabat.

Miller, J. B., and I. Pierce Stiver. 1997. *The Healing Connection*. Boston: Beacon Press.

Mindiola, T. J., and M. Martinez. 1986. Introduction to Chicano-Mexicano Relations. In *Chicano-Mexicano Relations*, ed. T. J. Mindiola and M. Martinez. Calhoun: University of Houston.

Mines, R. 1981. *Developing a Community Tradition of Migration to the United States: A Field Study in Rural Zacatecas, Mexico and California Settlement Areas*. La Jolla: University of California, San Diego.

Mines, R., and D. Massey. 1985. Patterns of Migration to the United States from Two Mexican Communities. *Latin American Research Review* 20(2): 104–23.

Missaoui, R. 1996. *Le secteur informel de l'énergie dans les pays en développement: Cas du Maghreb*. Paris: Agence de l'Environnement et de la Maîtrise de l'Énergie.

Moctezuma Longoría, M. 1989. Estructura económica de Zacatecas de la expulsión a la producción de fuerza de Trabajo (1893–1950). PhD diss., Universidad Autónoma de Zacatecas.

Moctezuma Longoría, M. 1999. Redes sociales, comunidades filiales, familias y clubes de migrantes: El circuito migrante Sain Alto, Zac. Oakland, CA: El Colegio de la Frontera Norte.

———. 2003. Territorialidad socio-cultural y política de los clubes de Zacatecanos en Estados Unidos. Unpublished paper, Zacatecas.

Moctezuma Longoría, M., and H. Rodríguez Ramírez. 2000. *Programas "Tres por Uno" y "Mi Comunidad": Evaluación con migrantes Zacatecanos y Guanajuatenses radicados en Chicago, Ill. y Los Angeles, Ca.: Informe final de investigación*. Zacatecas: Universidad Autónoma de Zacatecas.

———. 2002. Programas "Tres-por-uno" y "Mi Comunidad": Evaluación con migrantes Zacatecanos y Guanajuatenses radicados en Chicago, IL y Los Angeles, CA. Zacatecas.

Mohamed, J. 1998. Conditions d'un développement local d'une petite ville du Rif: Chefchaouen. In *Le développement du Maroc septiregionel: Points de vues de géographes*, ed. M. Berriane and A. Laouina. Neustadt an der Aisch: Justus Perthes Verlag Gotha.

Mohammed VI. 1999a. Discours de 46ème anniversaire de la révolution de roi et du peuple. August 20.

———. 1999b. Discours de trône de sa majesté le roi Mohammed VI.

———. 1999c. Lettre de s. m. le roi Mohammed VI au premier ministre, M. Abderrahmane el-Youssoufi définissant le cadre et les orientations du Plan Quinquennal.

———. 2000a. Allocution de s.m. le roi Mohammed VI devant les membres de la communauté marocaine en France.

———. 2000b. Allocution de s.m. le roi Mohammed VI devant les membres de la communauté marocaine en Espagne. September 18.

———. 2000c. Discours du throne de sa majesté le roi Mohammed VI.

———. 2001. Discours à l'occasion de deuxième anniversaire de l'intronisation de sa majesté le roi Mohammed VI.

———. 2002a. L'allocation de s.m. le roi Mohammed VI à l'occasion de la nomination des membres du conseil d'administration de l'Institut Royal de la Culture Amazighe (IRCAM).

———. 2002b. Texte intégral de l'interview accordée par s.m. le roi Mohammed VI à la revue "La Medina."

Monnard, C. 1998. L'éternel retour: La population marocaine dans le monde. In *Jeune Afrique*, May 24.

Morelli, A. 2004. Préface: L'histoire des migrants et l'histoire. In *Trajectoires et dynamiques migratoires de l'immigration marocain de Belgique*, ed. N. Ouali. Louvain-La Neuve: Bruylant-Academia.

Morocco. 1961. Dahir 1.60.232 1961.

———. 1990. *Loi 19/89 portant création de la Fondation Hassan II pour les MRE. Dahir 1.90.79. July 13.*

———. Ministère de la Communauté Marocaine à l'Etranger. 1993. Compte-rendu de l'entretien avec Monsieur Pasqua, Ministre de l'État, Ministre de l'Intérieur, et de l'Aménagement du Territoire. Internal document. June 23.

———. Ministère de la Communauté Marocaine à l'Etranger. Lettre d'information. February 1992–September 1995 (series). Rabat.

———. Ministère de l'Information. 1991. Discours et interviews de S. M. le Roi Hassan II. March 3, 1990–March 3, 1991. Rabat.

———. Ministère de l'Information. 1993. Discours du trône de sa majesté le roi Mohammed VI. Rabat.

———. Ministère de l'Information. 1996. Discours du trône de sa majesté le roi Mohammed VI. Rabat.

———. Ministère de l'Information. 1997. Discours du Trône de Sa Majesté le Roi Mohammed VI. Rabat.

———. Ministry of Employment. N.d. Yearly number of emigrants through guestworker contracts, issued 1915–79. Data series. Rabat: Hassan II Foundation archives.

———. Ministry of Foreign Affairs. 1968–2002. Record of Moroccans Living Abroad. Data series. Rabat.

———. Ministry of Foreign Affairs. 2003. Stratégie du Ministère Délégué Chargé de la Communauté Marocaine Résidant à l'Étranger. Rabat.

———. Ministry of Information. 1990. Discours et interviews de s.m. le Roi Hassan II. March 3, 1989–March 3, 1990.

———. Ministry of the Interior, Direction of Collectivities. 1988. Programme pilote de pre-électrification rurale: Dossier du project préliminaire. No. SAI-88-CDG/101.

———. Ministry of the Interior. 2003. *Electrification décentralisée: Evaluation et enseignements stratégiques.* Rabat.

———. Ministry of the Interior, Direction of Collectivities. N.d. *Programme pilote de pré-electrification rurale: Convention.* Rabat.

———. Ministry of the Interior and Agence Française pour la Maîtrise de l'Énergie (AFME). 1987. *Programme de pré-electrification rurale en coopération franco-marocaine.* Rabat.

———. Ministry of Labor. 1963a. *Champ d'application de la convention du 21 mai 1963.*

———. Ministry of Labor. 1963b. *Convention de main d'oeuvre entre le Maroc et la France.*

———. Ministry of Labor. 1964. *Convention de main d'oeuvre entre le Maroc et la Belgique.*

———. Ministry of Labor. 1969. *Convention de main d'oeuvre entre le Maroc et la Hollande.*

———. Office des Changes. 1963–2006 (series). Data on Remittances—Sources and Types. Rabat.

Mossadaq, F. 1996a. Electrification rurale décentralisée: Un programme pilote est prévu pour 3600 foyers. *L'Économiste*, January 11.

———. 1996b. La réorganisation de l'ONE démarre. *L'Économiste*, July 31.

Munzele Maimbo, S., and D. Ratha. 2005. *Remittances: Development Impact and Future Prospects.* Washington, DC: World Bank.

Nakamura, R. 1987. The Textbook Policy Process and Implementation Research. *Review of Policy Research* 7(1): 142–54.

New York Times. 1974. France Restricts Foreign Workers. July 5.

———. 1978. Chicanos Meet Mexican President in an Effort for Closer Relations. February 12.

———. 1984. Pechiney Counting on Quebec Plant. March 19.

——. 1986. Mexican Opposition Breaks Its Blockage of Bridge at El Paso. July 30.

Nobles, M. 2000. *Shades of Citizenship: Race and the Census in Modern Politics*. Stanford: Stanford University Press.

Noiriel, G. 1996. *The French Melting Pot: Immigration, Citizenship, and National Identity*. Minneapolis: University of Minnesota Press.

Nootebloom, B. 2000. *Learning and Innovation in Organization and Economies*. Oxford: Oxford University Press.

Nuijten, M. 1998. *In the Name of the Land: Organization, Transnationalism, and the Culture of the State in a Mexican Ejido*. Wageningen: Ponsen en Looijen.

Oakes, J. 1984. In Morocco, a Fuse Is Slowly Burning. *New York Times*, April 28.

Obukhova, E. 2009. Brain Circulation and Organizational Performance: Longitudinal Evidence from Shanghai's IC Design Industry. Industry Studies Association Conference, Chicago, May 27–29.

Office Nationale de l'Électricité (ONE). 1999. *PERG: Programme d'Electrification Rurale Globale*. Casablanca.

——. 2002. *Le programme d'electrification rurale globale: L'électricité pour tous*. Casablanca.

——. 2005. *L'électricité pour tous*. Rabat.

——. 2006. Official Web site. http//:www.one.org.ma.

——. N.d. *Programme d'electrification rurale*. Casablanca.

Olivares, J. 1994. Urgen reunir fondos y registrar votantes para derrotar iniciativa antiimigrante. *La Opinión*, August 8.

Ollman, B. 1992. Going beyond the State? *American Political Science Review* 86(4).

La Opinión. 2001. Vale la matrícula consular. November 12.

Oppenheimer, A. 2000. Los planes de Fox con Estados Unidos. *El Nuevo Herald*, July 6.

Orlikowski, W. J. 2002. Knowing in Practice: Enacting a Collective Capability in Distributed Organizing. *Organization Science* 13s(3): 24.

Orozco, G. 2001. Pasado, presente y futuro de nuestra relación con las comunidades mexicanas y de origen Mexico en Estados Unidos. *El Mercado de Valores* (July 7): 28–37.

Orozco, G., E. González, and D. d. Cossío. 2000. *Las organizaciones mexico-americanas, hispanas y mexicanas en Estados Unidos*. Mexico City: Fundación Solidaridad Mexicano-Americana.

Orozco, M. 2001. Globalization and Migration: The Impact of Family Remittances in Latin America. In *Approaches to Increasing the Productive Value of Remittances*. Washington, DC: Inter-American Foundation.

——. 2002. Globalization and Migration: The Impact of Family Remittances in Latin America. *Latin American Politics and Society* 44(2): 26.

——. 2003. *Hometown Associations and Their Present and Future Partnerships: New Development Opportunities?* Washington, DC: U.S. Agency for International Development.

Osterman, P. 2002. *Gathering Power: The Future of Progressive Politics in America*. Boston: Beacon Press.

Ostrom, E. 1996. Crossing the Great Divide: Coproduction, Synergy, and Development. *World Development* 24(6): 1073–87.

——. 2000. Collective Action and the Evolution of Social Norms. *Journal of Economic Perspectives* 14(3): 137–58.

Ouaked, S. 2002. Transatlantic Roundtable on High-Skilled Migration and Sending Countries Issues. *International Migration* 40(4): 153–66.

Ouali, N. 2004. Le mouvement associatif marocain de Belgique: Quelques repères. In *Trajectoires et dynamiques migratoires de l'immigration marocain de Belgique*, ed. N. Ouali. Louvain-La Neuve: Bruylant-Academia.

Padilla, J. M. 1998. *La población de Zacatecas*. Guadalajara: Ediciones Cuéllar.

Palazzoli, C. 1974. *Le Maroc politique*. Paris: Sindbad.

Pa'l Norte. 1994–2001 (series). Newsletter of the Dirección General de Atención a Comunidades Guanajuatenses in el Extranjero (DACGE).

La Paloma magazine. 1990–95 (series).

Palomo Acosta, T. 2005. Chicano Literary Renaissance. In *Handbook of Texas Online.* Austin: University of Texas. http://www.tsha.utexas.edu/handbook/online/articles/CC/kzcfa.html.

Paul, J. 1981. Riots in Morocco. *MERIP Reports,* no. 99.

———. 1984. States of Emergency: The Riots in Tunisia and Morocco. *MERIP Reports,* no. 127.

Pear, R. 1981a. Advisor in Mexican Government Assails Reagan Immigration Plan. *New York Times,* August 5.

———. 1981b. Plan Would Let Mexicans Work as U.S. Guests. *New York Times,* May 11.

———. 1981c. White House Asks for a Law to Bar Jobs for Illegal Aliens. *New York Times,* July 31.

———. 1986. Hard Times in Mexico Cause Concern in U.S. *New York Times,* October 19.

Pelham, N. 1999. Morocco's King Out to Heal Wounds in Drug-Growing Area. *Independent,* October 18.

Peteraf, M. 1993. The Cornerstones of Competitive Advantage: A Resource-Based View. *Strategic Management Journal* 14(3).

Piore, M. 1979. Qualitative Research Techniques in Economics. *Administrative Science Quarterly* 24:560–69.

Polanyi, M. 1967. *The Tacit Dimension.* New York: Doubleday.

Poniatowska, E. 1971. *La noche de Tlatelolco.* Mexico: Biblioteca Era.

Portes, A. 1999. Globalization from Below: The Rise of Transnational Communities. In *The Ends of Globalization: Bringing Society Back In,* ed. D. Kalb, M. Land, and R. Staring. Boulder: Rowman and Littlefield.

———. 2003. Conclusion: Theoretical Convergences and Empirical Evidence in the Study of Immigrant Transnationalism. *International Migration Review* 37(3).

Portes, A., C. Escobar, and A. Walton Radford. 2007. Immigrant Transnational Organizations and Development: A Comparative Study. *International Migration Review* 41(1): 242–81.

Portes, A., L. E. Guarnizo, and B. Landholt. 1999. Transnational Communities. *Ethnic and Racial Studies* 22 (special issue).

Powell, W., and P. DiMaggio. 1991. Introduction to *The New Institutionalism in Organizational Analysis.* Chicago: University of Chicago Press.

Power, J. 1974. Europe's Defenseless Immigrant Workers. *New York Times,* March 23.

Preston, J. 2000. The Mexico Election. *New York Times,* July 3.

Prichard, R. 2000. Know, Learn and Share! The Knowledge Phenomena and the Construction of a Consumptive-Communicative Body. In *Managing Knowledge: Critical Investigations of Work and Learning,* ed. R. Prichard, R. Hull, M. Chumer, and H. Willmott. New York: St. Martin's Press.

Pries, L. 2001. The Approach of Transnational Social Spaces: Responding to New Configurations of the Social and the Spatial. In *New Transnational Social Spaces: International Migration and Transnational Companies in the Early Twenty-First Century,* ed. L. Pries. London: Routledge.

Quiñones, S. 1999. Death of Voting-Abroad Bill in Mexico Was Simple Math. *San Diego Union-Tribune,* July 3.

Ramírez, R. 1969. *El movimiento estudiantil de México.* Mexico: Ediciones Era.

Ramírez Paredes, G. 1991. Los políticos mexicanos miran hacia el norte. In *El sistema político mexicano visto por los mexicanos de Afuera,* ed. G. Ramírez Paredes. Mexico City: UNAM.

Randal, J. 1974. Morocco Finds New Stability. *Washington Post,* October 8.

Ratha, D. 2005. Workers' Remittances: An Important and Stable Source of External Development Finance. In *Remittances: Development Impact and Future Prospects,* ed. S. Munzele Maimbo and D. Ratha. Washington, DC: World Bank.

Rebellyon. 2008. Pennaroya: Les travailleurs immigrés occupent l'usine-poison. February 9. http://www.rebellyon.info.

Reinhold, R. 1989. Mexican Politicians Look North of the Border. *New York Times,* December 8.

Revue du Liberal. 1992. Le Maroc et la question identitaire de ses jeunes en Europe: Interrogations et enjeux. October 1992.

Ribeiro, N., Laika el-Wardi, Mustapha Khyar, and Pedro de Vasconselos. 2005. Annexe de la Partie II: Les infrastructures financières de transferts de fonds via le système bancaire et les autres circuits financiers: Les cas du Portugal, du Maroc, et de l'Amerique Latine et des Caraïbes. In *Migrations, transferts, et fonds et développement*. Paris: OECD.

Riding, A. 1977a. Mexicans Are Vexed by U.S. Migrant Plan. *New York Times*, August 28.

——. 1977b. President López Portillo Has Recognized the Inescapable, That His Country Is Economically Dependent. *New York Times*, November 13.

——. 1978. Mexico, Upset at U.S., Awaits Mondale's Visit. *New York Times*, January 20.

——. 1980. Mexico's Count of Migrants in U.S. Is Lower Than Others. *New York Times*, October 13.

——. 1989. Spain's Quibble with Success: Moroccan Migrants. *New York Times*, August 24.

Robles, F. 1994. Condena México campaña en contra de inmigrantes. *La Opinión*, August 14.

——. 2000. Fox y Cárdenas visitan a los mexicanos de California. *La Opinión*, May 6.

——. 2002. Fox nombra al encargado de los migrantes mexicanos. *La Opinión*, September 17.

——. 2005. México aprueba voto postal. *La Opinión*, June 28.

Rodríguez, V. 1997. *The Politics of Decentralization in Mexico: from Municipio Libre to Solidaridad*. Boulder: Westview Press.

Roett, R. 1993. At the Crossroads: Liberalization in Mexico. In *Political and Economic Liberalization in Mexico: At a Critical Juncture*, ed. R. Roett. Boulder: Lynne Rienner.

Rohter, L. 1987. Dissidents in Mexico's Ruling Party Challenge Half-Century of Tradition. *New York Times*, August 16.

——. 1988a. In Mexican Race, Debate (in U.S.) Hits Home. *New York Times*, June 18.

——. 1988b. Mexican Party Practices Protests over Vote Fraud. *New York Times*, June 29.

——. 1988c. Stiff Setback Seen for Ruling Party in Mexican Voting. *New York Times*, July 8.

——. 1988d. New Campaign Begins after Mexican Elections. *New York Times*, July 22.

——. 1988e. 200,000 in Mexican Capital Protest Vote Count. *New York Times*, July 17.

——. 1988f. Mexican Shift on Economy Seen. *New York Times*, August 8.

Rosenberg, H. 1993. Snapshots in a Farm Labor Tradition. *Labor Management Decisions* 3(1).

Rosenblum, M. 1999a. Moroccans Bury Their King as World Leaders Look On. *Associated Press*, July 25.

——. 1999b. Moroccans Quietly Mourn Hassan—King, Spiritual Leader and Godfather. *Associated Press*, July 24.

Ross Piñeda, R. 2002. *Derechos políticos de los mexicanos en el extranjero*. Mexico City.

Sabagh, G. 1997. L'analyse du retour des émigrés: Les expériences du Maghreb et du Mexique. In *Migration internationale et changements sociaux dans le Maghreb*, ed. A. Benchérifa, L. Michalak, H. Hmzabi, and G. Sabagh. Tunis: Université de Tunis.

Safi, H. 1990. Essai sur l'économie de la sécheresse au Maroc: Passé, présent et perspectives. Master's thesis, Université Mohammed V, Rabat.

Salazar, R. 1998a. Growers Hit "Meddling" with Bracero Program, October 23, 1963. In *Border Correspondent*, ed. M. Garcia. Berkeley: University of California Press.

——. 1998b. Last Braceros Leaving as Job Program Ends, January 1, 1965. In *Border Correspondent*, ed. D. Maciel. Berkeley: University of California Press.

Saldaña-Portillo, M. J. 2003. *The Revolutionary Imagination in the Americas and the Age of Development*. Durham, NC: Duke University Press.

Samora, J. 1969. *Los Mojados: The Wetback Story*. South Bend, IN: University of Notre Dame Press.

Sanchez, R., and J. Mahoney. 1996. Modularity, Flexibility, and Knowledge Management in Product and Organization Design. *Strategic Management Journal* 17 (special issue: Knowledge and the Firm).

Sandos, J., and H. Cross. 1983. "National Development and International Labour Migration." *Journal of Contemporary History*. 18(1): 43–60.

Sans Frontière. 1979–84 (monthly series). Nos. 10-31. Paris.

Santamaría Gómez, A. 1994. *La política entre México y Aztlán: Relaciones chicano-mexicanas del 68 a Chiapas 94.* Cuiliacán Rosales: Universidad Autónoma de Sinaloa.

———. 2001. Mexicanos en Estados Unidos: La nación, la política y el voto sin fronteras. In *Mexicanos en Estados Unidos: La nación, la política y el voto sin fronteras,* ed. A. Santamaría Gómez. Cuiliacán: Universidad Autónoma de Sinaloa and Partido de la Revolución Democrática.

Santín Quiroz, O. 2001. *The Political Economy of Mexico's Financial Reform.* Aldershot: Ashgate.

Sawyer, K. 2007. *Group Genius: The Creative Power of Collaboration.* New York: Basic Books.

Saxenian, A. 2002. Transnational Communities and the Evolution of Global Production Networks: The Cases of Taiwan, China and India. *Industry and Innovation,* Fall (special issue).

———. 2007. *The New Argonauts: Regional Advantage in a Global Economy.* Cambridge: Harvard University Press.

Schmidt di Friedberg, O. 1994. Historique de l'immigration marocaine en Italie. In *L'Annuaire de l'émigration,* ed. K. Basfao and H. Taarji. Rabat: Fondation Hassan II.

Schon, D. 1971. *Beyond the Stable State.* New York: Random House.

Scott, J. 1998. *Seeing Like a State: How Certain Schemes to Improve the Human Condition Have Failed.* New Haven: Yale University Press.

Secretaría de Desarrollo Social (SEDESOL). 2005. Acuerdo por el que se emiten y publican las Reglas de Operación del Programa 3x1 Para Migrantes, a cargo de la Secretaría de Desarrollo Social, para el Ejercicio Fiscal 2005. Diario Official. Mexico City. February 18.

Secretaría de Relaciones Exteriores (SRE). 2002a. Funcionamiento del Consejo Nacional para las Comunidades Mexicanas en el Exterior. Mexico City. August 6.

Secretaría de Relaciones Exteriores (SRE). 2002b. Internal planning documents on IME. Various. Mexico City. January–August.

Secretaría de Relaciones Exteriores (SRE). 2003. Decreto por el que se crea el Instituto de los Mexicanos en el Exterior, con el carácter de órgano administrativo desconcentrado de la Secretaría de Relaciones Exteriores. Mexico City. April 13.

Secretaría de Relaciones Exteriores (SRE). Dirección General para las Comunidades Mexicanas en el Extranjero (DGCME) Archives. 1990–93. Organization documents, internal documents, promotional materials, press releases, newspaper clippings, memos. Mexico City.

Seddon, D. 1984. Winter of Discontent: Economic Crisis in Tunisia and Morocco. *MERIP Reports,* no. 127.

Shah, S. 2000. Sources and Patters of Innovation in a Consumer Products Field. Working Paper. MIT Sloan School of Management.

Shain, Y. 1999. The Mexican-American Diaspora's Impact on Mexico. *Political Science Quarterly* 114(4): 661–91.

Shapira, Y. 1977. Mexico: The Impact of the 1968 Student Protest on Echeverria's Reformism. *Journal of Interamerican Studies and World Affairs* 19(4): 557–80.

———. 1978. *Mexican Foreign Policy under Echeverría.* Beverly Hills, CA: Sage Publications.

Sherman, R. 1999. From State Introversion to State Extension in Mexico: Modes of Emigrant Incorporation, 1900–1997. *Theory and Society* 28(6): 835–66.

Shirk, D. 2005. *Mexico's New Politics.* Boulder: Lynne Rienner.

Silen, I. 1995. Mexico: La crisis de la democracia. *Impacto,* February 29.

Singer, D. 2002. *Prelude to Revolution: France in May 1968.* Cambridge, MA: South End Press.

Skocpol, T. 1992. *Protecting Soldiers and Mothers: The Political Origins of Social Policy in the United States.* Cambridge: Harvard University Press.

Slobodzian, J., and M. Rhor. 1993. 500 March in Chesco to Back Strikers. *Philadelphia Inquirer,* April 25.

Slyomovics, S. 2005. *The Performance of Human Rights in Morocco.* Philadelphia: University of Pennsylvania Press.

Smith, M. P. 2003. Transnationalism, the State, and the Extraterritorial Citizen. *Politics and Society* 31(4): 467–502.

Smith, M. P., and L. E. Guarnizo. 1998. The Locations of Transnationalism. In *Transnationalism from Below*, ed. M. P. Smith and L. E. Guarnizo. New Brunswick, NJ: Transaction Publishers.

Smith, R. 1995. "Los ausentes siempre presentes": The Imagining, Making and Politics of a Transnational Migrant Community between Ticuani, Puebla, Mexico and New York. PhD diss., Political Science, Columbia University.

——. 2003. Migrant Membership as an Instituted Process: Transnationalism, the State and the Extra-Territorial Conduct of Mexican Politics. *International Migration Review* 37(2): 232–52.

——. 2008. Contradictions of Diasporic Institutionalization in Mexican Politics: The 2006 Migrant Vote and Other Forms of Inclusion and Control. *Ethnic and Racial Studies* 31(4): 708–41.

Stork, J. 1990. North Africa Faces the 1990s. *MERIP Reports,* no. 163.

Suárez-Orozco, C., I. Todorova, and J. Louie. 2005. Making Up for Lost Time: The Experience of Separation and Reunification among Immigrant Families. In *The New Immigration*, ed. C. Suárez-Orozco, D. Qin-Hilliard, and D. Baolian Qin. New York: Routledge.

Suro, R. 2005. *Survey of Mexican Migrants, Part 2: Attitudes about Voting and Ties to Mexico*. Washington, DC: Pew Hispanic Center.

Swearingen, W. 1985. In Pursuit of the Granary of Rome: France's Wheat in Morocco, 1915–1931. *International Journal of Middle East Studies* 17(3): 347–63.

——. 1987. Morocco's Agricultural Crisis. In *The Political Economy of Morocco*, ed. I. W. Zartman. New York: Praeger.

Talha, L., ed. 1983. *Maghrébins en France: Émigrés ou immigrés?* Paris: Éditions du Centre National de la Recherche Scientifique.

Tamayo, J., and F. Lazano. 1991. The Economic and Social Development of High Emigration Areas in the State of Zacatecas: Antecedents and Policy Alternatives. In *Regional and Sectoral Development in Mexico as Alternatives to Migration*, ed. S. Díaz-Briquets and S. Weintraub. Boulder: Westview Press.

Tapinos, G. 1975. *L'immigration etrangère en France*. Paris: Presses Universitaires de France.

Taylor, J. E. 2002. Do Government Programs "Crowd In" Remittances? In *Sending Money Home: Hispanic Remittances and Community Development*, ed. B. L. Lowell and R. de la Garza. Lanham, MD: Rowman and Littlefield.

Telquel. 2003. De la jemaâ aux ONG. December 20–26.

Tendler, J. 1997. *Good Government in the Tropics*. Baltimore: Johns Hopkins University Press.

Thompson, J. 1995. Participatory Approaches in Government Bureaucracies: Facilitating the Process of Institutional Change. *World Development* 23(9): 1521–54.

——. 2007. *Organizations in Action: Social Science Bases of Administrative Theory*. New Brunswick, NJ: Transaction Publishers.

Togman, J. M. 2002. *The Ramparts of Nations: Institutions and Immigration Policies in France and the United States*. New York: Praeger.

Torres, F. 2001. *Las remesas y el desarrollo rural en las zonas de alta intensidad migratoria de Mexico*. Mexico City: CEPAL.

Touraine, A. 1968. *Le mouvement de mai ou le communisme utopique*. Paris: Éditions du Seuil.

Tozy, M. 1999. *Monarchie et Islam politique au Maroc*. Paris: Presses de la Fondation Nationale des Sciences Politiques.

Traversian, P. 2004. L'histoire d'une émancipation ouvrière. *Genevilliers Magazine*, September.

Treaster, J. 1988. Mexican Political Foes Block Bridge in El Paso. *New York Times*, July 11.

Triki, L. 1993a. Déficit électrique: Des délestages jusqu'au deuxième semestre 1994. *L'Économiste*, June 10.

——. 1993b. Électricité: Calendrier des coupures à Ain Sébaa-Hay Mohammadi. *L'Économiste*, September 9.

——. 1993c. Électricité: Le ministre de l'Énergie et des Mines "dénonce les reticences des industriels" à la réorganisation. *L'Économiste*, January 7.

——. 1994. L'ONE change de peau. *L'Économiste*, April 14.

Troin, J.-F., ed. 2002. *Maroc: Régions, pays, territoires*. Paris: Maisonneuve et Larose.

True, J., B. Jones, and F. Baumgartner. 2007. Punctuated-Equilibrium Theory. In *Theories of the Policy Process*, ed. P. Sabatier. Boulder: Westview Press.

Tucker, D. S. 1967. *Evolution of People's Banks*. New York: AMS Press.

Turner, F. 1979. Violence and Social Change: The Cases of Mexico and Curacao. *Latin American Research Review* 14(3): 251–55.

United Press International. 1999. Moroccan Prince Announces King's Death. July 23.

Valabrègue, C. 1973. *L'homme déraciné: Le livre noir des travailleurs étrangers*. Paris: Mercure de France.

Valdes, D. 1995. Legal Status and the Struggles of Farmworkers in West Texas in New Mexico, 1942–1993. *Latin American Perspectives* 22(1): 117–37.

Valencia García, G. 2001. The PAN in Guanajuato: Elections and Political Change in the 1990s. In *Party Politics and the Struggle for Democracy in Mexico: National and State-Level Analyses of the Partido Acción Nacional*, ed. K. Middlebrook. La Jolla: Center for U.S.-Mexican Studies, University of California, San Diego.

van de Walle, D. 2004. *Do Basic Services and Poverty Programs Reach Morocco's Poor?* Washington, DC: World Bank.

Van der Valk, I. 2004. Vie associative des marocains aux Pays-Bas. In *Trajectoires et dynamiques migratoires de l'immigration marocain de Belgique*, ed. N. Ouali. Louvain-La Neuve: Bruylant-Academia.

Van Maanen, J. 1988. *Tales of the Field: On Writing Ethnography*. Chicago: University of Chicago Press.

Vásquez, C., and M. García y Griego, eds. 1983. *Mexican-U.S. Relations: Conflict and Convergence*. Los Angeles: Chicano Studies Research Center, University of California.

Vaughan, D. 1992. Theory Elaboration: The Heuristics of Case Analysis. In *What Is a Case? Exploring the Foundations of Social Inquiry*, ed. C. Ragin and H. Becker. New York: Cambridge University Press.

Velasco, J. 1997. Selling Ideas, Buying Influence: Mexico and American Think Tanks in the Promotion of NAFTA. In *Bridging the Border: Transforming Mexico-U.S. Relations*, ed. R. de la Garza and J. Velazco. Lanham, MD: Rowman and Littlefield.

Velasco-Mondragón, H. E., J. Martin, and F. Chacón-Sosa. 2000. Technology Evaluation of a USA-Mexico Health Information System for Epidemiological Surveillance of Mexican Migrant Workers. *Pan American Journal of Public Health* 7(3): 7.

Vermeren, P. 2001. *Le Maroc en transition*. Paris: La Découverte.

Vernez, G., and D. Ronfeldt. 1991. The Current Situation in Mexican Immigration. *Science* 251 (4998): 1189–93.

Vidal, G. 2005. Du syndicat à la camera. Ligue Communiste Révolutionnaire, www.lcr-rouge.org (accessed October 2, 2005).

Vittas, D. 1995. *Thrift Deposit Institutions in Europe and the United States*. Washington, DC: World Bank.

von Hippel, E. 1994. Sticky Information and the Locus of Problem Solving: Implications for Innovation. *Management Science* 40:429–39.

——. 2005. *Democratizing Innovation*. Cambridge: MIT Press.

von Hippel, E., and R. Katz. 2002. Shifting Innovation to Users via Toolkits. *Management Science* 48(7): 821–33.

Waterbury, J. 1970. *The Commander of the Faithful*. New York: Columbia University Press.

Wavell, S., and D. Cunningham. 1999. Morocco Mourns Its Ruthless King. *Sunday Times*, July 11.

Weintraub, S. 1998. IRCA and the Facilitation of U.S.-Mexico Migration Dialogue. In *Binational Study/Estudio Binacional: Migration between Mexico and the United States*. Washington, DC: Mexican Ministry of Foreign Affairs and the U.S. Commission on Immigration Reform.

Weisberg, R. 2006. *Creativity: Understanding Innovation in Problem Solving, Science, Invention and the Arts.* Hoboken, NJ: John Wiley.

White, G. 2001. *A Comparative Political Economic of Tunisia and Morocco.* Albany: State University of New York Press.

Woodruff, C., and R. Zenteño. 2001. Remittances and Micro-Enterprises in Mexico. UCSD working paper.

World Bank. 1953. *The Economic Development of Mexico.* Baltimore: Johns Hopkins University Press.

———. 1966. *The Economic Development of Morocco.* Baltimore: Johns Hopkins University Press.

———. 1979. *Staff Appraisal Report: Morocco, Village Electrification Project.* Washington, DC.

———. 1981. *Morocco: Economic and Social Development Report.* Baltimore: Johns Hopkins University Press.

———. 1988. *Project Completion Report: Morocco, Village Electrification Project.* Washington, DC.

———. 1990. *Staff Appraisal Report: Morocco, Second Rural Electrification Project.* Washington, DC.

———. 1998. *Implementation Completion Report: Morocco, Second Rural Electrification Project.* Washington, DC.

———. 2001. *Morocco: Social Development Agency.* Washington, DC.

———. 2002. Project Appraisal Document on a Proposed Loan in the Amount of f5.8 Million (US$5 Million Equivalent) to the Kingdom of Morocco for a Support for the Social Development Agency Project. Washington, DC.

———. 2003. Morocco: A Watershed for Education and Health. Washington, DC.

———. 2004. Rural Roads Project for Morocco: Project Appraisal Document. Project ID P082754. Washington, DC.

———. 2005. *Rural Water Supply and Sanitation Project: Morocco.* Washington, DC.

Yabiladi. 2003. Interview with Samir. http://Yabiladi.com (accessed May 13, 2005).

Zabin, C., and L. Escala Rabadan. 1998. *Mexican Hometown Associations and Mexican Immigrant Political Empowerment in Los Angeles.* Aspen, CO: Aspen Institute.

Zabin, C., and S. Hughes. 1995. Economic Integration and Labor Flows: Stage Migration in Farm Labor Markets in Mexico and the United States. *International Migration Review* 29(2): 395–422.

Zacatecas. Secretaria de Planeación y Desarrollo Regional (SEPLADER). 1993–98 (series). Dos por Uno: Seguimiento de Proyectos. Zacatecas: SEPLADER archives.

———. Secretaria de Planeación y Desarrollo Regional (SEPLADER). N.d. [c. 1996]. Programa Dos por Uno: Actividades y Proyectos. Zacatecas: SEPLADER archives.

———. Secretaria de Planeación y Desarrollo Regional (SEPLADER). N.d. [c. 1997]. Programa Dos por Uno: Actividades y Proyectos. Zacatecas.

———. Secretaría de Planeación y Finanzas. 1993–98. Two for One program records. Zacatecas.

Zahariadis, N. 2007. The Multiple Streams Framework: Structure, Limitations, Prospects. In *Theories of the Policy Process,* ed. P. Sabatier. Boulder: Westview Press.

Zancarini-Fournel, M. 2002. La question immigrée après 68. *Plein Droit,* March, 53–54.

Zartman, I. W. 1987. King Hassan's New Morocco. In *The Political Economy of Morocco,* ed. I. W. Zartman. New York: Praeger.

Zazueta, C. 1983. Mexican Political Actors in the United States and Mexico: Historical and Political Contexts of a Dialogue Renewed. In *Mexican-U.S. Relations: Conflict and Convergence,* ed. C. Vásquez and M. García y Griego. Los Angeles: Chicano Studies Research Center, University of California.

Zelizer, V. 1997. *The Social Meaning of Money: Pin Money, Paychecks, Poor Relief, and Other Currencies.* Princeton: Princeton University Press.

Zermeño, S. 1993. Intellectuals and the State in the "Lost Decade." In *Mexico: Dilemmas of Transition*, ed. N. Harvey. London: University of London.

Zerrouky, H. 2004. Le Maroc face à son passé. *L'Humanité* (January 9). Paris.

Zisenwine, D. 2007. From Hassan II to Muhammed VI: Plus ça change? In *The Maghreb in the New Century: Identity, Religion, and Politics*, ed. B. Maddy-Weitzman and D. Zisenwine. Gainesville: University Press of Florida.

Index

Page numbers in *italics* refer to figures and tables.